ACHILLES

FIGURE 1. Achilles

ACHILLES

PARADIGMS
OF THE WAR HERO
FROM HOMER
TO THE MIDDLE AGES

KATHERINE CALLEN KING

ILLUSTRATED BY
DEBORAH NOURSE LATTIMORE

UNIVERSITY OF CALIFORNIA PRESS
BERKELEY
LOS ANGELES
OXFORD

University of California Press
Berkeley and Los Angeles, California

University of California Press, Ltd.
Oxford, England

© 1987 by
The Regents of the University of California

First Paperback Printing 1991

Library of Congress Cataloging-in-Publication Data

King, Katherine Callen.
Achilles: paradigms of the war hero from Homer through
the Middle Ages.

1. Classical literature—History and criticism.   2. Achilles
(Greek mythology) in literature.   3. Homer—Characters—
Achilles.   4. Homer. Iliad.   5. Trojan War in litera-
ture.   6. Literature, Medieval—History and
criticism.   I. Title.
PA3015.R5A375   1987   809'.93351   85-28868
ISBN 0-520-07407-6 (alk. paper)

Printed in the United States of America

1   2   3   4   5   6   7   8   9

For my sons,
ERIC
and
ETHAN,
who have grown like young trees,
in good hope that they need never be war heroes

And to the memory of
JOHN ARTHUR HANSON, 1931–1985,
teacher and friend

CONTENTS

ILLUSTRATIONS

PREFACE

If Achilles has been granted lasting fame, it has not always been the fame he sought in the *Iliad*. Glory, mass-murder, honesty, sado-masochism, idealism, ruthlessness, friendship, lust—all have been attributed to the "best of the Achaians" by authors who have drawn on the hero's reputation for their own literary purposes. This book attempts to elucidate these purposes while describing the actual variations in Achilles' literary fortune.

My initial purpose in undertaking this study was to deepen my analysis of Renaissance authors who used Homer's Achilles. In order to appreciate the complexity with which these authors deploy Achilles in their own poetry, I felt it necessary to know as much as possible not only about Homer's hero but also about the numerous other presentations of Achilles that might influence an audience's evaluation of his heroism. But as I proceeded, the inquiry took on an interest of its own. Those other presentations, many and varied beyond my original imaginings, together with the *Iliad* create a rich network of traditions and transformations, offering at each intersection glimpses into Achilles' literary and social functions as a paradigmatic war hero.

In offering the results of this intriguing journey from the archaic Achilles of the Epic Cycle to the medieval Achilles of *El Libro de Alexandre* and Guido delle Colonne, I have kept two objectives in mind: to demonstrate the continuous importance of Achilles in European literature and, more importantly, to establish the varying moral or political significance attached to the hero and to particular episodes of his career in response to shifting mores and contemporary issues. Consequently, my study provides a focused approach to several periods of literature and can function as a microhistory of the classical tradition that informs them, revealing continuity while detailing the variations that finally produce radical changes in how a character is perceived—changes such as that which placed Achilles in the company of lustful Paris in the second circle of Dante's inferno rather than in the first with noble Hektor or in the fifth with other irascible spirits. I have tried, that is, to analyze each manifestation of Achilles both as part of the tradition and as a specific historical event tied to poetic and societal values. My inclusive approach, reflected in an initial lengthy and comprehensive analysis of Homer's Achilles, in numerous quotations, and in copious notes, should make this study useful also as a reference work through which scholars can locate Achilles' major appearances in early European literature as well as for important discussions relevant to these appearances.

It is hoped that this study of Achilles' literary career will be of value to classicists, medievalists, scholars of Renaissance literature, comparatists, and the lay reader. All, I hope, will find it interesting to follow the changes in the valuation of Homeric heroism and the consequent transformations in the character of the figure who more than any other exemplifies that heroism. In order to make my material accessible to all these groups, I have assumed no specialized knowledge on the part of my reader, I have translated all quotations into English, providing the original language in footnotes, and I have transliterated all Greek words used in the text except in the case of a very few long quotations deemed necessary for extensive close readings. All translations, except where otherwise noted, are my own. For the sake of consistency, the names of most characters that appear first in Greek texts receive Greek spelling throughout (for example, Hektor, Hekabe, Odysseus) instead of the different spellings of the several languages in which they later occur. The main exception is Akhilleus himself, for whom I have adopted the popular Latin form, Achilles.

The illustrations were drawn after original vase paintings, sculptural reliefs, and illuminated manuscripts by my good friend Deborah Nourse Lattimore, whose skill as both artist and art historian has added much beauty to my scholarship.

Many have helped in the research and shaping of this book. Chapters One and Two, which first came into being as part of my doctoral dissertation in comparative literature at Princeton University, benefited greatly from the guidance of my advisors Robert Fagles and John Arthur Hanson. More recently, I am indebted to Peter Dronke and my colleagues Franz Bäuml and Joaquin Gimeno for their largess in sharing their vast knowledge of medieval Latin, German, and Spanish. Margaret Alexiou, Arnold Band, A. R. Braunmuller, Jean-Claude Carron, Michael Haslam, Kathleen Komar, Steven Lattimore, Edward Mitchell, Seth Schein, and Ross Shideler all read drafts and offered criticism that has improved the work greatly.

Research, as well as the onerous task of constant retyping and proofreading, was expedited by the help of several research assistants: Mary Eichbauer, Thomas Haeussler, Jeffrey Haus, Angelika Lee, Linda Paulson, Alison Taufer, and, especially, Marc Wiesmann. Final editing and verification were aided greatly by the tireless efforts of Karen Strickholm, who also created the index. My thanks to them and to the Academic Senate of UCLA, whose generous funding through research grants over the past six years made their help possible. I am grateful, too, to sponsoring editor Doris Kretschmer, project editor Mary Lamprech, and copy editor Ellen Setteducati of the University of California Press, whose skill and careful attention to detail have produced a book that is a joy to behold.

Finally, I want to thank the graduate students and faculty of the Program in Comparative Literature at UCLA whose demanding temperaments, fertile minds, unflagging interest, and supportive energies functioned collectively as a most skillful midwife to bring this book to birth.

INTRODUCTION

The figures of classical literature survive and exert influence not only in works that present them directly but also in works that borrow their characteristic motifs to enhance the portrayal of other heroes. Generally, such borrowing can be effective only when the association between a particular figure and a particular theme or episode is a strong and lasting one. Sometimes such an association results in the creation of an enduring stereotype such as the "fierce and indomitable Medea, lamentable Ino, treacherous Ixion, wandering Io, and miserable Orestes" described by Horace (*Ars Poetica* 123–124). Sometimes, however, the original, more complex portrait retains the power to engender complex literary offspring, as Homer's Odysseus engendered Joyce's Leopold Bloom. In both cases, of course, the hero's fortunes are closely tied to how his or her major characteristics and achievements are valued in the society for which the new poet is writing. How the original portrait is read is conditioned not only by this social context but also by poets who, writing to promote or resist dominant social values, may use a well-known figure to reinforce, to attack, or to undermine. Such poets will reconfigure traits and episodes, emphasizing some, downplaying others.[1]

In about 700 B.C. a poet in Asia Minor, whom I, like his fellow Greeks, shall call Homer,[2] created out of traditional Greek saga an unforgettable portrait of the hero of a pan-Hellenic war that was supposed to have taken place some five hundred years earlier. By skillful manipulation of the oral-formulaic language and themes that he had inherited from generations of epic singers, Homer turned a celebration of martial valor into a critical exploration of heroic values[3] and made godlike Achilles, famous for his power to inflict pain in war,[4] into a multifaceted human being coming to grips with human mortality. This Achilles, the Achilles of Homer's *Iliad,* has proved an excellent example of all forms of literary survival, direct and indirect, stereotypical and complex. In addition to the power of his Homeric characterization, his immortality is due to the popularity of the Trojan War story from antiquity through the Renaissance and to the martial excellence that has ensured the attention of poets and propagandists, both pro- and antiwar, through our own century.[5]

Educated Greeks and Romans knew Homer's story practically by heart, and parts of it could thus be easily evoked by post-Homeric poets to enrich the meaning of their own works. These new poets were not, however, limited to using Homer, who had sung the most famous but not the only story of Achilles. The well-known poems of the Epic Cycle contributed to the tradition exploits performed before the point at which Homer began his story and after the point at which he ended it. Achilles' appearances in classical Greek poetry and prose, therefore, often combine Homeric and Epic Cycle events. Most often such appearances are one-sided and skewed to fit in with the later author's point of view. Pindar and Sophokles, for example, evoke only the positive aspects of Achilles' epic career; Euripides evokes only the negative.

The earliest lyric poets sang the glory of Achilles without the tragic undertones orchestrated by Homer. Aristocratic Pindar, for instance, who continually pointed to Achilles as an exemplar of innate greatness, ignored the passion and the disillusioned questioning of the heroic code that motivate Homer's hero. The poems that patriotically celebrate young athletes' victories in pan-Hellenic games celebrate Achilles' wondrous power to kill in verses that evoke only the beauty inherent in any demonstration of human excellence in any arena of honest competition. Achilles' own death is presented equally without melancholy, for Pindar appears to accept uncritically the heroic view that martial glory is ample compensation for loss of life.

Like Pindar, Sophokles used Achilles as a symbol of natural nobility. Although Achilles is not among Sophokles' surviving dramatis personae, his Iliadic character, particularly that displayed in Books One and Nine, is evoked insistently in the *Philoktetes* as his son agonizes over whether to serve the army and its crafty agent, Odysseus, or to obey his paternally transmitted instinct for physical action and honesty. Homeric passion is thus admitted into Sophokles' world, but its complexity is reduced to a black-and-white opposition between a noble ghost from the Homeric past and a base forerunner of Athens's modern politicians. This split between physical and mental abilities, which was post-

Homeric but not original to Sophokles, would for centuries pit Achilles and Odysseus against each other as "types": doer versus speaker, honesty versus duplicity.

Euripides, whose tragedies were contemporary with Sophokles', also drew heavily on *Iliad* 1 and 9 for his portraits of Achilles in both the *Hekabe* and *Iphigeneia in Aulis,* but he did so not to praise but, rather, to critique the concept of self-aggrandizing "heroic" behavior that Homer's work had come to sanction. And he went beyond them in *Elektra* to evoke aspects of Homer's epic that both Sophokles and Pindar ignore: the terror, the ugliness of death. For Euripides employed Achilles in plays whose focus was victims: victims of a temper that could be called heroic only because it had belonged to men from the so-called heroic age—the victims of war. By means of parody and skewed evocations of Iliadic scenes, Euripides attempted to convince his fellow Athenians, who continued to invoke Homer to rouse up fervor for war, of the grim reality that lurked behind the glorious beauty of their beloved national epic. His attempts did not succeed, for as Plato's later invocations and attacks confirm, the Pindaric-Sophoklean valuation of Achilles was the one that prevailed in Athens. Plato, in his conviction that the true hero is the dispassionate philosopher, not the passionate warrior, carried Euripides' battle against the seductiveness of Homer on into the fourth century, but the effort did not bear lasting fruit until some three centuries later, when the center of literary creativity had passed from Greece to Rome.

In Rome Achilles' career of wrath and revenge was viewed positively by military leaders but negatively by golden-age poets and philosophers. Catullus transformed Achilles' exemplary Pindaric brilliance into an exemplum of brutality, and Cicero pronounced his Homeric wrath, already criticized by Plato, a disease. Horace placed him in the company of Niobe and Tantalus as having earned his premature death by hubris, and Vergil portrayed him as synonymous with war, the great destroyer of human achievement and happiness. Ovid's *Metamorphoses* presents a similar Achilles; concerned only with battles and glory, he expresses in a more lighthearted fashion all the energy, ire, inexorability, fierceness, and extreme independence that Horace had said the Roman people expected from any literary re-creation of Achilles.

The expectations of medieval audiences were not so simple. In the late-antique Quintus of Smyrna and the medieval Joseph of Exeter the passionate belligerence that remained Achilles' predominant trait was made part of a new characterization that effectively merged Achilles with the classical subtype of Kapaneus. But there coexisted with this new subtype Statius's influential silver-age Achilles, whose anger was linked to justice, and Simon Capra Aurea's twelfth-century Achilles, who, as a man of *pietas* and *virtus* standing in contrast to men of *consilium* like dishonest Odysseus, revived the fifth-century Greek opposition between man of words and man of deeds. Then, in thirteenth-century Spain, the anonymous author of the vernacular *Libro de Alexandre* rewrote the *Ilias Latina,* the uninspired Silver Latin verse abridgement of the *Iliad* that gave the Greekless readers of the Middle Ages their only knowledge of Homer, to make Achilles, great and noble warrior though he was, correspond to Alexander the Great as a negative exemplar of pride.

Throughout the above Iliadic tradition Achilles maintained his superiority over all other warriors at Troy; in the alternate tradition started by the "true accounts" of Dares and Dictys, however, this distinction passed to Hektor, who became the beneficiary of all the tragic stature that Achilles lost. Vestiges of his classical identity survived in Achilles' astonishing beauty, large size, and fierceness, but it was natural that poets writing for patrons who found it useful to trace their ancestry back to Troy should denigrate the Greek hero's prowess and character in favor of Trojan champions. Benoît de Sainte-Maure and Guido delle Colonne made so many disparaging changes that at the end of the thirteenth century Achilles rather than Odysseus would have leapt to mind if someone had referred to a perfidious scoundrel who had destroyed Troy.

Achilles would also have leapt to mind if someone had referred to a warrior who had destroyed himself through lust. Most surprisingly to the classicist, Achilles' passion in the Middle Ages was directed as much toward beautiful women as against hated commanders and enemy champions. The roots of the conception of Achilles as lover are found in the *Iliad* and the Epic Cycle, but the amatory motif does not take on serious importance until the first century A.D. Successive literary concentration on the three main objects of Achilles' affection—Homer's Briseis, Statius' Deidameia, and Dares' Polyxena—marks the progressive moralization of the hero's entanglement with love, as the relatively value-free classical opposition between lover and warrior becomes first an amusing and then a deadly serious lesson in the harmfulness of lust.

In the hands of Christian writers, who regarded concupiscence as a most deadly sin, the amatory tradition continued to take on increasing importance until finally, in the works of thirteenth-century redactors like Albert of Stade and Guido delle Colonne, love replaced wrath as Achilles' most characteristic passion.

Following the shifting fortunes of Achilles through periods of Athenian, Macedonian, Roman, and Christian imperialism in the hands of poets, generals, philosophers, priests, and patriots is fascinating in and of itself. But, more importantly, such a journey helps readers understand both the resources available in any particular period to writers who wished in some way to draw on the figure of Achilles and the ways in which their audiences might be expected to respond. I have therefore tried to present many details from each re-creation of Achilles in the hope that they will help make possible more sophisticated readings of some of the major works produced in ancient Rome and Renaissance Europe.

The best classical and Renaissance poets experienced their literary past as not so much a burden as a challenge, a resource rather than a source of anxiety. This resource consisted in much more than just the stock of exemplary phrases, images, and ideas that has furnished so much detective work to generations of scholars. More than mere models, the well-known words, phrases, and motifs of predecessors are incorporated as the raw material of a new master poet's system of imagery, bringing connotations that either support the primary message of the poem (thereby functioning as a source of authority) or oppose it (thereby creating tension and/or irony).[6]

Homer provided an abundant amount of striking raw material to poets who would revive Achilles in the person of their own heroes: the youthful warrior, the brutally vengeful warrior, preeminent prowess, wrath, obsession with honor, the quarrel between king and best warrior, the choice of imperishable glory over long life, the divine shield, fire-star imagery. All these became *topoi* that could instantly create an Achillean context. Certain similes, such as the one in *Iliad* 22 comparing Achilles to the Dog Star, had the same power. In addition, the poet steeped in Homer and writing for an audience equally conversant with the Greek epics might allude analogically to Achilles by incorporating details of scenes that cannot themselves be classified as *topoi*. An example of such a detail can be found in the last scene of Vergil's *Aeneid,* when

Turnus picks up and vainly heaves a rock at Aeneas, just as Aeneas in *Iliad* 20 picked up and was about to heave a rock vainly at Achilles.

Some poets use this raw material in complicated ways. Vergil, for instance, uses the stereotypic figure of Achilles initially as an exemplar of traditional epic heroism at its most violent. In the first half of the *Aeneid* he skews the reader's recollection of the Homeric original by interjecting details that evoke the least favorable non-Homeric traditions. Following Plato and Cicero, he sets up a new kind of spiritual heroism in opposition to the physical heroism exemplified by Achilles and explicitly uses the Iliadic Achilles as the archetype for Aeneas's opponent, Turnus. In Books One to Seven, Achilles is viewed as a manifestation of the irrationality that constantly threatens to destroy human civilization, and he functions as a simple foil to Aeneas's forced romanization. In Books Ten to Twelve, however, by using details, images, and *topoi* from *Iliad* 19–22, Vergil invests *pius* Aeneas with more Achillean nuance than his passionate opponent and thus re-creates the civil war in Italy as a continuing struggle between the old Homeric and the new Roman components of heroism within Aeneas's psyche. Surprisingly, the Roman does not win. When Vergil presents Aeneas's final act as one of personal vengeance conceived as religious duty, this synthesis of Achilles and *pietas*, in addition to perhaps making a political comment on the contemporary Caesarean mingling of power politics and religion, helps create a hero who has no self and a world view that has disturbingly little clarity—the perfect expression in microcosm of the effect of civil war on states.

The kind of analysis I have just outlined for reading Vergil is necessary for a more complete understanding of the many other poets who have wished to make contemporary statements about Homeric heroism. But for this method to be most successful, detailed knowledge about Achilles is indispensible, particularly so in the case of Renaissance poets like Tasso and Shakespeare, who had two equally strong traditions to manipulate. I hope, therefore, that the present systematic study of the varying political and moral interpretations attached to the many episodes of Achilles' career will be of use to all those scholars whose excellent analyses of Achilles in Renaissance poetry have stimulated my investigations by both their perspecuity and their necessary limitations.

THE ARCHETYPE

HOMER'S ACHILLES

In order to comprehend most clearly how later poets use Achillean motifs to animate their own heroes and political messages, it is necessary to have a thorough understanding of how these motifs function in the Iliadic portrait, which became archetypal because of Homer's great authority. My task in this chapter will therefore be to set forth these motifs—many of which for centuries had the power instantly to evoke Achilles—and to discuss them in the context of Homer's conception of his hero.

Of prime importance is Achilles' undoubted claim to the epithet "best of the Achaians," an epithet that comprises not only physical qualities but also a humanistic complexity that survives, if fitfully, into the Italian Renaissance. My analysis of Homer's use of Achilles' superlativeness leads naturally—but subvertingly—into an examination of the unsurpassed prowess displayed in Achilles' rampage, a period of total and uncharacteristic brutality that became an important motif for Euripides, Catullus, and Vergil as well as for Renaissance poets. Achilles' murderous heroics in this rampage are carefully nuanced by analogical allusion and simile to remove any sense of human nobility from the warcraft that eventually kills Hektor and thus creates another important motif: the effective conquering of a city by wreaking personal vengeance on that city's champion.

There remains the question of why Homer so nuanced Achilles' fighting. The first part of my answer discusses how Achilles' unique combination of qualities and behaviors functions as part of Homer's critique of heroic society and his exploration of what it means to be human, mortal. The famous wrath and the equally famous honor and

glory are the focal points of this section, which delineates Achilles' ago-
nizing reassessment of the kind of glory he is willing to die for. The next
part analyzes what becomes perhaps the most misrepresented motif in
Achilles' career: the final reconciliation with Priam, which in Homer's
version profoundly alters the reader's understanding of what it means to
be both human and "best."

All the images, speeches, and scenes that create powerful motifs for
later poets contribute in the *Iliad* to an original portrait that distinguishes Achilles as much for his self-awareness as for his wrath; as much
for his need for meaningfulness as for his pride; as much for his compassion as for his ability to kill. All contribute to the poignancy of the
last scene, which takes place under the shadow of Achilles' own imminent death. By prefiguring but not consummating this death within the
Iliad, Homer leaves us with the eternal poignancy of certain death waiting within a superlative living mind and body; he leaves us, that is, with
the essence of what it means to be mortal. But when in his later postwar
epic Homer shows us Achilles dead, the poignancy of his predicament is
gone. In the *Odyssey* it is Odysseus who engages our emotions; Achilles'
character is simplified so as to set in clear relief the now more complexly
developed portrait of the man who in many ways is his opposite. My
final brief look at Achilles' role in the *Odyssey* will thus adumbrate the
classical stereotyping of Achilles as a warrior of quick anger, stark honesty, superlative prowess, and obsession with worldly honor.

1. BEST OF THE ACHAIANS

When Achilles left to join the Greek army at Troy, his father's parting
charge was that he "always be best (*aristeúein*) and superior to others"
(11.784).[1] Among the bellicose Greeks, to whom, as Odysseus says,
"Zeus has given to wage painful wars from youth till old age" (14.85–87),
it is not surprising that *aristeúein* most often translates "perform greatest deeds of martial valor."[2] This is undoubtedly what Achilles has in
mind by the word *áristos*, "best," when he says that Agamemnon will
bitterly regret not honoring "the best of the Achaians" when without
his protection masses of Greeks fall dead at the hands of Hektor (1.240–
244).[3] There is no question even before he takes the field in the *Iliad*
that he is in fact the best warrior of them all.[4] But though both *aristeúein*
and Achilles have a bias toward war, neither is totally restricted to this.

Aristeúein can also describe Nestor's never-surpassed excellence in counsel (11.627), and Homer's Achilles fulfills Peleus's behest with almost every superlative imagined in the world of the *Iliad:* he is the swiftest, the most beautiful, the youngest, and, very importantly, the most complex of the heroes who fight at Troy.

The Swiftest Warrior: By far the most commonly employed of the six epithets used only for Achilles are the three that refer to his speed. He is *pódas ōkùs* (thirty-one times), *podárkēs* (twenty-one times), *podōkeos* (eleven times)—"swift-footed Achilles."[5] Diomedes may supply Achilles' place as *áristos* in the front ranks for a while in Book Five, and Aias may merit Idomeneus's supreme praise of being equal in fixed combat, but, we are told, no one can rival Achilles in running (13.324–325). This native speed, which is impressed upon us over and over through the traditional epithets, is made an essential part of the hero's terrible warcraft in Books Twenty-One and Twenty-Two when Achilles chases the stampeding Trojans nearly to the gates of Troy and when Hektor, even with the aid of Apollo, cannot outrun his maddened pursuer and escape to the protection of the walls.

The Most Beautiful Warrior: Achilles' beauty goes beyond that which seems to be the standard concomitant of nobility. The goodly appearance of a hero is regularly expressed by the word *eîdos,* "comeliness."[6] Achilles' beauty is expressed by the word *kalós,*[7] an adjective infrequently attached to male physiognomy though used regularly to express aesthetic appreciation of women and objects.[8] Among men it is used first of Nireus, a figure whose sole appearance is in the Catalogue and whose sole function seems to be to mark Achilles' extraordinary beauty. When we hear that "Nireus came beneath Ilium the most beautiful (*kállistos*) man of all the Danaans after flawless Achilles" (2.671–674), we learn that Achilles, in addition to his supreme valor, is also supreme in beauty. But in contrast to Achilles, who combines superlative beauty with superlative prowess, Nireus is "weak and has few followers" (2.675).[9]

Great beauty linked with slight valor is found also in Paris, of whom *kalós* is used twice in Book Three, once at the beginning when Hektor rebukes him for cowardice, pointing out the discrepancy between his *kalòn eîdos* and his minimal valor (3.44–45),[10] and then near the end when Aphrodite tells Helen to go to her vanquished husband, who is waiting on the bed, glistening in beauty (*kállei*) and looking as if he were going to or had just ceased from the dance (3.391–394). Two other young men possess this kind of beauty: Ganymede, "the most beautiful of mortal men," whose *kállos* (the noun form of *kalós*) earned him immortality as Zeus's wine pourer (20.232–235), and Bellerophon, whose *kállos* provoked adulterous lust and a vengeful charge of rape (6.156–165). It is clear that for Paris, Ganymede, and Bellerophon, *kalós* and *kállos* express a stunning and sexually enticing beauty rather than the comeliness that is the normal visible expression of nobility.

In one instance *kalós* seems to be used in a more neutral sense: Priam tells Helen he has never seen anyone so *kalós* and so dignified (3.169–170) as the Agamemnon she has just identified from the wall. We can either suppose that the unexpected adjective refers to the gorgeous armor described in Book Two, rather than the flesh and features, or feel the same contrast here as with Nireus and Paris, in whom beauty and valor were at odds. In Agamemnon's case it would not be physical but moral strength that was lacking. A lack of moral strength may be inferred also in Bellerophon's story, since Glaukos states that he became hated by the gods and ended his life miserably (6.200–202).[11] In any case, only in Achilles does *kállos* coexist with all the other excellences that a man and a warrior are expected to have if he is to be called *áristos*. Surprisingly enough, centuries later, when medieval authors have all but forgotten Achilles' surpassing swiftness, youth, and complexity, his marvelous beauty will still evoke comment.

The "Youngest" Warrior: When Achilles left for the war, he was, Phoinix says, *nḗpios*, "a child, inexperienced in either battle or assembly, where men (*ándres*) become distinguished" (9.440–441). Nine years, twelve sacked cities, and presumably many assemblies[12] later, he has in the *Iliad* firmly taken his place among *ándres* as the "speaker of words and doer of deeds" that Phoinix was sent to teach him to be (9.442–443). Yet there is ever present about him a sense of extreme youth. It comes not just from our being told that the older Patroklos was enjoined to act as advisor (11.786–789) or from Odysseus's politic remark that he surpasses Achilles in thought because he is older (19.218–219).[13] It emerges much more strongly from the presence of Thetis, the mother who comes to comfort her son when he grieves and who joins to his sorrow her own lamentation that, far from sharing her immortality, he has but a little portion of life (*aîsa mínuntha*), he is *ōkúmoros perì pán-tōn*, "swift-doomed" or "short-lived" beyond others (1.417, 505; 18.95, 458). Achilles is the only person in the *Iliad* to receive this adjective, and it is given him only by his mother, who, because she is a goddess, is privy to knowledge that her son will die young. Achilles is thus the only hero who knows absolutely that he will die at Troy,[14] and, as E. T. Owen points out, this knowledge plus Thetis's tender, mournful, and immortal motherhood accentuate the shortness of his life.[15]

Achilles' youth is associated with the general theme of life being cut short in war. Many men are short-lived in the *Iliad*, and four of them are described by the specific word *minunthádios*, "short-lived" or "of short duration," which Achilles uses of himself at 1.352. In a scene of utmost pathos, before Achilles kills him and throws his body into the river, Lykaon moans truthfully that his mother bore him *minunthádios* (21.84–85). *Minunthádios* again contributes to pathos when it is used twice of men who are killed by Aias, both times as part of a larger formulaic group (4.477–479 = 17.301–303):

> Nor did he pay back the nurturing care of his
> parents, but his life was of short duration (*minunthádios*),
> beaten down by the spear of great-hearted Aias.

In their second occurrence these verses stand almost alone to mark with a fleeting note of pity Hippothoos's dying far from his fertile homeland. But in Book Four they contribute to what Seth Schein terms the "richest and most exquisite" of many passages that make us "aware of what the war, with its splendid killing, costs in human terms."[16] They follow a brief vignette of the "blooming, unmarried" Simoeisios's birth beside a river and are followed by a carefully wrought simile that compares his death to the felling of a smooth poplar that lies drying, again beside a river. As Schein writes, "We get an idea of youth both blooming and potentially a husband, of warmth and energy which might have been directed toward a peaceful, procreative life but were instead turned to war, where death put an end to warmth, flowering, and potential." "This sense of unfulfillment," he adds, "is strengthened by the statement that Simoeisios didn't repay his parents for rearing him."[17]

All the young men whose deaths Homer has imbued with pathetic beauty contribute both to the poignancy of Thetis's cry, "And he shot up like a young tree nurtured in the best part of an orchard . . . but

I shall not receive him home again in the house of Peleus" (18.56–
60 = 437–441), and to the reflective sadness of Achilles' vision of Peleus (19.322–337),

> who now wasting away in Phthia weeps tears
> in bereavement of such a son as I, who in a foreign city
> on account of horrible Helen, wage war with the Trojans.
> . . . For I think by now Peleus is either wholly
> dead, or, clinging to life a little, grieves
> in hateful old age as he waits always for
> the miserable news, when he shall learn I am dead.

Achilles, the only hero who sees and mourns his own death in terms of
the effect it will have on others,[18] is the explicit and conscious carrier of
the sorrow that pervades his environment. Therefore, though he is not
precisely the youngest of the Greek warriors in actual years,[19] we cannot help feeling with Thetis that he is, in poetic fact, ōkumorótatos,
"shortest-lived" of the Greeks.

Being short-lived is associated not only with war's sorrowful cost but
also with its glorious rewards. The fourth man besides Achilles to receive the epithet minunthádios is Hektor, who is given honor and glory
by Zeus specifically because "he was destined to be minunthádios"
(15.612–613). Dying young is but the extreme expression of the unac-
ceptable fact that all human beings are mortal, that godlike heroes cannot be gods, cannot live forever. In endless cycles we bloom and wither,
no individual, no generation more permanent than leaves on a tree.[20]
The only compensation for this dreadful transience is timé, "honor,"
which one wins most often in the dangerous foreranks of battle. It is
clear from Sarpedon's famous remarks to Glaukos at 12.310–328 that
if youth were not bounded by old age and death there would be no
need to spend it in máchē kudiáneiran, "war that brings men honor"
(322–325). It is only because death in its myriad forms is inescapable
that it behooves a man to attempt to win honor, that is, to win the right
to have the tangible good things of life—ranking place, rich meat,
choice wine, and good farmland—and to be looked up to as the gods
one cannot be. All of this implies a recognition, here and now and by
one's society, of one's worthiness. This recognition, together with kléos,
the intangible companion of timé that disseminates and preserves one's
name and deeds even after death, is what gives life meaning.

A man wins honor and glory in battle specifically by risking that

brief life: "Let us go," says Sarpedon. "We will furnish matter for boasting to another, or someone will give it to us" (12.328). Thus the Homeric hero daily barters the certainty of fulfilling his natural length of
life, whatever it might be, in exchange for the achievement of meaningfulness. Achilles' famous choice, which we learn about in Book Nine,
is part of this theme. When he gave up a long, inglorious life in Phthia
for a short, glorious life on the battlefields of Troy (9.412–416), he was
exchanging, he thought, a meaningless life for a meaningful one, quan-
tity for quality. The difference between his choice and that of the other
heroes is that they have hope, at least, of surviving the war, of not having
to pay the ultimate price for the honor and glory they do and will enjoy.
Achilles knows he must pay. He is not just risking his life for honor like
the others; he is sacrificing it. Thus his reward ought to be all the greater.

If things were as they should be, Achilles' short life should be filled
with great honor. This is the point of his complaint in Book One:

> Mother, since you bore me wholly *minunthádios,*
> the Olympian ought to have given me honor at least,
> high-thundering Zeus; but now he has honored me not even a little.
>
> (352–354)

Thetis, when she has heard his story, responds in kind:

> Would that you were sitting by your ships without tears and without
>   misery,
> since indeed your portion is wholly *mínunthá,* not at all long.
> As it is, you are at the same time both *ōkúmoros* and miserable be-
>   yond all.
>
> (415–418)

When, in addition to these passages, we later hear Thetis request Zeus
to "honor my son, who is *ōkumorótatos* of all men" (505), it is clear that
the shortness of Achilles' life is directly proportioned to the great honor
he is supposed to receive. Achilles' foreknown, foremourned, premature
death thus crystallizes two major themes of the poem. His youth in the
Iliad is nothing more or less than the centralizing expression of both the
glory and the pathos of war.

The Most Complex Warrior: The Iliadic Achilles is not a monolithic
war hero. One legacy he holds from Cheiron is the murderous ash spear
(16.143–144 = 19.390–391); another is the gentle art of healing. Ho-

mer reveals that Achilles possesses this skill in a way that seems designed to enhance its significance. When Machaon, physician son of Asklepios (4.194, 11.518), is wounded near the beginning of the Great Battle, he is quickly taken back to the ships because "a healer is a man worth many others, for cutting out arrows and sprinkling on kindly (*épia*) drugs" (11.514–515). At this point Machaon's wounding seems only a minor incident, but after some seventy-five verses of further fighting, Achilles, who we learn has been standing on the prow of his ship watching the battle, sends Patroklos off to find out if the wounded man really is Ma-

FIGURE 2. Achilles as Healer

chaon. Patroklos ascertains that it is, and as he is running back, persuaded by Nestor to make another appeal to Achilles, he comes across a minor character named Eurypylos, who was wounded shortly after Machaon (11.583–584) and now asks for his help (11.828–832):

> Save me . . .
> Cut the arrow out of my thigh, wash away the dark
> blood with warm water, and sprinkle over it kindly drugs,
> good ones, which they say you have learned from Achilles
> whom Cheiron taught, justest of Centaurs.

Patroklos complies, and his medical activity is described in some detail. Homer does not simply give us a repetition of Eurypylos's request with the second-person imperatives changed to third-person aorists. Instead, he describes Patroklos laying him down, cutting out the sharp arrow, washing away the blood, and applying specific drugs: "He put on pungent root which he had crushed in his hands, a pain killer, which stopped all the pains" (11.844–848).

The healing motif supplies artistic unity and verisimilitude to events designed first to create hope that Achilles is softening and then to create suspense as Patroklos, drawn back into Greek society and intent on getting either Achilles or Achilles' armor to save the Greeks, is delayed in returning until fire has actually reached the ships and the situation is as desperate as it could possibly be.[21] It gives a nice finish to Patroklos's rebuke when he finally does get back to Achilles: "The healers, on the one hand, are working to help the wounded; you, on the other hand . . ." (16.28–29). But Homer manipulates the motif for more than unity; he weaves it into his narrative to mark his hero as different from the other warriors in yet a new way. Though the Iliad's two healers, Asklepios's sons Machaon and Podaleiros, perform also as minor war leaders (2.729–733, 4.200–202, 11.836),[22] the converse is not equally true: no other of the great chiefs besides Achilles is said to have any skill as a healer. Furthermore, Achilles' skill is presumably as great as the professional healers', since Cheiron was his and Asklepios's common teacher.[23] "Worth many men," says Agamemnon, "is the warrior whom Zeus loves" (9.116–117). Worth many men, too, is the healer (11.514–515). Achilles is both. His power to cure as well as to kill makes him more valuable not only to his society but to Homer's audience as well. Though the destructive power overwhelms the constructive one in this story of wrath and war, the gentleness of the healer's "kindly drugs" is there to draw our imaginations to a world of more kindly potential.

A similar pull on our imaginations is made by an earlier view of Achilles' gentler side in Book Nine. When Odysseus, Aias, and Phoinix arrive to supplicate the wrathful man of war, they find him

> delighting his heart with a clear-sounding lyre (*phórmingi*),
> a beautiful one, intricately carved, with a cross-bar of silver,
> which he took from the spoils (*enárōn*) when he destroyed the city
> of Eetion;
> with it he pleasured his heart, and he sang the glorious stories of men
> (*kléa andrôn*).
>
> (9.186–189)

Achilles is not the only man in the *Iliad* to sing. The Achaians as a group honor Apollo with song when they return Chryseis (1.472–474); they sing the paean (or at least Achilles urges them to) as they return to the ships after Hektor's death (22.391–392). But he is the only one to sing individually, and he is the only one except for the Trojan Paris[24] to have anything to do with the lyre. In Paris's case skill with the lyre (*kítharis*[25]) is associated with Aphrodite and is mentioned by Hektor, who sets it in opposition to warlike valor, specifically as a rebuke. In Book Nine one might be tempted to say that it is again opposed to warlike valor and to take the absorption in music as symbolic of Achilles' withdrawal from fighting. But we must note how he got the lovingly described lyre: he won it as part of the spoils (*énara*—a word elsewhere used only of the bloody armor of the slain) from a city he sacked. There is no opposition between lyre and battle here. They are both at home in the character of Achilles.[26]

The warrior won it, and the warrior sings. The subject of his song, *kléa andrôn*, "glories of men," also belongs to the warrior. We will soon learn that Achilles came to fight and die at Troy with the assurance of earning *kléos áphthiton*, "imperishable glory" (9.413). And soon after that we will hear Phoinix try to persuade Achilles by drawing from the "*kléa* of former heroes" (*tôn prósthen* . . . *kléa andrôn / hēróōn*, 9.524–525) an exemplary story analogous to his situation and conduct. Phoinix's use of the phrase fixes the referent for Achilles' song: Achilles is recounting martial deeds that won warriors like himself postmortem survival in glorious remembrance. But the word *kléa* here probably designates both glorious deeds and the songs that perpetuate them. If Gregory Nagy is right, *kléos* was originally "the formal word which the Singer himself (ἀοιδός) used to designate the songs which he sang in praise of gods and men, or, by extension, the songs which people learned to sing from him."[27] Therefore when Achilles sings we should think of him as both recalling *kléa* (deeds) and creating/performing *kléa* (songs). This is the function and art of every bard, but it has special point when the singer's primary function in life is to be creating *kléos* through performing his own glorious deeds. During his withdrawal from fighting into private status Achilles has stepped back from his role as doer of heroic deeds to become a shaper of heroic meaning.

He performs this shaping in an isolation that is intensified by the very fact of his singing. Song elsewhere in the *Iliad* is communal. The Achaians, as noted above, sing together in a group; the Muses sing for the enjoyment of the assembled gods (1.603–604); and on Achilles' shield a boy plays and sings for maidens and young men who respond joyfully to his music as they bring in the grape harvest (18.567–572). The singing of *kléa* ought to be no exception, since "glory" by definition demands a wide and consenting audience. But Achilles has no audience when he plays and sings; he pleasures only himself (*phréna terpómenon, thumòn éterpen*). There is but one other person present, his closest friend, Patroklos, and of him we are told only that he sits "in silence / awaiting the time when Achilles should finish singing" (9.190–191). Achilles has withdrawn into a realm so private that even Patroklos cannot fully share it. The mood seems one more appropriate to lyric songs of the self than to epic lays.[28] But this mood does not so much clash with the heroic subject as change that subject. Heroism for Achilles has become, like love, something intensely personal and, like love gone wrong, something intensely lonely.

Achilles' singing is the haunting prelude to the revelation of his disillusionment with the heroic code. It introduces the true subject of the embassy episode: What kind of story about myself, what action made eternally famous through song, what *kléos* is worth the sacrifice of my life?[29]

The Shield: When Achilles resumes his warrior role in Book Eighteen, Homer marks the extraordinary complexity of his hero by giving him an extraordinarily complicated shield. The two other shields described in the *Iliad* are things of pure terror. On Athene's shield (the aegis) are Strife (*Éris*), Prowess (*Alkḗ*), chilling Pursuit (*Iōkḗ*), and the terrible head of the monstrous Gorgon; Panic (*Phóbos*) is set all round it (5.739–742). The devices on Agamemnon's shield are equally focused on war, equally apotropaic: Fear (*Deîmos*) and Panic (*Phóbos*) surround a grim-looking Gorgon in the center, and a three-headed serpent is coiled on the strap (11.36–40). In contrast to these, Achilles' shield contains "a summary picture of the world,"[30] which tends to attract its viewers rather than to frighten them away.

FIGURE 3. Thetis Watches Hephaistos Make Achilles' Armor

In the center are sea, earth, and sky, sun, moon, and stars (18.483–489). There are two cities, one at war, the other at peace. In the city at peace there are two scenes, one of marriage and another of civil judgment over bloodprice (490–508). In the city at war there is debate, defense, and an ambush in which Strife (*Éris*), Confusion (*Kudoimós*) and Death (*Kér*) join in the bloody moil (509–540). Outside of the cities, agricultural scenes depict ploughing and harvesting both of grain and of grapes (541–568). The joyous singing of the grape-harvest scene (569–572) is balanced by the violence of two terrible lions who attack herds in a pastoral scene (573–586). Sheep flocks in a lovely meadow (586–589) and young men and women dancing (590–606) form the last scenes. The great strength of Ocean encircles all (607–608).

Unlike the devices on the shields of Agamemnon and Athene, which are limited to the terrifying images of war, Achilles' shield depicts human life in all its myriad changes. Bloodprice and wedding, war and harvest, sudden death and dancing are all present in its great dynamic circle. As J. T. Sheppard has said, "At the highest moment of his glory and his sorrow, strong young and beautiful, and so near death, the hero goes to fight his battle with a shield on which Hephaistos has emblazoned both the sweetness and the uncertainty of life."[31]

When the death of Patroklos takes away the sweetness of his own life, Achilles' vision becomes limited to violence. But as he carries the wondrous shield into his rampage, he carries also the promise that he will return to its complex human perspective, that he will not remain what he temporarily becomes: the incarnation of the Terrors that form the entirety of Agamemnon's and the war goddess's shields.

2. THE BE⟨A⟩ST OF THE ACHAIANS

The gentler side of Achilles that is revealed in his healing, singing, and shield finds an analogue in accounts of his earlier, pre-Iliadic fighting. These descriptions distinguish him not only for his prowess[32] but also for his mercy and regard for the suppliant. His past behavior provides the only instances mentioned in the *Iliad* of prisoners being taken or released for ransom (6.414–428; 11.104–106, 111–112), and this behavior stands in sharp contrast to that of the Greek leader Agamemnon, who thrice rejects the suppliant.[33] Homer, it seems, has deliberately led us to expect that Achilles, when he comes to fight in the *Iliad*, will be more

humane than Agamemnon and most of the other warriors, whose fighting has become increasingly savage as the Battle Books progress.[34] Instead, he is the most violent, most terrible warrior of them all.

The violence and terror of Achilles' battles may be best understood
by comparison with the *aristeía,* "extended display of martial prowess,"
of Agamemnon. Homer's art works by allusion and analogy, repetition
of generic scenes with additions of particular or recombinations of typical details.[35] In the case of Achilles, whether the allusion is to former self
or to another hero's actions, the effect is always intensification—for
better or worse. When, for instance, we compare his *aristeía* with that
of the brilliantly successful Diomedes, we find an escalation in brilliance, success, and seriousness.[36] But Achilles' monomaniacal desire for
vengeance also makes him capable of an *aristeía* worse even than that of
Agamemnon for its grimness and grisly detail.

Brutal and grisly slaying is associated most of the time with warriors
of the second rank.[37] It is interesting that of the major heroes only
Achilles and Agamemnon, his hated opponent (and, in Whitman's view,
"the nadir, as Achilles is the zenith, of the heroic assumption"[38]), kill
horribly with any consistency.[39] Interesting, too, is "the remarkable co-
incidence of structure and detail" that Bernard Fenik notes between that
part of Achilles' *aristeía* which I shall call his rampage (20.381–21.135)[40]
and Agamemnon's *aristeía* in Book Eleven:

1. *Aristeía* with quick and grisly slaughter of many Trojans.
2. Unhindered pursuit of the Trojans described by a fire simile.
3. Further description of the charging Greek, plus another simile,
   and the descriptive detail of the bloodstained hands.
4. Return to the account of the slaughter.[41]

Fenik offers no thematic interpretation of this correspondence, but
surely just as before Achilles' mercifulness was used as a foil to sharpen
our perception of Agamemnon's brutality, so here Agamemnon's previous brutality serves to deepen our sense of Achilles' descent into horror.
When Achilles' slayings go beyond Agamemon's both in number and in
grimness of detail, there is a dreadful sense that the man has crossed the
bounds of his own nature, has gone to the level of his opposite, the level
of a man who would bayonet pregnant women (6.58–59).

When Achilles leaps amid the Trojans after his fight with Aeneas and
his near fight with Hektor, he swiftly and brutally kills thirteen Trojans,

some named, some unnamed (20.382–489). There follow two similes in quick succession: Achilles' rampage is like raging, inhuman fire driven through the forests of a parched mountain (20.490–494). And as oxen thresh grain, so his horses trample bodies and shields together (20.495–499). The dark earth runs with blood (20.494); the axles and wheels of the chariot are splattered with blood thrown from the horses' hooves (20.499–502); his hands, as he strains to carry off glory, are mottled with bloody gore (20.502–503).

As Fenik pointed out, a fire simile (11.155–157) and the detail of the bloodstained hands (20.503 = 11.169) are found also in Agamemnon's *aristeía*. But though the function in both cases is to intensify the sense of grim destructiveness, the details within the simile and the context of the bloodstained hands mark the difference in the brutality of the two men. Achilles' fire is more intense, more active. It is not only divinely kindled (*thespidaés*), it races wildly (*anamaimáei*) through the mountain as the wind drives it in confusion (*klonéōn eilupházei*). The force of the simile is in the manic sweep of the fire: as it sweeps so sweeps (*thûne*) Achilles with his spear. Agamemnon's uncomplicatedly destructive (*aídē-lon*) fire simply falls upon (*empésēi*) the woods, where it is rolled along (*eiluphóōn phérei*) by the wind, both fire and killer being relegated to the dative case as attention is shifted to the bushes and heads that fall under their assault. Agamemnon's brutality is viewed from without as the simile emphasizes matter-of-fact destruction. Achilles' is viewed from within: the racing fire driven by the wind reflects not only his destructive action but also the wild grief that impels it. By using the words *anamaimáei* (a unique compound formed from the common *maimáō*, "shake with eagerness") and *klonéōn*, "throw into disorder," Homer here forges a strong link between the natural fire of the simile and the metaphorical "fire" of human passion,[42] and he thereby subtly shifts Achilles towards the elemental world of nature.

The detail of the bloody hands is placed at an almost equal distance from the fire simile in both cases,[43] but the intervening verses create greatly differing atmospheres. In Agamemnon's case there is the pathos of horses pulling empty chariots and the bodies of the drivers lying on the ground, a brief glimpse of Hektor's being led out of the moil by Zeus, then Agamemnon's exhorting the Danaans and screaming as he pursues the Trojans. In Achilles' case there is no such diversity: there is no sound, no other person but the mass of dead and dying. There is only Achilles, his spear, his chariot, his horses, his hands—and the blood that unites them.[44] Agamemnon's bloodstained hands are merely one significant detail in Homer's brutal portrait. In the depiction of Achilles' wrath they become almost emblematic. He is not just one example of a brutal man, he is brutality incarnate.

The blood spreads to the river (21.21), and there, when his hands grow tired with killing, Achilles takes twelve Trojan youths alive—not to ransom but to sacrifice on Patroklos's pyre (21.26–32). He then slays the naked and helpless Lykaon, whom he had captured and ransomed once before but who now begs in vain to be spared a second time. With Lykaon, as with the two brothers who asked mercy from Agamemnon in Book Eleven, "it is an unyielding voice he hears"[45] in reply (21.99–113):

> Poor innocent, do not keep speaking to me of ransom—
> For it was before death overtook Patroklos
> that it was dearer to my heart to spare Trojans,
> and I took many alive and sold them.
> Now there is not one who may escape death if a god
> casts him into my hands before Ilium,
> not one of all the Trojans, and especially the sons of Priam.
> Come, friend, die, you too. Why do you complain so?
> Patroklos, too, died, though he was a much better man than you.
> And me, do you not see how beautiful and tall I am?—
> my father noble, a goddess my mother.
> But still even to me belongs death and resistless doom.
> There will come a morning, or an evening, or a noontime
> when someone in battle will take the life even from me,
> striking either with his spear or with an arrow from the bowstring.

The ruthless inexorability of the words is sharpened by the pitifulness of the death that follows. Lykaon falls back, spreading wide his arms, while Achilles draws his sword and plunges it full into the unprotected neck.

Just before the sword pierces his neck, Lykaon is called "friend" (*phílos*) (21.106). There are two other times in the *Iliad* when enemies call each other *phílos*, both marking occasions when killing has *not* occurred. Diomedes tells Glaukos they should not fight, because each is a guest friend, *xeînos phílos* (6.224–225), to the other—there are plenty of others to kill. Hektor bids Aias exchange gifts with him at the end of their duel, so that others will say, "They fought in hate, parted in friend-

ship," *philótēti* (7.301–302). The first friendship is based on the guest-
host relationship; the second, it would appear, on a recognition of common humanity. Both are present in Achilles' "friend," and both are horribly transmuted to a kinship whose only bond is death.[46] As Michael
Nagler says, "one sees Achilles rejecting every compact of human intercourse: sympathy for one's age mate (20.465), *aidōs* for the guest, for the
suppliant, for him with whom one has broken bread, all these are flung
into the river with the body of Lykaon."[47]

When Achilles flings the dead youth into the river, Homer gives him
the familiar victor's vaunt that his unburied victim will be eaten by animals.[48] Such vaunting here and elsewhere reveals a particularly unpleasant aspect of the mood of men in war, that which James Redfield has
called the necessary "impurity" of the warrior wherein one's enemy is
"objectified, denied the privileges due to persons in community. He becomes mere nature."[49] Here the effect of the *topos* is intensified by
lengthy elaboration (21.122–127):

> Lie there now among the fishes, who, careless,
> will lick the blood off your wound. Nor will your mother
> lay you out on a bed and lament you. But Skamander
> will carry you, whirling, to the broad gulf of the sea.
> Leaping along the wave, there will dart from under a dark ripple
> a fish who will devour the white fat of Lykaon.

In this perversion of a funeral, blood will pass from man to fish, human
consolatory ritual will whirl into the obliterating processes of nature.
When Achilles repeats his determination that all Trojans die to pay for
the death of Patroklos and the destruction of the Achaians (21.133–134),
accumulated disgust makes the audience react even more negatively
than it did to Agamemnon's similar desire in Book Six.

Insofar as we see Achilles as still human, we may say that he has
crossed the bounds of his own character to that of his unheroic opposite. But there are indications that we must go further than this, or at
least in a different direction, that Homer wants us to see Achilles as
having somehow crossed the bounds of *human nature*. One such indication is the pattern of fire imagery, which, beginning with the divinely
kindled fire that blazes from his head in the trench and continuing
through the evening star that marks the end of his duel with Hektor,

contributes to our seeing Achilles as an increasingly deadly elemental force. Another indication is the series of lion similes, which suggests that Achilles' deadly force is not only elemental but bestial as well.

Both of these images—fire and lions—have been extensively associated with martial heroism before Achilles resumes his warrior role. Fire, as Whitman has shown, early becomes a "simple metonym for war,"[50] and, as the epic develops, it takes on connotations of heroic rage and valor. At their moments of greatest invincibility and inspired energy heroes are often compared to destructive fire. With Achilles, however, fire becomes "symbolic, from simply imagistic."[51] This is because Achilles is so much more intensely associated with fire that we come to think of him not merely as like but indeed *as* fire itself.

This conception of him is well begun in the arming scene (19.364–399), where Achilles becomes, as Whitman says, "all but identified with fire."[52] The brilliance of the armor is joined to Achilles' own inner fury by the word *sélas* ('brightness' or 'flash').[53] His eyes "flashed" (*sélas exepháanthen,* 19.17) in increased anger when he first saw the armor (15–17), and they again "flash like fire" (*lampésthēn hōs eí te puròs sélas,* 366) when he puts it on, gnashing his teeth and possessed by "unbearable grief" (365–367). The *sélas* of his shield is like that of the moon (374). It is also like the *sélas* of a fire that, blazing high in the mountains on a lonely steading, is seen by unhappy storm-swept sailors as they are borne out to sea far from their loved ones (375–378). Like this fire, the *sélas* of his shield "reaches to the sky" (379),[54] where the fire imagery now remains: his helmet shines (*apélampen*) like a star (381), and when he has completed his arming, Achilles is "all shining (*pamphaínōn*) like the Sun" (398).

The imagery continues in progressively more destructive similes through Achilles' rampage. The inhuman fire that sweeps in fury through mountain timbers (20.490–492), the blast that drives the locusts before it (21.12–14), the city burning with the wrath of gods upon it (21.522–524), all will culminate, as Achilles races "all-shining" (*pamphaínonth'*) from the field of indiscriminate slaughter to his single combat with Hektor, in an image that stretches from the positive to the negative poles of heroic action: Achilles shines like the Dog Star, the star that is brightest in the heavens, the star that is, on earth, a bane (22.26–31).

This fire imagery contributes to our seeing Achilles as an increasingly deadly elemental force. Fire, however, has already developed associations with divinity,[55] and with Achilles these associations increase. Not only does Athene kindle fire around his head when he appears unarmed at the trench to frighten the Trojans away from Patroklos's body (18.203– 214), but she also distills ambrosia, food of the gods, into his breast after he has vowed to eat nothing until he shall have killed Hektor (19.345– 354). Hephaistos, "the god of fire himself,"[56] creates the armor that imagistically clothes him in fire as he sets out to fulfill this vow. And when the angry Xanthos threatens to drown Achilles, Hephaistos becomes elemental fire to answer the waters' challenge.[57] We must, then, view fire in Books Eighteen through Twenty-Two as the symbol of Achilles' progression to the superhuman or divine.

The other image, however, that of the lion, insists simultaneously that we understand Achilles' deadly energy also as the brute force of beasts, that we view his ascent to the superhuman as simultaneously a descent to the subhuman. For the lion, too, though it occurs much less often in the rampage than fire, shifts from image to symbol when it is associated with Achilles.

The lion, as Bernard Fenik points out, is "the most common simile subject for describing fighting men."[58] All of the major heroes except Aeneas and Odysseus[59] have at least one such simile that is elaborated to three lines or more. The dispositions or inner states manifested by "lionness" are listed by Wolfgang Schadewaldt as "strong wildness, nobility, courage, dangerous thirst for blood, and mercilessness."[60] Though details in the similes, as both Schadewaldt and Hermann Fränkel point out, often form a bridge to the narrative,[61] and though very often the lion's action is fitted to the hero's personality,[62] still the lion normally is not anthropomorphized but is kept firmly within the bounds of his distinct realm of nature. The lion imagery that vivifies the Homeric warrior's more bestial side does not ever suggest a true merging of the animal's nature with the human's.[63] It does not, that is, until it is used to depict Achilles' grief and wrath.

Achilles' grief is expressed throughout Books Eighteen and Nineteen by repeated groaning.[64] At 18.318 a lion simile occurs that tells us that from this point on these groans, to use Fränkel's words, "should communicate not only sorrow, but also a wild thirst for vengeance."[65] The lion simile, as a matter of fact, marks the *genesis* of that thirst for vengeance.

Achilles first groans (*éstene*) as he lies in the dust, and his grief is such that Antilochos is afraid he will kill himself (18.33–34). He continues to groan (*stenáchōn*, 18.70, 78) as he tells his mother what happened, concluding with the declaration that he now has no purpose in life other than killing Hektor (18.78–81, 91–93, 98). Thetis takes his intent to re-enter the fighting in its most positive light: "It is a good thing to defend your friends" (18.128–129). And this positive interpretation is carried over into the simile that compares him to a besieged city's beacon fires when he shouts at the trench (18.207–213).

Achilles next groans over Patroklos's body, like a lion who, grieving (*áchnutai*) over his stolen cubs, travels far in hopes of tracking down the hunter: "For anger exceedingly bitter (*drimùs chólos*) seized him. / So Achilles, groaning deeply (*barù stenáchōn*), addressed the Myrmidons" (18.318–323). There follows an expression of pure grief, then a vow of untypically savage vengeance: he will not perform Patroklos's funeral until he brings back Hektor's head and armor; he will cut the throats of twelve Trojan youths (*tékna*) before the pyre "in anger (*cholōtheís*) over Patroklos's slaying" (334–337).[66] A lion, then, and a slightly personified one—*áchnutai* is not elsewhere used of animals—is the first image specifically to conjoin Achilles' grief and the anger of his uncharacteristically brutal rampage. Gone is any positive aspect (i.e., defending his friends) of his return to battle; pure destruction has come to the fore.[67]

A lion also introduces Achilles' entry into battle. But before I consider this simile, I should like to consider, of the thirty-four similes that are used of other heroes, Diomedes' at 5.136–142 and Sarpedon's at 12.299–306 to help elucidate what Homer is doing when he creates Achilles' lion simile at 20.164–173. I have chosen these similes in particular, first, because each introduces a hero's entry into the fighting (a reentry in Diomedes' case) and, second, because taken in combination they contain between them the basic elements of Achilles' simile: Diomedes' lion is wounded, as is that of Achilles, and the behavior of Sarpedon's lion is suggestive of the "heroic code," as is that of Achilles.[68]

Near the beginning of his *aristeía* Diomedes is wounded by Pandaros and withdraws from the fighting until he is healed by Athene. As he reenters the battle, a tripled rage seizes him

> like a lion
> whom a shepherd among wooly-fleeced sheep in the country
> wounds but does not subdue as he leaps over the pen.
> He has roused the lion's strength, and then he cannot stand in his
> defense

but retreats into buildings, and the sheep flee abandoned.
These are piled up on top of one another;
But he, enraged (*emmemaòs*), leaps out of the high-walled pen.
So enraged (*memaòs*) strong Diomedes engaged with the Trojans.

(5.136–143)

The lion in this simile is simple and straightforward. There is but one
point in the simile—the lion's rage—that finds a definite analogue in
the action.[69] The relevant point is that Diomedes is more dangerous
now, just as a lion is more dangerous when wounded. The details in this
simile look neither forwards nor backwards. The lion remains firmly in
the animal world of the simile, Diomedes in his heroic one.

The lion in the simile that describes Sarpedon when Zeus arouses him
to attack the Achaian wall shows some faint beginnings of personification:

He set off like a mountain-reared lion who has a
long time lacked meat, and his bold spirit (*thumòs agénōr*) urges him
to go even into a secure dwelling to try for sheep.
For even if he find there herdsmen
guarding the sheep with dogs and spears,
not even so is he minded to be chased from the farmyard without
   having made an attempt.
But leaping in, either he snatches or is himself struck (*éblēt'*)
in the foreranks (*en prótoisi*) by a javelin from a swift hand.
So at that time his spirit (*thumòs*) incited godlike Sarpedon
to leap against the wall and break the breastwork.

(12.299–308)

The lion's heart is *agénōr*, a word most often used of human courage and
connected by etymology (*aga* + *anér*) to the human realm. Armed
guards do not deter the lion from attacking the herd, but leaping in he
"either snatches or is struck (*éblēt'*) in the foreranks (*en prótoisi*)." This is
similar to what Sarpedon, when he explains the heroic code a few lines
later, says he expects to happen to him and Glaukos. It is an integral part
of the heroic code to fight *en prótoisi*,[70] as Sarpedon points out a few
lines later (318–321) when he says that he and Glaukos are not *akleées*,
"without glory," since they fight in the foreranks (*metà prótoisi*). Acceptance of the either-or proposition "kill or be killed" is equally important, as the audience has heard earlier in Odysseus's more abbreviated
statement of the heroic code: "The man who is a hero (*aristeúēisi*) must
stand firmly whether he be struck (*é t'éblēt'*) or strike (*é t'ébal'*) another" (11.409–410).[71] The heroic significance of this is brought out by

Sarpedon's formulation at 12.328: "Let us go: either we will furnish matter for boasting to another, or someone will give it to us."

The resemblances between a human hero and a lion in this simile are, however, superficial rather than organic. The difference in the formulation of the either-or clause is critical. The lion's "he snatches . . . or is struck," in the common gnomic aorist tense of similes, is a matter of (imaginative) fact. It lacks the generalizing *te*'s of Odysseus's phrasing[72] and, more importantly, it lacks the expression of intent in both his and Sarpedon's statements.[73] Therefore, though the simile is particularly suited to evoke Sarpedon's own characteristic courage, it does not confuse his nature with the animal's. Instead, it sets up the brute facts that Sarpedon's formulation will attempt to transcend by means of the specifically human constructs of honor and glory.[74]

We find something quite different when we look at Achilles' lion simile. It has elements common to both Diomedes' and Sarpedon's similes, but these common elements only reveal how different this simile and this warrior are. Achilles approaches Aeneas like a ravening lion

Πηλείδης δ᾽ ἑτέρωθεν ἐναντίον ὦρτο λέων ὥς,
σίντης, ὅν τε καὶ ἄνδρες ἀποκτάμεναι μεμάασιν
ἀγρόμενοι πᾶς δῆμος· ὁ δὲ πρῶτον μὲν ἀτίζων
ἔρχεται, ἀλλ᾽ ὅτε κέν τις ἀρηϊθόων αἰζηῶν
δουρὶ βάλῃ, ἑάλη τε χανών, περί τ᾽ ἀφρὸς ὀδόντας
γίγνεται, ἐν δέ τέ οἱ κραδίῃ στένει ἄλκιμον ἦτορ,
οὐρῇ δὲ πλευράς τε καὶ ἰσχία ἀμφοτέρωθεν
μαστίεται, ἑὲ δ᾽ αὐτὸν ἐποτρύνει μαχέσασθαι,
γλαυκιόων δ᾽ ἰθὺς φέρεται μένει, ἤν τινα πέφνῃ
ἀνδρῶν, ἢ αὐτὸς φθίεται πρώτῳ ἐν ὁμίλῳ.

whom men, when a whole community has gathered itself,
are furious to kill; he at first paying them no attention (*atízōn*)
goes on his way; but when some one of the war-swift young men
strikes him with a spear, he gathers himself, opening wide his jaws,
    froth
appears on his teeth, the courageous heart in his breast groans (*sténei*)
and he whips his sides and haunches with
his tail; he incites himself to fight
and, glaring, he carries himself straight on in his passion (*ménei*) if he
    might kill (*péphnēi*)
someone of the men, or he himself be killed (*phthíetai*) in the forefront.
                                                        (20.164–173)

This lion is highly anthropomorphic. *Atízōn,* "paying no heed," though we cannot compare it to any other epic uses, has definite human connotation through its root *tíō:* "to value," "hold in honor."[75] Unlike Diomedes' lion, whose wound merely rouses his strength, Achilles' lion "groans" (*stḗnei*). It is standard for a hero to groan (*stenáchō, stenachízō*) when wounded,[76] and though other animals and even the earth and rivers are said to "groan" or "make a heavy noise,"[77] this lion is distinguished from all of them by the detail that it is his heart (*ē̂tor*) that does the groaning.[78] "He incites himself to fight" (*heè d'autòn epotrúnei machḗsasthai*) is a variant of a phrase used of leaders exhorting their troops into battle,[79] and, as with Sarpedon's lion, his action takes place "in the forefront" (*prṓtōi en homílōi*). Finally, the idea of intent that was lacking in the earlier lion's either-or action is here present. Homer, by putting the verbs in the subjunctive and introducing them with *ḗn,* makes this lion's "kill or be killed" not the result but the purpose of his attack.[80]

This lion is not only manlike, he is remarkably like the particular man he images.[81] The lion is the enemy of a whole community (*pâs dêmos*); so is Achilles. The lion "pays no heed" to his enemies until he is wounded; so Achilles, after his quarrel with Agamemnon, paid no heed to the Trojans until he was "wounded" by Patroklos's death.[82] Once wounded, froth appears on the lion's teeth, his heart groans, and his eyes glare as he gets ready to spring at his attackers. These lines must recall the moment when Achilles armed:

> ἐν δὲ μέσοισι κορύσσετο δῖος Ἀχιλλεύς.
> τοῦ καὶ ὀδόντων μὲν καναχὴ πέλε, τὼ δέ οἱ ὄσσε
> λαμπέσθην ὡς εἴ τε πυρὸς σέλας, ἐν δέ οἱ ἦτορ
> δῦν' ἄχος ἄτλητον

> In the middle of them godlike Achilles armed.
> There was a grinding of his teeth, his two eyes
> shone like the glare of fire, and into his heart
> there entered unbearable grief.

> (19.364–367)

Both the lion and Achilles have no purpose in fighting other than to kill or be killed. Unlike the lions of Diomedes' and Sarpedon's similes, no hunger and no prey are mentioned—only the men whom he attacks because they have wounded him. So for Achilles death is the only thought—first death for Hektor and as many Trojans as he can kill, then death for himself.

There is not a single extraneous detail in this simile—such as prey for the lion, motivation for the attacking men, hunting dogs, etc.—to distract our attention and lure our minds away from Achilles. The resulting close approximation of total detail combined with the high degree of personification leads to a closer identification between man and lion than anywhere else in the *Iliad*.[83] When other heroes are compared to normal lions, we do not tend actually to picture them as lions. Instead we extract courage or fierceness or strength from the animal, who remains in its own world, and then add them to our composite image of the hero, who remains, however courageous, strong, or fierce he may be, a human being. The confusion of animal and human nature in Achilles' simile has the unique effect of drawing Achilles into the animal's nature. The first simile of his *aristeía* presents us with a lion who is as much a man as a lion; it images a hero who is not only as strong as or as courageous as a lion but as much a lion as he is a man.[84]

Unlike his identification with fire, Achilles' identification with the lion is not maintained by frequent similes. Lions recur only three times more and are reserved for crucial moments. They do not reappear in the rampage until the duel with Hektor, but it is interesting that each of the two fire similes that describe Achilles' inhuman slaughter before the battle with the river is followed by a simile of equal length which draws Achilles' behavior from its context of superhuman to that of subhuman. Raging inhuman fire (20.490–492) images Achilles' killing and rushing everywhere *daímoni îsos*, "equal to a divinity"; immediately thereafter his corpse-trampling horses are compared to oxen crushing barley (20.495–497). The merging of the productive agricultural scene with such a gruesome action has caused Michael N. Nagler to label the simile "near-grotesque."[85] Crushed barley and squashed bodies—this awful combination forces us to experience the squashing of these bodies as the very antithesis of civilized, that is, *human* behavior.[86]

Eighteen lines later, the Trojans fleeing from Achilles into the river are compared to locusts fleeing from the blast of weariless fire (21.12–14). After Achilles follows them into the river, again *daímoni îsos*, and starts flailing about with his sword, his victims are compared to terrified fish that try to hide from a "mighty-mouthed dolphin," who eats whatever he catches (21.22–24). It is reasonable that Achilles should be compared to a sea creature here, for, as the literal-minded Scholiast perceives, he is in the water.[87] Nonetheless, there is something ludicrous about the sim-

ile. Perhaps because no other hero in either the *Iliad* or *Odyssey* has an
aristeía in the water,[88] the predatory fish has not become a standard heroic image. On the contrary, fish similes elsewhere in the *Iliad* and *Odyssey* are used exclusively to describe unheroic, dead, or dying victims
similar to the Trojans being killed here by Achilles.[89] Achilles' "mighty-
mouthed dolphin," therefore, contains no intimations of heroism but
conveys only the simplest concept of predator and prey.[90] Neither, however, are Achilles' actions at this point heroic. Homer calls his indiscriminate slaughter *kakà érga*, "evil deeds" (19), and terms the groaning
that arises from the victims *aeikés*, "shameful" (20).[91] Then, just after
the simile, he describes Achilles, his hands "weary with killing," pausing
to pick out the twelve youths to be reserved for later slaughter on Patroklos's pyre (26–33).

There follows the brutal scene with Lykaon, which I have already discussed, and then the battle with the river and the *Theomachia* (Battle of
the Gods). During Skamander's attack, Achilles' divine (fiery) aspect is
more to the fore as he receives the aid of Poseidon, Athene, Herê, and
Hephaistos (21.284–297, 328–376). Immediately after the *Theomachia*
this superhuman status is reconfirmed in a simile that likens his wreaking havoc on Trojans to the wrath (*mênis*) of the gods burning a city
(522–524). Homer's very next comment on his activity, however, carries
the opposite connotation of subhumanness. Separated from the *mênis*-
fire simile only by a quick vision of Priam's opening the gates to let the
fleeing Trojans in is a metaphor which implies that Achilles is a mad
dog: "Strong *lússa* always held his heart" (542–543). *Lússa* is usually
translated "raging madness," but, as Redfield points out, its literal meaning seems to be "canine madness" or perhaps even "rabies."[92]

Fire and other normally heroic imagery holds sway in Book Twenty-
Two until the moment when the decisive duel between Hektor and
Achilles is about to take place. Hektor, deceived into standing firm by
Athene's appearance as his brother Deiphobos, tries to get his opponent
to agree to civilized rules of battle. Because he does not know what kind
of beings "Deiphobos" and Achilles really are, Hektor thinks that he
will be fighting in terms of the old heroic code—"I may slay, or I may be
slain" (253)—and he expects to set up the same civilized rules that governed his duel with Aias in Book Seven: whoever wins shall return the
loser's corpse to his people (22.254–259; cf. 7.76–91). Hektor's words
make the audience recollect that duel which ended in an exchange of

pleasant compliments; Achilles' response shows how far we have traveled from that civility.

In his response Achilles compares himself to a lion: "As there are no trustworthy oaths between lions and men . . . so there will be no oaths between us, until one of us is dead" (262, 265–267).[93] The syntax of this passage indicates that Achilles views himself as the lion and Hektor as the man, and his later words to Hektor confirm this. After Achilles strikes the fatal blow he says he wishes his spirit (*ménos* and *thumós*) would impel him to hack off Hektor's flesh and eat it raw (22.346–347). For the Greeks cannibalism was a mark of the nonhuman and is, in fact, Hesiod's means of differentiating between animal and human: "Zeus set down this law (*nómon*) for human beings, that fish and wild beasts and winged birds should eat each other, since there is no justice (*díkē*) among them. But to human beings he gave *díkē*, which is for the best" (*Works and Days* 276–280). Therefore, Achilles' words indicate that he would *rather* be a beast than a man.

Lions have attacked and been attacked by men in the *Iliad*'s similes, but never before have lion and human natures been explicitly contrasted as they are in the simile Achilles creates. By making their incongruity explicit and locating himself in the realm of the lions, Achilles confirms and intensifies the implications of his earlier lion similes. We are now to regard him not only as being as much a lion as he is a man; in this final battle with his most hated opponent we must regard his "lionness" as having superseded his humanness. Hektor, trapped between Athene and Achilles, thus epitomizes the fate of Achilles' previous victims: he is destroyed by a dreadful amalgamation of divine and bestial forces in human form.

The killing of Hektor marks simultaneously the peak of Achilles' military valor and the depth of his uncharacteristic brutality. Hektor's death initiates the fall of Troy and the end of the war. The mourning that greets his death is "most like that which would happen if all lofty / Troy were consumed top to bottom in fire" (22.410–411). This simile circles back to Priam's grim prediction of what would happen if Hektor did not retreat within the walls:

> Zeus
> will destroy me in a wretched fate, after I have seen many evils,
> my sons killed and my daughters dragged away,
> and bedrooms ravaged and innocent children

thrown to earth in terrible warfare
and daughters-in-law dragged off at the hands of the Achaians,
and me dogs will rend on the ground by the door.

(22.60–66)

These framing references make Hektor's destruction nearly equivalent to the destruction of Troy.[94] And Priam's horrific vision links that destruction with the savagery which has now practically overwhelmed the poem. Charles Segal believes that one of the broader implications of the corpse theme is illustrated here: "the destruction of civilized values, of civilization itself, by the savagery which war and its passions release." Troy, he says,

> embodies the stability and refinement of civilized life, with its settled families, palaces, temples, treasures, weaving, "long-robed" women. The closer we come to its fall, the closer we move to a vision of that total savagery of which man may be capable, the obliteration of those civilized sanctions which include respect for the bodies of the dead.[95]

FIGURE 4. Achilles and Athene Kill Hektor

As Hektor dies, he virtually embodies "civilization itself." Achilles, divine and bestial at the same time, virtually embodies "that total savagery of which man may be capable."[96]

The divine and the bestial in Achilles will become once again integrated into the human as Books Twenty-Three and Twenty-Four bring the *Iliad* to a quiet, civilized and sorrowful close. The poem does not end with the death of the Trojan champion and the brutal prefiguring of Troy's demise. For the *Iliad*'s main concern is not the Trojan War. We may, perhaps, say that it is concerned about what war does to people, but it would be more accurate to say that its concern is mortality, in other words, how the fact of death conditions what a man does with his life.[97] I have already touched on this theme in my brief discussions of *timé* (honor), *kléos* (glory), and the heroic code; it is time to return to it now, before we look at Books Twenty-Three and Twenty-Four, to examine how these concepts, *timé* and *kléos*, both give birth to and are affected by the inhuman wrath that we have been hearing the goddess sing.

3. THE WRATH: *TIMÉ* AND *KLÉOS*

Timé: King Agamemnon, because of his political power, and godlike (*dîos*) Achilles, because of his martial ability,[98] each possessed *géra*, special prizes that the Greeks selected from the human spoil of a sacked city and awarded by common consent[99] to the most valuable members of their community. This common consent had turned Chryseis and Briseis into measures of *timé*, the honor or due respect that binds the heroic society together. When Apollo's wrath forces Agamemnon to return his *géras*, Chryseis, to her father, Chryses, Agamemnon furiously demands another, for he feels it is not fitting (*oudè éoike*) for him alone of the Achaians to be *agérastos*, "a-person-without-a-prize" (1.118–120). But, as Achilles points out, the king's demand for an immediate replacement is unreasonable since there is no common store of booty at the moment (122–124) and there will not be any until another city (Troy) is sacked (125–129); it is not fitting (*ouk epéoike*) for the group (*laoùs*) to take back what it has already distributed (126).

Achilles is clearly standing for the established rights of the warriors who make up his society. But Agamemnon totally denies the code of his community (137–138):

> If the Achaians will not give me a prize, I myself
> will take one, either yours, or Aias's or Odysseus's.

Achilles' response, his attempt to maintain the community's violated code, forces him, paradoxically, to reject that very community. Though his first words still express his anger in a group context ("How can any of the Achaians wholeheartedly obey you?" 150), by the end of his speech he has threatened to leave the Greek alliance and go home (169). He joined the expedition to win honor (*timé*) for Agamemnon and Menelaos (152–160). Now he has himself been dishonored (*átimos eṓn*), and if he stays all he will be doing is "heaping up wealth and riches" for the king (171). It is clear that in Achilles' view the execution of Agamemnon's threat would strip possessions of all extramaterial value.[100] Agamemnon's reply, a belligerent assertion that he will take Briseis specifically to prove that he is the stronger, closes all traditionally acceptable modes of social interaction. If Achilles is to maintain his personal integrity, only two courses are open: either to assert himself violently within the group ("break up the assembly and kill Agamemnon," 191) or—the result of his obeying Athene and restraining his *thumós*—to withdraw from the group. He chooses the latter, and from this point on he grows more and more isolated.

Achilles is forced to withdraw because his violated society does not expel its violator but instead leaves Agamemnon's political power uncontested. The warriors betray their own code, a fact that is reflected first in Achilles' declaration that this would be Agamemnon's last insult were it not that he ruled over "nothings" (231) and again in the bitter sarcasm of *epaúrontai* when he requests Thetis to beg Zeus to "pen the Achaians back upon their ships, dying, so that all may 'have profit from' their king (409–410)."[101] Even though they know Agamemnon is in the wrong, as they admit later (9.105–111 and 19.181–182), the group does not join Achilles' revolt. They seem to accept Nestor's formulation that Agamemnon is automatically *phérteros*, "better," because he rules over more people (281). Since no one else renounces Agamemnon's authority,[102] the king is proved to have been at least half right when he boasted "there are others who will stay with me and honor me, especially Zeus" (174–175). So Achilles abjures them all and sets out to prove Agamemnon wrong in the second half of his boast. When Briseis has actually been taken, he withdraws alone to the beach and, weeping, calls upon his goddess mother to request Zeus to show whom he honors.

Twelve days later, in Olympus, Zeus finally nods his head and agrees to fulfill Thetis's request that he honor her son by putting might in the Trojans, thus causing the Greeks to be defeated in his absence (505–510). We expect now to see fulfilled, albeit on a grander scale, the paradigm of dishonor, divine reprisal, and reparation with which the *Iliad* opened.[103] Chryses was dishonored (*ētímasen*, 11) by Agamemnon's refusing to ransom his daughter; he prayed to Apollo, who honored (*tímēsas*) him by smiting the Achaian people (454); Agamemnon gave in and returned the woman with the addition of gifts. In the beginning of Book Nine this pattern seems indeed well on the way to completion. While Achilles remained wroth and unhappy by his ships (1.488–492), the Achaians were routed (Book Eight), and they recognize that Achilles has been honored by Zeus (9.110, 117–118). Briseis, gifts, and an embassy are readied to appease him (9.119–173). But from this point on the initial paradigm functions only as contrast.

Chryses got back from Agamemnon what he wanted: his daughter. Achilles cannot get back from Agamemnon what he wants: his *géras*. Agamemnon offers him a list of chattels, among which is Briseis. Though she herself is intrinsically dear to Achilles—he loves her from the heart as any good, sensible man loves his woman (9.341–343), and he calls her his wife (336)—she is no longer a *géras*, a gift from the Achaians in reward of his outstanding *aretē*. Though Agamemnon is willing to swear an oath that he has not slept with her (9.132–134), she is not, nevertheless, to be returned intact, because she is, in fact, not to be *returned*. Agamemnon says he will *give* her, along with seven other women,[104] with no mention that he is restoring the *géras* awarded by the sons of the Achaians. There is no mention at all of *géra* in Agamemnon's speech and no apology for the dishonor he has done Achilles. Though he says he is willing to make "atonement" (*arésai*, 120), his use of the optative in his concluding sentence, "These things would I do (*telésaimi*) if he desists from his anger" (157), shows that the gifts, including Briseis, are not atonement but rather the price for Achilles' future services.

Achilles is not willing to be bought. He knows that no true reparation is being offered, and it is unclear whether it could be.[105] Agamemnon's idiosyncratic action has destroyed the source (society's communal agreement) of the honor he came to Troy to win. That Achilles believes honor no longer exists to be won among men is clear from his "misuse"[106] of the word *timē*. Immediately after he says there was no gratitude (*cháris*) for his endless fighting (316), he states his new understanding of the system of honor: "In a single *timḗ* are both the coward (*kakós*) and the brave (*esthlós*)" (319). Since *timḗ* measures relative value, such a statement effectively denies its existence. It no longer accrues to the gifts men give to each other, and Achilles is not willing to sell his life for mere possessions (401, 406–409):

> Not of equal value to my life are all the possessions held in Troy . . .
> cattle and fat sheep may be had for the taking
> tripods may be won and the tawny heads of horses,
> but a man's life cannot be taken or seized
> to return again once it has crossed the teeth's barrier.

Achilles here denies the social (heroic) code which before gave purpose to life, reasons for action: he fought *because* of his mortality, that is, to win the *timḗ* and concomitant glory (*kléos*) that give quality to one's transient stay on earth and create of it something meaningful. Now this code is itself meaningless.

Achilles remains passionately concerned with the concept of *timḗ* throughout the embassy. His long speech to Odysseus refers three times to his lost *géras* (334, 344, 367), and in his concluding reply to Aias's appeal his rage at Agamemnon's treating him like a dishonored (*atimḗton*) vagabond (648) overwhelms his feelings of responsibility toward his personal friends. But the only *timḗ* which now has any value for him is that from Zeus (607–608).[107] Agamemnon's deceptions[108] have left him no alternative but to turn away from the human world to that of the gods. This forced and unhappy turning away from mortal society is the cause of his great wrath.

Achilles' isolation from his fellow mortals is announced by the very first word of the poem: *mênis*. The goddess is asked to sing not just any wrath but divine wrath.[109] Achilles is the only human whose anger is termed *mênis*, and then only in crucial passages: the invocation; Phoinix's reply to Achilles' speech here in the embassy (517); the formal retraction of the original wrath (19.35, 75); and lastly the simile which identifies him with the *mênis* of the gods as he rages in blood through the Trojan ranks (21.523). Phoinix's application of the term to Achilles' anger allows us to see most clearly how it sets him apart from other men. He says (515–517, 524–527):

> If Agamemnon were not bringing gifts and naming others
> for later, but continued to be violent furiously always,
> I would not bid you cast away your wrath (*mênin*) . . . .

> Thus also we have learned from the famous stories of
> heroes of old, when furious anger (*chólos*) came upon one of them,
> they accepted gifts and were persuaded by words.
> And I remember this of old.

He then begins a story about the hero Meleager that functions as a foil to Homer's greater story of a greater hero precisely in terms of the difference between the *mênis* used of Achilles and the *chólos* used of paradigmatic heroes. Ordinary heroes like Meleager who felt *chólos* (see 553–554) were persuaded by gifts to fight and win honor or were impelled to fight at the last moment without gifts and without honor. Achilles says consciously that he chooses to fight at the last moment (651–655); that he does not need Meleager's kind of honor (*taútēs timês*) because he has been honored by Zeus (607–608). He is not just another "angry" hero.[110]

Because he cannot get back what was taken as Chryses did, Achilles moves from the role of dishonored man into the role of Apollo, whose *mênis* (1.75) has to be understood before it can be appeased. Unfortunately, the Greeks have neither the perspicuity nor the seercraft to understand what would appease this god/man. The conflation of human and divine roles throws not only Chryses's but also Meleager's paradigm into confusion. The latter's paradigmatic loss of honor does not, in fact, predict what will happen to Achilles, for when Achilles finally chooses to fight, his fellow heroes will insist that he take their gifts, whether he wants them or not, in a ceremony designed to reintegrate him into their society (19.172–275). Achilles, who can never again be totally one of them, will take his place among them in Book Twenty-Three, but only after, as the climax of his inhuman *aristeía* in Books Twenty to Twenty-Two, he has killed Hektor and thereby assured his own imminent death.

Kléos: The second of the two specific components that make heroic life meaningful is *kléos,* which reports the deeds that won *timé* to all men even to after generations (7.87–91, 22.304–305) and is the compensation if in risking one's life for *timé* one actually loses that life. *Timé* is the more important component while one is alive; *kléos* is, of course, the more important after death. Achilles' complaints about the misery of his life without *timé* recur again and again (e.g., at 16.52–59) until Patroklos's death makes life not worth worrying about. Achilles mentions his *kléos,* on the other hand, only twice and only in conjunction with his death: first, in the famous description of his choice between *kléos* and long life (9.412–416), and second, when he decides to rejoin the fighting and kill Hektor even though this means his own death will swiftly follow (18.120–121).

Achilles' description of his choice comes immediately after his emphatic statement that nothing in this world is so valuable as his life (9.406–409). His mother, he says, has revealed to him that he has a twofold fate (412–416):

> If I stay here and fight around the Trojans' city
> my homecoming is lost, but my *kléos* will last forever.
> If I come home to my own fatherland
> my excellent *kléos* is lost, but life will continue long
> for me and my end in death will not arrive swiftly.

Since he chooses to go home, it is clear that the *kléos* of martial deeds pure and simple is not sufficient reason to stay. Now that *timé* no longer provides fighting with a meaningful context (real *timé* can now be won only by *not* fighting), there is no deed, no story about himself that is worth giving up years of life. But before the embassy is over, we see him acknowledge a different context for fighting as he begins to understand what kind of story about himself *will* be worth death.[111]

Achilles' reply to Odysseus shows him newly concerned with the reasons for the war itself. He draws a parallel between his loss of Briseis and Menelaos's loss of Helen (9.336–343):

> He keeps my beloved wife. Let him enjoy
> sleeping with her. But why must the Argives fight
> with the Trojans? Why did Atreides gather and bring
> an army here? Was it not on account of fair-haired Helen?
> Are the Atreidai the only ones of mortal men who love their wives?
> Since any man who is good and sensible
> loves and cares for his own, as also I
> loved her from my heart, though she was won by my spear.

The parallel between his loss of Briseis and Menelaos's loss of Helen implies a parallel between Agamemnon and Paris. The implications of this parallel can be best understood if we look at the goal formulated by Nestor in Book Two as he exhorted the Greek army to keep fighting until the Zeus-promised victory is achieved and every man "has slept with a Trojan wife to avenge the struggles and groans over Helen" (354–356). This unglorified goal is unconcerned with the system of heroic *timḗ* and *kléos* perhaps because it is formulated for the common soldiers whose participation in that system may be limited to winning *timḗ* for their chiefs or voting on which prince is to get a particular prize of honor.[112] In any case, since Nestor describes the women not as *géra* but rather as a means to ultimate vengeance after the Greeks complete the initial project of slaughtering the Trojan men (352), sleeping with them must be seen as punishment, a perversely simplistic kind of justice in which their rape avenges the "raped" Helen. Nestor's emphatic assertion that Zeus approved the Greeks' setting out for this goal implies that some principle beyond the chiefs' *timḗ* is at stake, and this principle is made explicit in Menelaos's later charge that the "evil Trojan dogs" had failed to fear the wrath (*mênis*) of Zeus *xeínios* ("protector of the guest-host relationship"), who would consequently destroy their city (13.623–625).

For the grandson of Zeus-born Aiakos, who was a man known for his justice,[113] such a concept of just punishment might possibly have provided a context for winning *kléos*. This possibility is perhaps why Achilles, who has been "wasting away his heart / waiting there, while he longed ever for the clamor and the fighting" (1.491–492) and who while longing has been rehearsing the traditional "glories" of other heroes (9.189), even bothers to consider a subject to which all the other princes except the wronged Menelaos and the statesman Nestor seem oblivious. But justice cannot give Achilles the context he is seeking; it turns out that Agamemnon in destroying honor has also destroyed the justification for attacking Troy. If the leader of the Achaians is merely a rapist like Paris, there remains not even a principle to fight for.[114]

Achilles' view that there is no moral differentiation between Greek and Trojan is based on his view that there is no difference in importance between Menelaos's queen and his own spear-won concubine, a view radically different from that held by the rest of his society.[115] As Paolo Vivante says, the world that before was subjected to the hero's arms is now being subjected to the man's own personal perspective.[116] His new way of interacting with the world will demand an immediate and personal, as opposed to a mediated, social context for the creation of his *kléos*. He will not fight for men's false *timḗ*, as Odysseus and Phoinix ask, and he cannot fight to save his friends, as Aias asks, since this would in effect be yielding to their leader and would thus vitiate his *timē* from Zeus.[117] He will, however, fight when personally attacked (9.650–655):

> I will not take thought for bloody war
> until the son of wise Priam, godlike Hektor,
> comes killing Argives to the huts and ships
> of the Myrmidons and consumes the ships with fire.
> About my hut and black ship
> I think I w'll hold Hektor, furious as he is for battle.

This, then, is the kind of *kléos* he is willing to create at the cost of his life: the story of his fighting and conquering not a representative of the collective enemy of his society but an individual enemy, personally his own. He does not yet guess *how* personal.

Before he brings Achilles to the point at which winning this kind of *kléos* will take specific form, Homer increases our sense of his isolation. We discover in Book Sixteen that he has been estranged not only from the leaders of his larger society but also from the Myrmidons, members of his own group that followed him from home. They have obeyed, but they have not understood. We learn from Achilles' exhortation to them as they arm to follow Patroklos into battle that they have stayed back with him "unwillingly" (*aékontas*, 204) and that they consider his anger "evil" (*kakós*, 206). Patroklos, too, no longer understands. He rebukes Achilles with the epithet *ainarétē*, "terrible in excellence" (31), and he denies Achilles' humanity, declaring that grey sea and rocks were his parents (34–35). Achilles, torn first between Patroklos's insistence that he relieve the *áchos*, "grief," of the Achaians (22) and the equally great imperative of his own terrible *áchos* over being dishonored (52, 55) and then between his desire to send Patroklos as surrogate and his great fear for his friend's safety, calls for the destruction of the whole heroic world (16.97–100):

> O father Zeus, Athene, and Apollo, would that
> no one of all the Trojans might escape death,
> no one of the Achaians, but that we two might put off destruction
> so that alone we might break the holy citadel of Troy.

He would eliminate everybody so that there would be no interference in the pure expression of his human attachments (exemplified by his love for Patroklos) conjoined with the pure expression of his heroic calling (exemplified in the destruction of Troy). Achilles can envision himself as acting in concert with only one other man. That one man is partly removed from him even now by the difference in temperament that does not permit Patroklos to sympathize with his friend's implacability; when Patroklos dies, Achilles will be totally alone.

It should be noted that Achilles' decision to send Patroklos to relieve the Achaians requires that he himself never fight again. He sends his friend in order to adhere to what he vowed before: not to fight until the Trojans came to his ships. If Patroklos drives them back, they never will get to the ships and Achilles never will be given a personal reason to fight. If Patroklos should obey Achilles' behest that he return immediately after rescuing the Greeks, the story would be at an impasse. But since Zeus—and the poet—is stronger than men's minds (16.686–688), Patroklos disobeys Achilles and is killed, and the story moves to a new plane.

The "black cloud of grief" (18.22) that overwhelms Achilles when he learns of Patroklos's death supersedes the grief that has actuated him since the quarrel. The original grief (1.188) engendered his *mênis* (absolute wrath), kept him out of battle, and turned him away from the human world to that of the gods. This new grief ends that *mênis*, impels him into battle, and drives him further away from his human nature. The word *timé* vanishes from his lips,[118] and we find there instead another manifestation of its root verb *tínō/tíō*, "set value on" or "pay what is owed": the friend whom he valued (*tîon*) equally with his own life has been killed (18.80–82) and that life is now worth nothing unless Hektor "pays back" (*apóteisēi*) life for life (18.90–93). The Greeks, on the other hand, will "pay back outrage" (*teisaímetha lóbēn*), that is, give outrage for the outrage they have received (19.208). After killing Lykaon, Achilles expresses the desire that Trojans continue to die at his hands "until all of you shall pay (*teísete*) for the murder of Patroklos and the destruction of the Achaians" (21.133–134). And as he is about to kill Hektor he declares, "Now you will pay back (*apóteiseis*) in one sum the griefs of my companions whom you killed" (22.271–272). This revenge, the negative manifestation of "value" as honor is the positive, forms the context in which he accepts the foreshortening of his life and says, "Now I would win excellent *kléos*" (18.121).

But in winning this "excellent *kléos*," Achilles' elemental fury takes him simultaneously far above all other heroes in numbers and quality of men killed and far below the most savage of men in brutality. As the imagery especially of fire and lions indicates, Achilles' vengeful response is so extreme that it invalidates the categories that give order to the world (god is to human as human is to beast) and against which humans define their being (for example, they are unlike gods in their mortality and unlike beasts in their mentality).[119] His *aristeía* pushes him to both of the extremes that, as Detienne shows, concurrently define the human condition,[120] and when he stands victorious over Hektor, simultaneously superhuman and subhuman, our human sympathies are engaged rather by Hektor's *kléos* (22.304) in defeat. Though Achilles' *aristeía* has just proved his claim to be *áristos Achaiôn,* best of the Achaians, his nonhuman status permits those who are hearing the *kléos* of that *aristeía* to reserve judgment on heroic victory per se as the supreme criterion of human worth.

4. RECONCILIATION

The disintegration of Achilles' human nature in the rampage helps us more clearly to recognize *essential* humanity when that human nature is reestablished in Book Twenty-Four through contrast with god and beast. In the course of this reestablishment Homer will offer some new criteria of human worth that we, outside of the poem, may use to make the valuation *áristos.* These criteria will have nothing to do with social position or the victory of one society's warrior over another's.[121] They will concern a new kind of victory. When Achilles killed Hektor in Book Twenty-Two, Homer portrayed his victory as a victory *over* humanity; when Achilles puts Hektor's body on Priam's wagon in Book Twenty-Four, it is a victory *of* and *for* humanity.

Homer returns Achilles to the human world in two stages. He returns him socially in Book Twenty-Three, spiritually in Book Twenty-Four. We see him moving again among men in the funeral games for Patroklos, which form a structural balance to the quarrel scene in Book One. The behavior of Achilles and his fellow Achaians during the various competitions is the comic correction of the dispute that began the *mênis* and wrenched Achilles from his heroic society.[122] Achilles presides over but does not really participate in this comedy. He remains an isolated figure among the social and lighthearted Greeks because of his agony, which remains in our minds from the scenes preceding the burning of Patroklos's body. As E. T. Owen says, "the figure of Achilles during the games, despite the fact that he is calm, self-possessed, even genial, is a mournful figure throughout because of this well-judged elaboration of his grief at the beginning." [123] Then, after the funeral, after the others disperse to their meals and their beds, his isolated agony stands out all the more sharply against their collective cheer. He neither eats nor sleeps like the rest but keeps remembering Patroklos and weeping during the night, keeps dragging Hektor's body around Patroklos's tomb during the day (24.1–18).

As with his impulse to kill Agamemnon in Book One, Achilles' treatment of Hektor's body provokes the intervention of the gods. Homer shifts the scene to Olympus, where Zeus listens to arguments that oppose and support Achilles' behavior, each by denying his humanity, and then begins the chain of events that will, in the process of uniting Achilles with Priam, reestablish that humanity and disentangle it from the bestiality and the divinity that all but obliterated it during the rampage.

Apollo, in condemning Achilles' endless revenge on Hektor's corpse, defines humanity as the opposite of "lionness" (24.40–45, 49–50):

> He has neither right understanding nor a bendable
> disposition, but is savage (*ágria oîden*) like a lion,
> who, yielding to his great strength and proud spirit (*agénori thumôi*),
> goes among the sheepflocks of men (*brotôn*) that he may feast (*hína
> daîta lábēisin*).
> So Achilles has killed pity, nor is there in him
> *aidòs* ("respect" or "shame"), which both greatly harms and benefits
> men (*ándras*).
>
> . . . .
>
> The Moirai have given a patient spirit to human beings (*anthrópoisin*).
> But Achilles . . .

In Apollo's view Achilles is behaving like a lion *rather than* a human being: his mental constitution (his *phrénes* and his *nóēma*) is not as it should be, for he is without the *aidós* that characterizes *ándres* and he is failing to exhibit the patience that characterizes *ánthrōpoi*. As in Achilles' own simile at 22.262 ("just as there are no trustworthy oaths between lions and *andrásin*"), Apollo creates an explicit contrast between human beings and lions that simultaneously locates Achilles in the nonhuman category.

Like earlier lion similes used to describe Achilles, this one, too, blurs the line between the animal nature of an anthropomorphic lion and the human nature of a bestial Achilles. As in the similes at 18.318–322 and 20.164–173, a word is used that elsewhere pertains only to human activity. The word here is *daís*, "feast," which names the specifically human practice of "dividing up" (*daíomai*) meat in correct portions for one's fellow human beings and for the gods.[124] The word is used only for human activity everywhere else in the *Iliad* except perhaps for 1.5, where *daîta* is written (instead of *pâsi*) by Zenodotos but athetized because ancient critics believed that *daís* could be used only for human meals.[125] As Redfield points out, the appearance of *daîta* in Apollo's simile implies that the lion feasts like a man.[126] *Daîta* thus has the same force as *áchnutai* in 18.320 and *atízon, êtor,* and the final subjunctives at 20.172–173 in obliterating boundaries between human and animal. Thus, once again, in contrast to the similes that use lions to vivify the martial temper or prowess of other heroes, Homer creates a simile for Achilles that merges his nature with that of the lion. The merging is all the more forceful here because the context explicitly calls Achilles' humanity into question.

Herê counters Apollo's differentiating Achilles from humans in terms of bestiality with her own differentiation in terms of divinity: "Hektor is a mortal and sucked a woman's breast, but Achilles is born of a goddess" (58–59). This difference disallows Apollo's threat to retaliate against Achilles, "great though he be" (*agathôi per eónti,* 53), for Achilles' divine parentage means that Hektor need not receive the same consideration; the two are not to be held in equal honor (*homên timên,* 57).

Herê's term "equal honor" and Apollo's phrase "great though he be" recall the moment in Book One when a venerable third party tried to reconcile the quarrel between King Agamemnon and godlike Achilles. Nestor was right in warning Agamemnon not to take Briseis, "great though you be" (275); he was wrong in suggesting that because a sceptered king does not share *homoíês timês* (278) Achilles therefore had less *timê* and should act accordingly; but, right or wrong, he did not have the power to enforce his opinions. Zeus will be able to achieve what Nestor could not, and his reconciliation of Apollo's claims against a bestial Achilles with Herê's claims in favor of a godlike Achilles will therefore be felt as providing a second, more serious correction of the dispute of Book One as well as initiating Achilles' return to himself and to full humanity.

Zeus agrees with neither and with both. He grants that Achilles shall have a different *timé* (66). But Hektor, too, is dear to the gods since he has never failed to honor their altars with wine and the savor of burning flesh, the *géras* of the gods (66–70). Zeus will not steal Hektor's body as Apollo suggested, for Achilles does indeed have a divine mother (71–73). He will, however, ask that mother to mediate the release of the body (74–76). Achilles' difference in degree does not constitute a difference in kind.

The appearance of the divine mother, Thetis, confirms the son's humanness by evoking, as usual, the motif of Achilles' own impending death. When Iris comes upon her to ask her to come to Zeus, she is "lamenting the fate of her son, who is going to die in Troy" (85–86). She wears the symbol of mourning: a dark veil "than which there is no raiment blacker" (93–94). For her here, as in Book Eighteen, Achilles is virtually dead,[127] and her grief makes her reluctant "to mingle with immortals" (91). This statement subtly undercuts Herê's distinction between Achilles and Hektor. Thetis cannot raise her son to divine status but is instead drawn away to his mortal nature. And insofar as she participates in that mortal nature (by her constant grief), she herself is *separated* from divinity. Her words move us one step closer to reestablishing the boundaries that Achilles dissolved in the rampage. In Book Eighteen the aura of death and Achilles' savage grief signaled a loss of humanity. Here his being virtually dead signifies the opposite, not loss but essence: as will become clearer and clearer, the essence of humanity is mortality—and the grief which is inherent in this mortality.

When Thetis comes to Achilles bearing the message of Zeus's anger, her first words focus attention on generic humanity. "How long," she asks,

> are you going to consume your heart
> with lamenting and grieving, remembering neither food
> nor bed? It is good even to lie in love with a
> woman. For you will not live long with me, but already
> death and strong fate stand near.
>
> (24.128–132)

THE ARCHETYPE: HOMER'S ACHILLES

How different this is from the code Sarpedon enunciated, in which the inevitability of death impelled the winning of *timé* and *kléos*. Achilles has finished with codes, and, standing now on the verge of death, he is urged not to heroic but to generic human activity: eating, sleeping, and sex. He will accept all three before the poem ends.[128]

Achilles, as usual, accedes to the gods' request and from this point on will himself, as both exemplar and interpreter, carry the burden of defining humanity as distinct from both god and beast. His partner in this endeavor is Priam, who, as the father of Hektor, is his worst enemy. Achilles' reconciliation with this worst enemy is carried out under the authority of Zeus, not of society; the only law is the transsocietal "spare the suppliant" (157–158, 186–187, 569–570, 586); value is placed only on personal interaction and recognition of a common human nature.

Priam supplicates Achilles in the person of a father and asks Achilles to remember his own father (486–492, 504). Achilles responds positively to this supplication (507), and as the two weep together, the

FIGURE 5. Ransom of Hektor

concept of fatherhood extends to Achilles himself: Priam bewailed man-slaughtering Hektor, "but Achilles bewailed his father, and also at other times Patroklos" (509–512). Four parent-child similes (9.323–325, 16.7–10, 18.318–322, 23.222–223), especially the one in Book Twenty-Three, which depicts Achilles grieving "like a father grieves as he burns his son's bones," have created an enduring feeling that Achilles' loss of Patroklos is equivalent to a parent's loss of a child.[129] Thus, when Achilles weeps with Hektor's father he weeps as both child of Peleus and "parent" of Patroklos.[130] He grieves both for and as a father, and this comprehensive grief transcends all previous personal response to the fact that Priam's child killed his own.

The generic grief that mingles his tears with Priam's issues in a new personal response, pity (*oiktírōn*, 516). This pity leads into an assertion of their common humanity in sorrow as distinguished from the carefree existence of the gods (525–526). Two urns sit on Zeus's threshold; one holds evils, the other good things. The best that human beings can hope for is not to be given a portion solely from the urn of evils but to receive a mixture of both (527–533). Peleus's life illustrates this truth (534–540); so does Priam's (543–548). The link between these two exemplars is Achilles himself: Peleus has no generation of strong sons in his house

> but one child be begat all-untimely. Nor do I
> care for him as he grows old, but very far from my fatherland
> I sit in Troy, bringing pain to you and your children.
>
> (540–542)

Gone is the brutal dispassion of his exhortation of Lykaon to die without a fuss since even better men than he must die (21.99–113). There his focal point was death, specifically his own death, which "justified" the death of everyone else. Here he focuses on life, specifically his own life as the admixture of evil in the lives of two otherwise fortunate men. Useless to his father, bringer of pain to Priam, Achilles seems the very embodiment of the sorrow that distinguishes human life from that of the gods.

Achilles attempts to comfort Priam with this exposition of generic human woe, but when Priam refuses comfort and asks only for the immediate return of the body, Achilles slips momentarily back into the anger that before had led to the merging of his human nature with that of god and beast. Human sympathy recedes. His mind reverts to the gods, who told him in the person of his divine mother to release the body and who, he knows, led Priam to his hut unhurt (560–567). His mood, on the other hand, is bestial: he threatens Priam that, if provoked, he might kill him, suppliant though he is, and transgress the commands of Zeus (568–570); then he leaps to the door "like a lion" (572). As W. C. Scott has perceived, this lion simile is the last mark of the hate that was born in Book Eighteen and that does not completely "die until the return of the body to Priam."[131] "Lionness" here is clearly associated with breaking the one law requisite to generically human interaction, respect for the suppliant, just as the motif of divinity marks the absence of the one necessary emotion, sympathy. But Achilles does not this time merge with the lion; he is merely *like* one for a brief moment. He does respect the suppliant, and thus his humanity wins victory. With one last cry of pain to Patroklos he himself places Hektor's body on the wagon, and when he returns to Priam his vision is again modulated by human sympathy. The momentary resurrection of the bestial and divine contexts by means of which Apollo and Herê condemned and justified Achilles' inhuman action thus serves finally to confirm the now distinctively human quality of Achilles' action.

When he returns from placing Hektor's body on the wagon, Achilles, echoing Thetis's earlier plea (129), says, "Now let us remember to eat" (601), and offers as exemplum another story that differentiates humans from gods. Even Niobe remembered food, he says, she whose twelve children were slain by Apollo and Artemis in anger over her comparing herself to Leto (602–608). Achilles urges Priam to act on her example: "Come now, let us too, godlike old man, remember food; then you may weep your dear son again as you bring him to Ilion. He will be worth many tears" (618–620).

Achilles' words echo but do not repeat Odysseus's practical advice in Book Nineteen. Odysseus said that men must bury the dead, mourn one day, then eat so they can fight again (228–232). Fighting, we may remember from Odysseus's words at 14.85–87, is a particular characteristic of heroic Greek society.[132] Achilles' advice is not so much practical as expressive of generic human necessity. He says, "Stop mourning, eat, mourn again." The paradigm is Niobe, who in utter isolation weeps eternally.[133] We must, therefore, interpret his words as Vivante does: one must pause and eat in order to renew one's "capacity for tears."[134]

The weeping rock symbolizes "a grief beyond redemption."[135] Here even more profoundly than in the earlier parable of the urns grief becomes the definitive condition of human existence. Understanding this condition and sharing one's understanding may not redeem, but it does assuage the grief enough to permit life to go on. Achilles and Priam are able to eat, then to admire each other, and then to prepare for the sleep that neither has enjoyed since the deaths of Patroklos and Hektor (627–648). Returned to his human nature and to humankind, Achilles' last appearance in the poem shows him in bed reunited with Briseis (675–676).

Before he goes to that bed, he makes one last jibe at the society which would prevent the kind of direct human-to-human response we have been witnessing (649–655), and he offers to Priam, in addition to the body itself, time to perform complete funeral rites for Hektor. These funeral rites will conclude the poem with a high tribute to both Hektor and Achilles. As Scholes and Kellogg point out, this funeral "glorifies his lesser antagonist Hektor, but because it does so through his sufferance alone, it glorifies Achilles more." [136] Let us remember now what Hektor said about his enemy's corpse before his duel with Aias in Book Seven (84–91):

> [If I win]
> I will give back the corpse to the well-benched ships
> in order that the abundant-haired Achaians may give it funeral rites
> and heap up a tomb on the broad Hellespont
> and perhaps some man of the later generations will say
> in his many-oared ship as he sails by on the wine-dark sea,
> "This is the tomb of a man who died long ago
> whom Hektor killed in heroic combat."
> So perhaps one will speak. And my *kléos* will never die.

So too Hektor's tomb will create never-ending *kléos* for the man who killed him. But in the difference between Hektor's hoped-for *kléos* and the *kléos* which his tomb actually affords Achilles, we can measure the distance Homer has brought us from the uncritically held heroic assumptions of both Greeks and Trojans. For the *kléos* Homer evokes with Hektor's tomb is not so much that of conquering an enemy in mortal combat as that of conquering one's own hate in shared suffering. By giving the Achilles who killed Hektor strong association with both god and beast and then by making the Achilles who weeps with Priam wholly and definitively a man, Homer makes us understand that transcendent personal sympathy, not martial prowess, represents quintessential human excellence. It is the *kléos* of this sympathy that wins Achilles in the hearts of later generations the valuation *áristos*, "best of the Achaians."

5. POSTSCRIPT: *TIMÉ* AND *KLÉOS* IN THE *ODYSSEY*

The best a human being can hope for, says Achilles in *Iliad* 24, is to be given portions from both urns that sit on Zeus's threshold, both the one that contains evils and the one that contains goods. The *Iliad* and its hero focus on the former; they define humanity through the evils, especially the fact of death, that make life's highest goods the source of deepest grief. In the *Odyssey* Homer's vision is quite different. Here he focuses on the urn of goods, on possibilities for wresting happiness out of the grief and death that threaten constantly, on human capacity for prolonging life and making it rich. The *Iliad*'s concern with limitation creates a vision of *essential* humanity that we may term "tragic"; the *Odyssey*'s concern with potentiality creates a vision of *comprehensive* humanity that we may term "optimistic." The *Odyssey*'s comprehensiveness does not exclude the tragic vision of the earlier epic but relegates it to Hades, where Achilles and other dead heroes from the *Iliad* form a mournful backdrop to Odysseus's success in overcoming evils and winning both *kléos and* homecoming.

In *Odyssey* 11, as he lingers in Hades to talk with figures from his past, Odysseus encounters Achilles in the company of Patroklos, Aias, and Antilochos, a group we may call the Big Four of those who died at Troy.[137] By way of greeting, Achilles asks how Odysseus dared to come down to Hades, "where live the senseless (*aphradées*) dead, phantoms of perished mortals" (475–476). Odysseus, quick-witted as ever, picks up the note of bitterness in *aphradées* and, after briefly summarizing his own troubles, responds (482–486):

> But as for you, Achilles,
> no man was or will be more fortunate.
> For before, while you were alive, we Argives honored (*etíomen*) you
>   equal with the gods,
> and now again in this realm you wield great power among the dead.
> Therefore do not be grieved because you are dead, Achilles.

But this attempt at consolation does not work. Achilles retains from *Iliad* 9 his fierce compulsion to view unadorned, unmediated facts;[138] in *Odyssey* 11 the fact is that he is dead, and there can be no compensation for this. He responds in an angry tone (488–491):

> Illustrious Odysseus, do not speak consolingly to me about death.
> I would rather be above the earth a servant to another
> in the house of a landless man who had little substance
> than to rule among all the withered dead.

Achilles here displays the same extremism in his response to Odysseus's words about honor and power as he did when similar words on Odysseus's lips in the *Iliad* (9.296–298, 302–303) provoked a declaration that not even so many gifts as grains of sand or dust could persuade him to change his mind (*Il.* 9.385–386).

As in the *Iliad,* this interchange between Achilles and Odysseus highlights their difference in character. Odysseus will try to make the best of any situation, do something to improve it. Achilles continually focuses on what he *cannot* do,[139] on the limitations of the situation he finds himself in. In the *Iliad* he could not win both *kléos* and homecoming; he could not enjoy both *timé* and his human society. Here death cancels out any joy he might get from his present power and remembrance of past honor. He focuses on the power he cannot have, the honor he can no longer guarantee. He cannot, as he would like, come as the killer of heroes, strong and invincible as he was in life, to rout the men who may be vexing his father and depriving him of honor (*atimásdousin,* 496; *eérgousin t'apò timês,* 503).

Timé here does not reverberate with the absolutist associations it acquired for Achilles in the *Iliad* but is, rather, that basic mundane rewarding of relative worth, either because of social position or martial prowess, which was accepted without question in all its human imperfection by the ordinary heroes in Achilles' society. The heroic code remains intact, and Achilles' persistently intense concern with *timé* and martial prowess reinforce rather than disrupt it. In addition to wanting to know if his father still enjoys honor among the Myrmidons (495), he asks if his son became a *prómos,* "champion in war" (492–493). When Odysseus answers that Neoptolemos fought heroically in the forefront (*polù prothéeske,* 515) and then, unscathed, departed from Troy with a *géras esthlón,* "noble prize of honor" (506–537), Achilles strides off happy (538–540).

Both Achilles and Agamemnon, who had encountered Odysseus just before Achilles, represent types of experience that set in relief the career of Odysseus. Agamemnon's immediate and unsuccessful homecoming provides a foil to Odysseus's delayed but successful homecoming. Achilles' martial heroism and death provide a foil to Odysseus's new heroism of survival. In a second vision of the underworld in Book Twenty-Four, Homer presents these two figures again, now together and oblivious of their quarrel in the *Iliad,* to represent the negative and positive poles of heroic experience and death.

As Hermes leads the slaughtered suitors down to Hades, Achilles, who is again standing with the other members of the Big Four, begins to converse with Agamemnon. He says he wishes that Agamemnon had died in Troy while enjoying his *timḗ:* then he would have won great *kléos* for his son. This *kléos* would presumably come from the great tomb Achilles says the Achaians would have heaped up for him.[140] As it is, Agamemnon was taken by a most pitiful death (28–34). Note that Achilles says nothing about Agamemnon's winning *kléos* for his son while alive through being king of the many strong men who fought at Troy (26–27). He says merely that Agamemnon was said to be dear to Zeus because of that fact (24–25). In the heroic world, it seems, what is said about you in your lifetime does not become immortal *kléos.* The manner of one's death supersedes all the deeds one may have performed; *kléos* comes only from the grandeur of one's tomb or funeral.

This conception of *kléos* is confirmed and amplified in Agamemnon's response to Achilles. "Fortunate Achilles," he begins, "you who died at Troy" (36–37). He then launches into a description of the grandest funeral of all: the Muses themselves sang Achilles' dirge (60–62) and Thetis set out immortal prizes for his funeral games (85–92). Agamemnon says that thus Achilles, though dead, did not lose his name but would always have noble *kléos* among all men (93–94).

The versatile ethic of the *Odyssey* provides other ways besides martial death to win valuable *kléos* (craft, 9.19–20; hospitality, 19.332–334; chastity, 24.196–198) and differentiates men not just in terms of *kléos* won but also in terms of length of life. In this respect the suitors, who did not participate in the heroic ethic but instead thought only of pleasure

FIGURE 6. Muses Mourn for Achilles

and winning a wife, represent the negative pole of nonheroic experience and death. They have, like Agamemnon, a short life and no *kléos*. Odysseus, who we expect will live long and meet a nonviolent (*ablēchrós*) death from the sea (11.134–136 = 23.281–283), represents the positive pole of nonheroic experience.[141] He is both like and unlike Achilles. Like Achilles he will have *kléos*—good fame in epic song, that is, in the *Odyssey* itself. Unlike Achilles he will also have a long life. The immortals are now fashioning not a dirge, as the Muses did for Achilles, but a lovely song to celebrate Penelope's imperishable *kléos* (24.196–198). Odysseus is "fortunate" in his wife's excellence (*ólbie Laértao pái*, 192) just as Achilles was "fortunate" in his death at Troy (*ólbie Pēléos huié*, 36).

An emphasis on life itself is what differentiates the nonheroic from the heroic mode of being. In the *Odyssey* a person does not have to create meaning for life by risking that life; sufficient meaning is available in roles of spouse, parent, and responsible member of society. Glimpses of such roles in the *Iliad* created only sorrow—sorrow that young men would not fill them, sorrow that older men such as Hektor would not return to them. Homer used Achilles' marvelous complexity to create a like sorrow: with this complexity he showed the cost of being heroic, the essential tragedy of being human. In the *Odyssey* Homer leaves Achilles the pain but does not ask us to recall the complexity. Anger, honesty, prowess for killing, and an uncritical concern for *timḗ* are all that remain of the *Iliad*'s hero. His immortal *kléos* comes not from Hektor's funeral but from his own. Thus simplified he can represent the summit of the old either-or heroic economy that pitted *kléos* against homecoming. His is the grandest funeral, Odysseus's the richest life.

· 2 ·

CLASSICAL VISIONS OF THE HOMERIC WARRIOR

As we trace Achilles in what remains of the epic, lyric, and tragic poetry composed in the seventh through fifth centuries B.C., we will see fully delineated the stereotype adumbrated by the *Odyssey*'s simplifications of the Homeric character. This stereotype is composed of several traits that are either taken from more simplistic alternate traditions or singled out from the *Iliad*'s complex portrait by artists who then endow them with varying political and philosophical content. Alkaios and Pindar, for example, extol Achilles' superlative prowess and aristocratic heritage, Sophokles his honesty and righteous anger. Using Achilles to portray a cosmic morality in which war and the aristocracy have a continuously positive part to play, all three ignore the bestial imagery that colors the seemingly limitless passion of his Iliadic grief. Euripides, on the other hand, whose contributions to the stereotype critique the ongoing war necessitated by Athenian imperialism, focuses precisely on this uncontrolled passion, condemning the destructive uses that the hero's prowess serves and attacking what is now portrayed as an obsession with honor. Plato, who uses Homer's Achilles in opposition to a new heroism—the ability to suffer steadfastly and to reason about what action is correct—reinforces the idea of uncontrolled and ultimately selfish passion.

Four figures who have left a substantial amount of material on Achilles—Pindar, Sophokles, Euripides, and Plato—will be the focus of this chapter. I will attempt here to establish an Hellenic stereotype (wrath, honesty, prowess, honor), the traditional deeds (both Homeric and non-Homeric) with which the stereotype becomes associated, and the political and philosophical context in which the classical Greek visions of Achilles are expressed.

1. THE EPIC CYCLE AND LYRIC

Homer composed the most powerful but not the only archaic epic about Achilles' role in the Trojan War. The *Kypria, Aithiopis, Little Iliad, Sack of Ilium, Nostoi,* which together make up what is called the Epic Cycle, provided pre- and post-Iliadic details to later poets who wished to recreate or evoke Achilles in their own lyric, tragic, or epic poetry. From the few existing fragments and the summaries made by Proclus for his *Chrestomathia* in the second or fifth century A.D.,[1] we can be reasonably sure that the loss of these poems does not represent a literary disaster;[2] indeed, their literary inferiority has been certified by ancient scholars (e.g., Aristotle *Poetics* 23.1459 B) and by the overwhelming popularity of the *Iliad* and the *Odyssey* in fifth-century Athens. Their loss does, however, limit our understanding of how Achilles was viewed, for the cycle transmitted many popular legends, providing him with a fabulous boyhood, superhuman strength and swiftness, an additional set of Hephaistean armor, two semidivine opponents, three or four sexual intrigues, and miscellaneous adventures both at and on the way to Troy.[3] The popularity of these incidents in early sixth-century vase painting—especially that of Achilles being turned over to Cheiron and of Thetis bringing the budding hero armor before he leaves for Troy—demonstrates Achilles' wide appeal in northeastern Greece even before universal knowledge of Homer's epics catapulted him into supremacy as a tragic as well as martial hero.[4]

Since we can never recapture the details and nuance of the above incidents, I do not wish to linger over the poems of the Epic Cycle. I will discuss particular episodes later as they are re-created by subsequent authors. A brief summary of the cycle's contributions to Achilles' biography will be useful, however, if only to show how closely every episode in the hero's life is bound to the war in which he must die.

Achilles and the Trojan War are engendered simultaneously, for, according to the *Kypria,* Zeus uses the marriage of Peleus and Thetis to put his plan for population control into effect. By the time the divinely matched pair retire to the nuptial couch, Strife has stirred up the quarrel between wedding guests Herê, Aphrodite, and Athene that will eventually produce the elopement of Helen and Paris to Troy and the subsequent vast numbers of war deaths required to lighten Earth's burden

(*Kypria* frag. 1, *Chrestomathia* 1, pp. 102–103).[5] Peleus's wedding gift from Cheiron, Athene, and Hephaistos is the ash spear that Achilles, born within the year (Alkaios 42), will use in his role as principal wreaker of such deaths (*Kypria* frag. 3).

Having been reared like other legendary heroes by the centaur Cheiron, between the ages of fifteen and twenty[6] Achilles sets off to war and along with the rest of the Greeks sacks his first city in error, mistaking the unfortunate Mysia for Troy.[7] After this false start, which surely must have warmed the cockles of Zeus's homicidal heart, a storm scatters the ships, and there follows, first, the romantic interlude at Skyros that produces Neoptolemos; next, at a second mustering of the chiefs at Aulis, the luring of Iphigeneia to the sacrificial altar under the pretense of marrying her to Achilles; and finally, after a brief stop at Tenedos and a quarrel with Agamemnon over "being consulted late,"[8] the arrival at Troy, where Achilles kills the first of his famous demigod victims, Kyknos, son of Poseidon. After some city sacking and a mysterious meeting between Achilles and Helen, something causes the Greeks to desire to return home, but Achilles unwittingly saves Zeus's plan by restraining them. There follow events important as background for the *Iliad:* Achilles' driving off the cattle of Aeneas; the sacking of Lyrnessos, Pedasos, and many neighboring cities; the killing of Troilos; the capture and selling of Lykaon; and the awarding of Briseis to Achilles and of Chryseis to Agamemnon. The *Kypria* ends with a new plan of Zeus to relieve the Trojans by detaching Achilles from his allies (*Chrestomathia* 1, pp. 103–105).

The *Aithiopis,* picking up the story after the *Iliad,* tells of Achilles' final heroic deeds: the slaying of the Amazon queen Penthesileia and of Memnon, himself the son of a goddess and clad like Achilles in armor made by Hephaistos. Shortly after killing Memnon, Achilles himself is slain by Paris and Apollo while pursuing the routed Trojans into the city (see figure 7). Aias and Odysseus rescue the body, Thetis and the Muses mourn, and the Achaians heap up a tomb and hold funeral games (*Chrestomathia* 2, p. 106).

Events in the *Little Iliad, Sack of Ilium,* and *Nostoi* are only peripherally pertinent to Achilles' story. The three most closely related matters are the contest between Aias (brawn) and Odysseus (brain) over his armor, the brutal warfare of his son, and the sacrifice of Priam's youngest

FIGURE 7. Death of Achilles

daughter on his tomb by the departing Greeks. Of these, only the slaughter of Polyxena will achieve great importance in valuations of Achilles' character.[9]

According to one early legend, Achilles' mortal remains were enclosed in a golden urn wrought by the same god who had made his armor.[10] An immortal urn, like the immortal song of the Muses, would have been appropriate to Homer's tragic hero. But it was not enough for the Epic Cycle's romantic hero. Before the Achaians heap up his tomb in the *Aithiopis,* Thetis carries him off to immortality on Leuke, an island near the mouth of the Danube (*Chrestomathia* 2, p. 106). This granting of immortality—which is conferred also on Achilles' rival, Memnon—points up what Griffin has described as "profoundly different attitudes to the fundamental nature of human life and death" in the *Iliad* and the Epic Cycle poems.[11] Gone is the difficult choice between glory and long life, gone is the poignant cost of martial heroism, gone is all sense of tragedy and of the waste of human potential. In their place is an uncritical vision of a supreme warrior beloved by beneficent gods and functioning as an inspiration to all right-thinking men. (See figure 8.)

Most later poets preferred this uncritical vision and freely granted Achilles the immortality that he in fact enjoyed in cult.[12] Alkaios is a good sixth-century example, for he indicates immortality in a fragment (Alk. frag. Z 31) that addresses Achilles as *Skuthíkas médeis* "Lord of Skythia," a title nearly equivalent to the hero's cult title "Ruler of the

FIGURE 8. Immortal Achilles

Hellespont";[13] and he reveals an uncritical vision in a short poem (Alk. 42) that draws a sharp moralistic contrast between the fruit of Helen's adultery and that of Thetis's legal union with Peleus:

> Story tells that because of wicked deeds bitter
> grief came to Priam and his children
> from you, Helen, and Zeus destroyed holy
> Ilium in fire.
> Not like you was the delicate maiden taken from the
> halls of Nereus and led to the house of
> Cheiron by the illustrious Aiakid when he had
> invited all
> the gods to his wedding. He loosed her
> pure maiden girdle; love bloomed
> between Peleus and the best of the Nereids,

and in a year's time
a child was born, best of the demigods,
happy driver of tawny colts. But the
Phrygians perished for the sake of Helen, they
and their city.[14]

ὡς λόγος, κάκων ἄχος ἔννεκ' ἔργων
Περράμωι καὶ παῖσι ποτ', Ὤλεν', ἦλθεν
ἐκ σέθεν πίκρον, πύρι δ' ὤλεσε Ζεῦς
Ἴλιον ἴραν.

οὐ τεαύταν Αἰακίδαις ἄγαυος
πάντας ἐς γάμον μάκαρας καλέσσαις
ἄγετ' ἐκ Νήρηος ἔλων μελάθρων
πάρθενον ἄβραν
ἐς δόμον Χέρρωνος· ἔλυσε δ ' ἄγνας
ζῶμα παρθένω· φιλότας δ' ἔθαλε
Πήλεος καὶ Νηεΐδων ἀρίστας,
ἐς δ' ἐνίαυτον
παῖδα γέννατ' αἰμιθέων φέριστον
ὄλβιον ξάνθαν ἐλάτηρα πώλων
οἱ δ' ἀπώλοντ' ἀμφ' Ἐλέναι Φρύγες τε
καὶ πόλις αὔτων.

The fruit of Helen's lust is grief for Priam and his children; the fruit of
Thetis's marriage is the best of demigods. How are they related? Thetis's
child, the happy (*ólbion*) semidivine driver of colts, is, of course, the one
who brings grief to Priam's children and thus carries out Zeus's willed
destruction. Achilles is here portrayed as the godlike and *ólbios* instrument of Zeus's vengeance. War is seen as tragically destructive only for
his sinful victims.

One need only compare this poem to an Iliadic passage describing a
similar situation to see how different Alkaios and Homer are in spirit.
In Book Twenty-Four Achilles proves his point that grief is a generic
component of human life by using Peleus and Priam as paradigms: both
were formerly *ólbios* (539, 543), but now they are both wretched because
Peleus's only son, instead of taking care of his aging father, is at war far
from home bringing griefs to Priam and his children (541–545). Alkaios,
though he knew the *Iliad*,[15] chooses not to invoke its mood along with
its hero, for he is more interested in clear moral oppositions than in
generic insights. His audience is not encouraged to remember that be-

fore Ilium sinks in flames Peleus's child, as well as Priam's, will fall in battle. Instead of creating a sorrowful linkage between Peleus and Priam, Alkaios heightens the disparity between Helen and Thetis. By using only negative words (*kákōn*, "evil"; *áchos*, "grief"; *apólonto*, "perish") for Helen and the Trojans and only positive words (*phériston*, "best"; *ólbion*, "happy"; *génnato*, "give birth") for Achilles and his parents, Alkaios sharpens a sense of difference between the two sets of people. Achilles as supreme warrior functions as a symbol of divine concern for human behavior: war may be bitter but it is just, and the supreme warrior provides simultaneously a dire warning to those who contemplate *kakà érga* like Helen and the promise of reward for virtuous parents like Peleus and Thetis.

We do not know for what occasion Alkaios composed this short poem about the Trojan War, one of the few surviving Lesbian poems to employ heroic themes. Its positive view of Achilles, as D. L. Page suggests, may be due to the fact that Achilles' tomb was among the heroic monuments of the Troad, in which the nearby Lesbians felt a proprietary interest. "No more patriotic theme," he says, "could inspire the poet, and delight his audience, than the praise of Thetis and her gallant son." [16]

A kind of patriotism also inspires much of Pindar's fifth-century praise of Achilles. Though his *epiníkia*, or victory poems, celebrate specific individual performances in lands not his own, Pindar's vision is a communal one and tends always to intertwine the excellence of the victor with the excellence of his city and its heroes. [17] Thus, in four of his odes addressed to Aiginetan victors (*N*. 3, 6; *I*. 5, 8) Achilles figures prominently as one of the Aiakidai, the famous sons and grandsons of Aiakos whose "great-hearted spirits (*orgaí*)" are worshipped as heroes in Aigina (*I*. 5.30–35).

Heroes, who are always of divine descent, are particularly important to Pindar's message because they illustrate his firm belief that excellence is something in one's blood, not something learned. [18] Achilles, son of a father "of ancient valor" (*palaiaîsi en aretaîs*) and great-grandson of Zeus, provides a good example of such inherited excellence, for he showed forth his illustrious genes even as a young boy, performing feats that carried him far above the realm of ordinary mortals (*N*. 3.43–53):

> Blond Achilles while still in the house of Philyra
> did great deeds even in boyish play, often poising a
> short-tipped javelin in his hands, wind-swift he

wrought death in battle with wild lions,
and he would slay boars and carry their panting bodies
to Cheiron, son of Kronos,
first at six years old and then all the time.
To the amazement of Artemis and bold Athene
he killed deer without dogs or entrapping nets
for he overpowered them on foot. This story of mine is
told by men of old.

ξανθὸς δ' Ἀχιλεὺς τὰ μὲν μένων Φιλύρας ἐν δόμοις,
παῖς ἐὼν ἄθυρε μεγάλα ἔργα χερσὶ θαμινὰ
βραχυσίδαρον ἄκοντα πάλλων ἴσα τ' ἀνέμοις,
μάχᾳ λεόντεσσιν ἀγροτέροις ἔπρασσεν φόνον,
κάπρους τ' ἔναιρε σώματα δὲ παρὰ Κρονίδαν
Κένταυρον ἀσθμαίνοντα κόμιζεν,
ἑξέτης τὸ πρῶτον, ὅλον δ' ἔπειτ' ἂν χρόνον·
τὸν ἐθάμβεον Ἄρτεμίς τε καὶ θρασεῖ' Ἀθάνα,
κτείνοντ' ἐλάφους ἄνευ κυνῶν δολίων θ' ἑρκέων
ποσσὶ γὰρ κράτεσκε. λεγόμενον δὲ τοῦτο προτέρων
ἔπος ἔχω·

Nothing could better prove the concept of untaught "weightiness" than this wonder-child able to kill lions and boars at age six, strong enough to drag the carcasses back to Cheiron's cave, his swiftness exaggerated to the ability to outrun deer.[19]

Evidence from vase painting (see Figure 9) shows that the story of Achilles' fantastic childhood in the cave of the centaur Cheiron was indeed told by men of old—as old, at least, as the sixth century B.C.[20] We cannot know whether the legend was fully developed at the time Homer composed the *Iliad*—he tells us only that Achilles was taught medicine by Cheiron (*Il.* 11.830–832), not when and where—but if it was, he chose not to use it. Homer gave Achilles a normal infancy to humanize the inexorable hero, to emphasize his common mortality: Phoinix's account of baby Achilles eating on his lap reminds us of all babies as we hear of his being given little pieces of meat and spitting up all over his tutor's shirt (*Il.* 9.486–491). Pindar, however, is not interested in *all* babies, only in extraordinary ones who can illustrate his belief in innate excellence. The Epic Cycle story is highly appropriate to this interest.

The excellence that Achilles exhibits as a child is that of killing. The mighty child shows all the marks of growing up to be the beautiful, swift, strong, and bloody hero of the *Iliad*. But he is limited to this de-

FIGURE 9. Cheiron Receives Young Achilles

structive role. Pindar relates that Cheiron taught Jason to be wise; he taught Asklepios, son of Apollo, "the tender touch of healing" (*N.* 3.53–55); both youths, we can assume, had their innate excellence developed. Achilles, it appears, is developed only as a warrior—no mention is made of the healing skills he has in Homer, no mention is made of his skill on the lyre. We are told only that Cheiron strengthened his spirit (*thumós*) with all things fitting

> so that when sent on the sea-blasting winds
> to Troy he might stand firm against the
> spear-thudding battle cry of Lykians, Phrygians,
> and Dardanians, and in hand-to-hand combat with
> sword-bearing Aithiopians might fix it in their hearts
> that their ruler would not return again home
> with them, Memnon the mighty, cousin of Helenos.
>
> (*N.* 3.59–63)

ὄφρα θαλασσίαις ἀνέμων ῥιπαῖσι πεμφθείς
ὑπὸ Τροΐαν δορίκτυπον ἀλαλὰν Λυκίων τε προσμένοι καὶ Φρυγῶν
Δαρδάνων τε, καὶ ἐγχεσφόροις ἐπιμείξαις
Αἰθιόπεσσι χεῖρας, ἐν φρασὶ πάξαιθ᾽, ὅπως σφίσι μὴ κοίρανος ὀπίσω
πάλιν οἴκαδ᾽ ἀνεψιὸς ζαμενὴς Ἑλένοιο Μέμνων μόλοι.

This supreme ability to kill is the kind of excellence (*aretàs megálas*) that has caused the name of the Aiakidai to fly far over sea and land (*N.*

6.46–49). Other praiseworthy excellences do exist: we learn in another ode that Cheiron was said to have advised his powerful ward[21]

> to revere the son of Kronos, deep-voiced
> ruler of lightning and thunder,
> first among the gods,
> and as long as he should live,
> never to deprive his parents of this same honor.
>
> (*P.* 6.21–27)

> τά ποτ᾽ ἐν οὔρεσι φαντὶ μεγαλοσθενεῖ
> Φιλύρας υἱὸν ὀρφανιζομένῳ
> Πηλεΐδᾳ παραινεῖν· μάλιστα μὲν Κρονίδαν,
> θεῶν σέβεσθαι·
> ταύτας δὲ μή ποτε τιμᾶς
> ἀμείρειν γονέων βίον πεπρωμένον.

But even though we may understand Achilles to have such piety, it is not the material of his *kléos*. After telling us that Cheiron taught it to Achilles, Pindar chooses another as its exemplar: Antilochos, a *theîos*, a "divine" man who sacrificed his life to save his father, Nestor, from Memnon, the hero whose death *is* the theme of Achilles' *kléos*.

In *Isthmian 5* Pindar calls upon the Muse to drive his heart high from the earth and tell

> who killed Kyknos, who Hektor,
> who the fearless leader of the Aithiopians,
> bronze-armed Memnon. Who wounded noble
> Telephos with his spear by the banks of the Kaikos.
>
> (38–42)

> ἔλα νῦν μοι πεδόθεν·
> λέγε, τίνες Κύκνον, τίνες Ἕκτορα πέφνον,
> καὶ στράταρχον Αἰθιόπων ἄφοβον
> Μέμνονα χαλκοάραν· τίς ἄρ᾽ ἐσλὸν Τήλεφον
> τρῶσεν ἑῷ δορὶ Καΐκου παρ᾽ ὄχθαις;

Such is the tenor of nearly all Pindar's references to Achilles: homicide follows homicide as Hektor, Kyknos, Telephos, and Memnon fall beneath his sword on the bloody battle plains (*I.* 5.39–42; *I.* 8.54–61; *N.* 6.49–53). These are the deeds that in one ode win Achilles literal immortality on the Islands of the Blessed (*O.* 2.79–83):

And his mother, having persuaded Zeus,
brought there Achilles,
him who felled Hektor, invincible
pillar of Troy, who gave to death Kyknos
and the Aithiopian child of Dawn.

Ἀχιλλέα τ᾽ ἔνεικ ᾽, ἐπεὶ Ζηνὸς ἦτορ
λιταῖς ἔπεισε, μάτηρ.
ὅς Ἕκτορα σφᾶλε, Τροίας
ἄμαχον ἀστραβῆ κίονα, Κύκνον τε θανάτῳ πόρεν,
Ἀοῦς τε παῖδ᾽ Αἰθίοπα.

More importantly, perhaps, for the singer Pindar, it is such deeds that
prove Achilles' place among those heroes who by being "good fighters
(*polemistai*) / gained repute (*lógon*) and are sung (*kléontai*) to the lyre
and the full-toned call of the flute / for uncountable time" (*I.* 5.26–28).

The *kléos* of this excellent killer is a song without shadow. Unlike
the battle scenes in the *Iliad* with their similes and graphic gore, the
Pindaric verses that relate Achilles' killings are swift and evocative only
of the beauty inherent in doing extremely well whatever it is one does.
Pindar also ignores any personal motivation for the warrior's acts and
sidesteps the passion, at once so horrifying and so compelling, that is
the foundation of Homer's hero.

Achilles' friendship with Patroklos, mentioned only once, is set in a
context of military excellence (*O.* 9.70–79):

The child of Menoitios, going to the plain of
Teuthras with the sons of Atreus, stood alone with
Achilles when Telephos turned the valiant
Danaans, attacking their sea-going ships,
so that the strong purpose of Patroklos
was clear for the wise to see.
From then on the son of Thetis urged that
never in the moil of Ares should Patroklos
be stationed apart from his own
man-slaughtering spear.

. . . . Μενοίτιον. τοῦ παῖς ἅμ᾽ Ἀτρείδαις
Τεύθραντος πεδίον μολὼν ἔστα σὺν Ἀχιλλεῖ
μόνος, ὅτ᾽ ἀλκάεντας Δαναοὺς τρέψαις ἁλίαισιν
πρύμναις Τήλεφος ἔμβαλεν·
ὥστ᾽ ἔμφρονι δεῖξαι

μαθεῖν Πατρόκλου βιατὰν νόον·
ἐξ οὗ Θέτιος γόνος οὐλίῳ νιν ἐν Ἄρει

παραγορεῖτο μή ποτε
σφετέρας ἄτερθε ταξιοῦσθαι
δαμασιμβρότου αἰχμᾶς.

Achilles' great enemy Hektor is presented as *hypérthumon*, "vehement" (*I*. 8.60) and as Troy's "invincible pillar" (*O*. 2.81–82), never as the killer of Patroklos, and although his death is briefly described three times, no mention is made of Achilles' fierce motive. One might think that choosing death over allowing his friend to go unavenged would be a perfect example for Pindar of noble courage. The inclusion of this motif, however, might evoke all the unseemly events that surrounded Patroklos's and Hektor's deaths: Achilles' sending Patroklos to fight instead of going himself; the brutal rejection of the suppliant, Lykaon; the maltreatment of Hektor's corpse; the sacrifice of the twelve Trojan youths on Patroklos's pyre. It is best not to recall the Achilles of *Iliad* 16–23 in songs whose primary purpose is praise.

Only once do any sort of emotive words give a hint of the wrathful and vengeful hero of the *Iliad*. In *Nemean* 6, in the context of the non-Iliadic episode of Memnon's death, Pindar uses the word *neîkos*, "feud," for Achilles' fight with Memnon (50b) and characterizes his spear as *zákotos*, "wrathful" (53).[22] It is perhaps the circumstances of Antilochos's death that allow the implacability and passion of the Homeric hero to be a positive contribution to Pindar's aims. We know from Proclus's summary of the *Aithiopis* that Achilles killed Memnon immediately after Memnon killed Antilochos (*Chrestomathia* 2, p. 106).[23] Achilles, we can assume, killed Memnon in vengeance for his "dear companion" (*Il.* 23.556), the sorrowing friend who brought him the news of Patroklos's death and held his hands while he wept (*Il.* 18.1–34), the cheating, then charmingly repentant youngster who produced the only smile on Achilles' face in the whole *Iliad* (23.541–556). But the killing of Memnon evokes more than just friendship. As we have seen, Antilochos died to save his father, thus earning the highest reputation for filial *areté* (*P.* 6.28–42). It is only in the context of such totally positive connotations of piety and friendship that the anger that characterizes Achilles in every other poet makes its appearance, briefly, in Pindar's celebration of excellence.

FIGURE 10. Achilles Fights with Memnon

Another event the slaying of Memnon must have evoked for Pindar's audience was the death of Achilles himself, for according to the *Aithiopis* Achilles was slain directly afterwards by Apollo and Paris (*Chrestomathia* 2, p. 106). Although Pindar never elaborates on the slaying, telling us only that he was struck by arrows (*P.* 3.101), he mentions the death in three odes (*O.* 2.79–83; *P.* 3.100–103; *I.* 8.40, 62–66). For Pindar, as for Homer, "dirge" would seem to be the melancholic underpinning of songs of heroic glory. This underpinning is suggested most strongly in *Pythian* 3 and *Isthmian* 8, odes that attach just a hint of Homeric tragedy to the great hero.

Pythian 3, written for the ill Hieron as a consolatory epistle rather than as a standard *epinikion*, is by far the darker of the two. Similar to Alkaios 42 insofar as its comparison of two fathers and its concern with the presence of evil in the world remind the reader of *Iliad* 24, its brooding over the ubiquitous human yearning for immortality brings it much closer than Alkaios's poem to Homer's melancholic mood. After first using the myths of Koronis and Asklepios to reject the idea that mortals should strive, as they do, to go beyond the limitations imposed on them by the gods,[24] Pindar uses Peleus and Kadmos as exemplars of how even the most fortunate of men must endure "two pains for every blessing" (*hèn par eslòn pêmata súnduo*, 81).[25] These men, says Pindar, are said to have had the "highest happiness" (*ólbon hypértaton*, 89) of any mortal: each married a goddess and heard the Muses sing at his wedding (86–96). But their friendship with gods does not change the mortal status of either themselves or their children: the fate of Kadmos's three daughters deprived him of happiness, and

> Peleus's only son, whom immortal Thetis
> bore in Phthia, arrows having taken his life in war,
> roused the Danaans to funereal wailing
> as he burned on the pyre.
>
> (100–103)

> τοῦ δὲ παῖς, ὅνπερ μόνον ἀθανάτα
> τίκτεν ἐν Φθίᾳ Θέτις, ἐν πολέμῳ τόξοις ἀπὸ ψυχὰν λιπὼν
> ὦρσεν πυρὶ καιόμενος
> ἐκ Δαναῶν γόον.

Human *ólbos*, Pindar affirms, cannot last long (105–106).

Pindar's vision at first seems even bleaker than that of the Iliadic Achilles. When Achilles said that the best a mortal could hope for was to be given from both of Zeus's two jars of goods and evils (*Il.* 24.525–533), he implied that Zeus's gifts would be disbursed in equal proportions. Pindar, less optimistic, specifies two portions of suffering for each portion of good fortune. This unequal proportion, however, does not mean that a double portion of evil follows every success: in Peleus's case, the two portions of suffering are represented first by the vague *kamátōn* ("tribulations") he had before his fortunate marriage (96) and then by the premature death of his son after that marriage. Unlike *Iliad* 24, where Achilles envisions absolute happiness followed by permanent and unconsolable misery, Pindar sees an alternation in good and bad, with the gods sending consolation for the evil we cannot ward off. In the case of Kadmos, Pindar makes the consolation explicit: although the fate of three daughters destroys happiness, the fourth daughter is made the mate of Zeus (97–98). In the case of Peleus, the consolation is implicit. Even though men's *ólbos* cannot last long, Pindar continues, their *aretē* can endure if poets, who are *téktones*, "crafters" of harmony (113) just as Asklepios was a *téktōn* of anodynes (6), preserve it, as they did for Nestor and Sarpedon, in resounding poetry (*epéōn keladennôn*) and in glorious songs (*kleinaîs aoidaîs* (112–115).[26]

With his repetition of the word *téktōn* Pindar makes an implicit contrast between the doctor's art and the poet's. The fate of Asklepios, struck with lightning for bringing the dead back to life, represents, even as does Achilles' death, the ineluctability of god-ordained evils in our lives. But if the doctor's art must yield to our mortal condition, the poet's art need not. *Aoidaí* can make the departed live again and thus respond to the "common prayer" with which Pindar opened this ode (2–3). They can confer their immortality not only with impunity but also with the gods' approval and participation. As we learn in *Isthmian* 8, which also uses Achilles to grapple with questions of sorrowful mortality, the Muses can be present at human funerals as well as at divine weddings.

Pindar prefaces his "song" of Achilles in this ode by a prebirth prophecy of his death. His mortality shall be the price of extinguishing strife in Olympus,[27] says Themis, as she urges Zeus and Poseidon to heal their quarrel by having Thetis marry Peleus (39–41):

> Let her join the bed of a mortal
> and see her son dead in war,
> her son with hands like Ares, with feet like lightning.

> βροτέων δὲ λεχέων τυχοῖσα
> υἱὸν εἰσιδέτω θανόντ' ἐν πολέμῳ,
> χεῖρας Ἄρεί τ' ἐναλίγκιον στεροπαῖσί τ' ἀκμὰν ποδῶν.

Zeus agrees, and the result is that

> the voice of poets made known
> to the ignorant the new excellence of Achilles
> who covered the Mysian vineyard with gore
> sprinkling it with the dark blood of Telephos,
> forged the path of homecoming for the sons of Atreus,
> and released Helen, cutting with his
> spear the sinews of Troy, which ever tried to hold him off as he
>   marshalled
> the work of man-slaying battle in the plain: strong Memnon,
> vehement Hektor, and other champions to whom Achilles, scion of
>   Aiakos, showed the house of Persephone
> as he made manifest Aigina's own stock.

(52–61)

καὶ νεαρὰν ἔδειξαν σοφῶν
στόματ' ἀπείροισιν ἀρετὰν Ἀχιλέος·
ὅ καὶ Μύσιον ἀμπελόεν
αἵμαξε Τηλέφου μέλανι ῥαίνων φόνῳ πεδίον,

στρ. ς΄ γεφύρωσέ τ' Ἀτρείδαισι νόστον,
Ἑλέναν τ' ἐλύσατο, Τροῖας
ἶνας ἐκταμὼν δορί, ταί νιν ῥύοντό ποτε μάχας ἐναριμβρότου
ἔργον ἐν πεδίῳ κορύσσοντα, Μέμνονός τε βίαν
ὑπέρθυμον Ἕκτορά τ' ἄλλους τ' ἀριστέας· οἷς δῶμα Φερσεφόνας
μανύων Ἀχιλεύς, οὖρος Αἰακιδᾶν,
Αἴγιναν σφετέραν τε ῥίζαν πρόφαινεν.

Everything in this single sentence is subordinate to "the poets' voices made known," and we soon see that such poetic activity is the single most important facet of Achilles' deeds. When the ode circles back to Achilles' predicted death, that death is again set in a context of song (62–66):

Nor in death did songs (*aoidaí*) abandon him,
but around his pyre and tomb stood the Heliconian maidens
pouring forth the many-voiced dirge (*thrênon*).
Indeed, even the deathless ones (*kaì athanátois*) deemed it right
to give a noble man, even when dead (*kaì phthímenon*),
into the keeping of the goddesses' hymns (*hýmnois*).

τὸν μὲν οὐδὲ θανόντ' ἀοιδαί τι λίπον,
ἀλλά οἱ παρά τε πυρὰν τάφον θ' Ἑλικώνιαι παρθένοι
στάν, ἐπὶ θρῆνόν τε πολύφαμον ἔχεαν.
ἔδοξ' ἄρα καὶ ἀθανάτοις,
ἐσλόν γε φῶτα καὶ φθίμενον ὕμνοις θεᾶν διδόμεν.

The repetition of *kaì* ("even") in *kaì athanátois* and *kaì phthímenon* emphasizes the normally vast difference between mortals and immortals. But in the case of a noble mortal that distance can be bridged: in *Olympian* 2 it was bridged by immortality on the Island of the Blessed; here the distance between the dead and the deathless is bridged by the Muses. Because of his deeds, Achilles has been kept alive in their song just as the contemporary young boxer Nikokles is kept in memory by their "vehicle," Pindar (67–69).

As Carola Greengard has pointed out, the movement of the Achilles myth and that of the ode as a whole follow a parallel development that ends in an affirmation of the "necessity of song in the face of sorrow and death as an answer to the debate between grief and hope."[28] I would add that Pindar's choosing to end the ode with hope—as indeed is fitting for a victory celebration—effectively vitiates a second parallel Greengard describes, that between the events of the mythic narrative and the tragic themes of the *Iliad*.[29] Heroic fame and death may indeed be inseparable in both works, but Pindar's uncritical view of song as recompense eradicates any tragic conclusions about the human predicament that Achilles' premature death might otherwise have emphasized. Pindar's final vision replaces the mother forced to "see her son dead in war" with a choir of Muses whose "dirge" (*thrênon*) soon shifts to "festive songs of praise" (*hýmnois*), and by the time Pindar actually places Achilles in his Muse-encircled tomb, "poets" have proved his regeneration by filling our minds with his living deeds.

Killing, being killed, and the meed of song: these to Pindar are the ingredients of the heroic world in which Achilles was the greatest hero. They are essentially the same ingredients that make up Homer's heroic world, but Pindar does not probe critically into that world the way Homer does. He shows an Achilles born and bred for the battlefield without any of the complexity we saw in Homer's hero, an Achilles whose actions are governed by his genes rather than by passion, an Achilles whose *kléos* is ample compensation for his early death. Pindar acknowledges the splendor in Achilles' blood but denies the agony in his heart.

2. SOPHOKLES

No more than Pindar does Sophokles show what is in Achilles' heart—at least not when he invokes Achilles by name. That tempestuous heart does beat in the breasts of almost all Sophokles' focal heroes—Oedipus, Antigone, Elektra, Aias, Philoktetes; the prototype of them all, as Bernard Knox demonstrates in his superb introductory chapters to *The Heroic Temper*, is the brooding, angry, obstinate, and death-scorning Iliadic Achilles.[30] But Achilles himself is not among Sophokles' heroes: no play survives in which he is even a secondary character.[31] His image, however, is kept constantly before our mind's eye in the *Philoktetes*, a play that is concerned with the Pindaric issues of natural nobility versus learned behavior. In this play we watch Neoptolemos, who is announced and subsequently addressed thirteen times as "son of Achilles," struggle between the conflicting claims of his "teacher" Odysseus, here portrayed as the master of words and expediency, and of his genes, which impel him toward physical action and honesty. Because the play portrays a clash of principles, both Odysseus and Achilles lose their Homeric complexity in the interest of dramatic clarity. Whatever soul-searching there is, is done by the young Neoptolemos as he chooses, in situations parallel to those in which his father acted in the *Iliad*, between the two compelling models. Achilles is hardly a real human being in this play, but he is, as Knox puts it, "the measure of Neoptolemos' fall from heroic virtue and the ideal to which he must in the end rise again."[32]

Except for Neoptolemos's statement that his father is honest (88–89), the play's references to Achilles are rather bland, broadly judgmental rather than discriminating, and merely indicate that, in fact, this person is appropriate to take as an ideal. All we learn from what Odysseus and Philoktetes say is that he was the strongest (*krátistos:* Odysseus, 4) and best (*áristos:* Philoktetes, 1284, 1313) of the Greeks, noble (*esthlós:* Odysseus, 96), and, of course, well-born (*eugenēs:* Philoktetes, 336, 874). The specific actions to which we are meant to apply these adjectives can be seen only through the foil of his son's choices. Therefore, for the purposes of this study we must reverse Knox's formulation and say that Neoptolemos's fall is the measure of his father's heroic virtue, his rise the restatement of that virtue. As we examine Neoptolemos's actions we shall find that our attention is directed to *Iliad* 1 and 9, the quarrel with Agamemnon and the rejection of the embassy.

The plot of the *Philoktetes* is briefly this: because the Greek army has learned through a prophecy that Philoktetes and his bow are essential to the capture of Troy, Odysseus has come to Lemnos to get the man whom he had abandoned nine years before when the stench from his festering wound and his cries of agony were driving everyone in the army mad. Since he knows Philoktetes hates him and will shoot him on sight with the invincible bow and arrows of Herakles, he has brought Neoptolemos with him to perform the trickery that he says is necessary to get Philoktetes on board their ship. Odysseus's first on-stage action, persuading his young companion to take part in this trickery and lie, establishes the conflict between birth and education that is only resolved in the last scene of the play.

"Son of Achilles," Odysseus begins, "in the business on which you came, you must be loyal (*gennaîon*) not with your body (*tôi sômati*) only, but—even if you hear something new, something you did not hear before, render assistance (*hypourgeîn*); since you are here as an assistant (*hyperétēs*)" (50–53). *Gennaîon,* the word I have translated as "loyal" (following Jebb), is double-edged in this context. Although its common meaning is "well-bred, noble"—whence the concept "loyal"—the basic meaning of *gennaîon* is "true to one's birth or descent." Thus, T. B. L. Webster translates "behave like your father."[33] On Odysseus's lips the word creates a subtle Sophoklean irony and embodies the tension that will inform all of Neoptolemos's choices: if he is truly to behave like his father, he cannot be loyal to the mission in the way Odysseus is about to ask; practicing deceit will preclude being true to his birth.[34]

The clause that follows the exhortation to be *gennaîon* "not only with your body" is jarring both rhetorically and syntactically. Syntactically one expects a phrase parallel to "with your body" (*tôi sômati*), but, instead of balancing the instrumental dative with either another dative or a circumstantial participle (for example, "by rendering assistance"), Odysseus concludes his exhortation with an imperative infinitive "render assistance" (*hypourgeîn*).[35] Such an abrupt change in syntax, though certainly not rare in fifth-century Greek, is meant, I think, to draw attention to the rough joinings in Odysseus's thought and to back up the unnaturalness of the request that is to follow.

On the rhetorical level the frustration of expectation is somewhat more complicated. The Athenians loved antithesis: it was a favorite rhetorical device to couple or contrast word and deed, thought and action. Implicit almost always in such antitheses is a deprecatory contrast between the slippery value of words and the solid actuality of deeds, between possible falsehood and provable reality. When Odysseus says "not only in body," the audience should expect the completion "but also in words."[36] This reverses the normal polarity "not only in word but also in deed," relegating physical action to the inferior position. This reversal will become explicit fifty lines later when Odysseus says, "It is not deeds but the tongue that holds command in everything" (99). It is in keeping with Odysseus's wily character that he does not complete his inverted antithesis now. But Sophokles has given his audience enough to make them suspect what will soon become clear: in this play Achilles and Odysseus are meant to be viewed as polar opposites.

In Homer there was no real dichotomy between word and deed, brain and brawn; when the two were coupled they were most often complementary. So, too, Achilles and Odysseus were not seen as having opposing characters but as having different talents within the same heroic mold. Martial heroes were not supposed to be tongue-tied in the assemblies where policy was decided. Phoinix, Achilles' tutor, was sent along to Troy with his young charge to complete his education into manhood. This involved, he tells us, teaching Achilles "to be a speaker of words and a doer of deeds" (*Il.* 9.443). Achilles excels more at doing deeds; in his own words: "I am such a one as no other of the bronze-greaved Achaians in battle; in council many others are better" (*Il.* 18.105–106). Odysseus is one of those who are better. We know what kind of an orator he is from Antenor's remarks in *Iliad* 3.221–223:

> But when he sent the great voice from his chest
> and words like snowflakes coming thick in winter,
> then you would not compare any other mortal to Odysseus.

However, when Odysseus comes to compare himself to Achilles, he does not say anything like "Your province is the battlefield, mine is the mind." Instead, he asks him politely to endure the force of his words, for

> You are stronger and much more powerful than me with the spear, but
> I am far ahead of you in intelligence since I am older and know more.
>
> (*Il.* 19.217–220)

This implies that Achilles, when he grows older, may achieve equal power with thought and words.

But of course Achilles never did grow older, and if his speeches were remembered, it was for the passion that lay behind their eloquence rather than for rhetoric. Odysseus, however, lived on to show himself master thinker, bard, and creator of fiction in the *Odyssey*. His verbal dexterity is wholeheartedly admired by Homer, who complements it with a martial heroism equal to that of any of the Iliadic heroes except perhaps Achilles and Diomedes.

The vision of later poets was not so inclusive.[37] In a fragment from Euripides' lost *Telephos*,[38] produced in 438 B.C., Achilles and Odysseus are clearly opposed as doer and speaker. This fragment presents a dialogue between Achilles, who has just landed at Argos to rejoin the Greek expedition against Troy, and Odysseus, who had arrived there earlier with the rest of the Greek host after a storm had scattered the ships. Achilles, who does not know that Telephos, directed by the oracle at Delphi, has come and seized the infant Orestes in order to compel the Greeks to get Achilles to heal the wound he gave him, expresses amazement that the host is not prepared to sail. "Why the delay?" he asks impatiently. "We should get moving" (13). Odysseus, obviously unwilling to tell him immediately that he must cure his enemy, stalls and says that it is not the right time to make haste (18). Achilles launches into a disgusted comparison between himself as an actor and the rest of them as idle talkers (19–24):

> Always you are sluggish and put off acting,
> and everyone, immobile, makes a million speeches
>   (*rhēseis légei*),
> but nothing (*tò érgon*) ever gets under way.
> I, however, as you see, am here ready
> to act, I and the host of Myrmidons,
> and I will sail, leaving behind
> the delays of the two sons of Atreus.

> αἰεί ποτ᾽ ἐστὲ νωχελεῖς καὶ μέλλετε,
> ῥήσεις θ᾽ ἕκαστος μυρίας καθήμενος
> λέγει, τὸ δ᾽ ἔργον οὐδαμοῦ περαίνεται.
> κἀγὼ μέν, ὡς ὁρᾶτε, δρᾶν ἕτοιμος ὢν
> ἥκω, στρατός τε Μυρμιδών, καὶ πλεύσομαι
> τὰ τῶν Ἀτρειδῶν οὐ μένων μελλήματα.[39]

We do not know precisely how Euripides judged the merits of the two types of character. I will speculate, however, that if one was singled out for admiration, it was Odysseus. This play was written during the great days of Athenian democracy under Perikles, when optimism was high about the working of the assembly and delight in the power of words had not yet been soured by the perversions of demagogues and the usurpations of meaning induced by wartime despair.[40]

We can do no more than guess about Euripides' opinion on the relative merit of words and deeds, Odysseus and Achilles, in 438. But there is evidence that in the last quarter of the fifth century the separation of physical from mental abilities was seen in Athens as an ever wider split between unthinking, wholesome nobility and decrepit, rationalistic immorality. Aristophanes' debate between *ho kreíttōn lógos* and *ho hếttōn lógos*, "Right" and "Wrong,"[41] makes a caricature of this split in the year 423.[42] Says Right (*Clouds* 1009–1021):

> If you devote yourself to following my precepts, your chest will be stout, your color glowing, your shoulders broad, your tongue short, your buttocks big, but your penis small. But if you follow the fashions of the day, you will be pallid in hue, have narrow shoulders, a narrow chest, a long tongue, scrawny thighs, and a big thing. . . . You will be persuaded also to regard as splendid everything that is shameful and as shameful everything that is honorable.[43]

At approximately the same time as Aristophanes was differentiating men of action from men of words in this comic way, Hippias the Sophist (if we can believe Plato) was expatiating in all seriousness on the profound difference between Achilles and Odysseus: "I will show you by means of careful reasoning and many proofs," he assures Sokrates in the *Hippias Minor*, "that Homer made Achilles better than Odysseus and honest (*ameínō . . . kaì apseudê*) and that he made Odysseus more guileful, full of lies, and worse (*dolerón te kaì pollà pseudómenon kaì cheírō*) than Achilles" (369c). Here the difference between the two is cast in terms of the standard corollary to the deeds-versus-words antithesis: honesty versus duplicity. The judgment—Achilles better, Odysseus worse—survived for centuries. We have our first complete literary expression of it here in the *Philoktetes*.

Odysseus does not complete the words-deeds antithesis at line 51 because he wants to instill the idea of obedience into Neoptolemos before he reveals his intentions completely. Webster explains: "Odysseus knows Achilles would never have consented to lying; he might, however, have obeyed an order, so Odysseus continues 'but also you must obey orders, even if they are strange.'"[44] Sophokles' Odysseus may indeed hope to convince Neoptolemos that Achilles might have obeyed an order; Sophokles' audience would never believe it. When the phrase *hos hyperétēs párei* ("you are here as an assistant," 53) occurs, one is surely being invited to recall Book One of the *Iliad*. *Hyperétēs*, which does not occur in Homer, is used in Attic Greek to designate someone or something in *subordinate* relationship to another, and a subordinate relationship to someone he thinks morally wrong or inferior is precisely what Achilles rejects in *Iliad* 1. Early on in his quarrel with Agamemnon, Achilles questions whether any of the Achaians now can be wholeheartedly obedient to their obviously shameless king (1.149–151). Later, disregarding Nestor's plea that he not stand against a man who by virtue of being a scepter-bearing king and ruling over more people is *phérteros,* "more powerful, superior in rank," Achilles declares (1.293–296):

> Indeed I should be called craven and worthless
> if I submit to you (*hypeíxomai*) in everything whatsoever you ask.
> Give your orders to others; don't command me.
> For I, at least, intend no longer to obey you.

Though made in passion, this decision to disobey an unjust leader is not portrayed as an easy one for Achilles. It entails not only isolation from the Greek community but also loss of his heart's desire, the action of fighting: while he stays in his camp he "pines away, continually longing for the cry and clash of battle" (1.491–492). Upholding this decision entails, in Book Nine, sacrifice not only of the enormously rich gifts Agamemnon offers but also of his promised glory.

Such is the Achilles our young hero's actions throw ever more into relief. Though Neoptolemos does finally accept the role of *hyperétēs* his father spurned, he does not do so easily. He does not immediately acquiesce to Odysseus's request for obedience but forces Odysseus to tell him what he is supposed to do before he agrees to do it (54–55). And though responsibility to the army weighs on him, he phrases the feeling thus: "Since I was sent with you as a co-worker (*sunergátēs*), I shrink from being called a traitor" (93–94). Neoptolemos has made a subtle but significant shift in prefixes. The *hyp-* in Odysseus's *hyperétēs* means "under"; the *sun-* in Neoptolemos's *sunergátēs* means "with." Linguistically, at least, Neoptolemos insists on a "co-" rather than a "sub-" status.

Neoptolemos's first response to the request that he give himself to Odysseus "for one small shameless day" (83–84) and "steal Philoktetes' soul with words" (54–55) sounds very much like his father. He declares passionately that ends do not justify means (89–90, 94–95):

> I am not one to do anything by evil means,
> nor, so they say, was he who fathered me.

. . . .
I would rather, my lord, do right and
lose, than win by doing wrong.

ἔφυν γὰρ οὐδὲν ἐκ τέκνης πράσσειν κακῆς,
οὔτ' αὐτὸς οὔθ', ὥς φασιν, οὔκφύσας ἐμέ.

. . . .
βούλομαι δ', ἄναξ, καλῶς
δρῶν ἐξαμαρτεῖν μᾶλλον ἢ νικᾶν κακῶς.

"Doing wrong" at this stage does not mean to Neoptolemos what it might mean to us: taking unfair advantage to get someone to do something against his or her will. The son of the man of action is quite willing to use physical strength to force Philoktetes back to Troy. Why not just attack him, he suggests: a cripple cannot possibly prevail against us (90–92).[45]

"Doing wrong" means specifically lying. "What are you ordering me to do except lie (*pseudê légein*)?" he protests (100). His reluctance to lie is what reminds us most of his father. Achilles announced to Odysseus his intention to speak the truth, no matter what the consequences, with the ringing lines: "Hateful as the gates of Hell to me is that man / who keeps one thing hidden in his heart and speaks another" (9.312–313). But that father seems far away when Neoptolemos finally must make his choice between abandoning the mission and abandoning his own principles. After Odysseus has convinced him that neither force nor persuasion but only deceit will work, Neoptolemos asks if Odysseus does not think it shameful to lie. "No," says Odysseus, "not if the lie brings salvation" (108–109). Neoptolemos's response captures both the struggle and the incipient defeat we are meant to feel within him: "With what face, then, does one dare to utter those things aloud?" (110). He is saying simultaneously: "I can't possibly do this!" and "Teach me how to do this."[46] Odysseus answers, "Whenever you do something for gain (*kérdos*) it is not proper to shrink (*okneîn*)" (111). *Okneîn* could be translated either "scruple" or "hang back," depending on whether one wished to convey moral strength or physical cowardice. Here it expresses both. At the same time as Odysseus is saying that morality is not an issue in this matter he is telling Neoptolemos he will be a coward if he does *not* lie. The one word thus pits Neoptolemos's innate bravery against his innate honesty.

The motive for this bravery, however, is to be something most un-Achillean. *Kérdos,* which means "gain," "profit," always has somewhat shady connotations in the *Iliad,*[47] and though it fares better in the *Odyssey* where Athene uses the plural to denote the intellectual acuity that links her and her favorite (*Od.* 13.296–299), it never ceases to evoke the idea of getting the better of someone in not particularly heroic ways and for not particularly heroic goals (e.g., money, possessions). It is a far cry from the *timê,* "honor," and *kléos,* "glory," that motivated Achilles, and although the word itself is never specifically opposed to these loftier concepts in the *Iliad,* it was precisely such an opposition that Achilles had in mind when he reviled Agamemnon as *philakteanôtate pántōn,* "most greedy for gain of all men" (1.122), and *kerdaleóphron,* which comes from the same root as *kérdos* and also means "greedy for gain" (1.149). These epithets heralded accusations that Agamemnon was more concerned with his own personal profit than he was with the good of the people he led (1.225–231), that he had turned the war into a source of wealth rather than of honor (1.170–171).

Neoptolemos, who has already been wavering, falls into Odysseus's trap. "What *kérdos* is it for me, what do I gain, if Philoktetes goes to Troy?" he asks, and the fatal answer comes: "You can't take Troy without his bow" (112–115).[48] This appeal to his ambition, as Knox calls it,[49] is what finally pushes Neoptolemos to give up his principles: "They would, I grant you, become things one must hunt, if this is so" (116). Unlike his father, who decided that if the leader was bad, the cause was bad too and must be abandoned, Neoptolemos cannot even think of foregoing the promised glory of being the one who destroys Troy.[50] He accepts without question Odysseus's statement that he will be called "wise and good" (119) if he agrees to lie and "casts off all shame" (120). Odysseus has wrenched Neoptolemos completely away from his initial brave pronouncement that he would rather fail doing right than win doing wrong. He now lets the ends he desires justify the means.

Once he has made up his mind to it, Neoptolemos lies beautifully. The lie he tells is doubly degrading because he uses the traits of his father to give it verisimilitude.[51] Philoktetes readily believes that Achilles' son, furious at Agamemnon because of an insult to his honor, is abandoning the war and sailing home. How like a fifth-century version of his father Neoptolemos sounds when he proclaims:

Where the inferior man is stronger than the good one,
where honesty perishes and the vile man prevails,
these men are not the ones I will hold as friends.

(456–458)[52]

ὅπου θ᾽ ὁ χείρων τ᾽ ἀγαθοῦ μεῖζον σθένει
κ᾽ ἀποφθίνει τὰ χρηστὰ χὠ δειλὸς κρατεῖ,
τούτους ἐγὼ τοὺς ἄνδρας οὐ στέρξω ποτέ·

The irony of these lines is not lost on the audience: every word confirms
the fact that Neoptolemos has *become* the "inferior man," the "vile man"
that his father would have in truth hated. But Philoktetes has no reason
to doubt their honesty and begs Neoptolemos to take him home with
him. The degenerate son of Achilles has as good as accomplished his
mission.

The festering wound in Philoktetes' foot flares up, however, before
they can get to the ship, and Neoptolemos sees firsthand the terrible
suffering of the man his comrades-in-arms deserted so long ago. Also,
he is asked to and does give Philoktetes his hand in pledge of friendship
and trust. After these events, it is impossible for him to maintain his
pretense in the face of Philoktetes' grateful insistence on the noble (*eugenēs*) nature he has inherited from noble (*eugenōn*) parents (874). Just
before they start for the ship Neoptolemos cries, "All is disgusting when
a person has left his own nature and does things that are not like him"
(902–903). He reverts to honesty and tells Philoktetes he must go to
Troy. He thus confirms what he said in his original Achillean utterance:
"It is not in my nature to do anything by evil means" (88–89). But he is
still hampered by the same feeling he also expressed then: "I shrink
from being called a traitor" (93–94). Although so carried away by the
pity and shame evoked by Philoktetes' prayers and imprecations that he
very nearly gives the bow back, he allows himself to be stopped by the
appearance of Odysseus. As Philoktetes says during his following bitter
exchange with Odysseus, Neoptolemos's "only thought has been to
carry out orders" (1010). Honesty is not enough; if he is to become
truly like his father, Neoptolemos will have to free himself of feeling a
greater responsibility to the army than he does to his own principles.
This he finally does in the next scene.

"I am going to undo the wrong I did before" (1224), he says firmly to

Odysseus as he strides back on stage. "I did wrong when I obeyed you and the whole army and captured a man by shameful deceits and tricks" (1226, 1228). He says he is going to give back the bow. Odysseus tries to talk him out of it. "The whole Achaian host and I among them will prevent you" (1243), declares the man whose first words on stage had justified his cruel abandonment of Philoktetes by an appeal to "orders from above" (6). Neoptolemos replies that this is not a *sophós*, "clever" or "wise," thing to say. Odysseus rejoins that Neoptolemos and what he is about to do are not *sophós* (1245). This harks back to when Odysseus told Neoptolemos that he would be called *sophós* and good if he performed the trickery. Neoptolemos did not question the adjectives then. Now he says simply that a just (*díkaios*) act is better than a *sophós* one (1246). He holds to this firmly when Odysseus once again threatens him with the enmity of the Greek army. "I am not afraid," says the son of Achilles, "as long as justice is my ally" (1251). To the further threat that the army will turn from fighting Trojans to fighting him, he replies, "So be it" (1254).

Neoptolemos not only has set himself apart from the army, he is willing to face their physical hostility. The latter is something Achilles never had to face in the *Iliad*. In Book Nine he had to disregard Odysseus's appeal to pity the weakening *Panachaioi* (301–302) and to risk losing the goodwill of his personal friends who had stayed active in the army (639–642). The latter, which involved rejecting Aias's appeal that he soften his spirit for the dear friends who were under his roof, was difficult, but the claims of the *Panachaioi* seem to have caused him no hesitation at all.[53] Although the reader's sense of Achilles' isolation builds throughout Book Nine until at the end Diomedes responds to Odysseus's report with the curt dismissal: "We never should have pleaded with him at all. . . . Let him go or stay as he wishes" (698–703), isolation is all. Homer's hero is never threatened with violence from the army.

Sometime during the second half of the fifth century, tradition turned Achilles' rejection of the claims of the army into a more dangerous defiance. The quarrel with Agamemnon spread to become a quarrel with the whole army. A fragment from an unknown play[54] presents an embassy scene in which threats seem to have been the means of persuasion. Achilles reacts hotly to the threat of being stoned:

> Shall I, through fear of the Achaians, set my hand to the spear,
> the hand that is raging with anger because of a vile leader?[55]

φόβωι δ' Ἀχαιῶν χεῖρ' ἐφορμήσω δορὶ
μαιμῶσαν ὀργῇι ποιμένος κακοῦ διαί;

Neoptolemos is not so violent here in the *Philoktetes* as his father was in the unknown play, but he has been placed in and rises to a similar situation. The one is singled out from the many; Achilles' Iliadic individualism, even in the more extreme version of extra-Homeric tradition, is affirmed.

When Neoptolemos tells Philoktetes to take back his bow, Philoktetes, remembering the previous discrepancy between word and deed, qualifies his joy: Neoptolemos's words are *phíltata,* "most welcome," he says, if they are true (1290). Neoptolemos responds: *t'oúrgon paréstai phanerón,* "The deed shall soon prove the word" (1291),[56] and thereby corrects the inversion Odysseus had created in the valuation of words and deeds. By carrying out his promise, Neoptolemos shows forth the nature that engendered him; he is, as Philoktetes says, the child not of Odysseus "but of Achilles, who was called best when he was among the living, and still is among the dead" (1310–1313).

Achilles, the ghost from the heroic past, is all good; Odysseus, the modern politician, is all bad. There are no shades of grey in the *Philoktetes.* Our judgment of Achilles is not confused by any problematic traits from the *Iliad.* The brutality of the great rampage is not evoked; neither is the sorrowful complexity of the meeting with Priam. Although the wrath is recalled in Neoptolemos's lie to Philoktetes, honesty takes its place as the characterizing trait. Achilles' insubordination in *Iliad* 1 and his refusal to rejoin the army in Book Nine are the actions Sophokles seems to have singled out for praise. The heroic virtue of Sophokles' "Achilles" is his strong individualism, his willingness to go against the commands of his leader, the wishes of his group, and the imperative of winning glory in war, in order to do what he feels is inherently right.

3. EURIPIDES

Sophokles seems to have looked back with some regret at the past heroic age, seeing it as a purer time than the present, a time when motives could be simple and actions direct. This is, at least, the impression created by his two extant Trojan War plays, *Ajax* and *Philoktetes,* in which such a past conflicts with the compromised present. It was the absolute temper of its heroes that interested him, not the martial *aretē*, "excellence," demanded of them by virtue of their heroic medium, war. It is thus those books of the *Iliad* that show Achilles' erupting emotions as he interacts with his king and his friends that contribute most importantly to Sophokles' purpose. The sad reality of the war setting is rarely evoked, never commented on. The opposite is true for Euripidean drama, at least for that drama written during the long-drawn-out years of the Peloponnesian War.[57] In *Elektra* (413 B.C.?) Euripides evokes negative aspects of Homer's epic that Sophokles ignores, and although he draws heavily on *Iliad* 1 and 9 for both *Hekabe* (c. 424 B.C.) and *Iphigeneia in Aulis* (406 B.C.), he does not, unlike Sophokles, accept their issues at Homer's valuation. Instead of appropriating the *Iliad* as an authority to validate the ideas in his own text, he seems intent on destroying the authority it and its hero Achilles enjoyed in Athens.

The popularity and power of Homeric epic among the Athenians who made up Euripides' audience can be adduced from the numerous citations of the *Iliad* and the *Odyssey* in the histories and comedies of the fifth century and in the dialogues, orations, and treatises of the fourth. We know that both epics were recited in full at the Great Panatheneia every four years,[58] and there is evidence that the Brauronia, an annual festival to Artemis, included a recitation of the *Iliad*.[59] In between festivals numerous rhapsodes offered Athenians the opportunity to hear daily recitations if they wished (Xenophon *Symposium* III.6), and even when they were not listening to rhapsodes they could well have been pondering illustrations of the *Iliad* at home on various vessels.[60] The ubiquity of the poems reflects their authority, and we find them cited as proof for matters as various as the effect of cold on Skythian cattle (Herodotos 4.29), the unequaled magnitude of the Peloponnesian War (Thuc. 1.10.3), the legitimacy of spending time in the *agorá* (Ar. *Clouds* 1055–1057), and the respectability of homosexuality (Aischines *Against Timarchos* 142–150).

Xenophon reports that a young Athenian friend of Sokrates was forced by his father to learn the complete *Iliad* and *Odyssey* by heart (*Sym.* III.5). Such a feat was unusual enough to be a great source of pride to Xenophon's young man, but, given the wealth of information, both moral and practical, the poems were thought to contain, it was probably not unique. Plato indicates that many people considered Homer the educator (*pepaídeuken*) of Greece because his poems provided a guide to conduct in every aspect of life (*Republic* 606e). Isokrates, writing in 380, confirms Plato's statement:

> I think also that the poetry of Homer acquired a greater reputation than the others because it praised those who fought with the barbarians, and on account of this our forefathers wished to give his art a place of honor (*éntimon* . . . *poiêsai*) both in musical contests and in the education of the younger generation, in order that by often hearing the epics we might learn by heart an already existing hatred against them (the barbarians) and that by emulating the excellences (*aretás*) of those who waged war we might desire to perform the same deeds. (*Panagyrikos* 159)

And what, according to this passage from Isokrates, did Homer teach above all? Not the "military tactics, excellences, and armings" that Aristophanes' Aischylos admires (*Frogs* 1034–1036);[61] not the art of generalship that Plato's Ion thinks he has learned (*Ion* 540d–541b); but, more important, the frame of mind most conducive to waging war, the inner spirit that, fired by magnificent examples of heroism, impels one actually to *like* fighting hard and dying well in battle.

Homeric epic, in particular the *Iliad*, had clearly become both an incitement to and a justification for war. At some point during the war that Athens had first undertaken to maintain her empire, then extended into conquest, and finally doggedly continued for self-preservation, Euripides ceased to find this use of the *Iliad* satisfactory. In days of seemingly endless conflict and growing brutality Euripides turned in loathing from the self-assertion of epic heroes and the self-aggrandizing militarism of Athens's leaders to give his praise to a new, nonaggressive heroism, the heroism of self-sacrifice. The warm and loving purity of Polyxena and Iphigeneia, young women who walk willingly and with dignity to have their throats cut by men whom we could generously label criminally insane, shines brightly if all too briefly against the dark greed, chauvinism, and egoism that control Euripides' dramatic world in the guise of patriotic purpose and traditional ideals. Euripides' versions—or perversions—of Homer's Achilles are very much a part of this darkened world. They debase the wrathful hero's passionate demand for honor to monstrous egoism (*Hekabe*) and petty vanity (*Iphigeneia*). When Euripides calls Achilles forth from the heroic past into the *Elektra*, a play devoid of heroic characters, it is to transmute the seductive brilliance of that hero and that past into the steely glint of murder.

Although neither setting nor psychology is in any way grand or heroic, traditional heroism is not entirely absent from the world of Euripides' *Elektra*. Agamemnon's sacking of Troy is ever present in the memory of Euripides' unheroic characters, where it is consistently evoked as a prime factor in the hate felt for Klytaimestra and Aigisthos (2–10, 161–162, 186–189, 314–316, 916–917), as an exemplary model for Orestes (336–338, 880–881), and as a necessary source of potency for the bloody desires of Elektra and Orestes (660–681). Achilles' martial excellence functions briefly in much the same way.

Achilles is the subject of a magnificent ode sung by the Chorus of peasant women in the interlude between Orestes' and Elektra's first encounter and the arrival of the old servant who will effect their reunion and set their murderous plot in motion. The most obvious purpose of its surprising and beautiful lyrics is to heighten the stature of Agamemnon and thus make more awful, more deserving of vengeance, Klytaimestra's crime: she murdered a great king, the "king of such warriors" as Achilles (479–480). But if we read the ode as carefully as we would a lyric poem, noting the subtle progression from the joyously romantic to the terror-filled mythic and epic modes of the heroic tradition, it becomes clear that Euripides has put into the mouths of the Chorus a song that is far from being merely a celebration of the supreme warrior of the Trojan War.[62]

The most remarkable feature of the lyrics that introduce Achilles into the tattered world of Elektra and Orestes is their wonderful ebullience (432–451):

> Famous ships who traveled once to Troy
> with innumerable oars
> moving in dancing procession with the sea nymphs
> where the flute-loving dolphin leaped
> rolling about the dark blue prows,
> conveying Achilles, light-springing
> son of Thetis,
> with Agamemnon to the coasts of
> Troy, where the Simoeis flows.

Nereids, leaving the cliffs of Euboia,
bore the shield-toils, golden[63]
armor, from Hephaistos's anvils,
up Pelion, up the holy
groves of sturdy Ossa,
watch-places of the nymphs,
searching out the youth, where the father[64]
centaur reared Thetis's sea child
to be a light to Greece,
swift-runner for the Atreidai.

κλειναὶ νᾶες, αἳ ποτ' ἔβατε Τροίαν
   τοῖς ἀμετρήτοις ἐρετμοῖς
πέμπουσαι χοροὺς μετὰ Νηρῇδων,
   ἵν' ὁ φίλαυλος ἔπαλλε δελφὶς
   πρῴραις κυανεμβόλοισιν εἱλισσόμενος,
   πορεύων τὸν τᾶς Θέτιδος
κοῦφον ἅλμα ποδῶν Ἀχιλῆ
σὺν Ἀγαμέμνονι Τρωίας
ἐπὶ Σιμουντίδας ἀκτάς.

Νηρῇδες δ' Εὐβοΐδας ἄκρας λιποῦσαι
μόχθους ἀσπιστὰς ἀκμόνων
   Ἡφαίστου χρυσέων ἔφερον τευχέων,
   ἀνά τε Πήλιον ἀνά τ' ἐρυμνᾶς
   Ὄσσας ἱερὰς νάπας Νυμφαίας σκοπιὰς
   ματεῦσαι κόρον, ἔνθα πατὴρ
ἱππότας τρέφεν Ἑλλάδι φῶς
Θέτιδος εἰνάλιον γόνον
   ταχύπορον πόδ' Ἀτρείδαις.

The Achilles who is here sent off to Troy is taken from a romantic tradition[65] that is unconcerned with the sorrows of war. Thetis's sisters, the Nereids, aid Achilles' career as his mother does in the *Iliad;* the difference is they do not weep. One can imagine Homer's Thetis sending her son off to war; it is impossible to imagine her dancing as she does so. The exuberance of the opening strophe is the perfect expression of the optimistic, high-hearted mood that often seems to prevail in the initial stages of a war, especially when that war is to be fought far from one's own home.[66]

The next stage of war, actual conflict, is revealed from the perspective of one whose home was lost—as Elektra and Orestes, themselves victims of the heroic tradition, will lose theirs—through Achilles' heroism (452–457):

> From a Trojan come to Nauplia harbor,
> son of Thetis,
> I learned of these
> emblems, terrors for
> Trojans, wrought
> in the circle of your famous shield.

> Ἰλιόθεν δ' ἔκλυόν τινος ἐν λιμέσιν
> Ναυπλίοισι βεβῶτος
> τᾶς σᾶς, ὦ Θέτιδος παῖ,
> κλεινᾶς ἀσπίδος ἐν κύκλῳ
> τοιάδε σήματα, δείματα
> Φρύγια, τετύχθαι·

The hero remains un-Homeric: instead of the Iliadic scenes of human life in all its happy and unhappy manifestations, Euripides puts monsters on his Achilles' shield and armor (458–475):

> On the circuiting rim
> Perseus, throat-cutter, above
> the sea on winged sandals held
> the Gorgon
> in company with Hermes, messenger of
> Zeus, Maia's
> country child.

> In the center of the shield there shone radiant
> the circular sun
> with his winged horses
> and the lofty choirs of stars
> Pleiades, Hyades, turning to rout
> the eyes of Hektor.

> Upon the helmet wrought of gold
> were Sphinxes, bearing in talons
> their song-won prey. In the hollow of
> the breastplate a fire-breathing

lioness sped her flight
on claws while she looked at
the Pirenian colt.

περιδρόμῳ μὲν ἴτυος ἕδρᾳ
Περσέα λαιμοτόμαν ὑπὲρ
  ἁλὸς ποτανοῖσι πεδίλοισι
φυὰν Γοργόνος ἴσχειν,
Διὸς ἀγγέλῳ σὺν Ἑρμᾷ,
τῷ Μαίας ἀγροτῆρι κούρῳ·

ἐν δὲ μέσῳ κατέλαμπε σάκει φαέθων
  κύκλος ἀελίοιο
ἵπποις ἂμ πτεροέσσαις
ἄστρων τ' αἰθέριοι χοροί,
Πλειάδες, Ὑάδες, Ἕκτορος
  ὄμμασι τροπαῖοι·

ἐπὶ δὲ χρυσοτύπῳ κράνει
Σφίγγες ὄνυξιν ἀοίδιμον
  ἄγραν φέρουσαι· περιπλεύρῳ
δὲ κύτει πύρπνοος ἔσπευδε
δρόμῳ λέαινα χαλαῖς
Πειρηναῖον ὁρῶσα πῶλον·

These images link martial heroism with the heroism of monster slaying,
man against malformed beast. This linkage suggests a dehumanization
of the victim in the eyes of the conquering hero. But the fact that the
images of the Gorgon, Sphinxes, and Chimaera are described as seen by
his terrified victim suggests further that the terrifying conqueror has
also become a monster,[67] an unnatural force rather than a human being.
These monsters are as alien to Homer's world[68] as is the joyous romanticism of the opening strophe.

The only images Euripides draws from Greece's most beautiful song
about the Trojan War are those that focus on the victim. The sun and
stars that shine from Achilles' shield into Hektor's eyes recall the stark
terror of *Iliad* 22. Then, on Achilles' weapon, Euripides evokes not a
specific Iliadic scene but all the dying men, who, "Trojans and Achaians . . . lay stretched out by one another, face down in the dust" (*Il.*
4.543–544). All the *Iliad*'s battle scenes contribute to the grim merging

of all heroes and all victims in the blood-dusty image that concludes both description of the armor and "celebration" of Achilles (476–477):

> along the bloody sword four-footed horses leapt,
> and black dust was cast on their backs.
>
> ἄορι δ' ἐν φονίῳ τετραβάμονες ἵπποι ἔπαλλον,
> κελαινὰ δ' ἀμφὶ νῶθ' ἵετο κόνις.

The supreme warrior of the supreme national war is, finally, just a killer.

Brilliance and horror are both present in this ode, but they do not occur in balanced simultaneity as they do in the *Iliad*. In portraying Achilles in the *Elektra*'s first *stasimon*, Euripides removes brilliance from its place on the Homeric battlefield and isolates it in another, much less realistic tradition. He then overwhelms its seductive, "unreal" charm with the monster-contaminated Iliadic killing that he places in the second half of the ode. In so doing he transforms Achilles' career from an example of human achievement to a paradigm of inhuman destruction.

In his earlier play, the *Hekabe*, Euripides also employs a kind of contamination, this time with the specific object of making Homeric heroism and Athenian war politics comment on each other to the detriment of both. Euripides implicates Achilles in an ugly incident taken from the Epic Cycle: the sacrifice of Polyxena on his tomb. Since in Euripides' version of this incident it is a recognizably Homeric ghost who demands the sacrifice, Homer's own hero is drawn firmly into whatever moral disapproval is engendered by the incident.

Euripides may or may not have been the first poet to make Achilles' ghost demand the sacrifice of Polyxena.[69] Proclus's summaries of the Epic Cycle poems merely state that the sacrifice took place on his tomb subsequent to the burning of Troy and that Achilles' ghost tried to prevent the victorious army from sailing home by foretelling the events that were to happen (*Chrestomathia* 2, p. 108).[70] Ibykos and Simonides, lyric poets of the late sixth and early fifth centuries, each dealt with one of these two incidents, but we know too little to determine whether or not they made a connection between the ghostly visitation and the sacrifice of the young woman. We learn from a scholiast on *Hekabe* 41 that Ibykos, like Euripides, said Neoptolemos performed the slaughter,[71] but this does not necessarily mean that Ibykos made him do it at the command of his father. Neoptolemos, who killed the aged Priam on the altar of Zeus and hurled Hektor's child Astyanax from the city walls,[72] might certainly be thought capable of initiating the deed himself. We are told by "Longinus" that Simonides described vividly the scene of the ghost's appearance,[73] but we have no clue as to what else he may have included in his poem. Sophokles is the first who we can be sure joined both incidents in one work. The scholiast to *Hekabe* 3 indicates that Sophokles' *Polyxena* presented the events surrounding the maiden's death,[74] and one of the fragments from this lost play makes certain the presence of a ghost.[75] It is therefore quite possible that Sophokles depicted a causal link between ghost and sacrifice.[76] However, since we do not know the date of Sophokles' play, we cannot say whether or not it antedated Euripides'.

It is not difficult to see why the simple conjunction of human sacrifice and of beneficent apparition (if this is all it was in the Epic Cycle) became a single incident in which a hostile ghost demanded the woman's blood. First, there is Achilles' temporary but overwhelming ruthlessness in the *Iliad* in Books Twenty through Twenty-Two and his sacrifice of twelve young men (*koûroi*) on Patroklos's funeral pyre. Second, there is the frequently vengeful nature of Greek hero-ghosts, such as the warrior at Temesa who forced the community who had executed him for rape to give him in recompense a virgin bride every year (Paus. 6.6.4–11).

FIGURE II. Sacrifice of Polyxena

Achilles' ghost in later tradition seems scarcely more endearing than the rapist's. Though he helped pious mariners who were washed up on the shore of Leuke where he lived with some other heroic spirits, he never forgot his grudge against the descendants of Priam. He asked a passing merchant to procure for him from Ilion a young slave woman who had made the mistake of boasting that her lineage went back to the ancient king, and when he got her, he tore her to pieces (*diaspōménou*).⁷⁷ These hero-ghosts seem to have been pure ego: kindly toward ministering kin and friends, ferocious towards those who are, no matter how peripherally, their enemies.⁷⁸

It is also true, however, that in the fifth century human sacrifice was *not* part of the cult worship offered to keep these irascible spirits happy.⁷⁹ Therefore if Euripides was the one to fuse the two incidents, he did so in order that the original heroism of Achilles, distilled into a savage egoism, might be condemned for its effect on human morality. But even if he received the combined incident from Sophokles or the lyric poets, we can be sure he changed it drastically to achieve the same end. One change can surely be found in his descriptions of the ghost's appearance.

The author of *On the Sublime* couples Sophokles' description of the appearance of Achilles' ghost with his description of Oedipus's death and self-burial "amid heavenly portents" (*metà diosēmeías*). Both are "consummately imagined" (*ákrōs . . . pephántastai*). "Longinus" also singles out Simonides' "image making" (*eidōlopoíēse*) in the ghost scene as the "most vivid" (*enargésteron*) of all versions (15.7). "Longinus" does not, alas, give quotations here, but from his previous examples of "sublime imagination," from our knowledge of the *Oedipus at Colonus* scene, and from his statement that the end (*télos*) of imagination in poetry is *ékplēxis*, "to awe, astound, shock" (15.2), we may infer that both Sophokles' and Simonides' descriptions were filled with grandeur and supernatural terror. Such versions would make Achilles' demand divinely or elementally awful rather than humanly immoral—and this would be consistent with the feeling Homer created in the great rampage of *Iliad* 20–22.

The *Hekabe*'s three descriptions of the apparition are not mentioned by "Longinus," and no wonder, for they include little that could be called sublime. The first is given by another ghost, that of Polydoros, Hekabe's son, who is hovering about waiting for his mother to find his body and give it burial.[80] As part of the prologue of the play, Polydoros recounts a brief history of the Trojan War and then matter-of-factly states Achilles' demand for Polyxena as the reason his mother is still in Thrace and thus able to find his body. He says (37–41),

> For the son of Peleus, Achilles, appearing above his tomb,
> stopped the whole Greek army when they were setting their
> sea-splashed oars toward home.
> He asks to take my sister Polyxena for his own,
> a victim on his tomb, a prize of honor (*géras*).

> ὁ Πηλέως γὰρ παῖς ὑπὲρ τύμβου φανεὶς
> κατέσχ' Ἀχιλλεὺς πᾶν στράτευμ' Ἑλληνικόν,
> πρὸς οἶκον εὐθύνοντας ἐναλίαν πλάτην·
> αἰτεῖ δ' ἀδελφὴν τὴν ἐμὴν Πολυξένην
> τύμβῳ φίλον πρόσφαγμα καὶ γέρας λαβεῖν.

He adds that Achilles will in fact get what he wants; his friends will not leave him "giftless" (*adórētos*, 42–43). Hekabe's later description is briefer and less specific (94–96):

> The ghost of Achilles came on the very top
> of the tomb; he asked for a prize of honor (*géras*)
> one of the much-suffering Trojan women.

> ἦλθ' ὑπὲρ ἄκρας τύμβου κορυφᾶς
> φάντασμ' Ἀχιλέως· ᾔτει δὲ γέρας
> τῶν πολυμόχθων τινὰ Τρωιάδων.

The problem of whether Achilles is supposed to have asked for Polyxena specifically, as Polydoros reports, or whether he merely asked for a Trojan woman, as Hekabe says, need not concern us here.[81] What is important is the absence of anything that could produce terror and awe.

Terror and awe are conpicuously absent even from the longest and most explicit of the descriptions, the one given by the Chorus after they tell Hekabe that the Greek assembly has resolved to sacrifice her daughter to Achilles (109–115):

> Having mounted on his tomb
> he appeared—you remember—in his golden armor
> and checked the sea-going ships
> when their sails had been set on the ropes,

crying (*thōüssōn*) this aloud:
"Whither, Danaans, do you prepare to go,
leaving my tomb without a gift of honor (*agéraston*)?"

τύμβου δ᾽ ἐπιωὰς
οἶσθ᾽ ὅτε χρυσέοις ἐφάνη σὺν ὅπλοις,
τὰς ποντοπόρους δ᾽ ἔσχε σχεδίας
λαίφη προτόνοις ἐπερειδομένας
τάδε θωῦσσων·
ποῖ δή, Δαναοί, τὸν ἐμὸν τύμβον
στέλλεσθ᾽ ἀγέραστον ἀφέντες;

The one word with possibly terrifying import is *thōüssōn*, "crying aloud" (113), the same verb Sophokles uses to describe the supernatural voice that calls Oedipus to his miraculous end in the *Oedipus at Colonus* (1624–1625). *That* voice makes everyone's hair stand on end in terror. But the line following Achilles' cry says only that "a huge wave of strife crashed down" (116). The succeeding line then specifies the opposing opinions that comprise that strife, and from there we are led into the actual debate in the assembly. The Greek assembly with its normal acerbic confrontations thus frames and clothes Achilles' appearance not with supernatural grandeur and awe but with mundane politics.

However, though no one's hair may be made to stand on end by Achilles' appearance, an intellectual shock may have sped through Euripides' audience when it felt the impact of *agéraston*, "without a gift of honor" (115), and realized that Euripides was intent on deepening a parody of the *Iliad* that he began with Polydoros's opening description of the ghost's demand: in both Polydoros's and Hekabe's descriptions what the ghost wants is a *géras*, "prize of honor" (41, 94). The word *géras* in conjunction with the name Achilles can evoke only one thing: the uncompromising temper displayed by Homer's hero in *Iliad* I.[82] This is no simple ghost from the dark regions of Greek religion. This ghost is a literary caricature.

During Achilles' quarrel with Agamemnon the word *géras* occurs no fewer than ten times in eighty-six lines of dialogue, and one could say that it and its companion words *timḗ*, "honor," and *kléos*, "glory," the primary objects for which one fights, express the key concepts of the *Iliad*. *Géra* are the visible measure of heroic *timḗ*, as epic song is the embodiment of *kléos*. When *timḗ* is denied Achilles by Agamemnon's wrongful seizure of his *géras*—the woman Briseis who was awarded him by the army—he rejects the Zeus-appointed king and turns to Zeus himself for confirmation and manifestation of his worth. This confirmation equals disaster for his fellow Greeks.

As we have seen, Sophokles accepts Homer's valuation of Achilles' temper and uses the hero's wrathful rejection of Agamemnon and the Greek cause as an example of noble and principled self-respect. Euripides, however, by repeating the word *géras* with the demand for Polyxena, distills out of it a monumental, utterly self-centered pride. The egotistical nature of this pride becomes especially clear with the third repetition, the *agéraston* of the Chorus's description. This rare adjective,[83] formed from *géras* plus alpha-privative, is used in *Iliad* 1 not by Achilles but by his opponent Agamemnon. It is the point at which the quarrel begins. Agamemnon has agreed grudgingly to let Chryseis go back home. But he adds (1.118–120):

> straightway make ready another *géras* for me so that I
> may not be the only one of the Achaians *agérastos;* that
> wouldn't be fitting. For you all see that my *géras* goes elsewhere.

Homer implies that nothing is as important to the king—neither the established rights nor the opinion of his fellow Greeks—as is the loss of one of his accoutrements of honor.[84] His case is quite different from Achilles', whose *géras* was taken by a man, not a god, and who is therefore defending a principle, the very foundation of his honor.

In spite of this difference, an unsympathetic reader might extract a self-pitying pique similar to Agamemnon's from a later speech by Achilles (*Il.* 9.334–336):

> to the nobles and kings he gave *géra*
> and the others keep them, but from me alone of the Achaians
> he has taken away. . . .

Though the sense of injured ego that arises from "me alone" (*emeû . . . moúnou*) is immediately softened by the addition "and he keeps the wife (*álochon*) who is close to my heart" (336), still, if one concentrates on the idea of *géras* rather than on wife, and on material symbol rather than on ethical substance, it would be possible (wrongly) to conclude that Achilles' continuing wrath emanates from the same hollow vanity that prompted Agamemnon to call himself *agérastos* and to seize Achilles' *géras* as a substitute prize. The "heroic temper" on this reading would be nothing more than arrogant pride.

Arrogant pride in conjunction with the *géras* Briseis in the *Iliad* may be viewed as unpleasant; in conjunction with Polyxena in the *Hekabe* it is truly appalling. For Euripides' Achilles is dead, and if he gets the *géras* he wants, she will be dead too. Thus, through the word *géras,* which firmly roots Achilles' ghost in a most distasteful corner of the traditional heroic world, Achilles becomes a vehicle for carrying the Homeric system of using human prizes as a measure of *timé* to its logical and ultimate barbarity.

The doctrine that makes this system possible, namely "to the victor belong *all* the spoils," including the conquered civilians, is presented by Homer with neither palliation[85] nor overt protest. But harsh as the Homeric doctrine is, it does not include human sacrifice to either gods or dead heroes. The victor's power of life and death over captives in the *Iliad* is never exercised off the battlefield except by Achilles' "evil"[86] slaughter of the twelve Trojans on Patroklos's pyre, and this is a matter of revenge, not of *timé*. The *géras* of the dead, say Zeus and Herê, is burial (16.457, 675 and see 23.9). Euripides, however, is concerned not with being true to Homer's epic but with the truth of the war mentality that this most powerful of martial epics had come to sanction. To get at this truth and to make it unpalatable, he not only emphasizes the negative parts of Homer's work, as he did in the *Elektra,* but perverts the positive parts—such as Achilles' principled break with Agamemnon— that are inextricably tied up with or stem from the heroic code. Once his perversions have associated this "civilized" code of killing and enslavement with the ultimate barbarity of human sacrifice, his audience ought to shrink back from cultured Homer as they previously shrank from the primitive awe-inspiring gods of Aischylos's *Agamemnon.* It is to this end, association of heroic *timé* with barbarity, that Euripides extracts Achilles' ghostly essence specifically from Homer rather than from the Epic Cycle's merely irascible hero.

The terms of the debate in the Greek army over whether or not to accede to the ghost's demand reinforce our sense both of barbarity and of epic sanction. One might expect the debate to revolve around *anánkē,* the necessity, that is, to choose between two evils: either to commit human sacrifice or to forfeit the return home.[87] Achilles is, after all, holding back the ships, and, when the sacrifice does take place, Neoptolemos will pray that his father's ghost drink the blood and release the ships (534–541). But *anánkē* is never mentioned. Instead, as the Chorus reports it, the issue is a political one.[88] The army sees itself as having finally to choose between the conflicting claims of Achilles and Polyxena: the dead hero's claim to honor versus the slave's right to life.

Agamemnon and Achilles are again pitted against each other over a slave woman as they were in the *Iliad*. Though Agamemnon's argument is not directly reported, the Chorus describes it as "sustaining the bed of the frenzied diviner" (120–122). The implication is that Agamemnon speaks against the sacrifice not out of any moral principle but mainly to win affection from his own war prize, Polyxena's sister Kassandra (cf. 826–830). This implication evokes the lustful behavior that started the tragic chain of events in the *Iliad*: Agamemnon's rejecting ransom from Chryseis's father with the words, "Sooner shall old age come upon her / in my house . . . / as she tends the loom and shares my bed" (1.29–31).[89]

Achilles' side in the debate is taken first by the two sons of Theseus,[90] who, agreeing that "Achilles' tomb should be crowned with living blood," say "Kassandra's bed should not be preferred to Achilles' spear" (126–129). This argument is clearly meant to "correct" (and thereby strongly evoke) the disastrous position adopted by the Greek army in the *Iliad* when they sanctioned Agamemnon's power as a scepterbearing king to put his personal desire over Achilles' military prowess.[91] Sex versus spear: these are the simplistic terms in which Euripides' audience is encouraged to (mis)remember the Iliadic scene that this debate recasts.

Euripides' debased version of the Homeric debate between Achilles' worth and Agamemnon's personal desire leaves the army still evenly divided. It takes a demagogue—one of Euripides' favorite targets—to tip the balance. Here, as in Odysseus's later confrontation with Hekabe, Euripides reveals the danger of having a sacred text: even the devil can quote Scripture; even Odysseus can quote Achilles. The "wily-minded, sweet-talking, mob-wooing liar" (*poikilóphrōn kópis hēdulógos dēmocharistḗs*) persuades the army

> not to spurn the best of all the Greeks (*tòn áriston Danaôn pántōn*)
> lest someone say in the realm of Persephone,
> standing among the dead,

how Greeks, ungrateful (*acháristoi*) to Greeks
who died for Helen,
departed from the plains of Troy.

(131–140)

Tòn áriston Danaôn ("the best of the Greeks") echoes Achilles' ringing
conclusion to his oath of withdrawal in *Iliad* 1: "And you will lacerate
your spirit / in anger at yourself that you did not honor the best of the
Achaians (*áriston Achaiôn*)" (243–244). *Acháristoi,* "ungrateful," recalls
the passage in Book Nine where Achilles reiterates his decision not to
fight "since there is no *cháris* ["gratitude"] for fighting endlessly, always, with enemy men" (316–317).[92]

Achilles' passionate rejection of a false society becomes a cold-blooded
justification for murder. But though Odysseus's audience is won over, it
is impossible to believe that Euripides meant his own audience to be
convinced when they heard Achilles' passionate words on Odysseus's
calculating lips, on the lips, that is, of one whom tradition had turned
into Achilles' diametric opposite. Euripides has here created a second
kind of grim parody. The earlier parody involved only extreme simplification and a logical if blunt extension of that simplification. "I want
my *géras*" may be utterly simplistic, but it sounds horrifyingly appropriate on the lips of Achilles' ghost. Simplification is involved in this
later parody too, but appropriateness is lacking. In Odysseus's speech
there is such a felt disparity between the form (the phraseology of the
honest Achilles) and the substance (the sentiments of a confirmed liar)
that it is impossible to take the argument seriously.[93]

The cold-bloodedness of Odysseus's argument becomes even clearer
in his second use of Achillean logic, which comes after two scenes designed to fix all sympathy on the suffering barbarian women as opposed
to the Greeks. By the time he brings Odysseus back to justify his actions
to Hekabe, Euripides has acquainted us with the warm nobility of Polyxena, who, when she hears that she is to be sacrificed, cries out in lamentation not for herself but for her suffering mother (197–204). And we
have heard the agonized mother plead (277–281):

Do not rip my child from my arms.
Do not kill her. Enough have died.
In her I rejoice and forget my sorrows;
She is my consolation, my
city, my nurse, my staff and guide on the road.

As the Chorus says, one would have to have a heart of stone to hear this and not weep (296–298).

Odysseus, of course, does not weep. His response is a slick sophistic disquisition on *timḗ* which begins with a subtly changed version of the lines that continued Achilles' complaint about gratitude in *Iliad* 9. Achilles said (318–319):

> There is an equal portion for him who waits and if someone fights
>   strenuously;
> The coward (*kakós*) and the brave (*esthlós*) are held in a single honor.

Odysseus, shifting the emphasis from individual to societal misfortune, says (306–308):

> Many cities are ruined because of this,
> that the brave (*esthlós*) and energetic man
> carries off no more than the cowardly (*tôn kakiónōn*).

He continues with an argument that makes honor solely a matter of po-litical expediency: Achilles is worthy of *timḗ* (310), and if others see that he is not honored (*ou timṓmenon*, 316) and that friends are not used well when dead as well as while alive, they will not come to fight when needed. The *cháris* (here to be translated both as "gratitude" and as "gratification") of a tomb endures long. He concludes by saying sar-castically that the Greeks may well incur the charge of stupidity for their custom of honoring the brave (*timân tòn esthlón*); but, he sneers, the issue of the war has proved them right: "Keep on failing to treat friends as friends and to honor those who have nobly died; so Greece will pros-per, and you barbarians will be in a state equal to your resolutions" (326–331). Again we hear the echo of the Iliadic Achilles in *cháris*, in *esthlón*, and in the repetition of words based on *timḗ*.

The man of duplicitous words has become an ally of the man of di-rect action. The separatist tradition—honest deeds (Achilles) versus clever words (Odysseus)—that Sophokles will continue to exploit in the *Philoktetes* some fifteen years after the *Hekabe* is here discarded. True, Achilles remains *haploûs* (his demand is direct and simple enough: "I want my *géras*") while Odysseus is *diploûs* (when reminded by Hekabe that he owes her the gratitude he promised when she saved his life dur-ing a spy mission, he replies evasively, "I said anything I could think of to save my life" [*pollôn lógōn heurḗmath', hṓste mḕ thaneîn*, 249–250]),

but these qualities are not the ones at issue. The two characters are conjoined, not juxtaposed, and in their conjunction they exacerbate the
negative aspects of the role each has come to represent. A double effect
is achieved thereby. Odysseus's successful twisting of Achilles' principled Iliadic outrage into an argument for expediential murder should
increase our distaste for politicians. But because this argument is made
specifically in the service of a Homeric ghost, it should also stimulate
distaste for and an accompanying critical reevaluation of the most
highly sanctioned self-assertive epic heroism.

The *Iphigeneia in Aulis*,[94] which is the only fully extant play to present Achilles as a living character upon the stage, is again an antiwar
play, and again it involves human sacrifice. It does not, however, involve
the kind of "monsters" we met in the *Hekabe*. Instead, as John Ferguson
has pointed out, all the characters in this play are quite ordinary.[95] We
are shown not the perverted effects of ten years of bloody war capped by
total and ruthless victory but examples of human imperfection in the
first stages of war-madness. Agamemnon is a loving and agonized father
who yet puts his desire to lead the greatest army in Greek history and
his paranoid fear of that army ahead of his affection for his daughter.
Menelaos, whose lust for his unfaithful wife overwhelms all other familial feelings, is capable of a last-minute change of heart, which comes too
late, however, to prevent Agamemnon's perpetrating the sacrifice.[96]
Though Klytaimestra hints that Agamemnon's distant homecoming
will not be all that he desires if he sacrifices their daughter for the sake
of revenge and recapture of Helen, she is not the famous virago of the
Agamemnon but a normally happy, then outraged and grieving wife and
mother. Iphigeneia is totally human in her first pathetic pleadings that it
is better to live badly than to die well (1252) and then equally human in
her self-deluding acceptance of a role as "savior of Greece" (1420).

Achilles, the young man whose name was used unbeknownst to him
as the lure to fetch Iphigeneia to Aulis, seems in introduction to promise something more marvelous than his fellow *dramatis personae*. The
old servant, incredulous at Agememnon's intent to put Achilles' "bride"
to death, mentions the characterizing wrath: "How, deprived of his
wife, will he not rise up in kindling anger?" (124–125).[97] And when the
Chorus enter with their heroic "Catalogue of Ships," meant, as Grube
says, "to make us feel the power and greatness of the expedition,"[98] they

devote twice as much space to the son of Thetis as to any other hero. With Pindaric verve (cf. *N*. 3) they describe his traditional swiftness (206—215):

Equal to the winds in speed
swift-running Achilles,
whom Thetis bore and Cheiron
reared to manhood, him I saw
by the pebbly shore
racing in his armor.
On foot he contested
with a four-horse chariot,
turned the laps toward victory.

τὸν ἰσάνεμόν τε ποδοῖν
λαιψηροδρόμον Ἀχιλῆα,
τὸν ἁ Θέτις τέκε καὶ Χείρων
ἐξεπόνησεν, εἶδον
αἰγιαλοῖς παρά τε κροκάλαις
δρόμον ἔχοντα σὺν ὅπλοις·
ἅμιλλαν δ' ἐπόνει ποδοῖν
πρὸς ἅρμα τέτρωρον
ἑλίσσων περὶ νίκας.

The horses in question are those of Eumelos; they are said by Homer to be the best after Achilles' own immortal team (*Iliad* 2.763–765). But this competition between swiftest man and swiftest horses is not Homeric. The equality of the contest displays the same romanticism we encountered in the opening stanzas of the *Elektra* ode (226–230):

Bounding beside them went
the son of Peleus in his armor
beside the rails and axles of the chariot.

οἷς παρεπάλλετο
Πηλείδας σὺν ὅπλοισι παρ' ἄντυγα καὶ σύριγγας ἁρματείους.

As in the *Elektra*, this romanticism will soon be brought down to earth. But before this, the audience's extraordinary expectations are further increased. In response to Klytaimestra's questions about her supposed future son-in-law, Agamemnon reveals that Achilles is not only the son of a goddess but also the great-grandson of Zeus and that he was reared by a centaur "so as not to learn the ways of evil men (*kakôn brotôn*)" (709). To the traditional anger, superhuman swiftness, and extrahuman upbringing there is added, when we first meet Achilles, the traditional impatience associated with the man of action. As in the *Telephos*, Achilles enters demanding to know why they are not getting on with the war. But the difference between his words here and those of the earlier play signals the reduction from high heroic to more common stature that will become ever more apparent the longer Achilles is on stage. In the *Telephos* Euripides had him erupt in staccato disgust, ending with the declaration that he was about to go on ahead with his Myrmidons, "leaving behind the delays of the Atreidai."⁹⁹ Here in the *Iphigeneia* Euripides makes him give an elaborate explanation of the relative desires of the different members of the army to get the war in progress and end with a statement that he is being pressured by his Myrmidons,¹⁰⁰ who are asking him to "act, if you are going to act, or lead your army home; / Do not wait on the delays of the Atreidai" (817–818).¹⁰¹

Achilles' wordy rhetoric dilutes the passionate impatience that is his trademark. Something similar will happen to his anger when it flares up over Agamemnon's misuse of his name. When Achilles learns what the king has done, he exhibits the violent anger we expect: "My temper rises greatly haughty!" (*hypsēlóphrōn moi thumòs aíretai prósō*, 919). Though *hypsēlóphrōn*, "haughty, high-minded," gives a rather more considered self-righteous tone to his anger than had the anguished cries of the Iliadic Achilles (e.g., at 9.646 and 16.52), still, what follows is traditional enough.¹⁰² Cheiron, he says to Klytaimestra, taught him simple (*haploûs*) habits,

> and I will obey the Atreidai when they command
> well (*kalôs*), I will not obey when they command ill.
> But here and in Troy I will maintain my free nature (*eleuthéran phúsin*)
> and adorn Ares with my spear.
>
> (927–931)

Χείρωνος, ἔμαθον τοὺς τρόπους ἁπλοῦς ἔχειν.
καὶ τοῖς Ἀτρείδαις, ἢν μὲν ἡγῶνται καλῶς,
πεισόμεθ', ὅταν δὲ μὴ καλῶς, οὐ πείσομαι.
ἀλλ' ἐνθάδ' ἐν Τροίᾳ τ' ἐλευθέραν φύσιν
παρέχων, Ἄρη τὸ κατ' ἐμὲ κοσμήσω δορί.

It is exactly such independence that Sophokles evokes as Neoptolemos's heritage in the *Philoktetes*, and Euripides will carry this motif to an even greater extreme than Sophokles when he later makes Achilles risk stoning and then volunteer to fight his own Myrmidons as well as the rest of the Greek army in defense of Iphigeneia (1349–1361).[103] More reminiscences of the Homeric wrath occur when Achilles states that it is Agamemnon's "outrageous insult" (*hýbrin es hēmâs hýbris*, 961)[104] that galls him so and when he cries, "Now I am nothing (*oudén*), and the commanders / find it easy to wrong me as they will" (968–969).[105]

νῦν δ' οὐδέν εἰμι, παρὰ δὲ τοῖς στρατηλάταις
ἐν εὐμαρεῖ με δρᾶν τε καὶ μὴ δρᾶν κακῶς.

The traditional Achillean pride is certainly not lacking from this long exposition of anger; what is lacking is a strong moral focus. The reasoning in this speech is disturbingly inconsistent, as moral fervor dwindles to egocentric bluster. Achilles declares that he himself will be defiled (*hagnòn d' oukét' estì sôm' emón*, 940) if Iphigeneia perishes, "suffering terrible and unbearable things, amazingly undeserved dishonor" through the agency of his name (941–943).[106] He invokes his father, grandfather, and city as proof that he cannot allow Agamemnon to lay a hand on his daughter even to the extent of touching her dress with the tips of his fingers (944–951). He threatens Kalchas, reducing all who profess the mantic art to mere guessers and liars (955–958). But, we soon discover, the "outrageous insult" that causes this vehemence is nothing more than the king's failure to ask permission before using his name (962–967):

> He should have asked my name from me
> snare for his daughter . . .
>
> . . . .
>
> I would have given it to the Hellenes, if our coming
> to Troy suffered because of it. I would not have refused
> to forward the cause of my fellow soldiers.

χρῆν δ' αὐτὸν αἰτεῖν τοὐμὸν ὄνομ' ἐμοῦ πάρα,
θήραμα παιδός· . . . .
ἔδωκά τᾶν Ἕλλησιν, εἰ πρὸς Ἴλιον
ἐν τῷδ' ἔκαμνε νόστος· οὐκ ἠρνούμεθ' ἄν
τὸ κοινὸν αὔξειν ὧν μέτ' ἐστρατευόμην.

This is not an instance of noble self-respect. In the face of the murder about to be committed, such intense concentration on something so relatively insignificant as a name emerges as very ordinary, very petty vanity.

The reminders of his epic personality that occur throughout this speech only make Achilles' moral ambiguity all the more pronounced and place him all the more firmly in the ranks of common mortals. So, too, does his inordinate respect for convention and for reputation. When he first meets Klytaimestra, the dialogue becomes almost comic as she tries to take the hand of her new "son-in-law," and he, totally misunderstanding, tries to withdraw, saying that it would be shameful (*aischrón*) for him to converse with a woman and that he fears (*aidoímeth'*) Agamemnon if he touches that which he should not (*mḗ moi thémis*, 830, 833–834). He emphatically refuses Klytaimestra's offer to have Iphigeneia come out and clasp his knees, for the idle army is prone to foul-mouthed gossip (998–1001). He exhibits a similar concern when he says he will hover close by while Klytaimestra argues with Agamemnon so that if she fails to change her husband's mind and needs his help, she will not have to shame her lineage by searching for him through the crowd of Danaans: "It is not worthy of the house of Tyndareos to get a bad report; for it is a great one among the Hellenes" (1031–1032). Such concern for reputation is also behind his admirable (and most surprising) attempt to change Agamemnon's purpose by Klytaimestra's use of reason before resorting to his own force. If he succeeds by reason instead of force, he says, he will be a better friend and he will escape censure by the army (1012–1021).[107]

When such an Achilles assures Klytaimestra that he will become a great god (*theòs mégistos*) for her (973–974), the audience's immediate impulse must be to laugh. For this Achilles is not, as were his Sophoklean and Euripidean predecessors, the embodiment of heroic virtue and vice brought into collision with present-day mores. He is, rather, a young man, very much a part of contemporary society,[108] whose ordinariness is made all the greater by contrast with his own epic and romantic tradition. This emphatic ordinariness has, up until the Choral ode that follows his dialogue with Klytaimestra, made Achilles seem rather disappointing. He will cease to seem so after the Chorus next sings.

One effect of the Chorus's song is, again, ironic contrast with the mundane characters that have occupied Euripides' stage. It returns to the high heroic vision of Achilles that we were offered in their earlier "Catalogue of Ships." At the wedding of Peleus and Thetis, sings the Chorus, Cheiron, "who knows the Apolline song," prophesied the birth of "a child, great light to Hellas,"

> who will come with his spear-wielding, shield-
> bearing Myrmidons
> to the famous land of Priam, to burn it to ashes,
> having fitted to his body
> the golden armor of Hephaistos's labor
> given by his goddess mother,
> Thetis who bore him.
>
> (1063–1075)

> παῖδα σὲ Θεσσαλίᾳ μέγα φῶς
> μάντις ὁ φοιβάδα μοῦσαν
> εἰδὼς γεννάσειν
> Χείρων ἐξονόμαζεν,
> ὅς ἥξει χθόνα λογχήρεσι σὺν Μυρμιδόνων
> ἀσπισταῖς Πριάμοιο κλεινὰν
> γαῖαν ἐκπυρώσων,
> περὶ σώματι χρυσέων
> ὅπλων Ἡφαιστοπόνων
> κεκορυθμένος ἔνδυτ᾽, ἐκ θεᾶς
> ματρὸς δωρήματ᾽ ἔχων
> Θέτιδος, ἅ νιν ἔτικτεν.

In addition to evoking the heroism that is absent from the present version of Achilles, this passage forces the audience to remember the heroism that will in fact exist in the "future" version of Achilles. But there will be no heroic action at Troy unless a lovely young woman is sacrificed. The hero who "will come to Troy to burn it to ashes" *cannot* save Iphigeneia.[109]

The absolute incompatibility between Achilles' resolution to save Iphigeneia and the martial heroism that must be creates a mood that is dark indeed. But on the level of character something more positive happens. We are reminded that Achilles is willing, even though he will not be allowed, to give up the glory that is his birthright. This willingness is

similar to the choice Sophokles' Neoptolemos made when he decided to
take Philoktetes home instead of returning to Troy. The stakes, however,
though superficially similar (public honor versus private honorable-
ness), are substantively different, and the choice Sophokles' audience
would prefer that Neoptolemos did not have to make Euripides' audience wishes Achilles could carry through. In the *Philoktetes*, the Trojan
War functioned as a source of glory; in the *Iphigeneia at Aulis*, on the
contrary, it is the cause of societal collapse. Achilles' future heroism is
pitted against the survival of Iphigeneia both as person in her own right
and, in her roles of daughter and "wife," as symbol of the family, the
principal victim of war.[110]

The Chorus of Aulidan wives has even before this point modified the
feeling of "sweet pleasure" (234) that was their initial reaction to the
splendid host. Their second ode (751–800) viewed the war in terms of
blood and tears and wives brutally dragged from their destroyed homes
by their lovely hair. Now their third ode focuses specifically on marriage, comparing the blessedness of Thetis's true wedding with the un-
holiness of Iphigeneia's false one. It begins with a joyous vision of the
wedding of Achilles' parents, the archetype of rewarded virtue and divine approbation.[111] The strophe presents golden-sandaled Muses dancing to the hymeneal music of flutes and lyres while Ganymede pours the
sacramental wine into golden goblets. Thetis's fifty sisters whirl the cir-
cling marriage dance on the white sand (1036–1057). The antistrophe
introduces a boisterous band of centaurs, wreathed in pine branches and
shouting aloud Cheiron's prophecy about the city-sacking issue of this
marriage. Thus, sings the Chorus, the divinities (*daímones*) celebrated
the blessed nuptials of Peleus and Thetis (1058–1079).

"But you, Iphigeneia," begins the epode, "your lovely hair they will
wreathe as they would a dappled heifer brought down from the mountain, staining your human throat with blood" (1080–1084). Cattle are
the proper victims for sacrifice; a young girl should be with her mother
getting married, not having her throat cut (1085–1088). All human values have been turned upside down (1089–1097):

> Where does the face of *Aidôs* ("Reverence, Respect")
> have any strength? where that of Goodness (*Aretâs*)?
> when impiety holds
> power but Goodness is left behind and forgotten,

and lawlessness conquers laws,
and mortals do not struggle in common against
the coming of a jealous god.

ποῦ τὸ τᾶς Αἰδοῦς
ἢ τὸ τᾶς Ἀρετᾶς ἔχει σθένειν τι πρόσωπον,
ὁπότε τὸ μὲν ἄσεπτον ἔχει
δύνασιν, ἁ δ᾽ Ἀρετὰ κατόπισθεν θνατοῖς ἀμελεῖται,
Ἀνομία δὲ νόμων κρατεῖ,
καὶ [μὴ] κοινὸς ἀγὼν βροτοῖς
μή τις θεῶν φθόνος ἔλθῃ;

This last sentiment is reminiscent of Hesiod's characterization of his age of iron men, fifth and final age in the descent of humankind into wickedness (*Works and Days* 176–201). Hesiod, indeed, provides an instructive parallel to what is going on here.

Strophe and antistrophe bridge past and future. The epode describes the present that makes possible that future. The past is idyllic: the wedding of Peleus and Thetis is exemplary of the time when there was happy intercourse between gods and mortals.[112] The future is heroic: the destruction of Troy is the grand subject of seven epics and for Hesiod represented the time when men were "nobler and more just (*dikaióteron kaì áreion*), a godlike race of heroes" (*W&D* 158–159).

But in Euripides' ode the heroic future can come about only because in the present (dramatic) time lawlessness and unrighteousness prevail. Hesiod's sequence is reversed: the foulness of the Age of Iron is what makes the age of heroes possible. Nor is the idyllic past totally idyllic. When the centaurs enter the harmonious wedding scene, two jarring notes sound: they "scream out" (*anéklagon*)[113] the prophecy, and the prophesied son will come to Troy to "burn it to ashes" (*ekpurōsōn*), a most negative condensation of Achilles' heroic activities.[114] Furthermore, given the facts that Hesiod's poem with its Iron Age set in his present (real) time might actually come to the hearer's mind and that all of the characters seem more like contemporary Athenians[115] than grand figures from the past, a pregnant collapsing of time emerges. Future dramatic time (Troy) remains past real time, but present dramatic time (Aulis) draws into itself present real time (Athens). Euripides is in effect saying, "They were no better than we are"—human nature is eternally the same and its product is war.

A confusion in the audience's response to the concept of heroism ensues. However principled or splendid the Iliadic or Pindaric heroism of Achilles may have been, its expression in action at Troy is clearly antithetic to the normal processes of civilized life. When Achilles reappears on stage announcing his ignominious defeat in the assembly, we find ourselves no longer comparing him negatively to his heroic archetype. His willingness single-handedly to fight the whole army, including his own Myrmidons, seems not a ridiculous exaggeration of traditional heroism but a fine heroic gesture—which may be the most significant thing that a human being can produce in the depressing world of Euripidean tragedy. It is this very sense of wresting nobility out of futility that makes us admire Iphigeneia's decision to sacrifice herself to "save" Greece even as we lament it.

Affirmation of spiritual significance as distinct from practical effect is well brought out in the scene that follows Iphigeneia's renunciation of life for a war that, in Kenneth Reckford's words, is being "fought for empty ambition and lust; for Helen; that is, for nothing."[116] The Chorus comments: "Your part, on the one hand, is noble (*gennaíōs*); that of chance and the goddess, on the other hand, is sick (*noseî*)" (1402–1403). Achilles' reaction is similarly twofold. Iphigeneia's decision is worthy of her country and wise (1407–1409); it shows her to be *gennaía* (1411). However, she should reconsider: "Death is a terrible evil (*deinòn kakón*)" (1415). When she reiterates her desire to die and save Greece, he applauds *o lêm' áriston* ("O best spirit") and says he can say no more about it, "for your intent is noble" (*gennaîa gàr phroneîs*, 1421–1423). He does, nevertheless, say more and ends by calling her decision *aphrosúnē*, "foolishness" (1430). As the audience must also realize, her willingness to die is noble; her death is terrible folly.[117]

Gesture is pitted against gesture in this scene. Each remains ultimately futile; each remains admirably intact. Euripides, as he works toward the story's compulsory ending, prevents Achilles from carrying out his bravura heroics in a way that only deepens our appreciation of their moral worth. Achilles remains willing and ever more eager to save Iphigeneia. He now admires her and wants her as his bride. She, however, asks him to allow (*éa*) her to save Greece (1420). His personal desire is not to allow this: he is grieved (*áchthomai*) at the thought of not saving her (1412–1415); he will take his arms to the altar "so as *not* to allow (*hōs ouk eásōn*) but to *prevent* her dying" (1426–1427); he will certainly not allow (*oúkoun eásō*) her to die through her foolishness (1430). But though he judges her decision foolish and desires to prevent her death, he subordinates this judgment and this desire to her will. He grants her the same autonomy he earlier claimed for himself. For the first time in extant literature, Achilles makes his own actions dependent on another's free choice. The moral focus that was lacking in the first half of the play is here present as the earlier egotistical devotion to reputation is replaced by a deeper *aidōs,* true respect for another person. Heroic self-assertion has been, through this more ordinary Achilles, transformed into a responsible individualism that might, if taken as a model, end war altogether.

But in this play, of course, it does not end the war but furthers it by removing the last obstacle in Iphigeneia's sacrifice. Achilles now seems to be not so much unworthy of his traditional stature as a victim of it. He may try to become bridegroom instead of warrior, but he is limited to a life-negating role (burning Troy to ashes) by the purposes of others. It is a role inextricably linked with the destruction of marriages both as cause and effect (Helen, Trojan wives, Iphigeneia) and with the death of children (Iphigeneia, Achilles himself). He is limited, that is, to the role termed heroic by tradition.

In previous plays Euripides made Achilles the embodiment of this awful heroism and set it in iconoclastic contrast to more ordinary civilized values. In this play Euripides is iconoclastic in a new way. He undermines traditional heroism first by portraying its prime exemplar as ordinary in every way except perhaps physical strength and belief in his own prowess. He then shows, in the Peleus and Thetis ode, that traditional heroism is not only useless for positive life-preserving action but is made possible only by the worst of human failings. Finally, having convinced his audience that they would rather Achilles not be a traditional hero, he gives the ordinary young man new moral stature. The hollow and almost parodic action of a superhuman hero is replaced by genuinely human "heroic" gesture. The movement seems somehow positive—even though it contributes to a feeling of futility unsurpassed in any other Euripidean play.

This positive movement bears no fruit either in the play or in the succeeding tradition. In the play Achilles must revert to and grow into the role that war and tradition have created for him. And the traditional typology created by Pindar, Sophokles, and Euripides himself will not be revised through this momentarily likeable Achilles.

4. PLATO

Despite Euripides' best efforts, the martial Achilles retained his commanding power as an inspirational figure for the Athenians. A year after Euripides died, the audience at the Greater Dionysia saw Aristophanes' Aischylos praise the *Iliad* as winning "divine" Homer "honor (*timế*) and glory (*kléos*) from things he taught most excellently: military tactics, excellences, armings of men" (*Frogs* 1034–1036) [118] and subsequently be chosen over Euripides as the poet to save Athens. Forty years later Isokrates' followers would learn that Achilles was still a viable exemplar of *aretế* in fighting barbarians (*Euagoras* 17–18):

> Aias, Teucer, and Achilles gave the greatest proof of their *aretế;* for . . . when the Hellenic armament against the barbarians was formed and many others gathered with no one of the most famous left behind, in these dangers Achilles excelled all.

Twenty years later still, in 344 B.C., Aristotle, who had lived and studied in Athens from 367–347, would invoke the epic warrior in a hymn to an heroic friend, judging the cause of Achilles' death to be a "passionate love (*póthois*) of *aretế*." [119] And in 341 B.C. the then famous playwright Astydamas would win first prize at the Greater Dionysia with his *Achilles,* a play that possibly included the following highly heroic verses from a messenger's speech:

> When Achilles saw Hektor's black spear
> fall vainly to the ground he cried out
> joyfully. And he pierced the arms, honored
> once, through which he had never been
> wounded. But the shield did not allow
> the sword to pass but held it there and
> did not betray the armor's new master. [120]

> ὡς δ᾽ εἶδ᾽ Ἀχιλλεὺς Ἕκτορος πεσὸν μάτην
> εἰς γῆν κελαινὸν ἔγχος, ἡδονῆς ὕπο
> ἀνηλάλαξεν καὶ δι᾽ ὧν διέπρεπε ὅπλων

οὐδ' αὐτὸς αὐτὰ πρόσθετο, ἀλλὰ φασγάνῳ
ἔπαισεν· ἀσπὶς δ' οὐ διῆκ' εἴσω στόμα
ἀλλ' ἴσχεν αὐτοῦ δεσπότου νιν, ὅπλα γὰρ
τὸν καινὸν οὐ προύδωκ' ἄνακτα . . . .

Hektor's casting first and the seeming absence of Athene makes this fight fairer than the one Homer depicted and demonstrates that Astydamas apparently took Pindar rather than Euripides as his model for dealing with dubious myths about national heroes.

Plato, too, attests to the power Achilles continued to wield in Athens after the death of Euripides. More eloquent even than the *Republic*'s disapproving testimony to the common belief that Homer was the educator of Greece are two early passages that may, in fact, represent the actual words and thoughts of Sokrates in 399 B.C. The first occurs midway through the *Apology* just after Sokrates has confuted Meletos's charge of atheism and just before he launches into the challenging assertion that nothing will induce him to change his ways. At this juncture, when Sokrates is intent on demonstrating that his only concern should be to consider whether his actions are just or unjust, he avails himself of what we must believe is the most powerful exemplar available:

> Achilles, who so much despised danger in comparison with submitting to anything shameful that when in his eagerness to kill Hektor his mother, a goddess, spoke to him to the following effect: "O child, if you avenge (*timōréseis*) Patroklos and kill Hektor you yourself will die"—for "straightway after Hektor," she said, "your fate stands ready"—he when he heard this made little of death and danger, but much more fearing life as a coward (*kakós*) without avenging his friends said, "May I die straightway when I have penalized the wrongdoer (*díkēn epitheìs tôi adikoûnti*) so that I may not remain here a laughingstock beside the beaked ships, a burden on the earth." (*Ap.* 28b–d)

In thus comparing his own resolve to that of Achilles, Sokrates uses a mixture of paraphrase and quotation from *Iliad* 18.88–121. The paraphrase is fairly accurate, but there are two changes in language that shift the tone significantly. When the Iliadic Achilles declares that life is not worth living unless Hektor "pays me back for spoiling Patroklos" (*Patrókloio d' hélōra Menoitiádeō apoteísei*, 18.93), when he says that he accepts death as the price of killing Hektor (*autíka tethnaíēn*) because he himself was intentionally (*ouk émellon*) not present to protect Patroklos

(18.98–99), and when he reiterates that he will die whenever Zeus wishes (18.115–116) but now he is going to find the "destroyer" (*oletêra*) of his friend (18.114), he displays motives of guilt and simple retaliation. Such motives are of little use to Sokrates, whose whole concern is just action. He therefore recasts the emotions of his exemplar as a combination of fear of living as a *kakós* ('evil person', 'coward') without avenging his friends (*polù dè mâllon deísas tò zên kakòs òn kaì toîs phílois mè timōreîn*) and desire to impose *díkēn*, "justice" or "penalty," on *tôi adikoûnti*, "wrongdoer" or "inflictor of hurt."

Since Sokrates has just contended that the only consideration proper to a man of any worth is whether his actions are *díkaia*, "just," or *ádika*, "unjust," and are those of an *agathós*, "good," or *kakós*, "bad," man (28b), we must link Achilles' *kakós* with *ho adikôn* and assign to them as well as to *díkēn* their more ethical meanings of "evil person," "wrongdoer," "justice." Sokrates' subsequent argument about the common fear of death also colors our interpretation of Achilles' motivations. He says that though no one can know whether death is a good or an evil, he does know that acting unjustly (*tò adikeîn*) is evil and shameful; therefore he will not fear (*phobḗsomai*) death more than injustice (29a–b). Like Achilles, Sokrates fears only "living like a *kakós*"; but the *kakós* is no longer merely a coward but very specifically one who commits injustice.

Here in the *Apology* we see Sokrates using and ethicizing Achilles in the service of an effort to transfer the concept of heroism from the wreaking of vengeance to the avoidance of wrongdoing and from martial prowess to intellectual perseverance. As Sokrates says, when he was a soldier his duty was to remain where he was stationed, taking no account of death. It would be strange if, having fulfilled his duty, he were now to desert a post assigned him by Apollo himself, that of living as a philosopher and scrutinizing himself and others (28d–e).

A month later, as the death he scorns draws close, Sokrates has a dream, which he repeats to Krito (*Krito* 44a–b):

> A woman fair and shapely dressed in white seemed
> to approach me and call me and say, "O Sokrates,
> on the third day may you fertile Phthia reach."

The woman's speech is a direct quotation, with a simple change from the first to the second person, of Achilles' words in *Iliad* 9.363 as he rejects Odysseus's plea and states his determination to return home. Krito finds the dream "strange" (*átopon*) but agrees with Sokrates that its meaning is all too clear. This meaning is not spelled out, but it is indeed clear: Sokrates will die on the day after the morrow.

The meaning of the dream is not, of course, exhausted by this literal prediction. Again, as in the *Apology*, Sokrates is elevated to the stature of Achilles, Greece's greatest hero; this time, however, the comparison is at the same time less explicit and more evocative. By being made to exercise our minds in recognizing the quotation, interpreting it, and making the implied comparison, readers are invited down a path of discovery that may lead first to contrasting the quotation's Homeric meaning with its meaning in Plato's context and then to considering how the comparison comments both on familiar Sokratic themes and on Iliadic heroism.

The first fact to note is that for Achilles Phthia represents life specifically as opposed to death and that his statement is an emphatic reversal of his original decision to barter life for glory. To Homeric Greeks death meant the loss of all things good, but there had been one thing even worse for a hero of Achilles' caliber: dying without glory. Now that, by eradicating any differentiation between the base person (*kakós*) and the noble (*esthlós, Il.* 9.319), the Greek community has made *kléos esthlón* impossible to win, Achilles views death as absolutely the worst thing that can happen to a human being (*Il.* 9.401–409). The death of Patroklos will change this view and provoke the stirring statement previously cited by Sokrates in the *Apology*, but until then we can see that Achilles' focus is always *this* world of earth and air and sun and brain and sinews: he wants either glorious immortality on the lips of living poets as compensation for death or long years of contented physical survival at home as compensation for no glory.

This last is part of a second noteworthy point: Phthia is Achilles' *home*, a pleasurable place of return where he will live with a wife selected by Peleus, enjoying his father's possessions (*Il.* 9.393–400). Phthia as "home" represents a normal peaceful mode of life, in which a man acquires wife and goods from his parents rather than from sacking cities, and as such it is directly opposed to the heroic, martial mode of life.

For Achilles of *Iliad* 9, then, home and death are unalterably opposed, and when Achilles says that if the glorious earthshaker gives good sailing he will reach Phthia in three days, he is turning away from heroism and death to home and life. When the beautiful beckoning lady quotes these words to Sokrates, however, we must strain to unite the two antithetical concepts, for Phthia is here the equivalent of death. The use of these particular words of Achilles should make clear to Sokrates and to Plato's audience the very thing that Krito naturally finds "strange": far from being the worst thing that can happen, Sokrates' death will be a joyful return to an original, happier state of being. This idea will reappear throughout Plato's works, most explicitly in the *Phaedo,* where Sokrates instructs his grieving friends that all of life should be a preparation for death and that all philosophers desire death above all things (*Phaedo* 63e--69d, 84a–b).[121] Here indeed is a new kind of fearlessness, the fearlessness of the philosopher who expects a posthumous reward not in earthly glory but in precisely that permanent separation of soul from body so detested by Achilles, a separation now viewed as the sole means to communion with the divine (*Phaedo* 83d–e).

By comparing the Athenian philosopher to the hero of *Iliad* 9, Plato (or the *daímōn* who sent Sokrates' dream) makes it impossible not to interpret Sokrates' choice, as it is delineated in the following discussion with Krito, as a critique of Achilles' Homeric ethics. Achilles spoke his original words in rejection of heroism and of a community whose unjust actions had negated the possibility of winning honor and glory. Sokrates applies Achilles' words to himself in accepting his community's unjust actions, in accepting a heroism that specifically involves an affirmation of that unjust community's claim upon his obedience. He rejects Krito's planned escape on the grounds that "acting unjustly [*toû adikeîn*], returning injustice [*toû antadikeîn*], and harming someone in self-defense is never right" (49d) and that the unjust actions of the community do not negate the just laws under which he was tried and condemned to death. Nothing could be more alien to Achilles' Homeric world view.

Sokrates' subtle critique of Achilles' motivations becomes explicit criticism in Plato's *Republic* (*Politeía*). First to be attacked is Achilles' expression of the Homeric view that death signifies the end of all possible happiness. Achilles' famous declaration to Odysseus that he would rather be a slave among the living than a king among the dead (*Od.* 11.489–91) heads a long list of passages to be expunged from Homer on the grounds that they might inculcate a fear of death among the future guardians of the republic (*Pol.* 386c–387a). Achilles' Iliadic behavior then figures prominently in an extended list of Homer's "erroneous" attribution of less than exemplary actions to his divine and semidivine characters. Homer is wrong to portray Achilles as extremely grief-stricken in *Iliad* 24.10–13 and 18.23–24, because a good man does not make a fuss over the death of a loved one (*Pol.* 388a–b). Achilles' abuse of Agamemnon in *Iliad* 1.225 will teach insolence instead of the self-control (*sōphrosúnē*) youths need to learn (389d–e). His acceptance of gifts from Agamemnon and ransom from Priam display the vice of greed (390e). Plato alleges disobedience to Skamander in *Iliad* 21, and he characterizes Achilles' angry words to Apollo (*Iliad* 22.15–20), his giving to Patroklos's body the lock of hair consecrated to the river Sperchios (*Iliad* 23.140–153), his dragging of Hektor's body around Patroklos's pyre, and his sacrifice of human captives thereon as examples of an unbelievable arrogance (*Pol.* 391a–c).

Some might agree with Plato's characterization of the last two examples, but his inversion of Skamander's deception into Achilles' disobedience and of acts of civil concession and magnanimity (accepting Agamemnon's gifts and Priam's ransom) into ones of greed are gross misreadings.[122] Plato, in his conviction that true heroism is the ability to do no wrong, is carrying forward the radical battle begun by Euripides. But the philosopher's object goes beyond that of the tragedian: Plato does not attempt to turn his fellow citizens' emotions against the Homeric Achilles—Plato does not trust emotions—but instead argues him out of existence:

> We will deny that any of these incidents is told correctly, nor will we allow our youth to believe that Achilles, who was the son of a goddess and Peleus—himself descended from Zeus and most temperate of men—and was reared by Cheiron, was so deranged as to contain within himself two opposite diseases: servile greed (*philochrēmatía*) and at the same time arrogance (*hyperēphanía*) toward gods and men. (391c)

Argument, however, is not enough, for Plato is not confident that in the majority of even highly intelligent people reason can prevail against Homer's emotional appeal. He therefore banishes altogether from his republic the revered "educator of Greece" (398a–b, 606e–607a) and with him, of course, his Achilles.

· 3 ·

LOVER OF WAR

CLASSICAL ROME
TO MEDIEVAL EUROPE

In spite of Plato, the *Iliad* was not banished from any republic until the Middle Ages, and until at least the first century A.D. readers continued to believe in the truth of Homer's story. Although their interpretations seem occasionally to have been skewed by those of Euripides and Plato, and although Stoics and Epicureans in particular, heirs of Plato's antipathy to passion, were never overly fond of Homer's hero, nonetheless Achilles maintained his inspirational ascendancy, moving apace with the center of political and military power as it passed from Greece to Hellenistic Egypt to Rome and the greater Roman empire.

I. CLASSICAL PASSION

Achilles was quite literally carried into Egypt by Alexander the Great (356–323 B.C.), who reputedly considered the *Iliad* so essential to his martial existence that he always slept with a copy of it under his pillow (Plut. *Life of Alexander* 8.2).[1] Though he did not become a favorite of the Hellenistic poets, who in general preferred more delicate subject matter,[2] Achilles lived on in the old epics and tragedies that were newly edited and copiously discussed by Alexandrian scholars as part of their effort to establish a complete collection of "classical" Greek literature.[3] He was transported to Rome in the third century B.C. when Livius Andronicus, himself a transplanted Greek, began the translations of Homer and Athenian poets that would make the Greek heroes as familiar in Rome as they had been in Athens.[4]

Livius recreated in Latin the *Odyssey* and eight tragedies, but the surviving fragments reveal nothing about how he might have portrayed

Achilles. One line that survives from his tragedy *Achilles* shows that cowardice versus manly behavior is someone's concern, but we cannot tell whose.[5] Livius's *Achilles* may well have been an adaptation of the lost *Achilles* of Aristarchos, an Athenian contemporary of Euripides. It is known that Ennius (239–169 B.C.) adapted Aristarchos's play, though the ten surviving fragments tell us little more than that his *Achilles Aristarchi* contains the Embassy of *Iliad* 9.[6] The only line that can definitely be attributed to Achilles is the Latin rendering of *Iliad* 9.312–313, in which Achilles' declaration "I hate like the gates of Hades the man who hides one thing in his heart and says another" emerges as "I was born with this nature: I show friendship or hostility visible on my face" (*Eo ego ingenio natus sum: amicitiam atque inimicitiam in frontem promptam gero,* frag. 7).[7] In addition to suggesting that the Roman Achilles may have lost his bardic ability to make similes, this verse indicates that honesty continues to characterize the hero.

The twenty-one fragments of Ennius's *Ransom of Hector* (*Hectoris Lytra*)[8] yield nothing so clear about the personal characteristics of Achilles. One of them, however, sets up a provocative opposition between "prowess" (*virtus*) and "justice" (*ius*): "Justice is better than prowess, for often evil men possess prowess; but justice and fairness (*aequum*) keep themselves far from evil men" (*Melius est virtute ius: nam saepe virtutem mali / Nanciscuntur: ius atque aecum se a malis spernit procul,* frag. 19).[9] It is difficult to assign these lines to a speaker; one can imagine them said to Achilles by an either hypocritical or rehabilitated Agamemnon during a quarrel scene (cf. *Iliad* 1.177–178, 185–188), by a reproachful Patroklos in an adaptation of the initial scene of *Iliad* 16, by a pleadingly philosophical Priam in the ransom scene, or by others. If they were indeed spoken to Achilles, they would provide us with an explicit statement of Plato's implicit critique, in other words, that ethical values are more important than Achilles' physical might.[10] But it is also just possible to imagine them spoken by an Achilles who feels he has both *virtus* and *ius* against an Agamemnon who has only *virtus*. In the absence of any indication of speaker we cannot judge what importance this sentiment may have had in the play as a whole.

My speculation that the speaker of Ennius's moralistic verses might be Achilles himself seems less fantastic when we examine the fragments of the *Iphigeneia* and find a similar inclination to *sententia* in a passage clearly assigned by Cicero to Achilles:

Astrological signs are carefully observed in the sky
When the goat or scorpion or other beast rises.
No one regards what is before his feet; they search out zones in
the skies.[11]

Astrologorum signa in caelo quid fit observationis,
Cum capra aut nepa exoritur nomen aliquod belvarum.
Quod est ante pedes nemo spectat, caeli scrutantur plagas.

These verses appear to have been derived from an anecdote about the
sixth-century Greek philosopher Thales that is said by Plato to represent the average person's unsympathetic attitude toward philosophers
(*Theatetus* 173d–174d). They apparently became proverbial in the criticism of abstract thinkers as opposed to doers of good deeds in the community, for we owe their survival to Cicero's awareness that they were
constantly quoted by Aelius Sextus, consul of 198 B.C., whenever he
would discuss astronomical speculations (*Republic* 1.18.30). Cicero's
Laelius quotes Aelius's quoting of Ennius's Achilles to bolster his own
argument against more than minimal study of the pure sciences. Since
Laelius also provides the information that Aelius was thought "extremely wise" (*egregie cordatus*, loc. cit.) by Ennius himself, we may
guess that the tragedian portrayed sympathetically Achilles' position on
the anti-philosophy side of this renewed version of the fifth-century opposition between words and deeds.

Four tragedies of Accius (170–after 90 B.C.) provide us with fragments more fruitful for assessing the Roman Achilles. The *Myrmidons*
shows us that unshakeable purpose and alienation are clearly still part of
his character. In this play Achilles' young friend Antilochos apparently
accused him of stubbornness, whereupon Achilles accused Antilochos
of maligning his character:

You call this obstinacy (*pertinaciam*), Antilochos;
I say it is firmness (*pervicaciam*), and I wish to practice it:
The one attends the brave, the other dolts possess.
You attribute to me a vice which halves my glory:
For I am happy to be called firm and to win;
I don't care to be called obstinate.

Tu pertinaciam esse, Antiloche, hanc praedicas,
Ego pervicaciam aio, et ea me uti volo:

> Haec fortes sequitur illam indocti possident.
> Tu addis quod vitio est, demis quod laudi datur:
> Nam pervicacem dici me esse et vincere
> Perfacile patior; pertinacem nil moror.[12]

Achilles' Iliadic isolation has survived, but his lonely idealism has lost all its magnificence. This Achilles is not content to get his honor from Zeus, and his concern with how others regard his action is a distant cry from his passionate rejection of his friends' pleas in Homer.

Indeed, Accius's fragments embody little passion, though they do indicate that strong emotion is still meant to be part of Achilles' character. Grief is clearly still a motivating force, for in the *Battle at the Ships* (*Epinausimache*) Achilles complains that "the death of a friend, which is the sharpest of sorrows, conquers me" (*Mors amici subigit, quod mi est senium multo acerrimum*).[13] Anger, too, is still a driving passion. In the *Telephus* someone is told to restrain his angry temper,[14] in the *Achilles* someone's breast is boiling with anger,[15] and in the *Myrmidons* someone is urged to bridle his wrath, stand up to his passions, and repress his rashness.[16] The "someone" described and rebuked in these passages is undoubtedly Achilles, who, equally undoubtedly, makes his own verbal contribution to the anger motif in a fragment from the *Battle at the Ships*. He says, perhaps to a Thetis who has advised waiting to avenge Patroklos until after she has brought new arms (see *Iliad* 18.134–135), "Ah, now when I go in wrath I go with sufficient arms" (*Ut nunc cum animatus iero, satis armatus sum*).[17]

Achilles' extraordinary battle prowess is evident in a fragment that describes the Trojans fleeing toward their city, none of them able to face his gleaming arms.[18] Accius may well have been influenced by Plato's criticism of Achilles, for this prowess provokes an impious arrogance quite absent from Homer's hero. Fragment 12 of the *Battle at the Ships* gives us the following boast: "I covered sacred Skamander's wave with salty blood / and piled heaps of enemy corpses in his deep stream" (*Scamandriam undam salso sanctam obtexi sanguine, / Atque acervos alta in amni corpore explevi hostico*).[19] The Iliadic Achilles did in fact fill Skamander with "foam and blood and corpses" (*Il.* 21.325–326, 218), but Homer did not make his hero tell of it. Nor did Achilles' original action violate something "sacred": Homer's Skamander is merely *dîos*, "divine" (*Il.* 12.21)[20] and not protected by the awesome aura of Accius's *sanctam*.

The character that emerges from the tragic fragments is familiar from the Attic simplifications we have already seen. Achilles is honest, wrathful, more concerned with reputation than with ideals, an incomparable warrior, and arrogant. Except for the last quality, which may, however, have been excused on the grounds of archaic mores, there is nothing here that average Romans, heirs of Romulus and his father Mars, would not approve. But neither do any of the fragments suggest that these plays are what created the continued fascination with Achilles that is attested at least as late as 90 A.D. in the writings of Quintilian.[21] His popularity, as indeed Quintilian's own references indicate, remains the responsibility of Homer—the original Homer for those who could read Greek, a Latinized Homer for those who could not.

We have already mentioned Livius Andronicus's *Odissea* of the late third century. We do not hear of a Roman *Iliad* until the early part of the first century, when Cnaeus Matius translated the entire work into Latin hexameters. The seven meagre fragments that remain from this popular work show a fidelity to Homer's text that would not have permitted gross distortions,[22] although one cannot believe that important changes did not occur in moving from the Greek language and culture to the Roman. One would like to know, for instance, how Matius translated *dîos Skámandros* of 12.21, whether he translated the *állēkton thumòn* of Aias's accusation (9.636–637) as *pervicacia* or *pertinacia,* and how he phrased Achilles "slaughter" (*deióōn*) of human captives on Patroklos's pyre (23.176). Most unfortunately for our purposes, none of the fragments touches on Achilles. Nor do the two fragments of another early-first-century translation, that of Ninnius Crassus.[23] Ninnius also shows no great deviation from Homer's text, but since the sample from both translations is so small, we cannot draw any conclusions about subtle shifts in attitude toward Achilles' career of wrath and revenge.

Catullus (84–54 B.C.) gives us our first extant complete Roman recreation of Achilles in Poem 64, an epyllion ("miniature epic") of 408 dactylic hexameter verses. The Fates' prophecy of Achilles' brief and bloody career, which plays a striking role in the celebration of his parents' wedding, shows that the brutalized archetype used by Euripides in the *Elektra* and the *Hekabe* is alive and well. It also shows that Catullus, though not perhaps as militantly antiwar, has the same ironic sensibilities as the Greek tragedian.

The subject of Poem 64 is the wedding of Peleus and Thetis. Its theme is the excellence of the heroic age (*o nimis optato saeclorum tempore nati / heroes*, 22–23) when men were demigods (*deum genus*, 23) and gods were willing to mingle with mortals (*sese mortali ostendere coetu . . . solebant*, 385–386), even to the point of marrying them (*tum Thetis humanos non despexit hymenaeos*, 20).[24] The blessedness of this age is brought at the end into Hesiodic contrast with the modern-day sinfulness (*omnia fanda nefanda malo permixta furore*, 405) that has put an end to such happy commerce (*quare nec talis dignantur visere coetus*, 407). Catullus's antithesis between semidivine past and all-too-human present is no more absolute, however, than was Euripides' in the *Iphigeneia*'s Peleus and Thetis ode. As Leo Curran has shown in detail, Catullus portrays "a tragic constancy in human nature" that transcends the fundamental antithesis in the poem.[25] Undercutting the idyllic portrayal of the wedding of Peleus and Thetis are a vision from the past (Ariadne) and another of the future (Achilles) that tarnish the Age of Heroes with brutal insensitivity and disallow Hesiod's view that there was a distinct age when men were *dikaióteron kaì áreion*, "nobler and more just."[26]

On the bridal bed of the goddess there is a coverlet whose embroidered scenes illustrate *heroum virtutes* (51). As Kenneth Quinn notes, the natural meaning of these words is "the courageous deeds of heroes,"[27] and it is even possible to take them as a translation of Homer's *kléa andrôn*, "famous deeds of epic heroes." Illustrations of such deeds would be fitting decoration for the bed used to engender Achilles. But what we find, in Catullus's long *ekphrasis* of the first of these scenes, are two "forgetful"[28] deeds—Theseus's abandonment of Ariadne and his sailing into Athens with unchanged sails—and their consequences: Ariadne's long lament and Aegeus's suicide (52–250). The second scene, which is shorter, reveals Bacchus, *incensus amore*, seeking Ariadne with a group of frenzied worshippers, some of whom are tossing about the limbs of a rent bullock (251–264). Terrifying rather than joyful, this scene portends not rescue but final degradation and is no more noble than the earlier scene of Theseus's forgetfulness.[29] These *ekphrases* associate *heroum virtutes* with a hero's causing wretchedness and misery to spouse and parent. Later, the shrill song of the Parcae[30] will associate the same concept with the brutal killing of sons and daughters.

The Achilles of the Parcae's prophecy seems at first to be the Achilles of Pindar. The first stanza tells us that he will be fearless, never run from an enemy, and be able to outrun deer (338–341).[31] The second stanza tells of his heroism on Phrygian fields flowing with Teucrian blood (344)—a description similar to that of the Pindaric Achilles, "who stained the Mysian vineyards / with the dark blood of Telephos, drenching the plain" (*I.* 8.54–55).[32] "Surpassing valor" (*egregias virtutes*) and "famous deeds" (*claraque facta*) open the third stanza in the same Pindaric vein, and, by analogy with the "valor" (*aretàn*) that Pindar's "lips of poets" (*sophôn stómat'*) published for Achilles (*I.* 8.52–53), as well as with the *heroum virtutes* Catullus earlier described as depicted in "wondrous art" (*mira arte,* 51), the reader expects the stanza to tell how Achilles' valor and deeds will be made known to all. It does, but not in the way we expect. Catullus mentions no tapestry, no epic poem; funerals are the medium here. Achilles' *virtutes* and *facta*

> will often be confessed by mothers at the funerals of sons
> when they loosen their uncombed hair from their heads and
> beat their withered breasts with feeble palms.

> saepe fatebuntur gnatorum in funere matres,
> cum incultum cano solvent a vertice crinem
> putridaque infirmis variabunt pectora palmis.
>
> (349–351)

Pindar's *Isthmian* 8, which hovers everywhere in the background of the Achilles section of Poem 64, also uses deaths as a means to reveal innate virtue: disclosing the House of Persephone to Memnon, Hektor, and other champions is the means by which Achilles displayed (*próphainen*) his (divine) stock (*I.* 8.59–61). But with the pitiable details of disheveled hair, flabby breasts, and feeble hands, Catullus interjects a pathos and horror quite alien to his aristocratic Greek predecessor. Furthermore, Achilles, the creator of the funerals, is not the grammatical subject of Catullus's sentence; neither are artists, be they poets or weavers, who traditionally celebrate the cause of such funerals. Instead, in Catullus's presentation of the epic world, it is mothers, helpless and grieving, who are given the role of affirming Achilles' valorous deeds. Here, as in Euripides, we have suddenly switched to the point of view of the victim: the *virtutes* of the son of Thetis is synonymous with the extinction of other mothers' offspring.[33]

Achilles' brutality escalates through a Homeric simile that juxtaposes the early reaping (*praecerpens . . . demetit*) of corn with the destructive (*infesto . . . ferro*) cutting down (*prosternet*) of men (353–355)[34] and through a Homeric vision of the Skamander, whose choked and blood-warm waters are a *testis,* "witness," to his *magnis virtutibus* (357–360). Then the final *testis* is the ultimate brutality: the beheading of Polyxena on his tomb (361–370). Catullus fuses the red-white color imagery and the fluid imagery that he established earlier in the poem to emphasize the passage in which Achilles' tomb receives the "snow-white limbs" (*niveos . . . artus*) of the virgin and is drenched with her blood (*Polyxenia madefient caede*). As Curran says, "We have passed from the sea's white foam of the opening lines, to the river stained red with gore, to a final horrifying vision of the pouring of an innocent girl's blood on the tomb of a ruthless killer."[35]

Achilles may be a ruthless killer, but he is also the son of the wedding couple. No matter how we are to suppose they react to the human sacrifice of a young girl, its location on their son's *tomb* can hardly be thought pleasing to Peleus and Thetis. We may now remember that both Homer and Pindar used Peleus as exemplar both of human happiness (his divine wedding) and of human misery (the young death of his only son).[36] Like the very presence of the Parcae, this reminder of Achilles' death undercuts the joyful mingling of human and divine that this poem is supposedly celebrating. For both Achilles' death and the Parcae, who cut as well as weave, are reminders of mortality, that is, of the *distinction* between gods and humans.[37]

The word *virtutes* does not create an immediate irony in the Parcae's song of Achilles' life and death as it did earlier when *heroum virtutes* introduced the story of Thesus's forgetfulness and Ariadne's misery. Achilles' bloody deeds and his own death are a perfectly true expression of heroic courage. Irony enters when the song is over and Catullus uses the word *felicia,* "auspicious, fertile," to signify our "expected" response to those brutal, life-destroying deeds (382). The irony carries over into the epilogue, in which Catullus contrasts those days when gods visited the "guiltless" (*castas,* 384) homes of heroes with these days of "unspeakable crime" (*scelere . . . nefando,* 397).

Of the three examples used to illustrate those happy days, two are irrevocably tainted by earlier images in the poem.[38] Bacchus's coming to Delphi with his orgiastic worshippers (390–393) recalls his lustful search for the abandoned Ariadne amid hysterical music and the torn limbs of the *sparagmós*. The presence of Mars, Minerva, and Nemesis urging on the troops in the death-dealing contest of war (394–396) can hardly inspire nostalgia after what we have seen of Achilles on the battlefield. It would seem that both the "dutiful conduct" (*pietas*, 386) that earlier drew these gods down to earth and the benefit that they conferred while here are equally suspect. We may not be better off without these gods in our midst, but we are probably no worse.

Through flashback and prophecy, Poem 64 extends from the voyage of the Argonauts to the end of the Trojan War. It thus becomes, as Curran says, "an epitome of the whole age of heroes." [39] By maintaining a guise of praise the poet forces us to create along with him our own judgment on this age; the sharp irony produced by the application of the terms *virtutes, felix, pietas,* and *castus* to the perpetration of suffering and brutality ensures that this judgment will be a severe one. Theseus's forgetfulness is the very opposite of valorous behavior; Achilles' perfect *virtutes* are the opposite of "auspicious." It would be difficult to grant that either of them has a "guiltless" house.

Catullus's brutal portrait did not tarnish Achilles in the eyes of those who would themselves find brutality useful in their pursuit of power and glory. In 44 B.C. the eighteen-year-old Octavian successfully used Achilles as an exemplar, invoking the identical scene from *Iliad* 18 that Sokrates had invoked at his trial. The object of Octavian's suasion was his mother, who, fearing for his life, wanted him to hide his relationship with his assassinated uncle. As Appian tells the story, Octavian refused to deny his relationship with Caesar but rather proclaimed it, saying that it would be noble (*kalón*) not only to risk danger but also to die since he had been singled out by Caesar, who was a born risk-taker. He then quoted Achilles, "turning to his mother as if she were Thetis: 'Straightway may I die, since I was not there to defend my friend when he was killed.' And then he said that this speech and consequent act were what above all else had earned Achilles eternal honor (*kósmon*)" (Appian 3.2.13). Octavian's mother, more receptive than Sokrates' jury, was so thrilled by his words that she immediately changed her mind and actively encouraged his vengeance (App. 3.2.14). The vengeance taken was often brutal and may even have included human sacrifice of not just twelve but three hundred victims on an altar to his father Julius.[40]

Cicero (106–43 B.C.) was an admirer neither of Octavian[41] nor of
Achilles, for as a republican he was categorically against dictators and
as a philosopher he was categorically against all passions, including
anger. Passions were not universally condemned by philosophers—the
Peripatetics, heirs of Aristotle, thought that wrath (*iracundia*) was occasionally useful and refused to consider anyone a man (*vir*) who was in-
capable of feeling it[42]—but both Stoics and Academics, who were
Plato's heirs and Cicero's teachers and colleagues, believed that passion
interefered with the life of the mind and had a deleterious effect on the
well-being of the soul. For the Stoics the well-being of the soul involved
living in peaceful accordance with reason (*ho lógos*), which was identical
to living in accordance with nature. For the Academics the well-being of
the soul meant eventual total separation from the body and an eternity
of bliss after death. Cicero utilized both schools of philosophy in his
own late philosophical works, whose intent was to romanize the Greek
philosophy he had learned. Homer's Achilles enters one of these works,
the *Tusculan Disputations*, three times, each time as a negative exemplar.

Cicero thought it necessary to add a Latin work on philosophy to
those already existing in Greek, because it had always seemed to him
that in addition to being wiser than Greeks in inventing things Romans
improved upon whatever the Greeks gave them (1.1). The Homeric
Achilles soon provides proof of this as Cicero proceeds, in the First Disputation, to discuss the immortality of the soul, to reiterate Plato's theory that life is but a preparation for death, and to counsel indifference to
the body. He cites with approval several philosophers to whom disposi-
tion of their bodies after death was irrelevant because they would no
longer be in those bodies, and he then turns to famous examples of
foolish people who did not understand this elementary fact. Achilles
heads the list: "Achilles drags Hektor bound behind his chariot and
believes, I think, that Hektor is being torn to bits and feels it" (*Trahit
Hectorem ad currum religatum Achilles: lacerari eum et sentire, credo,
putat*, 1.44.105). Much better (*melius*) is the Roman version of Achilles,
who, "finally wise" (*aliquando sapiens*) in Accius's tragedy, says: "Rather,
in truth I gave the body to Priam; Hektor have I taken away" (*Immo
enimvero corpus Priamo reddidi, Hectora abstuli*, 1.44.105).[43] Cicero then
chidingly corrects the Homeric Achilles: "Not therefore did you drag
Hektor, but a body, which had been Hektor's" (*Non igitur Hectora
traxisti, sed corpus, quod fuerat Hectoris*, 1.44.105).[44]

Accius's Achilles (in one play at least) may have been "finally wise," but as we have seen he was also at times full of anger. Indeed, a generation later Horace sums up his schoolboy reading about Achilles, be it from the *Iliad* or from the dramatists, as "how much damage angry Achilles did to the Greeks" (*iratus Graiis quantum nocuisset Achilles*, *Ep.* 2.2.42). Such an *iratus* Achilles could not by definition be *sapiens*, a fact Cicero is at great pains to prove in the Third and Fourth Disputations, which are concerned with *perturbationes*, "disturbances," of the soul. The wise man (*sapiens*) does not suffer such *perturbationes* as sorrow (*aegritudo*) and desire (*cupiditas*), fear (*formido*), lust (*libido*), and wrath (*iracundia*); he alone is *sanus* in mind. Those who do suffer from such emotions are *insanus*. *Insania* is specifically defined as "sickness of the mind," following, Cicero says, Stoic doctrine derived from Sokrates (3.4).

Each of the *perturbationes* is discussed in turn, and after proving that the *sapiens* is free from sorrow Cicero moves on to the proposition that he is also free from anger. He quotes in Latin Achilles' words to Aias at *Iliad* 9.646–647 (3.9.18), "My heart swells (*turgescit*) deep in bitter anger / when I remember that I am reft of honor and glory" (*Corque meum penitus turgescit tristibus iris, / cum decore atque omni me orbatum laude recordor*), and brings to bear on the quotation the Stoic argument of Dionysos of Heraclea (3.9.19):

> Can a hand be in good condition when it is swollen (*in tumore*)? or can any other member that is swollen and enlarged (*tumidum ac turgidum*) not be in a defective (*vitiose*) condition? So therefore a soul (*animus*) that is puffed up and swollen (*inflatus et tumens*) is in a defective condition (*in vitio*).

Since the *animus* of the *sapiens* is never defective, never swollen, but the *animus* of the *iratus* is swollen and defective, it follows that the *sapiens* is never angry (*numquam irascitur*).

Insofar as anger remains Achilles' main characteristic, then, he is, in the Stoic and Ciceronian view, unwise. But as the analogy with the swollen hand indicates, he is more than merely unwise, he is sick. Now, to the Stoics all *perturbationes* produce *insania* as we noted above, but to Cicero anger is the closest thing to mental illness that there is. In arguing against the Peripatetic view that anger is useful as an adjunct to courage Cicero avows that he, at least, has never acted in anger and asks,

"Is there anything more similar to *insania* than *ira?*" He says that Ennius called it *initium insaniae* ("beginning of madness")[45] and then asks another rhetorical question: "What more foul (*foedius*) than the Homeric Achilles, than Agamemnon, in their quarrel?" Then, as if responding to the fragment from Accius's *Battle at the Ships* in which Achilles says that if he goes in wrath he goes with sufficient arms (*Epinausimache* 1), Cicero concludes, "Courage therefore does not need the help of *iracundia*. She is sufficiently ordered, equipped, armed in herself" (*non igitur desiderat fortitudo advocatam iracundiam: satis est instructa parata armata per sese,* 4.23.52).

The only thing that can free humans from such *perturbationes*, such *insania*, such vileness, is philosophy, and this discipline Achilles clearly lacks. Cicero opens the Second Disputation with a paraphrased quotation from Achilles' son Neoptolemos from a play by Ennius to the effect that it was necessary to apply himself to philosophy but only a little, for it did not wholly please him (2.1.1). Cicero comments that he finds it necessary to apply himself to philosophy, but *not* just a little, since it is hard to learn a little without wanting to learn all. Yet, he says, in the busy life of a soldier even a little will help alleviate passions that hamper us (2.1.1–2). One can imagine (though Cicero does not) Achilles saying the very thing Ennius put in the mouth of his son, for the tragic fragments show both a tendency to play the "practical" philosopher (Ennius *Iph.* 12) and a lack of true idealism (Accius *Myr.* 1). In fact, in the *Republic* (1.18.31) Cicero makes an opponent of philosophy quote the Ennian fragment that shows Achilles "philosophizing" and follows it shortly by the very quotation from Neoptolemos that Cicero uses here in the Second Disputation. The old Athenian opposition between speaking and doing, which had become in Ennius an opposition between studying and acting, in Cicero becomes one between philosophy and passion. Despite the brief appearance of a "finally wise" Roman Achilles in Accius's tragedy, for Cicero Achilles remains on the wrong side of this opposition.

Vergil, who was twenty-seven years old when Antony's and Octavian's lust for power killed Cicero in 43 B.C., had received the same liberal education as the old republican philosopher and was influenced by the same Stoic and Academic currents. Passion in the *Aeneid*, whether it be Aeneas's grief at the loss of his wife[46] or Turnus's lust for slaughter,[47] is *insanus*. Anger in particular, as embodied in Juno, is the source of all evil. For Vergil as for Cicero, indulging or controlling one's passions is contingent upon training and environment (cf. *Tusc. Disp.* 2.27), and for Vergil as for Cicero the Roman environment is set up as morally better than the Greek. But while Cicero in the *Tusculan Disputations* was concerned with the effect of passions on the well-being of the individual person, Vergil in the *Aeneid* is concerned with the effect of personal passions on the well-being of the state, on the well-being, that is, of an environment that could promote the desired self-control. This self-control is the expression of Roman *pietas,* loving devotion to the state, the gods, and the family, eternal groupings whose importance far outweighs the ephemeral singleness of individual achievements. The program of the *Aeneid,* as developed in Books One to Six, is Aeneas's slow learning of Roman *pietas* against a backdrop of what is now seen as primitive Homeric heroism.[48] The symbol of this heroism is, as usual, Achilles.

Vergil evokes Achilles by name (including references to Phthia, Myrmidons, father of Neoptolemos, son of Peleus, or descendant of Aiakos) twenty-six times in the *Aeneid,* and almost every one of these references reflects Achilles' status as supreme martial hero. He is, for instance, the standard against which Aeneas's enemy Turnus measures both his own prowess (9.741–742)[49] and that of his Trojan opponent (11.438–440).[50] Together with Diomedes, his surrogate in *Iliad* 5, Achilles represents for Dido (1.752), Aeneas (2.196–198), and Turnus (11.403–404) the apex of the deadly warfare that harried Troy for ten years.[51] So too, when describing the joyful Trojan exploration of the falsely deserted Greek camp, Aeneas selects out the tents of *saevus* Achilles as their major interest (2.29), thereby making him almost an emblem of the Greek army.[52]

The deeds that earned Achilles his reputation among the troubled inhabitants of the *Aeneid* are not left abstract. In the course of reminding Venus that he has always cared for her son, Neptune also reminds Vergil's audience of the bloody rampage in *Iliad* 21–22, "when Achilles chased and dashed against the walls a breathless army, and when he gave many thousands to death, and the full rivers groaned, and Xanthus could not find a path and roll himself along to the sea" (5.804–808).[53] Neptune's evoking the mass slaughter of Achilles' grief-stricken sweep through the Trojan ranks complements the earlier pictures on the doors of Juno's temple, which also portray Achilles' awesome power to kill. These pictures put before Aeneas's eyes and ours individual people who are victims not of one uncharacteristically gruesome *aristeía* but of a whole career of slaughtering.

The temple pictures, which are drawn into an Iliadic context by the introductory picture of "the sons of Atreus and Priam, and Achilles ferocious to both" (*Atridas Priamumque et saevum ambobus Achilles,* 458), depict the Trojan War almost entirely in terms of Achilles' victims. The first scene (466–467) shows the Greeks fleeing and, in the Iliadic context created by verse 458, suggests the period of Hektor's temporary success during Achilles' withdrawal; the next picture (468) shows Achilles returned and pursuing the Trojans in a chariot. After a picture of Diomedes' night foray and murder of Rhesos, one of only two non-Achillean exploits pictured on the gates (469–473), the scene shifts to a pre-Iliadic episode: the slaughter of Troilos, "unfortunate boy and unequal to meet with Achilles" (*infelix puer atque impar congressus Achilli,* 475).[54] Whether Vergil means us to think of Troilos as ambushed by night or only cut down in battle is relatively unimportant; the poignancy of his youth and helplessness as he is dragged by his horses in the dust is the same in either case (476–478). Next (479–482), some Trojan women supplicate an unfavoring Pallas Athene as in *Iliad* 6.286–311, and then Vergil returns to the Iliadic Achilles with the dragging and ransoming of Hektor (483–486):

> Achilles had dragged Hektor three times around the walls of Ilium and was selling the dead body for gold. Then indeed Aeneas groaned hugely from deep in his chest when he saw the spoils and the chariot and the very body itself of his friend, and Priam stretching out his defenseless arms.

FIGURE 12. Achilles Pursues Troilos; Lion Pursues Deer

> ter circum Iliacos raptaverat Hectora muros
> exanimumque auro corpus vendebat Achilles.
> tum vero ingentem gemitum dat pectore ab imo,
> ut spolia, ut currus, utque ipsum corpus amici
> tendentemque manus Priamum conspexit inermis.

Vergil's reversing the order of these last two events, as he reversed the Homeric order of the death of Troilos, the supplication of the Trojan women, and Diomedes' night raid, destroys any sense of the progression of a life. Achilles died immediately after killing Memnon—again in vengeance for a friend, Antilochos—but Vergil buries this fact by placing the earlier victim, Penthesileia, last in his series of scenes. The result is a chaotic vision of the Trojan War as consisting predominantly of Achilles' victims, and a monolithic vision of Achilles' heroic career as nothing but endless killing. This combined vision is perhaps the proof of the commonplace that the first word of the *Aeneid, arma,* alludes to the *Iliad* as the second word, *virum,* picks up the first word of the *Odyssey.* The door panels provide the first "battle scene" in the *Aeneid,* and it would appear that *arma* in its extended meaning 'war' is virtually synonymous with Achilles, whose unmitigated murderousness is placed securely in the context of the *Iliad* by the introductory verse 458.

By mingling clearly Iliadic episodes ("Achilles ferocious to both," Diomedes' night raid, the Trojan women's supplicating Athene) with Epic Cycle episodes (Troilos, Memnon, Penthesileia) and by presenting alternative versions of two Iliadic incidents (the dragging and ransoming of Hektor) that depict Achilles in the worst possible light,[55] Vergil's version of the Trojan War strips Achilles and the *Iliad* of whatever tragic splendor they might have retained. Vergil invokes a similarly contaminated Iliadic event in Book Two when the ghost of Hektor appears to Aeneas in a dream looking just as he did after Achilles killed him (2.270–279):

> In sleep, lo! before my eyes sad Hektor seemed to stand by me and weep a flood of tears, as he once was, having been dragged behind the chariot, black with bloody dust, pierced with thongs through swollen feet. Alas, how he looked! How changed from that Hektor who returned having put on Achilles' arms or having thrown fire on Danaan ships! He wore a filthy beard and hair matted with blood and the many wounds that he received around his father's walls.

in somnis, ecce, ante oculos maestissimus Hector
visus adesse mihi largosque effundere fletus,
raptatus bigis ut quondam, aterque cruento
pulvere perque pedes traiectus lora tumentis.
hei mihi, qualis erat, quantum mutatus ab illo
Hectore qui redit exuvias indutus Achilli
vel Danaum Phrygios iaculatus puppibus ignis!
squalentem barbam, et concretos sanguine crinis,
vulneraque illa gerens, quae circum plurima muros
accepit patrios.

The references to putting on Achilles' arms and throwing fire on Danaan
ships explicitly evoke the *Iliad,* but, as Austin points out (*ad loc.*), the
detail of Hektor's "swollen feet" (*pedes tumentis*) shows that "Virgil has
adopted a version in which Hector was still alive when he was dragged
at Achilles' chariot wheels, as at Soph. *Ai.* 1031." We need only unite this
vision of Hektor with the picture on the temple doors of Priam's out-
stretched helpless arms (1.487) to feel its full gruesomeness. This passage reveals the glory of war (Hektor victorious in Achilles' armor)
overcome by its utter brutality, and it is an apt precursor of the brutality
that Aeneas is about to see wreaked on Troy.

Achilles, of course, is no longer around to participate in that brutality, but Neoptolemos, who presses on with his father's force (*instat vi
patria*, 491), more than fills the gap as, "raging with slaughter" (*furentem
caede*, 499–500), he bursts through the palace, slays Polites before his
father's eyes, and then drags the old man through his son's blood to
kill him on the household altar (526–533). Here amid the horrors of
Neoptolemos's limitless brutality, Vergil chooses, for the only time in
the *Aeneid,* to evoke the complex Iliadic Achilles. After Neoptolemos
has killed Polites, Priam reviles him and contrasts his actions with
Achilles' humane behavior when he returned Hektor's corpse (540–543):

But he, Achilles, whom you lyingly call your father, was not such to his
enemy Priam; but he respected the rights and trust of a suppliant, and he
gave back Hektor's bloodless corpse for burial and sent me back to my
kingdom.

at non ille, satum quo te mentiris, Achilles
talis in hoste fuit Priamo; sed iura fidemque

supplicis erubuit corpusque exsangue sepulchro
reddidit Hectoreum meque in mea regna remisit.

Vergil chooses to evoke here what he suppressed in Book One, Achilles' compassion in *Iliad* 24. This evocation, however, is meant not so much to make us think better of Achilles as to make us think worse of his son, to exacerbate Neoptolemos's traditionally nasty character. It is all very well for Priam to deny that Neoptolemos can be Achilles' son and for Bernard Knox to assert that "only the worst of the father is reborn in the son," [56] but the fact is that everywhere but here in the *Aeneid* "only the worst" is also evoked of Achilles, and he remains the symbol of the brutal destruction of Troy that his son actually carries out.

From first to last, Vergil's Achilles is the killer of Trojans, destroyer of Troy. Almost as if to frame the other references, Vergil introduces his Trojan protagonists as "the remnants left by the Greeks and unyielding Achilles" (*reliquias Danaum atque immitis Achilli,* 1.30) [57] and in the final battle has Turnus kill one who had escaped "Achilles, destroyer of Priam's kingdom" (*Priami regnorum eversor Achilles,* 12.545). He shares this role as implacable (*immitis,* 1.30, 3.87), ferocious (*saevus,* 1.458, 2.29) enemy of Troy with ferocious Juno, whose unforgetting anger (*saevae memorem Iunonis . . . iram,* 1.4) "wages war" with the "enemy race" (1.48, 67) until she gets Jupiter to agree that "fallen Troy shall stay fallen along with her name" (*occidit, occideritque sinas cum nomine Troia,* 12.828). It is entirely fitting that the scenes which make Achilles almost synonymous with the Trojan War appear on Juno's own temple.

Linked as warriors against Troy, Juno and Achilles are also linked as representatives of the uncontrolled passion that is both the cause and effect of war and that it will be the special mission of the Roman state to curb. According to Jupiter's prophecy in Book One, the following events will finally put an end to war: first, *aspera* "fierce," Juno will "improve her purposes" (*consilia in melius referet*) and cherish the Romans as Jupiter does (279–281); second, Homer's Greece—specifically Phthia (home of Achilles), Mycenae (home of Agamemnon), and Argos (home of Diomedes)—will be mastered and forced to serve Rome (*servitio premet . . . dominabitur,* 284–285); [58] third, a "Trojan Caesar" will be born (286) under whose rule centuries of fierce warfare will come to an end (*aspera tum positis mitescent saecula bellis,* 291) and *furor impius,* "limitless rage," will be bound fast within the closed gates of war

(294–296). Thus both Juno's amelioration and Rome's bringing the descendants of the *Iliad*'s heroes under her control are tied to the curbing of *furor*.

The third link between Juno, prime obstacle to the founding of Rome, and Achilles, exemplar of Greek heroism, clarifies their relationship: it is Juno who creates of Turnus the *alius Achilles*, "other Achilles," predicted by the Sibyl (6.89). Before Allecto hurls her firebrand into his chest, Turnus appears quite rational and not at all upset by Aeneas's appearance in Latium (7.435–444). But as soon as she hurls the firebrand, he acquires both the characteristic anger of Achilles and his preoccupation with fighting: "He howls madly for arms, searches for arms in bed and hall. Lust for the sword and the evil madness of war rage in him, and above all anger" (*arma amens fremit, arma toro tectisque requirit: / saevit amor ferri et scelerata insania belli, / ira super,* 7.460–462). Like Achilles, whom we saw "ferocious to both (*saevum ambobus*) Agamemnon and Priam," Turnus is soon ready to fight both his fellow Latins and enemy Teucrians (*se satis ambobus Teucrisque venire Latinisque,* 7.470).

Not only does Juno re-create Achilles, she also gives new life to the scenes on her temple. Once she sets the Latin war in motion every action portrayed on the doors except the mutilation and selling of Hektor's corpse will be replayed on the fields of Italy[59]—with various Trojans performing the roles of Achilles and Diomedes and with the Italians enacting the part of the Trojans. Aeneas will kill an *infelix puer*, Lausus, who confronts a warrior much greater than himself (10.811, 829); Nisus and Euryalus will reenact Diomedes' night raid (9.314–445); an Amazonian warrior, Camilla, will be killed by a Trojan (11.648–649, 803–831); the Italian women will reenact the Trojan women's offering and prayer to Athene (11.477–485); and a "Hektor," who also carries connotations of Memnon because of his Vulcan-made sword and immortal relative, will die again at the hands of a divinely armored warrior, *ira terribilis*, "terrible in anger" (12.946–947). It is clear that just as Achilles is synonymous with past war, so Juno, who is the very essence of personal passion as opposed to Jupiter's rationality and Aeneas's *pietas*, becomes synonymous with a replay of that war in the present.

If we think of Juno as wrath personified,[60] we can draw a useful parallel between her behavior and Achilles' *mênis*, "divine wrath," in the *Iliad*. Both Juno and *mênis* may be defined as limitless passion, and both wreak havoc on their respective epic worlds. But Homer's *mênis* and

Vergil's Juno are by no means equivalent. In the *Aeneid* divine wrath is the cause; Achilles and war are the joint and inseparable effect. In the *Aeneid* divine wrath does not emanate from one super- or subhuman hero but is incarnated in all men forced by Juno to take up arms. Limitless passion, in other words, turns a man into an Achillean, that is, destructive, martial hero. As it does so, we see revealed not Vergil's conception of the human essence of great individual heroes but his conception of human nature in general. We may legitimately see Homer's Achilles, especially in the rampage, as monomaniacal; Euripides revised this to egomaniacal; Vergil extracts from this the purely maniacal. Achilles, war, and the uncontrolled passion that underlies them are manifestations of the irrationality that constantly threatens to destroy human peace, human civilization.[61]

Vergil's ferocious killer of Trojans is not at odds with the oft-quoted dictum of his friend Horace, who, far from urging poets to adopt the "wiser Achilles" that serious Cicero would have preferred, lightheartedly advises retaining the hero's passionate belligerence (*Ep.* 2.3.120–122):[62]

> Writer, if you chance to bring back honored Achilles,
> let him be active, angry, inexorable, violent,
> deny that law was made for him, and arrogate all to his arms.

> scriptor, honoratum si forte reponis Achillem,
> impiger, iracundus, inexorabilis, acer
> iura neget sibi nata, nihil non arroget armis.

This advice was apparently followed by Aemilius Macer, whose poem about Achilles is described by his younger friend Ovid as a *carmen iratum* (*Amores* 2.18.1). Ovid's own *Metamorphoses* (c. 8 A.D.) evokes the characteristic wrath (12.102, 128) and pictures an Achilles totally engrossed in war: a relaxing after-dinner conversation with this energetic young city-sacker can turn only on *pugnas*, "battles," "for what indeed would Achilles rather talk about, what would others rather talk about in the company of great Achilles?" (*Meta.* 12.159–164).[63]

The belligerent anger of this Augustan Achilles continues to characterize the hero throughout late antiquity. Some forty years after Ovid's martial portrait, Seneca's *Troades* offers a grim retrospective of an Achilles who rages (*furens*) as he fills the Skamander with corpses (185–187) and who arrogantly (*superbo victor in curru*) maltreats Hektor's body

(188–189). When Seneca's Chorus conjures up a picture of the boy Achilles getting a music lesson from Cheiron, music does nothing to soften this hero: the songs Cheiron sings are of war (*bella,* 835), and their effect on the already fierce (*trux,* 832) youngster is only to "whet his immense ire" (*ingentes acuebat iras,* 834).

In Statius's *Achilleid* (96 A.D.) Thetis's adored child is again un-adorably *trux* (1.302) as well as hard (*durus,* 1.564) and savage (*ferus,* 1.852). Before he enters the poem in person, amusing himself by harassing two lion cubs whose mother he has just left dead in their cave (1.168–170), Cheiron introduces him through a worried account to Thetis of how the boy's violence to the Centaurs' herds and homes is getting out of hand (1.149–155). Unbeknownst to Cheiron, Achilles' worrisome acts are really the beginning of a magnificent career in violence: he is the future "destroyer of Asia" (*eversorem Asiae,* 1.530), the destined "ravager of Troy" (*vastator Troiae,* 2.32). Even while his love for Deidameia has him temporarily sidetracked from this career, he continues to show a most promising violence: since he cannot prove his manhood in Skyros by fighting enemy Asians, he proves it instead by raping his beloved (1.639–645). The predominant impression of Achilles left by the *Achilleid* can be summed up in a phrase Kalchas uses when he says that the massing Greeks, who are in love with war (1.412), are in love with Achilles as a *belligerum numen* "god of war" (1.504).

Statius did not live long enough to get his budding hero actually to Troy, and this is perhaps why he does not provide any explicit instances of the familiar Achillean wrath.[64] He foreshadows its presence, however, when he has Achilles tell Odysseus that he would like to work up a good righteous anger (*libet iustas hinc sumere protinus iras*) by listening to the causes of the war (2.46–48). Statius's qualification of the wrath by *iustus* ("righteous" or "just") has its roots in *Iliad* 9.337–341, where Achilles' disillusionment with the heroic code causes him to question the causes of the war itself.[65] Statius's transformation of this disillusionment into a spontaneous insistence on justice maintains a link between Achilles and justice, justice and anger, that will take on great importance in later Renaissance evocations of Achilles' temper.

Justice, however, has very little to do with the anger displayed by Achilles in Quintus of Smyrna's continuation of the *Iliad* (fourth century A.D.). The *Posthomerica*'s Achilles—who is bold, strong, swift, god-like, and pitiless[66]—displays intense wrath against Penthesileia for daring to fight him (1.611), against Thersites for his foul mouth (1.741–743), against Diomedes for rebuking his killing of Thersites (1.779–780), against the Trojans in general because of Antilochos's death (3.10–31), and against Apollo for trying to stop him as he sets out on another rampage (3.32–52). He is angry up until the moment he dies, fighting fiercely and making dire threats long after Apollo's fatal arrow has wounded him (3.147–179). After his death, in order to complete the process of making his corpse lifelike for his funeral, Athene adorns his face with an angry scowl (3.536–539):

> She made him dewy and as if he were breathing,
> and though dead she gave him a terrible scowl
> such as was on his fearsome face when he lay
> in wrath over his slain companion Patroklos.

> Θῆκε δ᾽ ἄρ᾽ ἐρσήεντα καὶ εἴκελον ἀμπνείοντι·
> σμερδαλέον δ᾽ ἄρ᾽ ἐπισκύνιον νεκρῷ περ ἔτευξεν,
> οἷόν τ᾽ ἀμφ᾽ ἑταροῖο δαικταμένου Πατρόκλοιο
> χωομένῳ ἐπέκειτο κατὰ βλοσυροῖο προσώπου.

The Greeks give Achilles the same offering that Achilles had given Patroklos: human victims slain on the pyre (3.679–680). The gentle Homeric Patroklos may or may not have appreciated the gift; Quintus's scowling corpse undoubtedly does.

2. THE ROMANTIC AND RATIONALISTIC TRADITIONS

Anger and belligerence thus remain Achilles' most prominent characteristics in late antiquity. The poetic atmosphere in which these qualities are expressed, however, bifurcates in the first century A.D. On the one hand, the romantic or miraculous elements that appeared in the Epic Cycle and Pindar now take firm hold of the tradition as it is developed by Statius and Quintus of Smyrna. At the same time, an alternate tradition, begun in the first century A.D. with the "histories" of the supposed Dares and Dictys, attempts to divest the Trojan War story of all miraculous elements, reducing the heroes who fought at Troy to just a little bit better or a little bit worse than ordinary men. In both branches of the tradition Achilles is stripped of his stature as a tragic hero, and often his very nobility is as much in question as it was in Euripides.

Statius's *Achilleid* provides us with a complete account of the fabulous boyhood that Pindar evoked in *Nemean* 3.[67] The Achilles of this advanced romantic tradition never sat in a palace dining hall burping up chopped meat and wine into the lap of a human tutor, as Homer would have us believe (*Iliad* 9.488–491); instead, his earliest baby food was "the entrails of lions and the marrow of half-dead wolves" (*leonum viscera semianimisque lupae . . . medullas, Ach.* 2.99–100) served up in a cave by a Centaur who provided the only nurturing Achilles knew. The reason for this extraordinary situation is that Thetis, as we are told by Apollonios and others, had found intolerable Peleus's interference in her attempt to make Achilles immortal and so had stalked out leaving him to deal with their screaming baby. Peleus immediately turned the baby over to Cheiron.[68]

Achilles' unusual baby food was but the precursor to an even more unusual childhood that Statius has him describe to Diomedes and Odysseus as they sail to Aulis. Achilles relates that he slept on a rock to keep his body tough (2.108–109) and was drilled in running, climbing, tracking, leaping, fighting, hunting lions and other savage beasts, catching rocks on his shield, and hand-to-hand combat (2.102–143). What makes these pursuits extraordinary is the degree to which they were pushed. For example, Cheiron insisted that the twelve-year-old Achilles run faster than galloping horses and hurled spears (2.110–113) and that he be able to seize and stop racing teams of horses (2.142–143). More extraordinary still is the incident in which Cheiron taunted him if he gave ground even a little while standing, as ordered, in a raging torrent that was sweeping away both boulders and trees (2.143–152). His motive for meeting this challenge, which is obviously a forerunner of Skamander's attack in *Iliad* 21, is his traditional desire for glory (*sic me sublimis agebat / gloria,* 2.152–153).

Though Cheiron's rigorous program is clearly designed to develop Achilles' semidivine body into a wondrous instrument of war, Statius does make some attempt to imbue his hero-in-the-making with some of the original Homeric complexity. At the end of Achilles' account of his education, four lines are devoted to medical arts (2.159–162), two to music (2.157–158), and three to philosophy, that is, the study of justice (2.163–165). The latter two curricula, music and justice, are not irrelevant to the poem's themes. Though Achilles' raids on his Centaur neighbors definitely show neglect of the "admonitions of sacred justice" used by the law-giving Cheiron and supposedly fixed in his pupil's heart,[69] still, as we have seen, Achilles wants to fight at Troy with a specifically "just" anger. In fact, the early raids represent a misuse of his military education that is corrected by his going to Troy. A similar misapplication of training is evident when Achilles takes his knowledge of heroic songs, the *virum honores* that translates Homer's *kléa andrôn* (*Iliad* 9.189), and turns them to good use in his seduction of Deidameia. His teaching her to sing and admire his own wonderful deeds (1.572–579) transforms a haunting Homeric scene into a comic portrayal of his squandering his education in the service of love instead of utilizing it, as would be proper, in war.[70]

FIGURE 13. Achilles Plays Lyre for Deidameia

His concern for justice and his skill in music draw Statius's Achilles away from the traditional monolithic fighter exemplified in Horace's dictum but do not give his character a depth that might be plumbed for tragic power. This Achilles does not ask questions about justice, and his singing is not introspective. His complexity is a superficial one, used for moral rather than tragic effect—to gloss his martial activity with righteousness and to help point a lesson in the amorous behavior that impedes it.

The *Achilleid,* which ends before Achilles gets to sack even his first city, remains essentially lighthearted, much like the first stanza of Euripides' Achilles ode.[71] The next major account of Achilles, in Quintus's *Posthomerica,* contains nary a chuckle. It returns Achilles to the rather limited role of brutal warrior and gives him a personality that not only lacks depth but also is devoid of charm. His most unappealing characteristic, conceit, can best be illustrated by juxtaposing with their Homeric sources two boasts Quintus puts in the mouth of his hero. First, the sources: In *Iliad* 1 Achilles calls himself the "best of the Achaians" (*áristos Achaiôn,* 244 and cf. 412) as part of his response to Agamemnon's threat to teach him how much better (i.e., "stronger," *phérteros*) he, Agamemnon, is (184–186). In *Iliad* 18 Achilles reviles himself for being an unequaled fighter and yet not having been a "light of safety" (*pháos*) to Patroklos and the others killed by Hektor (101–106). In both cases his statements that he is the best fighter, though immodest by today's standards, are not so much boasts as statements of fact; they reveal not egoism but self-knowledge. And in the second case this self-knowledge reverberates with tragic intensity throughout the scene of Achilles' discovery that being "best" no longer has any meaning except insofar as it ensures that he will succeed in killing Hektor and thus precipitate his own death. Quintus's Achilles, on the other hand, calls himself "by far the best of heroes" (*méga phértatoi eimen heróōn,* 1.649–650) and a "great light of safety" (*pháos méga*) to the Danaans (1.650), in the context of "laughing aloud" (*epikangchalóōn,* 1.643) at the dying Penthesileia's temerity in having dared, a mere woman, to fight him (1.643–653). His self-evaluation is, of course, as true as it was in the *Iliad,* but here it serves no purpose other than self-aggrandizement.

Aggrandizement, in fact, of self or otherwise, is the key to Quintus's vision of Achilles. In addition to giving Achilles the traditional Homeric similes of wild beasts, forest fires, torrents, and storms, Quintus compares him five times to Titans or giants (1.516–519; 2.205, 518–519, 3.392–398, 724–725). Aside from Achilles' cousin Aias and his semidivine opponent Memnon, who are apparently nearly equal to him in size (see, e.g., 4.457–460), no other fighter receives such a simile.[72] And even Memnon and Aias do not receive them independently but only jointly with Achilles (1.516–519, 2.518–519). Physical size seems to be the quality Quintus means to stress by the comparison: Achilles' corpse, which is likened to that of the Titan Tityos (3.392), is elsewhere called "huge" (*mégas*, 3.410, 419, 672), immense (*apeíriton*, 3.386), and "monstrous" (*pelṓrios*, 3.719), and when Quintus compares the bones left after cremation to those of a giant (3.724–725), it is to emphasize how easily they can be differentiated from those of the human sacrifices who were burnt with him.

The *Iliad*'s only reference to the fact that Achilles is bigger than most men occurs in Achilles' statement to Iris that none of the Achaians, except perhaps Aias, has armor that will fit him (18.192–193), but the idea that Achilles is huge probably antedates Homer. From the emphasis on superhuman strength and speed found in the more romantic versions of Achilles' life we can infer a correspondingly superhuman size, but nowhere is it explicitly mentioned in the extant fragments of the Epic Cycle, the lyric poets, or the tragedians. Theokritos calls him *mégas* (16.74), but the first explicit reference to extraordinary size is Lykophron's calling him "the nine-cubits one" (*tòn einápēchun*, 860). If we were to interpret this literally we would have to envision him at a minimum of twelve and a half feet tall, but since nothing in the *Alexandra* is meant to be taken literally, we may translate with a vague "huge." Catullus does not mention Achilles' size in his account of the hero's bloody career, but Vergil does. Dido's question to Aeneas at *Aeneid* 1.752 (*nunc quantus Achilles*) classes his size among the marvels of the Trojan War saga. Vergil uses the word *magnus* three times to describe Achilles, and Ovid uses it eight times, but this word, which like its most obvious English equivalent "great" can mean either "large" or "impressive," only once is used clearly to stress physical size: at *Metamorphoses* 12.615 Ovid contrasts the former *magnus* Achilles with the little, *parvus*, pile of ashes that remains after cremation.[73] The late-classical mythographers do not seem much interested in Achilles' physical size. The account of Achilles given by Apollodorus (*Epitome* 3.14–5.5) nowhere even hints at Achilles' size, and

Hyginus's *Fabulae* neither mentions it in the stories about Achilles nor lists him in the category *Qui amplissimi fuerunt* (*Fab.* 269)—though it should be noted that there is a lacuna in this category.[74] In the *Achilleid*, however, size is important. Statius, as O. A. W. Dilke says, "employs every artifice. . . , in a grandiose manner reminiscent of baroque art, to make him appear greater in size, impressiveness and character."[75] Achilles is *magnanimum* ("great-souled") in the very first word of the poem, has a *magna*, "natural capacity" (*indoles*, 1.276−277), and is elsewhere generally *magnus* (1.19, 513; 2.83). Physical size is definitely meant to be part of this impressiveness, for he is described as having *magna* arms (1.604) and an "enormous stride" (*immanis gradu*, 1.883).

Quintus, then, has authority for stressing Achilles' huge stature. But he moves far beyond Statian grandiosity when he compares Achilles to Titans, for in addition to emphasizing a giant bulk such comparisons associate Achilles with classic Titanic aggression and shift the context of his fighting away from notions of justice and closer to a philosophy of "might makes right." Of the five Titan similes, two extended ones in particular create this effect. In Book One, Achilles and Aias are compared to the raging (*memaôte*, 519) Otos and Ephialtes when they attempted to reach Olympus by piling three mountains on top of each other (1.516−519). Interestingly enough, these two giants, who were only nine years old when they undertook this feat,[76] were, according to tradition, killed by Apollo before they could grow any more and succeed. Apollo is the traditional slayer of Achilles too,[77] and in Quintus's version Apollo attacks only when Achilles arrogantly defies the Olympian by threatening to strike him if he does not get out of his way (3.37−62).[78] In retrospect, then, the simile comparing Achilles to the giant children who tried to storm Olympus is prophetic of Achilles' death.

Ideas of arrogant earthling defiance and Olympian retribution, which are only implicit in this earlier simile, become explicit in the second extended simile, which likens Achilles' dead body to that of the Titan Tityos (3.391−401):

> He lay by the shore of the deep-thudding sea,
> just as arrogant (*hyperphíalos*) Tityos fell, when he
> assaulted Leto as she travelled to Pytho, and, weariless though he

was, a wrathful Apollo quickly subdued him
with swift arrows; in grievous gore he
lay stretched for hundreds of feet (*poulupélethros*) along the wide-
surfaced earth,
his mother. And she lamented round her fallen son
who was hated by the blessed gods, but revered Leto laughed.
So the son of Peleus fell upon the land of his enemies
bringing delight to Trojans but endless grief to
the host of lamenting Achaians.

κεῖτο βαρυγδούποιο παρ' ἠόσιν Ἑλλησπόντου,
οἷος ὑπερφίαλος Τιτυὸς πέσεν, ὁππότε Λητὼ
ἐρχομένην Πυθῶδε βιάζετο, καὶ ἑ χολωθεὶς
ἀκάματόν περ ἐόντα θοῶς ὑπερδάμνατ' Ἀπόλλων
λαιψηροῖς βελέεσσιν, ὁ δ' ἀργαλέῳ ἐνὶ λύθρῳ
πουλυπέλεθρος ἔκειτο κατὰ χθονὸς εὐρυπέδοιο
μητρὸς ἑῆς· ἡ δ' υἷα περιστονάχησε πεσόντα
ἐχθόμενον μακάρεσσι, γέλασσε δὲ πότνια Λητώ·
τοῖος ἄρ' Ἀιακίδης δηίων ἐπικάππεσε γαίῃ
χάρμα φέρων Τρώεσσι, γόον δ' ἀλίαστον Ἀχαιῶν
λαῷ μυρομένων.

The point of this comparison is that just as huge Tityos's death brings
grief to his mother but joy to Leto, so huge Achilles' death brings joy to
the Trojans but grief to the Achaians. But the total effect of the simile
goes beyond this explicit analogy; the close correspondences between
the end of Achilles' life and the end of Tityos's—defiance of Olympians,
death from Apollo, responses of grief and gladness—forge a link between would-be rapist and would-be city-sacker that extends to the level
of character.

The repeated similes of giants in conjunction with Quintus's particular
version of Achilles' death have the ultimate effect of merging Achilles'
character with that of Kapaneus, the archetypal god-defying Greek hero
who is the model for Vergil's Mezentius. Kapaneus is described by
Aischylos as a giant (*gígas*) whose vaunts intend what is more than human[79] and who promises to sack Thebes whether the gods are willing or
not (*Seven* 424–428). Euripides describes him as loving war as much as
Ares does (*Phoinissai* 1128), gives him a shield whose emblem is a giant
carrying an uprooted city on his back (*Ph.* 1130–1132), and has him
boast that not even the lightning bolt of Zeus will stop him from de-

stroying the city (*Ph.* 1174–1176); just a few lines later, Zeus's lightning bolt burns him up (1180–1186). Statius's later depiction of Kapaneus in the *Thebaid* is unforgettable. The hero is again huge (4.165–166), so huge that his spear is a whole cypress tree stripped of its leaves and tipped with iron (4.176–177), and a giant adorns his helmet (4.175–176). He loves war, hates peace, despises the gods, is impatient of justice (3.598–603). As he pounds on Amphiaraus's door to force the reluctant priest to announce the omens for war, he is compared to a Cyclops (3.605). At one point during the fighting he gleefully kills an unarmed priest who is calling for peace (7.675–683), thus revealing in addition to his disrespect for priests a complete lack of concern for honor. While he climbs the Theban battlement, he is compared to the same Otos and Ephialtes (10.849–852) to whom Quintus will later compare Achilles. When he is at the top of the tower and gets bored with pulling it apart with his bare hands, he challenges first Bacchus and Hercules and then Jupiter himself (10.870–906). Jupiter obliges with a lightning storm and a thunderbolt that fries Kapaneus within his armor (10.913–939).

What links Quintus's Achilles with the tradition's Kapaneus is, of course, the giant size, which is assigned to Kapaneus by all poets, the association with pugnacious giants, which in Kapaneus's case is created by armorial emblems as well as similes, and the divine defiance that leads to their deaths. The two characters differ in their explicit motivations for fighting—for Kapaneus an outright love of war for its own sake, for Achilles glory or revenge—and in their attitude toward the gods: Kapaneus is contemptuous of all the gods, whereas Achilles shows contempt only for the specific god who tries to block his revenge. But the near fusion of the two characters in many passages of the *Posthomerica* makes possible a more general fusion that comprehends these differences and creates an Achillean subtype in which physical size and violent energy are the outstanding characteristics, revenge and glory are but aspects of the sheer love of war, and the hero's relationship to justice and the gods is either negative or of minimal concern. This subtype, which in no way contradicts Horace's dictum, will reemerge in a twelfth-century epic by Joseph of Exeter and in the sixteenth century will provide the model for Tasso's pagan hero Argante.

As we have seen, Quintus's Achilles is predominantly a man of enormous violence. His outstanding characteristic is his battle strength, and Quintus says that what causes the Achaians to grieve for him so heavily is their expectation that now they will all be killed by the Trojans (3.402–419). A few lines after this, however, Quintus makes the Myrmidons eulogize Achilles as "gentle" (*épios*) and a friend to all, as being "neither overbearing (*hyperphíalos*) nor malevolent, but preeminent in self-control (*saophrosúnēi*) and in strength (*kártei*) (3.424–426). These lines, which appear to be based on various characterizations of the dead Patroklos in the *Iliad*,[80] perhaps represent a nod to Achilles' Homeric complexity. So too, perhaps, does the captive women's lament, which praises Achilles as "kindly" (*eúphrōn*) and testifies that he treated them well despite the fact that their fathers were his enemies (3.549–551). But since gentleness and self-control are nowhere in evidence in the *Posthomerica*'s living Achilles, these passages contribute little toward recreating the complexity he had in the *Iliad*.

The same dual quality again appears when, on the night before the Greeks are to leave Troy, Achilles appears to Neoptolemos in a dream to give him some final advice and make one final request. The advice consists of a lecture on how valor must be coupled with virtue and on the importance of maintaining a dispassionate calm throughout the vicissitudes of life (14.189–203).[81] The request, however, exemplifies the very opposite of the advised Stoicism: Achilles "craves" (*eéldomai*, 14.213) Polyxena as his share of the spoils and threatens that if she is not quickly sacrificed on his tomb he will be even angrier at the Greeks than he was over Briseis (14.213–216).[82] This abrasive juxtaposition of Stoic philosophy and murderous passion adds no depth to Achilles' character but rather creates a character that has two halves but no whole, one that is more confusing than complex.

The tradition I have been tracing through Ovid, Statius, and Quintus, however it may vary in details and attitude, continues to portray Achilles as a superhero. Ovid may keep his tongue in his cheek, Statius incline to lighthearted moralizing, and Quintus veer between stoicism and bombast, but they all at least pretend to take the early epic tradition seriously and to start from the assumption that an heroically principled way of life—whether or not they approve of the principle—is exemplified in the stories of the battle for Troy. But not everyone was disposed to make this assumption. Horace, for example, the very creator of the dictum about Achilles that was to absorb and create character traits for centuries, had early made a frontal attack on the idea that the action of the *Iliad* revolved around any principles at all. In a verse epistle written in approximately 20 B.C.,[83] Horace declares that Homer is well worth reading, for his epics tell more clearly than some philosophers "what is lovely [*pulchrum*], what ugly [*turpe*], what useful, what not" (*Epit.* 1.2.1–4).[84] The *Iliad*, alas, is limited to teaching us what is *turpe*. As Horace puts it (*Epit.* 1.2.6–16):

> The story that tells of the Greeks' long war with
> the barbarians on account of Paris's love
> contains the passion of fatuous kings and commoners.
> Antenor proposes to cut off the cause of the war:
> What does Paris do? He denies that he can be forced
> to reign in safety and be happy. Nestor hastens to
> compose the quarrel between Achilles and Agamemnon;
> love burns the latter, a common anger burns each.
> The kings' derangements entangle the Argives.
> Sins of sedition, deceit, crime, as well as lust and anger,
> occur within the walls of Troy and without.

> Fabula, qua Paridis propter narratur amorem
> Graecia barbariae lento collisa duello,
> stultorum regum et populorum continet aestus.
> Antenor censet belli praecidere causam:
> quid Paris? Ut salvus regnet vivatque beatus
> cogi posse negat. Nestor componere litis
> inter Peliden festinat et inter Atriden;
> hunc amor, ira quidem communiter urit utrumque.
> Quidquid delirant reges, plectuntur Achivi.
> Seditione, dolis, scelere, atque libidine et ira,
> Iliacos intra muros peccatur et extra.

Though "sedition," "deceit," and "crime" may seem to apply more to the sins within the walls, and "lust" and "anger" to those without, Horace has made no clear distinction, and the reader is left with an impression of ubiquitous folly and treachery.

Two Greek-speaking writers of the first century A.D. seem to have concurred in Horace's judgment, but from different angles: one agreeing with his evaluation of what happened at Troy, the other only with his evaluation of what happens in the *Iliad*. They each decided that Homer and the heroic tradition needed correcting, and each wrote— possibly one in response to the other—what was supposed to be the "true" version of the Trojan War. We do not know who these writers were, for they did not acknowledge the works as their own but feigned them to have been written by actual participants in the legendary war, in the one case by Dictys of Crete, a follower of Idomeneus, and in the other by Dares, a follower of the Trojan Antenor.[85] This pretended authorship, which was taken seriously throughout the Middle Ages and Renaissance, gave the forgeries an authority that was equal or superior to that of Homer, for, as the letter appended to the Latin translation of Dares says, the translation was done "so that readers may know how the events happened: either they may judge to be truer what Dares the Phrygian committed to memory, he who lived and was a soldier during the time the Greeks besieged Troy, or they may decide that Homer is to be believed, he who was born many years after this war was waged."[86] Dictys' *Ephemeris Belli Troiani* (*Journal of the Trojan War*) was freely translated into Latin in the fourth century,[87] and Dares' *De Excidio Troiae Historia* (*History of the Fall of Troy*) was expanded and translated into Latin in the sixth century.[88] With the exception of one fragment of Dictys, the works exist only in these Latin versions, which together form the basis for a strong alternate tradition concerning the Trojan War and Achilles' part in it.

Within this alternate tradition, Dictys' *Journal,* though longer and better written, was less influential in the West than Dares' *History.*[89] The reason for this is, I think, that Dictys' anti-aristocratic bias makes sure that none of the traditional heroes, except perhaps Agamemnon, survives as such.[90] Although purportedly written by a Greek, its narrative does not redound to the glory of Greece.[91] If members of the Trojan royal family are shown to be faithless, greedy, lustful, and murderous in starting the war, the Greeks are shown to be utterly unprincipled in negotiating the false treaty that ends it with a complete sack of the city.[92]

Achilles does not participate in this last bit of treachery but only because he is dead. At the start of the narrative, his character is traditional: his bravery is stressed, and, in keeping with the Horatian dictum, we are told of "a certain thoughtless vehemence and ferocious impatience with customary modes of action" (1.14).[93] As the narrative proceeds, Achilles' "thoughtless vehemence" becomes progressively more shameful as he takes on the ends-justify-means mentality that infects everyone in the narrative. His two greatest traditional exploits, the slayings of Hektor and Memnon, are stripped of any heroic value: he ambushes Hektor at night while he is off guard crossing a river (3.15),[94] and he kills Memnon after the hero is already badly wounded by Aias (4.6). When he is angry at Agamemnon and the army for the loss of Hippodamia (Dictys' equivalent of Briseis), he does not simply brood in his tent but actually sneaks up to attack the Greeks while they are at dinner (2.37).[95] In addition, though Diomedes' behavior toward the dying Penthesileia must win that hero the story's first prize for cruelty,[96] Achilles' brutality in the *Journal* far exceeds any in the *Iliad*. Not only does he sacrifice fifty-two captives to Patroklos's spirit (versus the *Iliad*'s twelve) and ceremoniously slit the captive Troilos's throat in order to hurt Priam (3.14, 4.9), he also severs the hands of the single survivor of the ambush of Hektor before sending him back to Troy to report the news (3.15).

The Trojan Dares, on the other hand, makes the noble heroes of both sides even more noble than in the tradition. The war begins with both sides feeling that they are truly fighting for justice, and though it ends in a Trojan betrayal of the city, that betrayal is committed only because Antenor and Aeneas[97] are desperate in the face of Priam's intransigence. Hekabe, Kassandra, and Andromache and her two children are all set free after the capture, and the sole act of brutality is the sacrifice of Polyxena that will enable the ships to sail.[98] Agamemnon has become a paragon of forbearance, even to the extent of peacefully yielding his command to Palamedes at one point (25). There is no contest for the arms of Achilles; instead, Aias is offered Achilles' command and refuses it in favor of Neoptolemos, who is not yet even present (35).

Achilles' character and deeds are also improved by this positive atmosphere. In the Epic Cycle Achilles had wounded a hero named Telephos in the course of destroying Mysia, a city that he mistakenly thought was Troy. Some time later, back in Argos, Achilles himself cured the wound upon the promise that Telephos would guide the Greeks to the real Troy.[99] In Dares' account Achilles does not wound Telephos at all; instead, Telephos is his companion in arms and becomes king of Mysia through Achilles' exploits (16). Patroklos's death occurs on the second day after landing in Troy and provokes no monumental wrath; Achilles' mourning is described in one half sentence, the funeral games in one sentence (20). Achilles kills Hektor during a fierce general battle not to wreak vengeance but to prevent his slaughtering increasing numbers of Greeks; their fight is long and heroic, and Hektor wounds Achilles (24). Troilos is not the pretty youth, *infelix puer atque impar congressus*

Achilli,[100] that he is in every other account; he is a fierce warrior who fully supplies the place of the dead Hektor and manages to wound Achilles severely before he is killed (32–33).[101] The first battle between Memnon and Achilles ends in a draw; in the second Memnon wounds Achilles in a long and hard struggle before he is killed (33). Achilles' fierce temper is nowhere evident. His withdrawal from the fighting is caused not by a quarrel with Agamemnon but by his love for Polyxena (27–30);[102] during this withdrawal he yields to Agamemnon's prayers to send his Myrmidons, and then later he himself enters the fight to save the Greeks from Troilos (31–33). The two character traits among the hodgepodge of physical characteristics that compose Achilles' catalogue portrait fit what we see in his actions: Achilles is both *clemens,* "gentle" and *in armis acerrimum,* "most violent in battle" (13).[103]

Both Dares and Dictys portray Achilles' actions, whether cruel or kind, as totally human. He is neither a protégé nor an antagonist of gods, whose divine presence is felt only through the knowledge they reveal to their priests, never through interference in human action. Dictys, who is particularly concerned to rid his universe of the supernatural, even takes pains to point out that Achilles' mother is really an ordinary woman, daughter of a man named Cheiron. Dictys' explanation of why she was thought to be a goddess is ingenious: during her wedding banquet the many kings who attended

> had celebrated the bride with magnificent praises as if she were a goddess, calling her father Cheiron Nereus and herself a Nereid. And whenever one of these kings at the banquet had distinguished himself in dancing or singing, they had called him Apollo or Bacchus and they had called many of the women Muses. Whence to this day that banquet is termed a banquet of the gods (6.7).[104]

> multi undique reges acciti domum Chironis inter ipsas epulas novam nuptam magnis laudibus veluti deam celebraverant, parentem eius Chirona appellantes Nerea ipsamque Nereidam: et ut quisque eorum regum, qui convivio interfuerant, choro modulisque carminum praevaluerat, ita Apollinem Liberumque, ex feminis plurimas Musas cognominaverant: unde ad id tempus convivium illud deorum appellatum (Meister, 107).

With divine protection and parentage both eliminated, the invulnerability that Achilles' body has shown heretofore—whether because of divine armor, superhuman prowess, or a bath in the Styx—is also gone:

in both accounts he is wounded, once in Dictys (3.6) and three times in Dares (24, 33). He is clearly still the best Greek warrior,[105] but he has lost the Homeric fire that blazed among the stars at the same time as it scorched the earth.

3. THE *ILIAS LATINA*

We will be less surprised at the authority these new texts gained over Homer when we remember that after Byzantium and Rome drifted completely apart in the sixth century, knowledge of the Greek language declined in the West to such a point that almost no one could read the *Iliad* or the *Odyssey* in the original.[106] The "Greekless" reader had only the uninspired summary offered by the 1070 Latin hexameters of the *Ilias Latina,* itself created during the reign of Nero.[107] Though the gross plot of the poem follows Homer's, the details (or lack thereof) manage to strip the work and its hero of all tragic resonance. The result is an Achilles who may be as *magnus* as Statius's[108] but who is as pedestrian as Dares' and Dictys'. Two examples will suffice. First, though the poem devotes nearly one hundred verses to *Iliad* 3—Paris's duel with Menelaos and his bedchamber conversation with Helen (252–343)— *Iliad* 9 gets a grand total of ten verses, only five and a half of which are devoted to the embassy and none of which suggests a reason for Achilles' refusal of the Greek offer (686–695). Second, the return of Hektor's body in *Iliad* 24 is accomplished without the moving reconciliation between Achilles and Priam, and its entire philosophical content is encapsulated in Priam's "You have conquered Priam. Do you the victor remember the lot / of mortals and consider the changing fortunes of princes" (1041–1042) (*Vicisti Priamum: sortis reminiscere victor / Humanae variosque ducum tu respice casus*).

The *Ilias Latina* in combination with Vergil, Ovid, and Statius managed to inspire a number of Medieval Latin poems on the Trojan War. The most interesting of these in regard to Achilles are two short eleventh-century works, one written in France and the other in Italy, that focus on the battle in which he kills Hektor. In addition to carrying forward the standard Achillean characteristics of wrath and battle fierceness, both of these poems, Godfrey of Rheims's "Hektor and Achilles"[109] and an anonymous Roman's "Lament for Hektor,"[110] complicate the tradition further by their use of Vergilian motifs.

Godfrey recreates the events of *Iliad* 15–22 (*Ilias Latina* 790–946) in a third and apparently final *ekphrasis* (following a prewar biography of "Paris" and a description of "The Destruction of Troy") that describes pictures embroidered on the gown of Kalliope, Muse of epic poetry. He begins by portraying a Hektor who is the equal in battle of Minerva, Mars, and the giants who attacked Jupiter (441–449) and who is, as in the *Ilias Latina*, the sole stay of Troy (*solo securi fiunt hoc milite muri*, 451; compare *I.L.* 931–932). We see him "bound out of the city, rage, set the ships and sails aflame" (*exilit urbe, furit, naves et vela perurit*, 453), and return to the city "dressed in the spoils of terrible Achilles" (*intrat terribilis spoliis indutus Achillis*, 455). As Boutemy points out,[111] Hektor's wearing these spoils must refer to his having killed Patroklos. The time scheme gets somewhat confused at this point, just as it did earlier when Godfrey made Hektor's bounding out of the city dependent upon his ignoring "the prayers of his wretched father and mother" (*Non miseri patris flexus prece, nec prece matris*, 452), an act that is supposed to happen later when he is awaiting Achilles' onslaught *after* firing the ships and killing Patroklos (compare *I.L.* 933, 944). Although now, in verse 455, he has supposedly entered the city, the next couplet describes his devastating effect on the Greeks he encounters in battle (456–457):

> Where he turns his horse, he makes Greeks disappear,
> and all but those who hide in the ships fall dead.

> Qua detorquet equos facit evanescere Grecos
> Exanimesque cadunt, nisi qui se navibus abdunt.

These verses provide a transition to Achilles' entering the fray (458–459):

> Hektor would have routed the whole camp of Pelasgian men
> had not renowned Achilles seen their easy slaughter.

> Tota Pelasgorum pepulisset castra virorum
> ne vinci faciles clarus tueretur Achilles.

Once in battle, Achilles exhibits the passionate belligerence and prowess familiar from the Homeric tradition: he is "mad with fury" (*rabies*, 460) as he rampages over the field killing and wounding (460–463); his horses' hooves trample the bodies of one hundred thousand men who fall beneath his onslaught (464–465); and when he reaches the closed city walls he "seethes and is all inflamed with amazing anger" (*Estuat et mira totus succenditur ira,* 470).

The object of his anger is not Hektor but all the Trojans who by hiding behind their walls have "halted his fighting" and created "peace" (*quod male pugnatur, quod res in pace geratur,* 471). This emphasis on his desire for war per se seems to be the reason for skewing the Iliadic time sequence and putting Hektor behind rather than in front of the walls when Achilles arrives. Hektor's absence also produces a situation in which Godfrey can make Achilles act like Turnus's foolishly mistaken *macho* brother-in-law, who in *Aeneid* 9 insulted Aeneas's walled-in men with accusations of slothful hearts and love of dancing (*desidiae cordi, iuvat indulgere choreis,* 9.615), effeminacy in dress and behavior (9.616–619), and unfitness for arms: "yield arms to men and give up the sword" (*sinite arma viris et cedite ferro,* 9.620). Achilles' goading of the Trojans to come out and fight him is similar in tone and message (474–481):

> You cowards!—I hadn't thought you such—
> why are a thousand men afraid of the lone Achilles?
> Why so sluggish? Why do you, a multitude, fear a single man?
> O Phrygian nation! What chilly hearts you have!
> O folk fit for women's dances!
> O spineless people, men devoted to Venus!
> Certainly neither shield nor horse nor any kind of arms suits you!
> Bequeath them all to us!

> O ignaui, quod uos non esse putaui,
> Cur homines mille solo terrentur Achille?
> Cur ita torpetis? Hominem cur turba timetis?
> O Phrygie gentes! O frigida corda gerentes!
> O modo femineis plebs opportuna choreis!
> O populus lentus, Veneri deuota iuuentus!
> Certe nec parma, nec equus, nec quelibet arma
> Conueniunt uobis! Ea cuncta relinquite nobis.

For the educated reader who would recognize its Vergilian original, this speech colors Achilles' simple bellicosity with the hot-headed opposition to the Roman empire with which Vergil himself had insistently associated Homer's passionate Achilles. It creates, that is, an implied moral differentiation between the Greek and Trojan champions that is absent from the *Ilias Latina*. Unfortunately, the poem ends abruptly (and obviously incompletely)[112] at this point, so we do not know how Godfrey may also have colored Achilles' victory over his powerful and morally superior rival.

The anonymous "Lament for Hektor" does include this victory and gives it its own very different Vergilian coloring. The lament's twenty-four couplets, each punctuated by the refrain "Alas, terribly we yearn for you" (*Heu, male te cupimus*), begin with a dramatization of "conquering" (*victor*) Hektor's decision to confront "wrathful" (*indignatus*) Achilles and end with Achilles delivering the death blow as Hektor pleads for his life. Andromache's opening plea that he not face the semi-divine Greek, which revitalizes the *Ilias Latina*'s vague "paternal prayers" (*patriae preces*),[113] incorporates details from Statius's *Achilleid:* the rearing by a "Hippocentaur" (16), the capturing of lions (20), and the skin that is harder than iron (*cutis eius sic est dura, quod nec ferrum ibi durat,* 21–22).[114] Hektor's proud response, which states simply that he will fight and kill Achilles just as he previously fought and killed Patroklos in Achilles' armor (25–28), recapitulates material from the *Ilias Latina*. The ten couplets that describe their duel, however, draw on Vergil to alter significantly the tradition of Hektor's final heroic moments.

As in the *Ilias Latina* (951, 956–963) the initial confrontation takes place with spears ("Lament" 33–36):

> After they had come together
> joining weapons, they fought together.
> Alas, terribly we yearn for you!
> Hektor's spear broke in pieces;
> but, he said to the other: "Stand by!"

> Postquam se iunxerunt ambo
> Mixtis telis, pugnant ambo.
> Heu, male te cupimus!
> Hectori fracta fit hasta;
> Illi tamen dixit: "Asta."

The second, somewhat enigmatic, couplet, which may presuppose knowledge of Athene's deception (*I.L.* 947–950, 968–970), changes the mere failure of Hektor's spear to pierce Achilles' divine armor (*I.L.* 962–963) to a breaking (*fracta fit*) reminiscent of Turnus's shattered sword in the final battle of the *Aeneid* (12.731–732). Reminiscence of

Turnus's battle with Aeneas continues after Achilles' weapon meets with more success (39–48):

> When he perceived he was going to die,
> Hektor began to plead.
> > Alas, terribly we yearn for you!
> "O Achilles, keep clear of crime,
> grant my life to wretched me."
> > Alas, terribly we yearn for you!
> "Through me you have conquered my country
> and subjected my kin."
> > Alas, terribly we yearn for you!
> "My aged father entreats through me,
> Andromache implores you."
> > Alas, terribly we yearn for you!
> While Hektor was speaking thus,
> Achilles killed him.
> > Alas, terribly we yearn for you!

> Ubi se sentit necari
> coepit Hector deprecari.
> > Heu, male te cupimus!
> O Achille[s] scelus vita;
> mihi misero da vita[m].
> > Heu, male te cupimus!
> Per me patriam vicisti
> et parentes subiecisti.
> > Heu, male te cupimus!
> Senex pater per me plorat,
> te Andromache implorat.
> > Heu, male te cupimus!
> Talia dum Hector dicit,
> Eum Achilles occidit.
> > Heu, male te cupimus!

Hektor's pleading for his life instead of just for the return of his body, as was the case in the *Iliad* and the *Ilias Latina,* weakens the auditor's sense of his fortitude and nobility at the same time as it increases the impression of Achilles' cruelty at rejecting the suppliant. Simultaneously, when coupled with Hektor's statement that Achilles has conquered Troy by conquering him, it intensifies an identification between Hektor and

Vergil's Turnus, who also pleaded for his life and who considered the stakes of his duel with Aeneas to be conclusive victory in the war (compare 41–46 with *Aeneid* 12.934–938 and 13–17). This identification, which of course also makes the listener identify Achilles with Vergil's Aeneas, cleverly reworks an identification originally created by Vergil's own allusions to Book Twenty-Two of the *Iliad*.[115] In the *Aeneid* this identification created a complexity subversive of the epic's overt glorification of Augustus. In the medieval "Lament" it produces a similarly ambiguous message for the citizens of Rome: on the one hand, warm sympathy for the doomed human weakness and folly of Hektor ("weep his death, O reader," *mortem defle, lector,* 32) that is now linked with civilization (Troy, family) as well as with opposition to the Roman empire (Turnus); on the other hand, cold awe for the superhuman and destructive power of Achilles that is now aligned with the divinely guided founding of that empire. The one thing that is entirely unambiguous in the "Lament" is Achilles' clear martial superiority to Hektor, a superiority that remains unchallenged in the few poems that have survived from this branch of the medieval Trojan War tradition.

Other extant poems in this tradition add little to Achilles' character. Odo of Orleans (eleventh century) wrote a poem of several hundred verses, but the twenty-five line summary that is left to us[116] mentions Achilles only to say that he rose up *ferus* in behalf of the Greeks and that his counterpart on the Trojan side was *martius* Hektor.[117] That Hektor and Achilles are the only warriors singled out for mention by the summarizer indicates the "Iliadic" nature of Odo's work as opposed to the more diffuse heroics of Dares and Dictys. A short work (*Viribus, arte, minis . . .*)[118] by Pierre de Saintes (mid-twelfth century), a poet whose model is explicitly Homer,)[119] again concentrates on Achilles and Hektor, Hektor as the mainstay of Troy and Achilles as his killer (43–46).[120] This poem contains no epithets by which we might judge Achilles' character, but it does classify him once again as the preeminent warrior of the Homeric tradition (41–42): "Nestor by means of wisdom, Athene by means of divine command, Achilles by means of his sword, delivered Phrygians to destruction" (*Nestor consilio, nutu Tritonia dio, / Pelides gladio, dant Phryges exitio*).[121] This couplet is especially interesting as the first medieval statement of Achilles' role in the divinely sanctioned yoking of brain and brawn that issues in Tasso's beloved Christian allegory of head, hand, and body politic.

Simon Capra Aurea (or "Chevre d'Or," late twelfth century), who is
the fifth Medieval Latin poet in this tradition to mention Achilles,[122] dis-
solves Pierre's conjunction and reverts to the post-Homeric dichotomy
between brain and brawn. In the first, shorter version of his *Iliad*[123] he
makes a terse comparison between two sets of Greek princes (137–142):

> In the Greek camp, Palamedes, Nestor and Odysseus
>   Are leaders more in strategy [*consilium*] than in honesty
> Achilles, Aias, Diomedes, Pyrrhus, Agamemnon:
>   Here the flower, the light, the apex of piety (*pietas*).

> In castris Danaum, Palimedes, Nestor, Ulysses
>   Plus sunt consilio, quam probate, duces.
> Aeacides, Ajax, Diomedes, Pyrrhus, Atrides:
>   Hic flos, hic lumen, hic pietatis apex.[124]

Perhaps because Agamemnon's inclusion in a category labelled "pious"
might have seemed contradictory in the later, expanded version, which
describes the king as *reus*, "criminal" in repeating the *crimen* of Paris by
taking Briseis,[125] Simon there changes the second line of the second
couplet to read, "These men are the *virtus* of the Greeks, the dread of
the Trojans."[126] He thus allows the category to include both physical
and moral excellence, but this change does not affect the basic dichotomy. *Pietas* and/or *virtus* are assigned to the great killers, *consilium* and a
lack of honesty to the great strategists. The opposition inherent in the
groupings revives the fifth-century Athenian categorization of Achilles as
the honest doer of deeds, Odysseus as the deceitful wielder of words.[127]

Since Simon views Hektor as the sole safety of Troy (268), its hope,
its shield, its life force (*spes, clipeus, vigor,* 274), Achilles the conqueror of
Hektor is thereby, as in Homer and Vergil, the ultimate conqueror of
the city itself.[128] Hektor's greatness serves in the end only to measure
Achilles': "If you ask the courage, the strength, the battles of Achilles,"
says Simon, "a few words will suffice: he was greater than Hektor."[129]
Simon does not in his final version limit himself to these few words. His
praise of the hero is emphatic: Achilles is the "supreme warrior" (*miles
summus,* 215), a "prince of princes" (*dux ducum,* 210).

More exciting than any of these brief Latin poems is a 1712-verse
Spanish vernacular redaction of the *Ilias Latina* written in the early thir-
teenth century as part of a larger poem (10,700 verses) on Alexander the
Great.[130] Drawing on Alexander's traditional fascination with Achilles,[131]

the poet of the *Libro de Alexandre* expands the Macedonian hero's envy of Achilles' good fortune in having an incomparable poet like Homer around to record his deeds (Cicero *Pro Archia* 24) into a long digression that recounts the history of the Trojan War from the Apple of Discord to the Stratagem of the Horse. As Ian Michael has shown, the Trojan War digression plays an integral artistic part in the larger poem both as an *exemplum* of the worth of fame and as a standard by which Alexander's achievements can be judged and which they can be seen to surpass.[132] A close look at how the poet altered the *Ilias Latina* to make Achilles function more precisely as an exemplar for his Alexander proves beyond any remaining doubt that the redaction was created by the poet of the whole work.

On a first reading of the poem, it would appear that the poet's main concern was to exalt fame as a motivation to action,[133] for the importance of acquiring fame functions throughout the poem as Alexander's guiding principle, starting with the exhortations of his tutor Aristotle and continuing until his death at the hand of the jealous Antipater. But on a more careful reading, as Michael has demonstrated, it becomes clearer that Alexander, who is portrayed as the perfect medieval king in order to make the moral lesson clearer,[134] is so obsessed with the desire for fame that he succumbs to the sin of pride and is therefore punished by God with early death.[135] The main concern of this medieval poet is clearly a religious one, and the force that shaped his reworking of the two stories he inherited and combined is his Christian wariness of all things of this world, be they ephemeral material possessions or eternal fame.[136]

The key to Alexander's obsession with fame is Homer's account of the deeds done at Troy. Alexander is taught to desire fame by his tutor Aristotle, who uses Hektor, Diomedes, and Achilles as exemplars of the value of fighting courageously to gain a *preçio* that will endure forever in books (*en escriptura,* stt. 70–71)[137] and who then urges his pupil to attack Darius to win his own lasting *preçio* (st. 85). Alexander's telling the story of Troy to his tired men upon their arrival at the tomb of Achilles in Asia is an expanded version of Aristotle's exhortation, a full illustration of the fact that good deeds do ensure one's immortal survival (stt. 328, 764–765). When, after conquering Darius, Alexander wishes to set out on a more difficult enterprise to conquer the realms of the air and

sea, he compares himself to Achilles in order to justify his seeming reck-
lessness (st. 2288):

> I do not reckon my life by years and days,
> but by good accomplishments and by feats of arms;
> Homer did not record in his stories
> the months of Achilles, but his heroic exploits.

> Non conto yo mi vida por años nin por días,
> mas por buenas faziendas e por cavallerías;
> non escrivió Homero en sus alegorías
> los meses de Aquiles, mas sus barraganías.

Thus, Troy in general and Achilles in particular function as the heroic
exemplars for all action throughout the poem.

But Alexander's relationship with the heroes of the Troy Story is one
more of rivalry than of emulation. He does not want to survive in books
merely as good; he wants for himself and his army a *preçio* that is best: as
he says when he finishes telling them the story, if his men will keep their
wills intent on *preçio* they will surpass even the deeds of Troy, winning
fame so great that they will consider as small what men accomplished
there (stt. 769–770). When Alexander has completed his military conquest of the world, he feels that this goal has indeed been accomplished:
he tells his men that they have "darkened the story of Troy, honored
yourselves, achieved our glory."

> la hestoria troyana con esto la çegastes,
> honrastes a vos mismos, nuestro preçio alçastes (st. 2286cd).

The poet later makes it clear that this precise achievement, surpassing
the glory of Troy, has been the goal of Alexander's life. When Alexander
sees the scenes of Troy painted on his tent (stt. 2571–2574) he is inspired
and exclaims that he would rather die than not have surpassed them (*si
non se mejorasse, morir se dexarié*, st. 2575d). Clearly, by surpassing the
deeds at Troy Alexander has surpassed all, for it is a given in this poem
that the conquest of Troy represents the supreme achievement of human
history.

In the Homeric tradition that the *Alexandre* poet has chosen to follow Achilles is the supreme hero of this supreme achievement. It is he,
therefore, who inspires Alexander's actions and, indirectly, his physical

and spiritual death. This linkage between the two is emphasized by the alterations the poet made in the *Ilias,* alterations that create a more subtle interdependence of main story and digression than even Michael has suggested. Because of these changes, the *Alexandre's* Achilles provides more than just a standard to be surpassed; he demonstrates the same flaw as Alexander, an overweening pride that Alexander surpasses to the same degree that he surpasses Achilles' achievement.

The poet begins his account of Achilles' career with an incident taken from the *Excidium Trojae,* a prophecy given to the Greeks that "Achilles would be the one to conquer Hektor / and therefore would have to be present / or the Greeks could not take Troy" (st. 409bcd):

> . . . Aquiles havrié a Héctor a vençer,
> en cabo él havrié y a remaneçer,
> ca a menos de tanto non la podrién prender.

This prophecy, which makes explicit what in Statius was only implicit, that Achilles is divinely appointed to be the killer of Hektor and thus absolutely necessary to the taking of Troy,[138] is followed by another example of foreordination, his sorceress mother's knowledge that Achilles must die at Troy (st. 410), and by a description of her making him invulnerable to iron and hiding him among some nuns in a convent (st. 411). Next follows his discovery by Odysseus's trick and his joining the Greeks at Aulis (stt. 412–416). Then begins the retelling of the *Ilias Latina.*

The poet concentrates on Achilles' feelings of insult and betrayal when Agamemnon takes the woman he loves. The incident, which takes place while the Greeks are still at Aulis, is described as follows (stt. 417–418):

> He had a woman whom he very much loved,
> anyone who saw her would think her beautiful.
> King Agamemnon, because it seemed good to him,
> took her from Achilles, who did not merit ill.

> Heavy in spirit, he held himself dishonored,
> because the king had so wickedly shamed him;
> unwilling to endure it, he left him in anger,
> he began to war with him like a man despoiled.

> Havié una amiga que él mucho querié,
> teniéla por fermosa quiquier que la veié;
> el rey Agamenón, porque bién paraçié.
> tollióla a Aquiles, que mal non mereçié.
>
> Pesól de voluntad, tovos por deshonrado,
> ca lo havié el rey malament' ahontado;
> non lo quiso sofrir, partióse d'él irado,
> commençó darle guerra com' home despojado.

As we soon see, this warfare is quite literal. Achilles does not retire to his tent as he did in the *Ilias* (*I.L.* 586); instead, he begins to kill Agamemnon's vassals (st. 419):

> So valiantly was he able to fight him,
> so many of his vassals was he able to kill,
> that as Homer says—I don't want to exaggerate—
> there were so many dead that they could not count them.
>
> Tan denodadament lo pudo guerrear,
> tantos muchos le pudo de vassallos matar,
> que, como diz' Homero—non quiero yo bafar—
> cuantos eran los muertos non los podién contar.

When the next stanza reports that there were so many bodies that they could not cover them nor put them in shrouds (st. 420b), we begin to realize that the *Alexandre* poet has substituted Achilles' fierce response for the Apolline plague that had forced Agamemnon originally to give back Chryseis to her priest father (cf. *I.L.* 47–48). Achilles' warfare is as successful as the plague had been: the Greek barons call a council and force Agamemnon to give back the woman by threatening to leave if he refuses to do so (st. 421). This transformed incident demonstrates Achilles' absolute superiority to the rest of the Greeks without the poet's having to bring in pagan divine machinery, something he scrupulously excludes from Achilles' story despite his earlier goddess-filled account of the Judgment of Paris.

Agamemnon's acquiescence pacifies Achilles (st. 422ab)—to the displeasure of the devil, the poet is careful to add (st. 422c)—but though he stops killing the Greeks, Achilles does not rejoin them. We are told at this point that "for the future Lord Achilles was doubtful [*dubdado*]" (st. 422d), and much later, after the host gets to Troy and engages in the normal Iliadic battles of Books One through Eight, we learn that he has been so *irado* and wrathful (*despecho*) that he has retired with his *amiga* (she is never named) to a monastery in the hills (stt. 610abc, 614c) and has been ignoring repeated calls for help (stt. 610–611ab). It is here, in his response to the third embassy, that the analogy between him and the poem's Alexander begins to take clear shape. The third embassy's plea that if he does not help them, "Troy will not be taken, according to the diviners" (st. 611cd) is the acknowledgment of superiority that he has apparently been waiting for (st. 614):

> Achilles was delighted with the news,
> it pleased him that the Greeks recognized his
> superiority [*mejoría*];
> immediately he came from the monastery
> to win the glory [*preçio*] of his feats of arms.

> Aquiles con las nuevas hovo grant alegría,
> plogól quel conoçiessen los griegos mejoría,
> luego se vino, d'essa, de la ermitanía
> por acabar el preçio de su cavallería.

He then routs the Trojans and saves the day (st. 615).

The reader has encountered *mejoría* and *preçio* before in Aristotle's speech to Alexander: at the beginning the old philosopher had told his pupil that he had "great *mejoría* over all men living" (st. 52d), and at the end, as we have seen, he had sent him off to conquer Asia and win *preçio* like that of the heroes at Troy (st. 85d). The reader will encounter *mejoría* again much later when Alexander makes his comment about his need to have surpassed (*mejorasse*) Achilles' deeds. At this early point in the narration, with Achilles as with Alexander, the hero's desire for *mejoría* and *preçio* has not led to any behavior that one would term foolish or arrogant. Achilles' attacking Agamemnon may have pleased the devil, but it was deeply provoked—one cannot, after all, imagine the Cid maintaining his exemplary vassalage if Alfonso had taken Jimena—and Achilles' subsequent withdrawal, too, though definitely prideful, is directly linked to Agamemnon's insulting behavior. But though he never reaches the same degree of foolishness as Alexander, whose obsession to have *mejoría* finally carries him to the point where God himself terms him "crazy" (*lunatico*, 2329c), when Achilles becomes *dubdado* a second time his pride will reek of a similar folly and arrogance.

Achilles' triumphant return is followed by the night mission of Book Ten (stt. 616–623). When Diomedes and Odysseus appear back in camp with the horses of Rhesos and much other booty, the Greeks are as pleased as if they had conquered "all of France" (st. 624ab), a nice little anachronism that supports Michael's argument that the poet desires completely to medievalize the classical story. The poet's declaration that Diomedes and Odysseus themselves do not boast (st. 624d) then creates a medieval standard of humility against which we must judge Achilles' far from humble response to Nestor's exclamation "Now the Trojans are conquered" (625d).[139] Annoyed, it would appear, that the credit for conquering Troy may go to someone else, Achilles replies,

> Don't marvel so much at this,
> that Odysseus accomplished so great a thing with Diomedes;
> for he did a greater thing than this that you see
> when he extracted me from the monastery.

> "Desto"—dixo Aquiles—, "non vos maravilledes
> Ulises fer tal cosa, siquiere Dïomedes;
> que mayor cosa fizo éste que vos veedes
> cuando sacó a mí dentro de las paredes" (st. 626).

This clever reworking of Odysseus's own argument in Ovid's *Metamorphoses* (13.160–178) that he should get credit for sacking Lesbos, killing Hektor, and so on because he brought Achilles from Skyros makes it clear that Achilles wants everyone at all times to recognize his absolute *mejoría*. Only in the midst of the next day's battle do we comprehend the depth of Achilles' indignation at Nestor's ill-considered remark. The battle begins with Hektor and the Trojans explicitly terrified of Achilles, who, Hektor opines, "was born for our sins" (st. 627d). But Hektor rampages through the field for days with no one able to stop him until Aias makes a final stand at the ships (stt. 629–635). The reason? Achilles is again *dubdado,* as we find out in the next stanza when Patroklos, his "standard bearer" (*alfierzo*), is so upset that he puts on the armor of "his doubtful *señor*" and goes out to rout the Trojans (stt. 636–637) and to die at the hands of Hektor (stt. 638–645) as he did in the original *Ilias.*

The poet would have sacrificed verisimilitude if he had had Alexander, the supposed narrator of this episode, make any overt comment condemning Achilles for this arrogance. He guides our interpretation, however, both by drawing attention to Odysseus's and Diomedes' humility and by inserting a new item in his later description of the shield. After Achilles has lamented Patroklos "as if he were his father or his grandfather" (st. 647b) [140] and vowed revenge, he orders new arms made by a *maestro* who paints the shield so skillfully that merely looking at it would make a scholar out of an ignoramus (st. 659). The scholar's education would consist of an abbreviated version of the shield in the *Ilias:* the sea, with ships and fishes (st. 654); the earth, with mountains, lakes, and cities, and birds and beasts (st. 655); the sky, with wind and storm (st. 656); the four seasons, which are here personified rather than illustrated by human activity (st. 657); and the sun, stars, and seven planets (st. 658). As Michael notes, the pagan nymphs, Nereids, and deities are omitted.[141] But something Christian is also added; in stanza 655, which closely translates *Ilias* 875–876, the poet inserts the Tower of Babel so that instead of "high-walled cities in which quarrelling people go to law" (876–877), we have "walled towns and the tower which the traitorous folk built" (655bc). The poet shifts his vision from the cooperative legal system humans constructed to save themselves from bestial violence to the impious tower that was constructed to achieve godhood but instead caused eternal noncommunication and noncooperation. Achilles carries this prime Christian symbol of spiritual blindness [142] into his battle with Hektor, who now, for the first time in the poem, is portrayed in good Christian terms: he asks God to do with him as He will (st. 677d), he commends his soul to "el Padre Santo" (st. 678c) before turning to face Achilles, and he stops to pray in a most Christian fashion in the middle of the battle (stt. 685–688).[143] The battle between the angry [144] self-confident bearer of the tower and the humble suppliant of God comes very close to being an allegorical battle between Pride and Christian humility.

The tower is a minor element in the shield, but because it is the only Christian element its symbolism is significant, all the more so because it is a significant symbol in Alexander's career. Its most neutral appearance in this career is as part of a long Biblical sequence on the tomb Alexander had built for Darius's captured wife (st. 1241d), where its significance is religious in a general sense. Most often it is associated with Alexander's enemy Darius, who claims descent for himself and all Persians from the giants who built it (stt. 948ab, 1369ab), and whose pride in this descent makes him confident that he will conquer Alexander (stt. 948cd, 1369cd). Darius, like Achilles, carries a picture of the tower and its builders on his shield (st. 990cd), along with those of several other great sinners.

When Alexander takes possession of Babylon he takes possession of the tower, the folly (*locura*) of whose builders is now explicitly condemned by God (st. 1506), just as Alexander's will be later. The tower appears one last time just before Alexander is killed. After he has completed his mad ventures to conquer the air and the sea and has thereby prompted offended Natura to secure his condemnation for "pride" (*sobervia*, st. 2330a), the conquerer takes possession of a wonderful tent the ceiling of which first depicts Biblical scenes of punishment for the great sinners: Lucifer, Adam and Eve, the tower builders (st. 2552), and victims of the Flood, and ends with a holy man in one of his more fallible moments: the drunken Noah (stt. 2550–2553). On the walls of the tent are painted the greatest human achievements to date: the labors of Hercules, the Trojan War (in which Achilles figures prominently, stt. 2573–2574a), and Alexander's own deeds. We must, I think, agree with Michael that the pictures are meant to be interconnected and that they signify as a whole the "futility and fleetingness of human achievement and the vanity of human ambition *sub specie aeternitatis*."[145] We must further understand that Alexander's possession of the tower emblem, like Achilles' possession of his more abbreviated version, symbolizes the overweening pride that earns his early death by poison.

Achilles, like Alexander, is killed shortly after he takes possession of the tower emblem. Like Alexander, too, he is killed by poison with the aid of *el peccado*, "the devil." It is perhaps to this very end of making their deaths as similar as possible given their differing traditions that the *Alexandre* poet uses the story of Achilles' invulnerability, a story absent both from the *Ilias Latina* and from the redactions of Dares and Dictys.[146] The invulnerability, which is announced at the beginning of Achilles' story (st. 411ab), is mentioned twice more before it figures in the death scene. It appears first in Hektor's fight with Patroklos, whom he thinks is Achilles and whom he thinks he may have to poison (*hovieral dado venino a bever*) when he remembers "the story that he was enchanted and that no iron could harm him in any way" (*que le dixieran que encantado era, / que nol farié mal fierro por ninguna manera*; stt. 643cd–644ab). It is mentioned again during Achilles' arming, which the poet remarks is taking place despite the hero's being "enchanted" (st. 660a). This latter instance is perhaps motivated by a desire either to appear consistent and logical[147] or to lessen any admiration we might feel for Achilles' boldness in the ensuing battle with Hektor. The motivation of the earlier instance is clearly to foreshadow the final poisoning by Paris and to emphasize that poison is the only means possible to kill Achilles. As will be stressed later, poison is also the only means of killing Alexander (stt. 2332, 2431).

Achilles' arrogant killing of Hektor, which we can relate directly to the desire for *mejoría* that sent Patroklos into battle in his stead, is made his last action in the poem and the direct cause of Paris's vengeance. When, therefore, Paris, who is at a loss as to how to kill Achilles, is reminded by *el peccado* of Achilles' vulnerability in the soles of his feet (stt. 722d–724b), we can view this diabolic intervention in the same way that Michael interprets Satan's participation in the death of Alexander: as "the outer or allegorical presentation of Alexander's inner state. . . . On one plane the devil brings him down; on the other, he brings himself down by succumbing to pride."[148] In Alexander's case this interpretation is reinforced by the poet's comment that Alexander's *sobervia*, "pride," is as great as Lucifer's (st. 2327d); in Achilles' case it is reinforced by the devil's reminding us that the hero's invulnerability was a factor in his facing Hektor so boldly (st. 723d) and by the poet's reminding us that the devil's presence is gratuitous as far as Paris is concerned (st. 724cd).[149]

That Achilles presents his soles to the poisoned arrow while playing (st. 725cd) does not destroy the case for his deadly pridefulness. It merely creates another parallel with Alexander, who in one breath is explicitly condemned for the sin of pride (st. 2330) and in the next is called "a great light to the world" (st. 2457a). Both of these men are great heroes and are basically to be admired; only thus can the lesson be made clear about the dangers of centering one's hopes in the world. Desire for immortal fame is set in subtle opposition to Christian immortality and is identified with the major deadly sin of Pride (see st. 2406). Anger, which here as in every version of Achilles' story is associated with winning this glory, is also a deadly sin (see st. 2356). The *Libro de Alexandre* portrays Achilles as being at the zenith of the kind of human power and achievement that will send one straight to Hell.

4. THE DARES TRADITION

Joseph of Exeter's *Iliad of Dares Phrygius*,[150] written in the alternate Dares-Dictys tradition at about the same time as Simon's "Homeric" *Iliad*,[151] has elements in common with both Simon's work and the *Libro de Alexandre*. Though he at one point seems to undermine Simon's

ranking of Achilles over Hektor—it is only the insistent prompting of
Juno and Minerva that persuades a reluctant Achilles to challenge (and
subsequently kill) such a great man (*tanto viro*) as Hektor (5.485–
488) [152]—Achilles is elsewhere by far the greatest of heroes both Trojan
and Greek. He is compared to Herakles and is the standard by which all
the Greeks measure themselves (5.75–79). He three times routs an entire
army singlehandedly (4.378–382, 5.208–219, 6.361), once shouting *solus
eam, vincam solus*, "Let me go alone, alone I will conquer" (5.211). The
army in the second of these routs includes Hektor, who retreats in a
dignified manner but nonetheless retreats. Since Hektor himself is never
given a similar feat, it is quite clear that Achilles is the superior warrior.

Joseph is like Simon also in labelling Achilles "pious" (4.108). But
this adjective, which appears in the catalogue portrait as the equivalent
of Dares' *clementem*, "merciful," [153] is not supported by the narrative. On
the contrary, Joseph's highly rhetorical verse creates an Achilles who
seems little more than a hyperbolic embodiment of Statius's *belligerum
numen* (*Ach.* 1.504). [154] Love of war (*amor belli*) lives in him (4.267–268),
and, while the army is awaiting the results of Odysseus's diplomatic
efforts before attacking Troy, the war god's *furor* and his own "savage
mind" [155] impel him to attack Mysia (4.353–358). In Mysia, although he
has suffered no personal harm or insult, he is as maniacally brutal
as Homer's Achilles at his worst and more so than Vergil's Turnus.
Checked by his own friend Telephos in his desire to keep striking the
fatally wounded King Teuthras, Achilles grinds his teeth, rolls flaming
eyes in his angry shame, [156] and is ready to kill Telephos himself (4.396–
400). Though his ferocious behavior wins a new supply base for the
Greeks, it does not earn Joseph's praise: when Achilles finally comes to
his senses and stops trying to kill the dying Teuthras, Joseph comments
(4.426–428):

> Thus, for many, mercy [*clementia*] too late puts a check on their fury. Ap-
> peased at last by the supreme penalty, they put aside their savage pas-
> sions—but no praise lies in this. [157]

> Sic multis sera furorem
> temperat et penis tandem saciata supremis
> illaudata feros differt clementia motus.

Like Quintus of Smyrna, who had Athene fix the dead Achilles' face
in an undecaying scowl (3.536–539), Joseph immortalizes Achilles' angry
face (*irata fronte*, 4.484) in the sculpture on Teuthras's tomb. [158] And,

again like Quintus, Joseph implies that Achilles' character is similar to
that of the giant children who assaulted Olympus. While watching
Achilles rampage through a second murderous onslaught, in which the
hero's rage to kill is so impatient that it will not even allow him properly
to hold his hand until he can get to the fleeing leaders but forces him
immediately to attack masses of common soldiers,[159] Jupiter rejoices
that he himself did not marry Thetis, for "such a son would have given
him more to fear than all the piled up mountains and missiles of Phlegra"
(6.354–356).[160] Since Joseph regards these mountain-piling giants as the
pagan analogue of the insurrectionist tower builders of Babylon,[161]
Jupiter's words cannot be taken merely as hyperbolic praise. They and
the following lines about Thetis's pride as she counts her son's slaughtered victims, his present glory having obliterated her knowledge of his
impending death (6.357–358),[162] are surely designed to evoke thoughts
of how pride and worldly glory make one forget one's human condition
and place in God's universe. With them Joseph, like Quintus and the
author of the *Libro de Alexandre,* inclines his reader to judge Achilles'
extraordinary prowess—marvel of human achievement though it be—
as perilously hubristic. Apart from his lack of gigantic size, Achilles has
all the qualities—love of war, brutality, and a minimal concern for justice—to make him accord perfectly with Quintus's Achilles-Kapaneus
subtype.

The Achilles of Albert de Stade's *Troilus,* A.D. 1249,[163] is not so
extraordinarily violent as Joseph's. He routs an entire army only once
(2.542–545), and though there is much blood and gore on the plains of
Troy (e.g., 3.62–72), he goes on no individualized rampages. As in
Dares' *Historia,* Achilles attacks Mysia not for the fun of it but because
he is so ordered (2.319–320), and the episode of Teuthras's death is brief
and matter-of-fact.[164] Albert does, however, agree with Joseph in ranking Achilles' prowess superior to Hektor's. This willingness to grant superiority to Achilles aligns the German poet with the English one in
that both accept the evaluation of Dares and other classical sources,[165] as
opposed to the more independent-minded Benoît de Sainte-Maure,
whose mammoth *Roman de Troie* of A.D. 1160[166] from now on exercises
an overwhelming influence over the tradition both in its original 30,000
French verses and in Guido delle Colonne's Latin prose translation, the
Historia Destructionis Troiae of A.D. 1287.[167] Most redactions subsequent
to Albert's will follow Benoît and Guido in making Hektor—who

through his sons and nephew is, after all, the putative ancestor of several European nations[168]—superior to the best of the enemy Greeks.

Achilles' inferiority to Hektor is demonstrated over and over again in the *Roman de Troie*. In six of the eight combats between Hektor and Achilles[169] Benoît depicts Achilles as at least slightly weaker than the Trojan hero. In one fight, for example, Achilles is unhorsed first, in another he remounts more slowly than Hektor, in another he is wounded more severely. In addition, Benoît brings the two together off the battlefield in an entirely new incident that seems designed expressly to demonstrate Hektor's vast superiority. A verbal "combat" that takes place during a long truce when the champions meet to take each other's personal measure[170] gives Benoît's audience the opportunity to contrast the two warriors in terms both of character and of prowess.

Before giving us the details of their speeches Benoît says in summary that they discussed future encounters and projected the outcome, "the one in anger, the other laughing" (*Li un s'iraissent, l'autre en rient,* 13134). As the speeches proceed, we see that it is Achilles who becomes angry at Hektor's contemptuous laughter. Achilles speaks in deadly earnest about the hard blows Hektor has given him in battle, about the great pain (*grant duel*) that Hektor has put in his heart by killing Patroklos, and about his intent to kill Hektor in revenge the next time

FIGURE 14. Interview Between Hektor and Achilles

they meet (13135–13162). Hektor wastes few words on his reciprocal hate for Achilles but immediately delivers a challenge to single combat (13164–13168). He is willing to stake the whole war on the outcome: if Achilles loses, the Greeks will go home without Helen; if Hektor loses, the Trojans will leave, turning their city over to the Greeks (13169–13177). He offers two inducements: revenge (13178–13188) and the saving of a hundred thousand lives that will otherwise be lost (13189–13192); the former is offered in language that reeks of sarcasm and insult: "If you accept my challenge," he says,

> you would be able to take vengeance for your
> heart's great anger, and the numerous
> wrongs you say I've done you,
> for both the grief you feel for your companion
> from whom I've separated you,
> whom so often you have felt
> naked in your naked arms,
> and for other jousts vicious and shameful,
> of which the greater part are hateful
> to the gods, who will take vengeance
> by their divine power.

> L'ire grant que vostre cuers a
> Porreiz vengier e les mesfaiz
> Que tant dites que vos ai faiz,
> E la dolor del compaignon
> Dont j'ai fait la desevreison,
> Que tantes feiz avez sentu
> Entre voz braz tot nu a nu,
> Et autres gieus vis e hontos,
> Dont li plusor sont hainos
> As deus, quin prenent la venjance
> Par la lor devine poissance.

This sarcastic "laughing" produces anger and shame (*ire e vergoigne*) in Achilles, who calls for the combat, which now alone can save his honor, to take place immediately (13195–13206).

The combat cannot, of course, take place because Benoît cannot change the outcome of the war. Both armies, therefore, reject the terms of the duel. Benoît depicts a significant difference, however, in the Greek and Trojan rejections: Agamemnon leads a unanimous opposition to the duel, while Priam, who has complete confidence in Hektor's strength, rejects it only under pressure from his people. The effect of the episode as a whole, then, is to elevate Hektor both as a warrior (he proposes the duel and seems likely to have won it) and as a leader (his purpose is to save his people's bloodshed) in contrast to Achilles, who fights only for personal revenge and honor and who had been willing to wait until the next general battle to carry out his threats.

Benoît's episode does not significantly undermine Achilles' character; the Greek hero is still brave and his anger is the normal knightly response to insult. Guido's translation, however, introduces important changes that degrade Achilles' character at the same time as they elevate Hektor's even higher than Benoît's version. Guido's Achilles opens his conversation with Hektor by bluntly remarking that he would very much like to kill him. The reasons for this desire are the same as in Benoît: the many wounds he has suffered and the loss of his beloved Patroklos. Hektor, he declares, will be dead within the year. Guido expands Hektor's response from Benoît's simple "You have given me so much cause that I can't help hating you" (13164–13165) into a long philosophical disquisition. Hektor explains in tones of utmost rationality that he too hates and wants to kill Achilles not for any personal reason but only because Achilles hates him and is attacking his land, his family, and himself. It is neither just nor possible, he continues reasonably, that love can issue from war or affectionate esteem from hate. He suggests the single combat in the same reasonable tone, without even a hint of Benoît's sarcasm. Guido's dignified Hektor also omits the homosexual slur. Achilles' extreme reaction is therefore all the more striking because it is unprovoked: he flies into a heated rage (*ira totus caluit*) that drenches him in sweat (*madefactus totus in sui rore sudoris*). Guido thus re-creates Vergil's contrast between furious Turnus and calm, public-spirited Aeneas as they prepared for the single combat that was supposed to decide the fate of Rome (*Aen.* 12.101–112). By so modifying Benoît's episode Guido turns the outcome of the Hektor-Achilles vendetta into a reversal of the end of the *Aeneid:* rational man succumbs to an incarnation of *furor,* and as he falls he takes with him a great civilization.[171]

Allowing Hektor such clear moral and physical superiority over his Greek opponent, however, created a problem for twelfth-century nationalists similar to that faced by the first-century rationalists over Achilles' death at the hands of the effeminate and Apollo-less Paris. How could they make Hektor's death credible and still keep intact his status as the greatest warrior? They could have adopted the solution suggested by the eleventh-century Latin poem "Sub vespere," which added several opponents to help bring Hektor down. This Italian "popular romance," which C. P. Bock believes was a song meant to exalt military valor and rouse nationalistic sentiment,[172] describes the final encounter between Hektor and Achilles as follows:

> At twilight from the Trojan walls
> Hektor went forth, outstanding knight;
> as soon as the troops of Myrmidons saw him,
> they turned their horses and fled to camp.
> At once they shout, "Achilles, haste!   5
> Take arms and deliver your men!"
> Says Hektor, "Put to flight and wound
> the one whom Greece foully flees!"
> At these words, Achilles headlong
> seizes arms and rushes at him.   10
> Both Atrides run up together,
> also Diomedes, Aias and Odysseus.
> Hektor says, "Men, where are you rushing?
> I combat now with the son of Thetis—
> let him now feel Hektor's valor   15
> and see if he can be pierced with a lance."
> Hektor fights, fights without waver,
> casts his spear, draws his sword.
> He strikes Achilles' shield with his sword,
> then breaks it almost to its hilt.   20
> He contests in combat, but contests unevenly:
> one man bravely stands against many.
> Joyful the princes thus leap down
> to overwhelm him with cruel death.
> Thus falls now the jewel of Asia;   25
> Thus perishes the grief of Achaia.
>
> Sub vespere Troianis menibus [173]
> Prodit Hector, miles egregius,
> Quem ut visit turba Myrmidonum,
> Versis equis in castra fugiunt.
> Clamat simul "Achilles, propera! [174]

Arma cape et tuos libera."
Ait Hector "Fuga et saucia [175]
Quem turpiter fugit Achagia!"
Ad hec verba Achilles protinus
Arma capit, it ei obvius;
Concurrerunt uterque Atrides,
Diomedes, Aiax et Ulixes.
Ait [176] Hector "Viri, quo ruitis?
Mecum certat filius Thetidis—
Iam sentiet quid Hector valeat
Et si possit perfodi lancea."
Pugnat Hector, pugnat nec dubitat,
Iacit astam, ensem evaginat.
Ferit hense Achillis clipeum,
Frangit eum mox prope capulum.
Fit certamen, set fit dispariter:
Unus obstat multis viriliter.
Leti duces ita desiliunt
Ut crudeli funere obruunt.
Sic cecidit nunc decus Asie,
Sic occidit luctus Achagie!

The broken sword in verse 20 may be related to the broken spear in the "Lament for Hektor" (35), but though it must still evoke Turnus, its effect here is not to engender sympathy for an understandably foolish opponent of the Roman empire. Instead of continuing an identification with Aeneas's opponent, the poem follows Hektor's loss of a weapon with his being overwhelmed by "joyful princes," who are, we must assume, the five champions who ran up together with Achilles in verses 11–12. The result is a grossly unjust picture of an unarmed man killed by six armed men acting in concert. Hektor's superiority to Achilles is thereby in no way diminished.

This solution did not catch on. Twelfth-century authors preferred to keep Achilles and Hektor as single opponents and to modify Dares' episode by adding deceit rather than additional warriors. The first to do so was apparently the anonymous composer of an abridgement of Dares' *History* [177] written about 1150.

In Dares' version Achilles attacks Hektor to preserve the Greeks from wholesale slaughter.[178] While Hektor is stripping the body of one prince, Polypoetes, Achilles rushes up: "A great battle took place, and an outcry arose from the city and the whole army. Hektor wounded Achilles' thigh. In spite of [or because of] his pain, Achilles attacked harder, nor would he stop until he killed him."[179] In the twelfth-century abridgement Achilles prevents Hektor from stripping "Popetes," is wounded, rages more furiously, and (343–349):

> determines to follow the author of the wound and
> goes on foot, because this path suits secret injury.
> Just as when a serpent puts off old age in the warm glow
> of Spring and rejoicing lies green among the grass,
> then, wounded by a farmer, it gathers all its poison
> in its jaws and follows its enemy mindful of the blow.
> Achilles' impious hope prevails: Hektor dies.

> Auctoremque sequi proponit vulneris atque
> It pede, quod fraudi via congruit ista latenti.
> Sic, ubi deposuit senium sub vere tepenti
> Serpens et mediis gaudens interviret herbis,
> Lesus ab agricola mox colligit omne venenum
> In fauces sequiturque suum, plage memor, hostem.
> Impia Pelide spes prevalet: occidit Hector.

The implications of *fraudi latenti,* "secret injury," of *impia spes,* "impious hope," and of the poisonous snake deliberately awaiting its enemy strip Achilles' victory over Hektor of the heroic quality it had in Dares. The actual deed, however, is left to the reader's imagination, and Achilles' treachery remains, therefore, only implicit. Ten years later, when Benoît expands the scene, the treachery becomes explicit.[180]

In Benoît's *Roman* Achilles similarly attacks Hektor to rescue the Greeks and prevent the despoiling of Polypoetes (16121–16142), but there is the additional detail that prince Polypoetes is the close friend and future brother-in-law of Achilles (16155–16168). During their fight, Achilles is wounded so gravely in the thigh that he is forced to retire (16180–16204). Once the wound is bandaged, he returns to the battle *embronc et morne* with the single purpose of killing Hektor: he "spies out" (*aguaite*) Hektor, and when he finds him without a shield trying to drag off a captured king, he dispatches him immediately (16205–16230). Guido's almost identical version[181] is most explicit about the purposefulness of Achilles' taking unfair advantage:

FIGURE 15. Achilles Kills Hektor

When Achilles noticed that Hektor's breast was not defended by his shield, he took up a very strong spear and, while Hektor was not looking, attacked and fatally wounded him in the stomach so that he cast him down dead from his horse.

Achilles dum persensit Hectorem ante pectus scuti sui subsidium non habere, accepta quadam lancea valde forti, non advertente Hectore, in ipsum irruit et letaliter vulneravit in ventre sic quod eum mortuum deiecit ab equo.[182]

In Achilles' defense one might say that he is merely carrying out the mandate of the Greeks, who according to Guido earlier elected him to get rid of their prime enemy and instructed him to accomplish this not so much by strength as by cleverness (*non tantum suis viribus quam suo sagaci ingenio*).[183] Benoît's Greeks are no less pragmatic: the princes all approve Agamemnon's plan to have them gang up on Hektor so that Achilles can kill the Trojan hero when he is isolated from help (10988–11060). The germ of this nasty plot is a sentence at the end of Dares 20:

> At night Agamemnon calls all the leaders into council and persuasively exhorts all of them to go into battle and especially to pursue Hektor since he killed some of their strongest leaders.

> Agamemnon noctu in consilium omnes duces convocat suadet hortatur, ut omnes in aciem prodeant et maxime Hectorem persequantur, quia de his aliquos duces fortissimos occidit (Meister, 26).

There is nothing necessarily conspiratorial about Agamemnon's exhortation here, and a concerted attack on Hektor never takes place. The magnitude of the difference between Dares' exhortation and the conspiracy and instructions of Benoît and Guido respectively are further proof of how wrongly simplistic it has been to classify Dares as anti-Greek. Rather, this label must be reserved for the late-medieval redactors who removed the last vestiges of honor from the character of both Greeks and Achilles.[184]

The Achilles of these redactors takes even greater unfair advantage in order to kill Troilos and Memnon, waiting until they are completely surrounded by Myrmidons and helpless before moving in to the kill.[185] As with Hektor's death, it is Guido's account in particular that makes Achilles look bad. In Dares' "Troilos" episode Achilles was neither heroic nor unheroic (33):

> Achilles, who had chafed for several days at not going out to battle because of a wound inflicted by Troilos, drew up his Myrmidons in battle array and urged them strongly to attack Troilos. When the greater part of the day had passed, Troilos came out joyfully on horseback. The Greeks fled with huge clamor and the Myrmidons came up and attacked Troilos. Many of them were killed by Troilos, but while they were bitterly fighting Troilos's horse was wounded and fell, entangling him as it threw him. Achilles was on the spot immediately and killed him. He tried to drag him out of the moil but was unable to do so because Memnon intervened.

> Achilles, qui aliquot dies vexatus in pugnam non prodierat, Myrmidones instruit: alloquitur hortatur, ut fortiter inpressionem in Troilum faciant. Postquam maior pars diei transiit, prodit Troilus ex equo laetus. Argivi

maximo clamore fugam faciunt, Myrmidones supervenerunt, inpres-
sionem in Troilum faciunt, de quorum numero multi a Troilo occiduntur:
dum acriter proeliantur, equus volneratus corruit, Troilum inplicitum ex-
cutit. Eum cito Achilles adveniens occidit, ex proelio trahere coepit, quod
Achilles interventu Memnonis complere non potuit. (Meister, 39.)

Joseph apparently thought Dares' version too tame for his Titanic warrior, so he eliminated the Myrmidons and reworked the scene to make
Troilos's end similar to that of Mezentius, who was killed by Aeneas
also while trapped beneath his fallen horse (*Aeneid* 10.890–908). Like
Mezentius, Troilos has the advantage of being on horseback while
Achilles, like Aeneas, is on foot; also like Mezentius, Troilos hurls spears
until his horse is felled by his foe's weapon.[186] Albert reinstated the bat-
talion of Myrmidons and kept close to Dares' account, but, like Joseph,
he gave the battle more of an heroic flavor by adding two similes—lion
and boar—that play up the analogy between Troilos and Mezentius.[187]
Guido's intentions are quite the opposite; taking his cue from Benoît
rather than Joseph and Albert, his additions to Dares' account create a
most unheroic Achilles: upon instruction from their vengeful leader,
who is furious over his previous wound, two thousand Myrmidons surround Troilos, kill his horse, and snatch off his helmet before Achilles
runs up to cut off his head. Achilles' behavior toward Troilos's corpse is
equally deplorable: he ties the headless body to the tail of his horse and
drags it through the army.[188]

Benoît calls Achilles in these episodes a scoundrel (*coilverz*, 16222)
and perfidious (*reneié*, 21441); Guido condemns his lack of honor, nobility, and valor[189] and reviles Homer for having praised a man who
"never killed any vigorous man except by deceit."[190] Although in their
earlier catalogue portraits both Benoît and Guido retain the physical
beauty attributed to Achilles by all followers of Dares,[191] they make his
character as ugly as or uglier than it became in Dictys. Benoît is so concerned with establishing Hektor's superiority in particular and Trojan
superiority in general that he does not allow Achilles to take credit for
any of his three greatest exploits in Dares—the killing of Hektor, Troilos,
and Memnon. Instead of conquering by strength of arms, Achilles must
take unfair advantage to slay all three Trojan heroes. Dares provides the
germ of the incidents, but neither his nor the alternative Iliadic Achilles
is now recognizable in Benoît's villainous Greek soldier. Achilles is still

the strongest of the Greeks,[192] and, since he does kill the man whose single presence ensures the safety of his city throughout both traditions,[193] he remains the conqueror of Troy; but throughout the two centuries in which Benoît and Guido reign supreme over the Trojan War saga Achilles loses his Homeric claim to be termed the "best" of the heroes who fought at Troy.

· 4 ·

SOLDIER OF LOVE

ARCHAIC GREECE
TO MEDIEVAL EUROPE

Classical scholars rarely feel the need to concern themselves with Achilles' sex-life,[1] for to the classical poets of both Greece and Rome the hero's major importance lay in his behavior as the wrathful warrior either mowing down Trojans on the battlefield or adamantly refusing to compromise his honor by helping his fellow Greeks. In the Middle Ages, however, erotic passion closely rivaled the traditional wrath as the key to understanding Achilles' life and death, and by 1314 Achilles' lust had placed him in the company of Paris in the second circle of Dante's *Inferno* rather than in the first with noble Hektor or in the fifth with other irascible spirits. This change in the perception of Achilles is indeed a radical one, but it is produced not by a revolution in the tradition but by innumerable variations on amatory motifs that go back to the *Iliad* and the Epic Cycle. The purpose of this chapter is to provide a comprehensive study of these variations in Achilles' classical, late-antique, and medieval love-life and thus to demonstrate how the epic warrior evolved into the epic lover.

1. EARLY LOVERS

The Homeric roots of the theme of Achilles as lover are his relationships with Patroklos and Briseis. His friendship with Patroklos developed into homosexual love in the fifth- and fourth-century writings of Aischylos,[2] Plato,[3] and Aischines,[4] and as such seems to have given birth to the enigmatic verses in Lykophron's third-century *Alexandra* that make unrequited love Achilles' motive for killing Troilos (308–313).[5] By the fourth century A.D. this eroticism in at least one instance became elaborated into a story that Achilles killed Troilos by squeezing him too hard in a lover's embrace.[6] In most of the tradition, however, Achilles is firmly heterosexual, and his friendship with Patroklos becomes exemplary of devoted but asexual friendship between men.[7]

Achilles' relationship with Briseis is literarily much more fruitful. In the *Iliad* Achilles' love for the woman stolen by Agamemnon functions more to round out Achilles' appealingly complex character than to indicate a motive for the hero's desertion of the Greek forces; Briseis is the cause only in her role as *géras,* "prize of honor," not as love object. Most classical Greek poets followed this version. One apparent exception is Bacchylides, who, in his fifth-century victory ode to Pytheas of Aegina, ascribes Achilles' withdrawal to a "sexy blonde" (*xanthâs gunaikós himeroguíou,* 12.136–137).[8] Bacchylides' view must have had some currency, for when Propertius summarizes the *Iliad* in one of his amatory elegies four and a half centuries later, love for Briseis motivates everything that happens (2.8.29–38):

> And even the famous Achilles when his wife was stolen
> endured to keep his arms idle in his hut.
> He looked on the Greeks in flight, strewn on the shore,
> and the Greek camp alight with Hektor's torch;
> he looked on Patroklos stretched out hideously over the
> sand, his hair covered with gore,
> he suffered everything on account of beautiful Briseis,
> so great a grief raged in him for his stolen love.
> But when at last he was indemnified, the captive woman
> returned,
> he dragged strong Hektor behind his Haemonian horses.

> ille etiam abrepta desertus coniuge Achilles
> cessare in tectis pertulit arma sua.
> viderat ille fuga stratos in litore Achivos,
> fervere et Hectorea Dorica castra face;
> viderat informem multa Patroclon harena
> porrectum et sparsas caede iacere comas,
> omnia formosam propter Briseida passus:
> tantus in erepto saevit amore dolor.
> at postquam sera captiva est reddita poena,
> fortem illum Haemoniis Hectora traxit equis.

According to this poem, the career of the *Iliad*'s Achilles is an exemplum of the extreme power of love, which can force even the strongest man to act contrary to what he would normally do; its point is to ask how, then, can Propertius himself be stronger than love (39–40). The same exemplum for the same point is used by the Chorus in "Seneca's" *Octavia* when they say that Cupid "ordered fierce Achilles / to pluck the lyre, love crushed the Danaans" (*ferocem iussit Achillem / pulsare lyram, fregit Danaos,* 814–815).[9]

Ovid gives a contrary though equally stereotypical picture of Achilles as lover. In his *Heroides* Briseis complains that Achilles' love for her is not as strong as it should be (*Her.* 3.7–56), and she casts Achilles in the role of typical oath-breaking lover abandoning the woman who has been faithful to him (*Her.* 3.53–54, 115–120). Elsewhere, Ovid imagines the two of them in bed, Achilles' murderous hands now expertly engaged in giving her sexual pleasure (*A.A.* 2.711–716).[10] Ovid differs from the other poets in that he seems to see the roles of soldier and lover as quite compatible: hands that are expert in battle during the day should be equally expert at night, and true love, according to Briseis (*Her.* 3.25–42, 55–56), would in fact return Achilles to his role as warrior.

But Ovid's view does not prevail. The *Ilias Latina,* the Latin summary that carried the *Iliad* through the Middle Ages (see Chapter Three, part three, above), clearly and moralistically portrays love as incompatible with the successful waging of war. Dido's destructive love for Aeneas provides the model for Agamemnon's feeling for Chryseis: the king first refuses to return his captive because "fierce love clings deep in his bones and destructive lust spurns prayers" (*ferus ossibus imis / Haeret amor, spernitque preces damnosa libido,* 25–26); then he mourns his lost love (*amissos . . . luget amores,* 71) and takes Briseis from Achilles in order to solace his flame of love with someone else's flame (*solaturque suos alienis ignibus ignes,* 73). Had not Athena restrained Achilles, the poet comments, *caecus amor* would have left a *turpem famam* to the Greeks for eternity (78–80). This moralistic tone is continued in Thetis's plea to Zeus that if he does not avenge the rape of Achilles' "flame" (*flammas,* 91), "virtue shall perish shamefully overcome by lust" (*turpiter occiderit superata libidine virtus,* 92).

In the quarrel with Agamemnon, Achilles is not judged harshly, but, as is clear from the use of *ignes* and *flamma* in the passages quoted above, he is meant to be as hotly in love with Briseis as Agamemnon is with Chryseis or, as we learn later, as Helen is with Paris (cf. *flamma* in

320 and 338). In fact, when we come to this poet's one-line version of the Iliadic lyre-playing scene, we find that Achilles is strumming it not to accompany the reevaluation of an heroic code but to soothe the pangs of love (*et cithara dulci durum lenibat amorem*, 586). Since this line functions as the explanation of what Achilles is doing *instead of* fighting Trojans (585), we can infer that the poet of the *Ilias Latina*, like Bacchylides, Propertius, and "Seneca," sees an opposition between Achilles' role as lover of Briseis and as fighter for Greece, just as he sees an opposition between Agamemnon's love and his duty as commander-in-chief of the army. Only the latter opposition is moralized in the *Ilias Latina*, but when Statius's epic biography presents a lengthy treatment of Achilles' relationship with another woman, Deidameia, both the opposition and the moralization will become an irrevocable part of the Achilles tradition.

Deidameia is but one of several women whose connections with Achilles in the Epic Cycle and in the recondite verse of Lykophron indicate that Achilles may always have been considered susceptible to the ladies. References to her son (*Il.* 19.326–327, *Od.* 11. 492–493, 506–540) and to Achilles' sojourn on Skyros, her home (Allen, 104) prove that Deidameia's story was known in some fashion to Homer and the poets of the Epic Cycle. Allusions to other amorous affairs occur in the *Aithiopis*'s rumor, fatal to Thersites, about Achilles' love for Penthesileia (Allen, 105) and in the *Kypria*'s meeting between Achilles and Helen arranged by Thetis and Aphrodite at Achilles' request (Allen, 105). Something came of the meeting between these two most beautiful and most destructive characters in the Trojan War, for we find Achilles listed by Lykophron as the last of Helen's five husbands (*Alex.* 146, 171–179), and we read in Philostratos's *Heroikos* (third century A.D.) that Achilles and Helen are living in immortal wedded bliss on the White Island, spending their time drinking and singing of their love for each other and of the events at Troy (19.16–17).[11]

Lykophron includes two additional incidents that may have encouraged poets to conceive of Achilles as lover. The first is a marriage between Achilles and Iphigeneia, who becomes the mother of Neoptolemos before she is led to the sacrificial altar at Aulis (*Alex.* 183–185). After losing her, Achilles groans (*sténō*), mourns (*aiázō*), and yearns (*himeírō*) for a full five years (*Alex.* 186–201). The second incident is Achilles' lust for Hemitheia, the sister of Tenes. Lykophron alludes to

the story by mentioning that Achilles killed the pair of them (*Alex.* 232–
242). Plutarch provides some details: stricken by the beauty of Hemitheia when the Greeks landed at Tenedos, Achilles tried to rape her;
when her brother came to her rescue, Achilles killed him (*Quaestiones
Graecae* 28).[12]

Helen, Iphigeneia, and Hemitheia play no literary role in the developing tradition of an amatory Achilles, but the erotic beauty of
Penthesileia, after centuries of neglect,[13] does receive some poetic attention. In the *Aithiopis* of the Epic Cycle, Achilles had killed Thersites for
accusing him of loving Penthesileia. Lykophron paid no heed to this
erotic rumor but instead offered as motive for the murder Thersites's

FIGURE 16. Achilles Kills Penthesileia

stabbing the dying woman in the eye (*Alex.* 990–1001). Propertius, however, revives the love story in a poem (3.11) that attempts to justify his beloved Cynthia's power over him by citing several legendary couples in which the woman usurped the male part: Medea and Jason, Omphale and Herakles, Semiramis and Ninus, Cleopatra and Antony. Listed among these famous women is the slain Penthesileia (3.11.13–16):

> Fierce Penthesileia once dared to fight mounted
> with Scythian arrows against Greek ships.
> But after her golden helmet laid bare her face
> her shining beauty conquered the conquering hero.

> ausa ferox ab equo quondam oppugnare sagittis
> Maeotis Danaum Penthesilea ratis;
> aurea cui postquam nudavit cassida frontem
> vicit victorem candida forma virum.

Apollodoros's prose summary repeats the love story and adds that Achilles then killed Thersites for jeering at him (*Epit.* 5.1). A more detailed version is produced in the fourth century A.D. In Quintus of Smyrna's *Posthomerica* Achilles falls in love with Penthesileia when he takes off her helmet and sees how beautiful she is (*Post.* 1.666–668):

> Aphrodite herself, the lovely garlanded
> wife of strong Ares, made her wondrous in death
> so that even you, son of blameless Peleus, might grieve.

> αὐτὴ γάρ μιν ἔτευξε καὶ ἐν φθιμένοισιν ἀγητὴν
> Κύπρις ἐϋστέφανος κρατεροῦ παράκοιτις Ἄρηος,
> ὄφρα τι καὶ Πηλῆος ἀμύμονος υἱ ἀκαχήσῃ.

Grief-stricken, he wishes he had married her instead of killing her (1.671–674):

> And Achilles felt enduring pain in his heart
> because he had killed her and not led her, his wife,
> to Phthia rich in horses, since she was tall
> and shapely, faultless and like the immortals.

> καὶ δ᾽ Ἀχιλεὺς ἀλίαστον ἑῷ ἐνετείρετο θυμῷ,
> οὕνεκά μιν κατέπεφνε καὶ οὐκ ἄγε δῖαν ἄκοιτιν
> Φθίην εἰς εὔπωλον, ἐπεὶ μέγεθός τε καὶ εἶδος
> ἔπλετ᾽ ἀμώμητός τε καὶ ἀθανάτῃσιν ὁμοίη.

The mere sight of Penthesileia's inanimate beauty is enough to engender sorrow comparable to that which Achilles had felt for his lifelong friend Patroklos[14] (1.718–721):

> The son of Peleus grieved greatly as he
> looked on the strong girl's loveliness in the dust;
> wherefore baneful sorrow ate away his heart,
> sorrow as great as before when Patroklos was killed.

> μέγα δ' ἄχνυτο Πηλέος υἱὸς
> κούρης εἰσορόων ἐρατὸν σθένος ἐν κονίῃσι·
> τοὔνεκά οἱ κραδίην ὀλοαὶ κατέδαπτον ἀνῖαι
> ὁππόσον ἀμφ' ἑτάροιο πάρος Πατρόκλοιο δαμέντος.

We may see this instant devotion as typical of the universal superficiality of Quintus's characters, but it is also an example of a theme that will later be very dear to medieval and Renaissance hearts: love at first sight.[15] As we will see later, Achilles had already been strongly associated with this theme by Statius and in the alternate Trojan War tradition begun by Dares and Dictys.

Thersites seizes this opportunity to heap scorn on the whole of Achilles' relations with women. According to him, Achilles has a "woman-mad" (*gunaimanés*) heart, and once he sees a woman there is no longer any care "in his baneful brains for glorious deeds of valor" (*phresìn ouloménēsin / amph' aretês klutòn érgon*, 1.726, 731–732). *Phresìn ouloménē-sin*, "baneful brains," is an obvious reference to the *mênin ouloménēn*, "baneful wrath," that sent hoards of Achaians to Hades in the *Iliad* (1.1–3), and it therefore alludes most specifically to Briseis's role in Achilles' quarrel with Agamemnon. This negative interpretation of Achilles' earlier withdrawal from the fighting is followed by an opprobrious generalization on the inherent opposition between foolish lover and sensible soldier (1.736–740):

> There is nothing more baneful to mortals than lustful
> delight in sex, which turns even a sensible man
> into a fool; but glory attends labor.
> For a spearman delights in glorious victory and the
> work of Ares; couching with women pleases the coward.

> οὐ γὰρ τερπωλῆς ὀλοώτερον ἄλλο βροτοῖσιν
> ἐς λέχος ἱεμένης, ἥτ' ἄφρονα φῶτα τίθησι

καὶ πινυτόν περ ἐόντα · πόνῳ δ' ἄρα κῦδος ὀπηδεῖ.
ἀνδρὶ γὰρ αἰχμητῇ νίκης κλέος ἔργα τ' Ἄρηος
τερπνά · φυγοπτολέμῳ δὲ γυναικῶν εὔαδεν εὐνή.

Achilles responds to the implication that he is a coward delighting in sex rather than a spearman delighting in victory by killing Thersites with a slap of his hand (1.741–747).

Thersites' statement recasts in moral terms the opposition between lover and warrior that was adumbrated in earlier poets' interpretations of Achilles' response to the loss of Briseis. Bacchylides, Propertius, and "Seneca" had all viewed Achilles' idleness as forced by the pain of frustrated desire, the absence of the beloved; Achilles was a victim and the issue was not a moral one. Thersites' formulation is specifically moral. *Eros* is not seen as a powerful god that through grief and pain forces Achilles to do his bidding but is instead viewed as a natural proclivity, an internal failing. Thersites sees in Achilles' feelings towards Briseis and Penthesileia what medieval and Renaissance poets will condemn as *cupiditas*.

The least sympathetic of epic characters interprets least sympathetically the opposition between Achilles the lover and Achilles the warrior. Perhaps more important for its later use in the Achilles tradition is an earlier, more sympathetic interpretation offered in Statius's first-century A.D. account of Achilles' affair with Deidameia. This earlier interpretation is as clearly moral as that of Quintus's Thersites, but Achilles' amorous feelings are depicted not as an ignoble defect of soul but merely as something a youth needs to learn to control. And, as opposed to the goatish lust implied in Thersites' appellation *gunaimanés,* Achilles' sexual desire for Deidameia may truly be termed love.

We do not know how most of Statius's predecessors handled the episode of Achilles' sojourn in Skyros and his begetting Neoptolemos on the daughter of King Lykomedes before heading off to Troy. A verse in the *Iliad* (9.668) indicates that Skyros was one of the seven cities sacked by Achilles en route to Troy and therefore that Deidameia was originally a war prize.[16] The *Kypria,* according to Proclus's summary, converted the war prize into a bride and the preliminary maneuver into a displacement of Achilles' military career: it told of a storm at sea that scattered the Greek ships and blew Achilles to Skyros, where he married (*gameî*) Lykomedes' daughter.[17] This accidental interruption soon became a de-

FIGURE 17. Achilles Bids Farewell to Deidameia

liberate one, and we know that by the fifth century Thetis's maternal fears had supplanted the Epic Cycle's storm. Unfortunately, all examples of this new version, including Polygnotos's famous painting of Achilles among the maidens of Skyros (Pausanias 1.22.6) and Euripides' tragedy about his being extracted by Odysseus and Diomedes,[18] have disappeared.

The earliest, pre-Statian literary treatment occurs in a thirty-two-verse fragment of a poem traditionally ascribed to Bion (c. 100 B.C.). The poem consists of a song about Achilles and Deidameia sung by a shepherd who, luckily, first summarizes its subject (2.5–9):[19]

> love at Skyros,
> Achilles' secret kisses and lovemaking,
> how the boy put on a dress to change his looks,
> and how among Lykomedes' daughters, careless
> Deidameia came to know Achilles in her bedchamber.

> Σκύριον . . . ἔρωτα,
> λάθρια Πηλείδαο φιλάματα, λάθριον εὐνάν,
> πῶς παῖς ἔσσατο φᾶρος, ὅπως δ' ἐψεύσατο μορφὰν
> χὤπως ἐν κώραις Λυκομηδίσιν ἀπαλέγοισα
> ἠείδη κατὰ παστὸν 'Αχιλλέα Δηιδάμεια.

What we have of the song itself tells how all the Greek men eagerly went off to war (10–14) except for Achilles, who, hidden among Lykomedes' daughters, learned to ply wool instead of weapons (15–16). The poet stresses Achilles' feminine appearance, remarking on his white (leukâi) hand (16), his maidenly (parthenikón) work (17), his girlish (éúte kóra) appearance (17), the blushes on his white cheeks that feminize (thēlúneto) him (18–19), and his maidenly (parthenikês) walk (20). Underneath it all, however, there lurks a masculine spirit (thumós) and a masculine erôs (21)—whence the seduction of Deidameia. This seduction begins with Achilles sitting next to her all day, kissing her hand, helping her and praising her weaving (22–24). Then, as he is trying to persuade her that it is silly for the two of them, maidens so alike, to sleep alone (25–32), the fragment breaks off. Most interesting is Achilles' complete external feminization, which is surely meant to be comic rather than judgmental. Since the song is erotic, not heroic, it probably included no stern moralizing.

Mock moralizing is the aim when Ovid invokes the episode in the Ars Amatoria (1.689–706) to prove the wisdom of a man's pressing his sexual attentions vigorously without waiting for the woman's consent. Ovid begins by chiding the obedient son for shamefully (turpe) concealing his manhood (virum . . . dissimulatus erat) under a long dress: Achilles' art is war, not wool; his hand should be carrying a shield, not be stuck in a sewing basket; this hand is destined to kill Hektor, to brandish the Pelian spear, not to wind spindles (689–696). The scene then shifts abruptly to the bedroom that Achilles happened (*forte*) to be sharing with a royal virgin (697), an unfortunate young woman who becomes the locus for proving the potent masculine reality behind Achilles' effeminate appearance. The means of establishing Achilles' true virility is rape, which act is immediately succeeded by a complete return to the masculine role (698–702):

> she learned he was a man, to her disgrace.
> By force, indeed, was she conquered (thus we must believe);
> she wished, however, to be conquered by force.
> Often she said, "Stay!" when now Achilles would hurry off:
> for, the distaff put away, he had taken up strong arms.
>
> haec illum stupro comperit esse virum.
> viribus illa quidem victa est (ita credere oportet),
> sed voluit vinci viribus illa tamen.
> saepe 'mane' dixit, cum iam properaret Achilles:
> fortia nam posito sumpserat arma colo.

Lover and warrior express a parallel "manly" violence, a violence that is here presented as purely destructive. The picture of Deidameia vainly trying to prevent "the author of her disgrace" (*auctorem stupri*) from abandoning her (703–704) counters the narrator's overt purpose in introducing the episode as well as his initial moralizing.[20] Since the manly art that suits Achilles and will provide his claim to fame (*titulos petes*, 692) is that of killing and raping, the only lesson actually conveyed is that it is indeed dangerous to excite the manhood of heroes like Achilles.

In this telescoped version of the sojourn on Skyros, the opposition that emerges most strongly is one between woman's work and man's work, not between lover and warrior. Similar to the view we discussed above in connection with Briseis's lament in the *Heroides,* Ovid here suggests that sexual fulfillment is intimately linked to the warrior's correct functioning. Statius, on the other hand, presents the episode in a way that evokes the conventional moral lessons attached by earlier poets to Achilles' relationships with Briseis and Penthesileia. Achilles' using his knowledge of heroic song for the seduction of Deidameia, his teaching her to sing and admire his own wonderful deeds (1.572–579) much as Cheiron had taught him to sing and admire the *honores* (2.158) of other heroes (1.188–194, 2.156–158), represents him as squandering his education in the employ of love instead of utilizing it, as would be proper, in war. An additional lesson is implied when Achilles later decides that since he cannot prove his manhood (*mas*) in Skyros by fighting enemy Asians, he will prove it instead by raping his beloved (1.639–645). Achilles' explicit awareness that his sexuality is the only masculine potency left to him is clearly a moralization of Bion's amusing contrast between an ultrafeminine appearance and a masculine *thumós*.

But more important, perhaps, than these specific moralizations is the more general one under which they are subsumed: that Achilles' falling in love is not merely the result of an assumed effeminacy that allows him to move freely among beautiful maidens but is the *cause* of that effeminacy. It seems likely that Statius was inspired to introduce the causal relationship into Achilles' story by having read Ovid's skewed version of Herakles' enslavement to Omphale.[21] In any case, his narrative gives us our first and most delightful extant expression of the youthful Achilles sacrificing all to love.

It is love at first sight. Achilles sees Deidameia and immediately fire races through his body (1.302–306):

> The fierce youth, whose breast had never been shaken before,
> went rigid, and he drank new fire through all his bones.
> Nor does the imbibed love keep hidden, but quivering in his marrow
> the fire appears again in his face and colors his bright
> cheeks and moves over his aroused body with a light sweat.

> trux puer et nullo temeratus pectora motu
> deriguit totisque novum bibit ossibus ignem.
> nec latet haustus amor, sed fax vibrata medullis
> in vultus atque ora redit lucemque genarum
> tingit et inpulsum tenui sudore pererrat.

A simile comparing Achilles to a young bullock whose lust for a heifer produces joy in his herdsmen (1.313–317) indicates that such intense desire is both useful and natural to the male of the species. But its effect here, as manipulated by Thetis, is to produce the opposite of manly behavior: Achilles consents to put on female clothing and hide among the daughters of Lykomedes in the hope that he may thus achieve union with Deidameia (1.318–329). In short, all other expressions of manhood are subordinated to the basic biological one. The lesson is clear: uncontrolled love, the force that induces this subordination, produces effeminacy, turns a man into a woman.[22]

FIGURE 18. Achilles Discovered

The opposition between effeminate lover and masculine warrior is later made explicit as an opposition between love and *virtus* "manly virtue." After Achilles has reassumed his warrior identity through the machinations of Odysseus, he suddenly hears Deidameia weeping in the next room and his *virtus* is broken by his hidden love (1.888). The breakage is only temporary this time, and after making their marriage public and comforting her as best as he can, he sails off to war with Odysseus and Diomedes. But as they sail away, Achilles looks back at Deidameia, and when he thinks about her being left all alone, his *virtus* yields place to the reborn *ardor* that is hidden in his heart (*occultus sub corde renascitur ardor / datque locum virtus,* 2.29–30). Once again, he has to be brought back to his warrior identity by Odysseus.

What appears to be an opposition, however, is actually felt more as a tension. Achilles' stint as a lover has produced a marriage and a son, which are societally and generically useful and remain as objects of care after Achilles assumes his proper role as a warrior. Statius's morality is gentler than Quintus's will be. Love in the *Achilleid* is good and should be pursued—but in a properly subordinate way.

2. POLYXENA

A much more insidious version of this theme of love versus duty develops in a most interesting way through the story of Polyxena, which, as the centuries pass, becomes more and more intricately intertwined with that of Achilles. What begins as a simple sacrifice, the final horror of a ten-year war, ends up a fully developed romance in which Achilles' death is due directly to his love for the enemy woman. The progression of this love story is tricky to follow since there are often huge gaps between small pieces of evidence, but it is possible nonetheless to make some hypotheses as to how and why the love story grew.

It is difficult to tell how Achilles' relationship to Polyxena was represented in the Epic Cycle, but if we are to judge by the two fragments that mention her, the importance of the relationship centered on her death. Unfortunately, these two extant fragments give contradictory versions of that death. Proclus states that in the *Sack of Ilium* Polyxena was sacrificed on Achilles' grave just before the Greeks sailed home after destroying Troy (Allen 108). But if we are to believe the scholiast to *Hekabe* 41, the *Kypria* had her die as a result of wounds inflicted by Odysseus and Diomedes while the city was being sacked.[23] More interesting perhaps even than this difference in the mode and timing of her death is the scholiast's mention of her subsequent burial by Neoptolemos (*taphênai dè hypò Neoptolémou*). In Förster's view this burial is performed by Neoptolemos as "an act of piety towards his father" and indicates that Achilles' love for Polyxena occurred already in the *Kypria*.[24]

Förster's hypothesis of an early love story, which is shared by many scholars,[25] is based on no evidence other than the aforementioned burial and numerous archaic vase paintings that show Polyxena fleeing along with her brother in illustrations of Achilles' famous ambush of Troilos.[26] These archaic scenes are thought by some to indicate that Achilles tried to carry her off but failed.[27] At the very least, they show that Achilles was aware of Polyxena well before he died; therefore, what more natural than to assume that he lusted after her and that this lust is the reason either for the grave piously heaped or the sacrifice ruthlessly

FIGURE 19. Achilles and Polyxena at Well

performed by his son?[28] But natural though it may be, such an assumption is countered by the absence of any allusion to such a motif in classical Greek literature. Nor can the wedding imagery in Lykophron's third-century description of the sacrifice be used to buttress such an assumption for either archaic or Alexandrian poetry, although most scholars who deny an origin in the Epic Cycle for the love story believe that Alexandrian poets either invented or gave definitive shape to it.[29] Lykophron's describing the slain Polyxena as Achilles' bride can prove nothing because such description is a literary convention, a convention that in fact probably gave birth to the love story but only in combination with other factors in the first century A.D.

When a woman died before being able to marry, her death was frequently bewailed specifically as having taken the place of marriage. This view of death as a cruel substitute for marriage is revealed in numerous artifacts, epitaphs, and literary works that span the centuries from archaic Greece to postclassical Rome.[30] A sixth-century Athenian epitaph, for instance, portrays a young girl lamenting that the gods allotted her the eternal name of maiden (*koúrē*) instead of marriage (*antì gámou*),[31] and in another epitaph, perhaps also Athenian but much later, the dead girl complains that instead of parents or brother or husband, baneful Hades plucked the fruit of her youth.[32]

The poignant waste caused by premarital death seems to have been underscored by dressing the maiden corpse in what would have been wedding clothes. A Greek epitaph from Egypt declares that because a girl died untimely she wears bridal robes in Hades,[33] and memorial vases placed on the graves of unwed Athenian girls depict the dead girl dressed as a bride.[34] Euripides' Hekabe communicates the full pathos of such an action in her lament as she prepares what is left of Astyanax for burial (*Trojan Women* 1218–1220):

> This adornment of Phrygian robes which you
> should have worn when you married
> the noblest of Asian princesses, I place upon your body.[35]

> ἃ δ' ἐν γάμοισι χρῆν σε προσθέσθαι χροΐ
> ᾿Ασιατίδων γήμαντα τὴν ὑπερτάτην,
> Φρύγια πέπλων ἀγάλματ' ἐξάπτω χροός.

As Alexiou and Dronke state, this dressing of the unmarried dead in wedding clothes indicates "a deliberate fusion" between marriage and death,[36] a fusion that reflects the popular view of death and marriage as fundamentally similar occasions, signaling the transition from one stage in the cycle of human existence to another.[37]

One product of this fusion, especially in the most lamentable case of a virgin's dying unwed after she had attained the age for marriage,[38] is the conception of Hades as bridegroom. The earliest example of such a conception occurs in Sophokles' *Antigone* (c. 441 B.C.) when the heroine laments that she has had no share in wedding songs but "will wed Acheron" (*Achéronti numpheúsō*, 813–816), and this idea is later developed by the messenger who reports what they found in the cave, "the maiden's marriage chamber (*numpheîon*) of Hades" (1205).[39] The next example occurs in Euripides' *Orestes* (408 B.C.) when Pylades terms Helen's impending death at his and Orestes' hands as her "possessing Hades as a bridegroom" (*Haídēn numphíon kektēménē*, 1109).[40] And last, in Euripides' *Iphigeneia in Aulis,* Agamemnon in lamenting the fate of his daughter first calls her a maiden and then corrects himself: "Why maiden? Hades, as it seems, will marry her soon" (*tí parthénon? Háidēs nin, hōs éoike, numpheúsei tácha,* 460–461).[41]

This theme is continued in epigrams and inscriptions. Of the epigrams, Meleager's (c. 100 B.C.) about the maiden who died on her wedding night is perhaps the most famous; it begins, "Not a wedding (*gámon*) but Hades as bridegroom (*epinumphídion*) did Klearista receive when she loosened her maiden girdle" (*Palatine Anthology* 7.182.1–2). A Cretan inscription from approximately the same date makes the fusion of Hades and bridegroom more emphatic by making the maiden's death the explicit result of Hades' seeing her beauty and blameless character.[42] And then in the first century A.D., the furthest we need go for our study of Polyxena, there is an inscription from Pantikapaion (on the northeast coast of the Black Sea) that elaborates to twenty-two lines the conception of Hades as an active lover who snatches the maiden away from a human marriage to marry her himself.[43]

Bearing in mind this widespread fusion of death and marriage, Hades and bridegroom, we are now prepared to return and follow the development of Polyxena's relationship to Achilles.

There need have been nothing personal in Achilles' demand for Polyxena in the original legend, as indeed there seems to be none in Euripides' *Hekabe.* In the *Iliad* one of the rewards Agamemnon offered Achilles to induce him to return to the fighting was his pick of the Trojan women (*Iliad* 9.139–140); Polyxena would surely have been that pick since as the only surviving virgin of the royal house she is the most desirable human prize that Troy contains.[44] Who, then, could be more fitting as the prize of honor for the foremost Greek warrior? In the *Hekabe* the sacrifice is put firmly into this context by emphatic repetition of the word *géras* and by the whole sustained parody of *Iliad* 1 and 9.[45] In the *Trojan Women* Polyxena is in fact given to Achilles as part of a general allotment of female prizes to the Greek princes and is called a *dôron* (622–623).

In the *Trojan Women,* where Polyxena does not appear on stage and where pathos is concentrated on the fate of Kassandra and Astyanax, Euripides reserves wedding imagery for the latter two young people. But in the *Hekabe,* where Euripides wants to make Achilles' crime particularly revolting, Polyxena's death is made more poignant by evoking the traditional horror of death taking the place of marriage. Euripides' courageous heroine sees only two causes for lamentation in her untimely death. The first is her mother's bereavement (197–215); the second is her own unwed state: she will die "unwed without the bridal song I should have had" (*ánumphos anuménaios hôn m'echrên tuchein*, 416). Once she is dead, Hekabe addresses her as "bride no bride, maid no maid" (*númphēn t 'ánumphon, parthénon t 'apárthenon*, 612–613). In other words, she has left the stage of life she was in, that of being a maid, and therefore she must now be a bride; but in fact her transition was not from maid to bride but from life to death, so she is neither and both at the same time. Hekabe's contradictory words express perfectly the unspeakableness of her daughter's fate.

Nearly 150 years intervene between *The Trojan Women* and the next reference to Polyxena in Lykophron's *Alexandra*. Here in Kassandra's prophecy of her sister's fate, wedding imagery is to the fore (323–326):

> You to a cruel wedding and nuptial
> sacrifice the hateful lion, son of Iphis,[46] will lead,
> imitating the purificatory rites of his dark mother.[47]

> σε δ' ὠμὰ πρὸς νυμφεῖα καὶ γαμηλίους
> ἄξει θυηλὰς στυγνὸς Ἴφιδος λέων,
> μητρὸς κελαινῆς χέρνιβας μιμούμενος.

There is nothing to indicate that *numpheîa* and *gamēlíous* represent anything but a literary convention used to heighten pathos, no need to envision a lustful ghost waiting to receive what was denied him in life. In fact, Lykophron views Achilles as already having an underworld wife, Medea (*Alex.* 171–175, 798).[48] Although this odd marriage with Medea may in itself be of little value in determining Achilles' predeath relationship to Polyxena, when coupled with the existence of the death-marriage convention it should make us wary of using Lykophron's wedding imagery to support the theory of an early love story.

It is unlikely that Lykophron's description of Polyxena's death offers us more than the same "grim parody"[49] of marriage that we see in the funerary laments for young girls, for we find no hint of a love relationship in any of the poetry written in the next three centuries. This includes the poetry of Catullus, Propertius, Tibullus, and Ovid, none of whom ever mentions Polyxena in his amatory lyrics. Catullus and Ovid make striking use of her sacrifice in their hexameters, but in both cases the context is the brutality of martial heroism, not love.

Catullus uses the sacrifice of Polyxena to cap a grimly ironic prophecy of Achilles' futūre *egregias virtutes* in his miniature epic celebration
of the wedding of Peleus and Thetis. Polyxena's death is, as M. C. J. Putnam puts it, "the final witness to Achilles' prowess, the one particularly
gruesome achievement singled out from the nameless heap."[50] I quote
Catullus's lines in full (64.362–370):

> Lastly there will bear witness also the spoils given to the dead
> when the rounded tomb, heaped to a high mound,
> receives the white limbs of the stricken virgin.
> Run spindles run, weaving the threads.
> For as soon as fortune shall have given the weary Achaians means
> to loosen the Neptunian binding of the Trojan city,
> the high sepulchre shall be soaked with Polyxena's blood;
> she who, like a sacrificial beast falling beneath the double-edged ax,
> will cast forward a headless trunk from lowered knee.

> denique testis erit morti quoque reddita praeda
> cum teres excelso coacervatum aggere bustum
> excipiet niveos perculsae virginis artus.
> currite ducentes subtegmina, currite, fusi.
> nam simul ac fessis dederit fors copiam Achivis
> urbis Dardaniae Neptunia solvere vincla,
> alta Polyxenia madefient caede sepulchra;
> quae velut ancipiti succumbens victima ferro,
> proiciet truncum summisso poplite corpus.

Earlier, Achilles in battle had been likened to a reaper mowing unripe
corn (*praecerpens messor aristas,* 353); now his victim is likened to a sacrificial animal (*victima,* 369). Achilles kills with the same impersonality as
one acquires food for a meal; Catullus allows not the slightest hint of a
personal motive—neither revenge nor unrequited love—in any way to
redeem the hero's brutal actions. Furthermore, Polyxena is beheaded
(*truncum . . . corpus,* 370), not just stabbed as in previous versions. She
is thus treated as if she were a member of the enemy army whose bodies
Achilles had left in heaps (*acervis*) to block Skamander's waters (359–
360). Her body on top of the heap (*coacervatum,* 363) that forms Achilles' tomb is, as Putnam says, just one more body among the other war
dead.[51] It may be that in order to achieve this end, to portray the utter
inhumanity of war and the heroic age, Catullus excluded a love story
just as he excluded Achilles' grief for Patroklos. All we can say with certainty is that no love story is evident in Poem 64.[52]

Nor is there one evident in Ovid's version of the episode in Book Thirteen of the *Metamorphoses*. Ovid follows Euripides in basing Achilles' demand for Polyxena on the issues and mood of Books One and Nine of the *Iliad*, now making explicit what Euripides had indicated through parody. As the Greek army waits for calmer seas,

> suddenly the earth split wide
> and large as in life Achilles came out and
> showed a face as threatening as when he
> wildly and unjustly attacked Agamemnon with his sword.
> "Do you leave forgetful of me, Achaians?
> Is your gratitude for my prowess buried with me?
> No! So that my tomb be not without honor
> let the ghost of sacrificed Polyxena placate Achilles!"

> hic subito, quantus, cum viveret, esse solebat,
> exit humo late rupta similesque minanti
> temporis illius vultum referebat Achilles,
> quo ferus iniusto petiit Agamemnona ferro,
> "inmemores" que "mei disceditis," inquit "Achivi,
> obrutaque est mecum virtutis gratia nostrae?
> ne facite! utque meum non sit sine honore sepulchrum,
> placet Achilleos mactata Polyxena manes!"
>
> (*Met.* 13.441–448)

We recognize Ovid's *gratia* (446) as the *cháris* of *Iliad* 9.316–317 and of Euripides' parody (*Hekabe* 134–140, 320); it seems obvious that Ovid's *sine honore* (447), surely equivalent to *agéraston* at *Hekabe* 115, represents the theme of honor throughout the *Iliad*. One might, if desperate to find a love motif in this passage, select the verse about Polyxena's ghost (*manes*, 448) as evidence that there was to be an otherworldly marriage. But in the absence of any wedding imagery and in the presence, instead, of *honore*, we must understand the verse to mean that what will placate Achilles is the honor the Greeks' willingness to kill her will bring him. Ovid later has Polyxena ask that she be allowed to join the ghosts in the underworld (*Stygios . . . manes*) as a free woman (*libera*, 465).[53] This request is made purely for her own sake, but, hoping to dissuade the Greek men from touching her, she adds an argument based on possible benefit for Achilles (467–469): "More acceptable to him, / whoever he is, whom you are preparing to placate with my slaughter, / will be free blood" (*acceptior illi, / quisquis is est, quem caede mea placare paratis, / liber erit sanguis*). Not only does the *quisquis is est* deny any personal relationship with the demander of the sacrifice, it is clear that Polyxena believes Achilles to be interested only in her *sanguis;* her *manes* is strictly her own concern.

Nor does Ovid's Hekabe see any personal motive behind Achilles' demand for her daughter. To Hekabe, Polyxena is just one more of her beloved children that Achilles has killed, one she had thought exempt from Achilles' sword because of her sex (13.497–500). Hekabe laments that even Achilles' ashes rage against her family, that his enmity reaches them even from the grave (503–504).[54] The emphasis here, as throughout Ovid's reworking of Euripides, is on the familiar destructive wrath. There is no hint of a love story in this version of Polyxena's sacrifice.

An epigram by Statyllius Flaccus,[55] an obscure Greek who wrote at about the same time as Ovid or a little later, describes the sacrifice as a *pénthimon huménaion,* "mournful wedding" (*Palatine Anthology* 9.117.1– 2).[56] The word *huménaion* provokes Gow and Page to say that this epigram is "the first clear allusion" to "the story of Achilles' courtship of Polyxena."[57] But as with the wedding imagery in Lykophron, which Gow and Page either overlook or interpret metaphorically as I do, Statyllius's *huménaion* is similar to images found in funerary epigrams and epitaphs. We find the very word *huménaion,* "wedding" or "wedding song," employed to fuse death and the wedding it preempted in an epitaph that terms itself the dead virgin's "wedding song."[58] It is probably used in the same way by Statyllius and has nothing—as yet—to do with a love story. We are, however, now approaching the time when words like *numpheîa, gamélíous* and *huménaion* will pass from the realm of imagery to that of narrative fact and when Achilles, specifically named as Polyxena's bridegroom, will take his place in a parody much grimmer than that first exemplified in Lykophron's *Alexandra.*

Seneca provides us, I believe, with the major point of transition. His *Trojan Women,* as an interweaving of Euripides' *Hekabe* and *Trojan Women* combined with the narrative in Ovid's *Metamorphoses,* gives no indication that a love story was then in existence. It does, however, in Seneca's typically macabre fashion, make the wedding imagery so personal and concrete that the shift to a love story is made very easy.

The Achilles who demands Polyxena's sacrifice in Seneca's drama is the war hero earlier presented by Euripides and Ovid. Talthybius's description of his huge shade as it had flashed forth from the split earth summarizes Achilles' martial career from a preliminary victory in Thrace, through conquering Kyknos in the first battle of Troy, through the rampage that filled Skamander's waters with corpses, to the dragging of Hektor's body behind the chariot (178–189). When Talthybius reports the angry ghost's speech, motifs of honor and gratitude and a reference to the plot of the *Iliad* in the last two verses recall Euripides' and Ovid's versions of the scene (190–194):

> The sound of the angry one filled all the shore:
> "Go, go, sluggish ones, rob me of the honors due
> my ghost, let loose the ungrateful ships
> to sail over my sea. Greece paid greatly to appease
> the anger of Achilles, and she will pay greatly."[59]

> implevit omne litus irati sonus:
> "ite, ite, inertes, manibus meis debitos
> auferte honores, solvite ingratas rates
> per nostra ituri maria. non parvo luit
> iras Achilles Graecia et magno luet."

The subsequent demand for Polyxena's sacrifice is also similar to the demand for a sacrificial victim expressed both by Euripides (*prósphagma*, *Hek.* 41) and Ovid (*mactata*, *Met.* 13.448), but it is elaborated beyond the earlier stark simplicity by the addition of wedding imagery (195–196): "Let Polyxena, betrothed to my ashes, / be sacrificed by the hand of Pyrrhus to water my tomb" (*desponsa nostris cineribus Polyxene / Pyrrhi manu mactetur et tumulum riget*).[60]

Desponsa, apparently used only to emphasize the victim's wasted virginity, is not at this point shocking. With the conclusion of Talthybius's speech, however, Seneca indicates that this betrothal is not simply metaphorical. When Talthybius reports that after Achilles plunged back beneath the earth a chorus of Tritons sang the wedding song (*cecinit hymenaeum,* 202), we begin to suspect that Seneca's characters will literally act out the "grim parody" of marriage that was conventionally used in epigrams and vase paintings. We become sure of it when Kalchas not only confirms the need to sacrifice a virgin on Achilles' tomb but also specifies that she must be (362–365)

> . . . dressed as women are wont when they marry
> in Thessaly, Ionia, or Mycenae.
> Let Pyrrhus deliver a wife to his father.
> Thus she will be given correctly.

> . . . quo iugari Thessalae cultu solent
> Ionidesque vel Mycenaeae nurus,
> Pyrrhus parenti coniugem tradat suo:
> sic rite dabitur.

Of the three major elements in the funerary laments we now have two: wedding clothes and wedding song. The third, the deathly bridegroom, will soon make its appearance.

Helen is given the task of persuading Polyxena to put on wedding clothes, and she attempts to do so by telling her the "good" news that she is going to marry Neoptolemos (881–887). But when the prospect of this marriage only increases the gloom and hostility of the Trojan women—Andromache even suggests that the fires of burning Troy will provide appropriate torches for such a wedding (889–900)—Helen finally confesses that the man whom Polyxena must marry is not Neoptolemos but Achilles (942–944):

> Achilles orders that you must be delivered to
> him and sacrificed before his ashes
> so that he may be your husband in the Elysian Fields.

> . . . [te] tradi sibi
> cineremque Achilles ante mactari suum,
> campi maritus ut sit Elysio, iubet.

The parody is now complete as Achilles takes the role of Hades and Acheron in the epigrams.

Upon hearing the truth, Polyxena's recalcitrance vanishes and she joins in the parody. She puts on the bridal robes joyfully because she considers her impending death equivalent to marriage, whereas marriage to Neoptolemos would have been equivalent to death (*mortem putabat illud, hoc thalamos putat*, 948). The parody is sustained till the moment of sacrifice: as she walks to Achilles' tomb, torches and a bridesmaid (*pronuba*) precede her just as in a wedding (*thalami more*) (1132–1133).[61] This marriage does not, however, promise eternal bliss. Polyxena, who has met the knife proudly, falls with an angry thrust (*irato impetu*, 1159), as if to make the ground weigh heavy on Achilles (1158–1159).[62] As for Achilles, he is, as so often, ferocious: Polyxena's blood remains not even briefly on the surface of the earth but is instantaneously sucked down by the *saevus tumulus* (1162–1164).

If acting out the "marriage rite of death," as Lattimore terms the funerary convention,[63] makes Polyxena's sacrifice more macabre than pathetic, this sensation accords well with Seneca's usual aims. But, one might object, why assume that we are dealing merely with a convention? Since Achilles makes a clear demand for a bride, why not assume along with Förster and other scholars that the wedding imagery reflects the love story that is summarized, perhaps about this time, by Hyginus (*Fab.* 110), and that will soon be told in detail in Dictys' *Journal* and Dares' *History*? The answer is, first, that nowhere in the *Trojan Women* is there any suggestion that love has anything to do with Achilles' "marriage" and, second, that revenge, the only other possible motive in keeping with the love story, is equally absent.

If the notion of personal revenge were present, it would support the theory of an already existing love story because the story as we have it in Dares and Dictys implicates Polyxena in Achilles' death. Contrary to the standard account, which has him die in battle struck by an arrow shot from Paris's bow but guided by Apollo,[64] Dares' and Dictys' version has him murdered in a treacherous ambush that uses Polyxena as bait. Hyginus's brief account of the sacrifice of Polyxena after the ghost demands an unspecified share of the spoils (*praedae*) provides a convenient summary (*Fab.* 110): "And accordingly the Greeks took Priam's daughter Polyxena, a virgin of remarkable beauty on account of whom Achilles was killed by Alexander and Deiphobus when he came to confer about his request for her, and they sacrificed her on Achilles' tomb" (*itaque Danai Polyxenam Priami filiam, quae virgo fuit formosissima, propter quam Achilles, cum eam peteret et ad colloquium venisset, ab Alexandro et Deiphobo est occisus, ad sepulchrum eius eam immolaverunt*). In this version of Achilles' death, the Greeks select Polyxena as Achilles' portion for one of two reasons: she will be pleasing to the dead hero either because he still wants her as he had in life[65] or because he now hates her as the cause of his death and wants revenge.[66]

In Seneca's play the savage sucking down of his angry "bride's" blood certainly might engender suspicion that revenge was Achilles' motive for demanding her. But neither Achilles' demand nor Neoptolemos's lengthy and belligerent defense of that demand alludes to revenge. Neoptolemos's defense is merely a more debased version of the *Hekabe*'s "Homeric" debate over the hero's right to honor versus the slave's right to live (*Hek.* 120–140, 306–331). He sees Polyxena in the context of *merces*, "wages" (209), *praemium*, "profit" or "recompense" (292), and *spolia*, "booty" (305), and his justification of the proposition that Achilles, true conqueror of Troy, should get what he wants boils down to a "might makes right" doctrine that is stated baldly in the midst of his argument with Agamemnon (333, 335): "No law spares the captive or limits the penalty. . . . The victor may do whatever he wishes to do" (*Lex nulla capto parcit aut poenam impedit. . . . Quodcumque libuit facere victori licet*). Seneca is blatant where Euripides is subtle, but the issue remains the same: the brutality of the war-spoils ethic. Revenge is not made a part of this issue.

Nor does Seneca introduce any motive for revenge. Neither in his comprehensive account of his father's war career (210–243) nor anywhere else does Neoptolemos mention death by treachery even though it would have made an effective retort to Agamemnon's belittling Achilles' death *manu Paridis*, "at the hand of Paris" (347).[67] Instead of alleging ambush, Neoptolemos combats the slur by asserting that his father was one whom none of the gods would attack *comminus*, "in person" (348), alluding to the story that Apollo guided the arrow shot by Paris.

It seems clear either that Seneca chose not to use the love story or that the story was not yet in existence. In the absence of any evidence to the contrary, I will hypothesize that the latter is true and that Achilles' demand reveals not love but a conscious brutality, a full awareness of the human cost of his *debitos honores*. In this case, Seneca's concretization of conventional death-marriage imagery in his treatment of the sacrifice probably helped give rise to the love story, which finally appears in clear narrative form within fifty years of the playwright's death in A.D. 65.

3. DARES AND DICTYS

A look at another work produced within the same fifty-year period will contribute to our understanding of how the love story in Dares and Dictys took shape. The work is Dio Chrysostomos's Eleventh Oration, sometimes called the Trojan Oration, which refutes Homer's version of the Trojan War predominantly on the grounds of plausibility but also on the "authority" of an Egyptian priest with access to written records of the account Menelaos gave when he came to Egypt (37–38).[68] According to Dio, Helen was the legitimate wife of Paris (53), Hektor killed Achilles (96), and Troy remained unconquered (119–124). Most of the oration is devoted to the *Iliad,* but specific Epic Cycle events, particularly the ones having to do with Achilles, are also refuted. The more ordinary feats and deaths of Memnon and Penthesileia, for example, take place after Achilles is dead (114–117), and the shameful sacrifice of Polyxena never takes place at all.[69]

There is, however, no refutation of a love story, and nowhere is a death by treachery mentioned. Dio recognizes that Achilles' death in battle at the hands of the Paris depicted by Homer is indeed implausible (105–106) and that it is shameful that the best (*tòn áriston*) of the Greeks was killed by the worst (*toû phaulotátou*) of his enemies (152). But his solution to this disgraceful implausibility is not to posit an ambush but to choose a different killer, Hektor, who is both the greatest Trojan warrior and smart enough not to attack until Achilles is totally worn out from fighting and pursuing others (93–96). Thus a battle death for Achilles is made completely plausible and relatively credible.

Although Dio's neglect of the love story and death by treachery supports my contention that Achilles' amatory involvement with Polyxena was not traditional in the first century A.D., his pervasive concern with plausibility makes an even more important contribution to our understanding the evolution of Polyxena's story. His concern with the implausible shamefulness of Achilles' death at the hands of Paris makes explicit a problem that may perhaps have helped produce the variant in which Apollo alone, either openly or in the guise of Paris, kills Achilles as punishment for hubris.[70] As we have seen, Seneca's Agamemnon regards being killed by Paris as something shameful, and Neoptolemos must recoup his father's honor by invoking Apollo (*Tro.* 347–348). But if the gods are not to be regarded as intimately involved in the human action—as they were not in the rationalistic "histories" composed in the late first and early second centuries A.D.—solutions other than Apollo must be found. The one Dio Chrysostomos puts forward does not enter the tradition. But Dares and Dictys, two Greek-speaking writers of the first century A.D. who decided like Dio that Homer and the heroic tradition needed correcting, propounded a solution so replete with passion, intrigue, and moral lessons that it not only entered the tradition as an alternate but also soon superseded the version that had held sway since Homer.

The alternate version is, of course, that of the ambush in the temple of Apollo, the penultimate act of a love story that now receives a definite shape distinct from the funerary imagery that gave it birth. The accounts of this love story that Dares and Dictys included in their "true" versions of the Trojan War[71] are not identical, but they do contribute to what forms essentially a single version of the cause of Achilles' death— and, of course, of the subsequent sacrifice of Polyxena. Dares' simpler account, which made Achilles' death plausible by his being deceived and outnumbered, provided the basic outline for medieval redactors. Dictys' more complicated plot, which solved the problem of implausible shamefulness not only by means of the ambush but also by degrading Achilles' character to a level with Paris's, provided the moral grist for the redactors' Christian mills.

The story, according to Dares' *Historia*,[72] begins on the first anniversary of Hektor's death, when Achilles sees Polyxena at her brother's tomb and falls violently in love (27): "He gazes upon her, fixes her in his soul, and falls passionately in love with her. Then, constrained by ardent desire, he wastes away his life, now hateful, in love." (*Polyxenam contemplatur, figit animum, amare vehementer eam coepit. Tunc ardore compulsus odiosam in amore vitam consumit.*) He sends a servant to Hekabe, offering to go home if they will give him Polyxena as wife. Hekabe consults Priam, who replies that it would not be right to give his daughter to an enemy, but if a lasting peace (*pax perpetua*) were made with all the Greeks, then he would freely give her (27). Achilles then begins agitating for peace in the Greek camp (27) and in fact refuses to fight in the next two battles (28, 30). In his reply to the embassy that is soon sent to him, we see the same theme of lover versus soldier that we traced earlier in reference to Briseis and Deidameia: he refused them "because he had firmly decided not to fight because of what he had promised to Hekabe, and in any case he would fight less well because of his strong love for Polyxena" (*quod iam destinaverat in bellum non prodire ob id quod promiserat Hecubae, aut certe se minus pugnaturum eo quod Polyxenam valde amabat*, 30). The cause of the famous withdrawal is transformed from a quarrel with Agamemnon to desire to marry Priam's daughter. But unlike the roughly contemporary Achilles of Statius, Dares' Achilles is in no way condemned for refusing battle. One is led to feel that if Achilles' love had produced a *pax perpetua* between Greeks and Trojans it would in fact have been a good solution for this unfortunate war.

The Greeks, however, will not make peace, and eventually Achilles is compelled to reenter battle and kill Troilos in order to save his compatriots from destruction. At this point Hekabe turns against Achilles, and by means of a false message that Priam will meet him to settle his betrothal to Polyxena she lures him to a temple of Apollo that stands just outside the gates. When he arrives inside the temple with one friend, Antilochos, Paris attacks with a group of hidden Trojans. Achilles and Antilochos, using their folded cloaks as makeshift shields, fight back, and Achilles manages to kill several attackers. But Paris kills Antilochos and finally brings down Achilles with multiple stab wounds. "Thus, his courageous fighting useless, Achilles lost his life through treachery" (*ita Achilles animam ex insidiis nequiquam fortiter faciens amisit*, 34).

In this way, the story of Achilles' death is rationalized and his prowess remains unsullied. Apollo's agency is reduced to Paris's using his temple as the site of an ambush, and Achilles, essentially unarmed, is brought down not just by Paris but by several men and only at a great cost to his attackers. If there is a moral to Trojan Dares' account, it is that strength and courage are rendered powerless by deceit, a moral remarkably similar to that one might draw from the final treacherous conquest of Troy. Achilles' love for Polyxena is not presented as a weakness in character even though it did—like the heel of late tradition—make him vulnerable to the enemy.

The more complex account in Dictys' *Journal* offers not only a moral but explicit moralizing. Achilles' character is far from exemplary, and his love for Polyxena wreaks havoc on his psyche. Dictys also adds further to the intricate intertwining of traditional incidents with Achilles' love story by using Polyxena to motivate some famous Iliadic actions.

Achilles first sees Polyxena when he comes as a tourist to a Trojan religious ceremony during a truce, and again it is love at first sight (3.2):

> When Achilles happened to turn his eyes on Polyxena, he was captivated by her virgin beauty. Since his desire grew apace, so that his soul was uneasy, he went back to the ships.

> tum forte Achilles versis in Polyxenam oculis pulchritudine virginis capitur: auctoque in horas desiderio, ubi animus non lenitur, ad naves discedit.

Back at the Greek camp his *amor* grows progressively worse (*ingravescit*), and a few days later he confesses his *ardorem animi* to Automedon and sends him off to ask Hektor for Polyxena (3.2). Hektor, unfortunately, is an obstacle. His precondition for the marriage is that

Achilles betray the whole Greek army to him (3.2). Achilles counters with the more reasonable proposal that he will end the whole war, but Hektor flatly insists on either a betrayal or, alternatively, an assassination of Agamemnon or Menelaos (3.3). Achilles now grows angry and vows to kill him as soon as the fighting starts again (3.3). Thus, Polyxena is made the first cause of Achilles' particular anger against Hektor and of the next battle's rampage, clearly parallel to *Iliad* 20–22, when Hektor eludes him by fleeing (3.6).[73]

Achilles' anger at Hektor by no means cures his love. On the contrary, his frustration makes him begin wandering and burning like a bereft Dido or Turnus[74] (3.3):

> Wounded by the turmoil in his soul he wandered here and there, sometimes, however, considering how far he should go in the matter. And when Automedon saw that his soul was in turmoil, that his desire was growing hotter every day, and that he was spending the night outside his tent, he told Aias and Patroklos everything lest Achilles harm either himself or the above-mentioned kings.

> dein animi iactatione saucius huc atque illuc oberrans interdum tamen, quatenus praesenti negotio utendum esset consultare. at ubi eum Automedon iactari animo atque in dies magis magisque aestuare desiderio ac pernoctare extra tentoria animadvertit veritus, ne quid adversum se aut in supradictos reges moliretur, Patroclo atque Aiaci rem cunctam aperit.

As with Dido, Achilles' passion provokes him to consider actions that would destroy his good repute; unlike Dido, however, Achilles does not in fact commit such actions but eventually comes to his senses (*recordatus sui*) and tells everything to Agamemnon and Menelaos, who comfort him and counsel patience until Troy's fall shall make him master of what he wants (3.3).

Nothing more is said of Polyxena until after Hektor is killed and Priam comes to ransom the body, leaning for support on the shoulders of his daughter (3.20). This scene has little to do with Homer's original: Priam pleads and faints (3.21); Andromache pleads (3.22); Achilles lectures Priam on his responsibilities as a father (3.23) and then goes outside to consult with the Greek leaders (3.24). When he returns, having already decided to accept the ransom, he finds Polyxena at his feet offering herself in return for Hektor's body (3.24). It is she—plus, in a nod to *Iliad* 24.507–512, the thought of father and son—who moves Achilles to tears and motivates a reconciliation that differs from the *Iliad*'s mainly in its more mundanely moralistic topic of conversation.[75] Once again Dictys has interwoven the new love story into a traditional scene.

At the end of the reconciliation scene, attention returns to Polyxena when Priam, "either in gratitude for his having been granted a funeral or else so that he might feel secure about his daughter if something should happen to Troy, embraces Achilles' knees and begs him to take Polyxena for his own" (*in gratiamne impetrati funeris an si quid Troiae accideret securus iam filiae, amplexus Achillis genua orat, uti Polyxenam suscipiat sibique habeat*, 3.27). Does Achilles take advantage of this offer to seize his heart's desire? No. He shows his essential nobility and his desire for a legitimate marriage by putting off the matter to a more appropriate time (*aliud tempus aliud locum tractatumque fore*) and ordering her to return with her father (3.27).

This magnanimous gesture, however, leads to his downfall, first morally and then physically. First, when Priam is slow to act, Achilles is led to perform an act of dreadful brutality: he has the throats of Troilos and Lykaon, Priam's sons, cut in a public ceremony because he is angry that Priam has not yet sent him word about the marriage (4.9). Thus, his frustrated love for Polyxena draws him down to the same barbarous level he had reached twice earlier, when his anger at Agamemnon had provoked him to attack his fellow Greeks while they ate (2.37) and when his vengeful grief for Patroklos had impelled him to sacrifice fifty-two captives on Patroklos's ashes and to throw the bodies of two of them— Priam's sons Pisus and Evander—to be ripped apart by dogs (3.14). But then, when Priam finally does act, Achilles' love makes him careless of physical danger and provides his enemies with the means to kill him.

During the truce that succeeds the slaughter of Troilos, Priam, apparently in good faith, sends instructions about the marriage via Idaeus, whom Achilles meets in the temple of Apollo (4.10). Paris, however, has devised a plot with Deiphobos, and while Achilles is in the temple, "unarmed because he feared no attack in a place sacred to Apollo" (*inermem . . . quippe in sacro Apollonis nihil hostile metuentem*), they approach him under pretense of confirming Priam's agreement. Deiphobos gives him a long, tight embrace that makes it possible for Paris to stab him twice. As they leave him dying (4.11), Odysseus and Aias, who have been waiting outside the temple to talk to Achilles about the camp's anger at his secret meetings with the enemy (4.10), rush in. While Achil-

les bleeds to death, Aias somberly moralizes that no other human being
could have overpowered Achilles, but clearly his own thoughtless fool-
hardiness (*tua inconsulta temeritas*) betrayed him (*prodidit*). Achilles
barely manages to gasp out what has happened—"Deiphobos and Alexander overthrew me by deceit and treachery on account of Polyxena"
(*dolo me atque insidiis . . . Deiphobus atque Alexander Polyxenae gratia cir-
cumvenere*)—before he dies in his comrades' arms (4.11).

The adjective *inconsulta* is perhaps meant to recall Dictys' initial
qualification of Achilles' virtues at 1.14, where he had said that although
Achilles surpassed everyone in military zeal, prowess, and glory, still he
was not free from a certain thoughtless vehemence (*vis inconsulta*) and
ferocious impatience. His tendency to act from passion, be it from love
or anger, is dangerous both to Achilles himself and to the war effort.
But of the two motives, love seems to be the more harmful: it not only
kills him in the end but causes the whole Greek army to suspect treachery and turn against him (4.10).[76]

In Dictys' account the emphasis is on internal rather than external
treachery. If Dares' moral is simply that strength can be brought down
by treachery, Dictys' is that the highest virtues of the body and mind
can be brought down by the treachery of one's own passions. This latter
moral contributes most to the tradition, for although medieval redactors considered Dares' *History* to be the truer version of the Trojan War,
Dictys' emphasis on the enemy within is the more congenial to Christian interpretations of heroic success or failure.

4. MEDIEVAL LOVER

A conveniently succinct example of such Christian interpretation is provided by Fulgentius the Mythographer, who in the late fifth or early
sixth century explicates Achilles' life from birth to death as a lesson
in the danger of *libido*. His brief allegorization of the myth of Peleus
and Thetis (*Mitologiarum 3 Fab. 7*) relates that Peleus (who represents
earth or *caro*, "flesh"), Thetis (water or *humor*, "bodily fluids") and
Jupiter (fire or *anima*, "breath of life") together produced Achilles, a
complete man (*hominum perfectum*) whom Thetis then dipped in the
Styx to arm him against all troubles (721–722). Her failure to dip his
heel, whose veins are connected to organs of sex and passion, signifies
that "human virtue, no matter how strongly fortified, is open to attacks

of lust" (*humana virtus quamvis ad omnia munita tamen libidinis ictibus subiacet patula*, 722–723).[77] According to Fulgentius, Achilles' indulgent stay on Skyros represented the first such attack of *libido* (723); the second attack, his love for Polyxena, proved fatal:

> And then Achilles died through love for Polyxena and was killed for the sake of lust by means of his heel. Indeed, Polyxena's name in Greek means "much wandering" either because *amor* causes the mind to wander from its own nature or because *libido* wanders like a foreign traveler among many.

> Denique et amore Polixenae perit et pro libidine per talum occiditur. Polixene enim Grece multorum peregrina dicitur, seu quod amor peregrinari faciat mentes ab ingenio suo, sive quod aput multos libido ut peregrinabunda vagetur (723).

The treachery that destroys Achilles is here completely internalized.

Fulgentius's allegory depersonalizes Achilles' career, depicting sexual love as an inherent human weakness and Achilles as Everyman who fails to guard against it.[78] Polyxena becomes a mere personification of his susceptibility, the weak female part, as it were, of an otherwise strong, masculine, virtuous nature.[79] This late-antique allegory adumbrates the Christian misogyny that is strikingly exemplified in Bernardus's twelfth-century *Commentary on the first six books of Vergil's Aeneid*, a work that makes Dido the express equivalent of *libido* and likens her city to Babylon, a city of earthly disorder:

> This city is ruled by Dido, that is *libido*. . . . In this city one finds a woman ruling and the Phoenician men serving her because in this world the disorder is such that *libido* rules and virtues are overpowered like the strong and upright Phoenician men; and we understand that thus does a man serve and a woman rule. Therefore the Bible calls the world the "city of Babylon," that is the "city of disorder."

> In hac civitate regnum habet Dido, id est libido. . . . In hac civitate invenit mulierem regnantem et Penos servientes quia in mundo isto talis est confusio quod imperat libido et virtutes opprimuntur quas per Penos, fortes et rigidos viros, intellegimus atque ita servit vir et imperat mulier. Ideo in divinis libris dicitur mundus civitas Babilonis, id est confusionis.[80]

Such Christian perspective very early converted reaction to the "conquering hero conquered" *topos* (exemplified by Propertius's usurping heroines and Statius's effeminized adolescent) from pitying amusement to the stern "Detestabilis turpitudo!" with which Lactantius, a Christian apologist of the early fourth century, chides the subjugated Herakles (*Divinarum Institutionum* 1.9).[81] In a heroic world thus Christianized, a conqueror who lets his martial spirit be conquered by a lesser female—a *topos* that remains a favorite of Achilles' medieval redactors[82]—merits not pity but scorn, for, even if never explicitly portrayed as a Christian, he must be judged to have jeopardized not only his mind but his soul, not only his personal well-being but also cosmic order.

In this environment the most pointed analogues to Achilles' lovestruck behavior are found in the Bible. Benoît de Sainte-Maure's twelfth-century Achilles asks himself, "Who can be sensible in the face of love?" (18044), and then, like Propertius, invokes heroic exemplars to excuse his feebleness. But instead of Jason, Herakles, and Antony, Achilles invokes prominent Old Testament figures: Samson, David, and Solomon (18045–18046), all of whom betrayed through lust the cause of their people and/or the commandments of their God. The anonymous writer who transformed Benoît's *Roman* into prose (mid-thirteenth century) adds to this list Adam, the ultimate transgressor, and the Apocryphal Holofernes, who like Achilles actually lost his life through lust.[83]

The parallel between Samson's career and Achilles' is especially close in that Samson's love for an enemy woman resulted in his being successfully ambushed and his people's being deprived of their strongest warrior (*Judges* 13–16). One early medieval redactor, the anonymous author of the *Excidium Troiae*,[84] felt this parallel so strongly that he or she recast Achilles' entire relationship with Polyxena to make it correspond to Samson's with Delilah. According to this unique version of the story, Polyxena is requested as the price of the dead Hektor's ransom.[85] Priam agrees, and then,

when Polyxena was married to Achilles who loved her exceedingly, she got a message from King Priam her father or Hekabe her mother, saying, "We believe that because you must grieve so greatly for your youthful brother, whom none dared attack, you must also find out for us the secret place in which Achilles can be breached by steel; and when he is dead and your brother's death is avenged, we will be able to give you to a better husband who is our equal." When Polyxena heard this, she took Achilles in her arms and charmingly challenged him to show her the secret place where he could be harmed by steel; and because there is nothing that women cannot force men to confess when their dear spouses hold them, he showed her the secret place in the tendon of his heel where he could be

harmed by steel. When Polyxena learned this she told it to her parents,
who subsequently pretended to be having a service in the temple of
Apollo . . . and asked Achilles to join them at the service along with
Polyxena their daughter.

> Polyxena vero dum Achilli coniuncta fuisset et eam nimie diligeret, a
> Priamo rege patre eius vel ab Hecuba matre eius mandatur, dicens: "Cre-
> dimus quia debes dolere tante iuventutis fratris tui contra quem nec unus
> hominum manum ausus est levare, et ad secretam Achillis partem ubi po-
> terit a ferro adiri nobis prevenire; et dum occisus fuerit et mors fratris tui
> vindicata fuerit meliore coniugo coequali nostro te poterimus dare." Hoc
> dum Polyxena audiret, cepit Achillem per amplexus et blandimenta pro-
> vocare ut ei locum occultum ubi a ferro adiri poterat ostenderet. Et quia
> nichil est quod mulieres non extorqueant de viris ut eis fateantur ut con-
> iuges cari habent, secretum locum in tali nervo ubi a ferro adiri poterat
> ei ostendit. Hoc dum Polixena agnosceret parentibus suis nuntiavit, qui
> dum audissent finxerunt se devotionem in templo Apollinis habere . . .
> ad quam devotionem petierunt Achillem una cum Polyxena filia eorum
> interesse.[86]

The sequel is similar to the ambush in Dares and Dictys except that
Paris attacks Achilles while his brother-in-law is offering incense to
Apollo—thus making the sacrilege worse—and shoots him in the heel
with a poisoned arrow rather than overwhelming him with spears.[87] The
Trojans in this account are every bit as bad as the Biblical Philistines,
and, in comparison with them, Achilles' action in revealing his secret to
his enemy wife is, like Samson's, more foolish than consciously sinful.

Fortunately for Polyxena's reputation, but unfortunately for Achilles', the above account had little influence,[88] and Polyxena elsewhere is
almost universally proclaimed innocent of Achilles' death and is even occasionally said to have been in love with the Greek hero.[89] The beautiful
girl is merely the unwitting cause of his entrapment—the *causa penitus
impulsiva,* as Guido delle Colonne puts it[90]—and all blame falls on
Achilles himself, who can no more control his lust in these medieval
narratives than he could control his temper in classical poetry. His temper, which is no longer essential to a plot in which his withdrawal is
unrelated to a quarrel with Agamemnon,[91] diminishes in importance,
and a tendency toward lust takes its place as his basic character flaw. This
tendency is especially pronounced in Albert of Stade's *Troilus,* a mid-
thirteenth-century Latin poem of some 5000 elegiac verses, and Guido
delle Colonne's *Historia Destructionis Troaie,* the influential Latin prose

redaction of Benoît's *Roman* written in 1287. In these two sternest redactors of the Troy story even the "catalogue" portraits, which universally
prefer Dares' beautiful curly-haired cheerfulness, generosity, and martial
fierceness to Dictys' *vis inconsulta* and *effera impatientia*,[92] reflect this
new emphasis on lust: Albert adds *amorosus* to Dares' adjectives (2.74),
and Guido puts an amorous glance into a newly discovered pair of large
grey eyes.[93]

It is no accident that Guido locates Achilles' amorousness in his eyes,
for orthodox Christianity located the beginnings of lust in the organ of
sight. The first step in the development of this sin, writes Thomas Aquinas, "is the gazing of the eyes by which a beautiful woman is seen."[94] To
Christians the physical eye is the window by which worldly delight enters the mind and fatally disturbs its concentration on spiritual beauty.[95]
We can see this doctrine at work in the behavior of Albert's *amorosus*
Achilles (*Troilus* 3.707–708, 711–718):

> Hekabe and Polyxena went to the tomb with Priam
>   to honor Hektor with customary dirges.
>
> . . . .
>
> Some Greek men came, among them Achilles
>   idly curious with wandering eyes.
> The body's eye is such that, unless it shuts tightly,
>   it blinds the eye of the mind.
> Thus his bodily eye blinded Achilles' heart
>   so that his formerly sighted mind lost its vision.
> Thus the sight of Polyxena blinded his breast,
>   and past, present, and future fled his blind mind.[96]

> Hecuba cum Priamo tumulumque Polyxena visunt
>   Ut celebrent carmen funebre more suo;
>
> . . . .
>
> Graecorum juvenes accurrunt, his et Achilles
>   Intendens oculis vana videre vagis.
> Corporis est oculus talis, quod mentis ocellum,
>   Ni bene se claudat, exoculare solet.
> Sic cor corporeus Pelidae caecat ocellus,
>   Ut visum perdat mens oculata prius.
> Cuius tiresiat sic visa Polyxena pectus,
>   Transeat ut caeca tempora mente tria.

Achilles' idle curiosity (*intendens . . . vana videre*) and wandering eyes
(*oculis . . . vagis*) indicate that we are meant to judge Achilles as overly

receptive to things of this world. This receptivity, as Albert makes quite clear in verses 713–716, condemns Achilles to being not merely foolish but also spiritually blind. The emphatic metaphor of the mind's eye (*mentis ocellum, mens oculata*) and blinded heart (*cor . . . caecat*) links Achilles to numerous Biblical backsliders and refusers of the true faith. In the *Vulgate, caecus,* "blind," is a term of opprobrium for ignorant Old Testament Jews and New Testament disciples and for corrupt New Testament Pharisees and pagans.[97] According to Paul, Jesus often locates such blindness in the *cor,* which seems to be synonymous with the *mens* and which at one point (Ephesians 1.18) is said specifically to have *oculi.*[98] Paul himself uses the metaphor, positing *caecitas cordis* as the ultimate cause of abandoning oneself to *impudicitia* (Eph. 4.18–19).[99]

Albert sustains his metaphor with five repetitions of words for eye (*oculus, ocellus,* and *oculatus* 'furnished with eyes') and no fewer than four different verbs for blinding: *exoculare* (714), *caecare* (715), *visum perdere* (716), and *tiresiare* (717). The first three verbs are common; the last is a highly unusual medieval coinage from the name of the Greek seer Teiresias, a man who changed sex twice, first from a man into a woman and then from a woman back into a man, and who was stricken blind when he displeased Herê over the issue of the female's greater sexual pleasure. The verb made from his name must clearly be translated "blinded" in the context of Albert's metaphor, but in another context it could equally well mean "to change sex."[100] The undertone created by this possible second meaning reinforces Albert's moral by linking Achilles' blindness with the same loss of masculinity that we saw in the misogynist Christian allegories of Fulgentius and Bernardus. The sight of the female body gives the female part of Achilles, that is, his own body, so great a mastery over the male part, his reason, that he can more correctly be viewed as a woman than as a man.

Needless to say, the overlay of Christian doctrine in this passage weighs heavily upon Albert's subsequent depiction of Achilles as a typical Ovidian lover (721–738) and eradicates all its potential Augustan charm. The Christian opposition between physical sight and spiritual blindness operates similarly even in the relatively unmoralistic *Roman de Troie* of Benoît de Sainte-Maure. Benoît comments that love makes a man "blind, deaf and dumb" (*sort, cec e mu,* 22131) and attributes to Polyxena's splendid appearance (*resplendor de sa semblance*) and an irremediable ruin (*errance,* 22139–22141) that includes Achilles' ceasing to be concerned with justice, nobility, honesty, and proper appearance (*dreiture, noblece, honesté, parage*, 18446–18447). Achilles' abandonment of virtuous behavior is typical, for according to Simon Capra Aurea, a late-twelfth-century poet contemporary with Benoît, "every lover spurns himself and everything: / counsel, reputation, faith, laws, gods" (*sic est omnis amans: sic se, sic omnia spernit: consilium, famam, federa, iura, deos*).[101] But the Christian reader of Benoît and Simon would know that it is also the opposite of what one should do to avoid being destroyed by concupiscence.[102] According to the Apostle Peter, the only way to avoid such a fate is to *add* virtues to one's basic faith: *virtus, scientia,* abstinence, patience, piety, brotherly love, and *caritas;* not to have these is to be *caecus* and lost (2 Peter 1.4–7).

The best, most inclusive picture of the harmful effects of love is found in chapter 198 of the more moralistic prose redaction of the *Roman de Troie.* Commenting on the fact that Dares had expressed surprise at Achilles' change from his usual prudence and cleverness and courage to the opposite as soon as he fell in love, the author of the *Roman en prose* declares that he for one is not surprised:

> For whoever is as cruelly seized by love as was Achilles is in the power of another and not in his right senses nor in possession of his rational nature: for this reason he often takes the false for the true and the true for the false. His condition is the same as that of a sick person who refuses to take what will return him to health and wants to eat what will kill him. . . . Similarly do those men act who are utterly careless of the peril that could happen to them and care not whether what they do is honest or rational or unreasonable, but only that they may follow whatever their pleasure procures for them. And they choose to act so that their bad fortune or the devil, whatever it be, will give them the power to accomplish their desire. And when he has accomplished what he desired, what he has gained is as worthless as a false suit of armor, and if he has locked everything into it, both the power of his body and soul and also his good renown, which it is very important to hold dear, he perishes. And Achilles fell into such passion and folly over Polyxena . . . and put himself so thoroughly into the power of love that he abandoned and forgot all his sense and his rational nature.

> car qui est si cruelment espris d'amors come Achillès estoit entrés, il est en pooir d'autre et non pas en son droit sens ne en sa rasnable matiere: por coi il juge maintes fois le faus por voir et le voir pour faus. Et est en la

condition dou malade que il eschieve a prendre ce qui li peut torner a santé et desir au mangier ce que li peut doner la mort. . . . Tout ensi font tel maniere de gent qui ne considerent point dou peril qui avenir lor puet, ne ne gardent que la chose soit heneste ou raisnable ou encontre raison, mais que il porsivent ce que la volenté lor aporte; et eslisent chose a faire que lor male fortune ou dyable, quel qui soit, li donra pooir d'accomplir son desirier. Et quant il avra compliment de ce que il avra desiret n'avra il pas tant gaaignié que une fausse maille ne vaille plus, et si avra mis toute estuide et peril dou cors e d'arme, et sa bone renomee, qui mout fait a tenir chier, pert. Et en tel rage et en tel folie entra Achilles por le regart de Polixenaim . . . et se mist si dou tout en pooir d'Amors, que il en laissa et oblia tout son sens et sa raisnable matiere.[103]

After comparing Achilles to several Biblical figures—as well as to Merlin and Vergil[104]—the author concludes that he is therefore not surprised that Achilles lost the right path and behaved so badly (*fu si chaitif*), so much had Love blinded him (*auveuglé*).

The Christian bias in this passage is obvious. The worthless *fausse maille* begs to be compared to the New Testament spiritual armor of the person who is strong in Christian virtue (Paul, Ephesians 6.10–11). The Devil is explicitly mentioned, and what medieval reader, well-instructed by the pupils of St. Jerome, would not (to paraphrase Andreas Capellanus) recognize the Devil as the very author of carnal love?[105] God and *amor* are antithetical, and it is clear that Achilles, as a medieval soldier of love, sacrifices everything: blind, he takes the false for true;[106] he follows pleasure, not reason; he could (were it appropriate to the story) be induced to betray his God. As Andreas says, the fruits of love are a miserable life in this world and enormous punishment in the next.[107]

The basic image in the passage from the *Roman en prose* is that of the sick man who kills himself by refusing to do what he knows will heal him. The same image is found presented more vividly as metaphor in the accounts of Achilles' passion created by Joseph of Exeter, Albert of Stade, and Guido delle Colonne. Their Christian expropriation of the pagan *topos* of love as a physical disease or wound[108] is quite appropriate, for, as we have seen, the origin of this deadly mental illness is the physical body.[109] For Christian writers, using sickness and wounding as a metaphor is one means of stressing the carnality of Achilles' love.

The imagery and the carnality occur only briefly in Joseph's *Ilias*, a 3000-verse Latin poem written near the end of the twelfth century. The

FIGURE 20. Achilles Languishes in Love

image is used to describe Achilles' falling in love (6.84–85): Achilles "sees Polyxena, desires her, and, wounded with the golden dart of Venus, pants with sudden love" (*Hanc videt, hanc optat, et acuto Cypridis auro / Saucius Eacides subitos suspirat amores*). A subsequent message to Hekabe, in which he says he wants her daughter as a "bed-mate" (*consors tori*) and terms her a rather materialistic "price" (*precium*) of his withdrawal (6.93), implies clearly though mildly the physical nature of his desires. The implication is just strong enough to indicate that if Jean de Meun's Reason speaks truth when she informs us that "Good love must come from a pure heart over which bodily gratification lacks mastery" (*Bone amor doit de fin queur nestre: / don n'en doivent pas estre mestre / ne quel font corporel soulas*),[110] what Achilles feels is not true love.

Albert of Stade, whose work is roughly contemporary with the moralistic *Roman en prose,* as is Joseph's with that of the relatively unmoralistic Benoît, greatly expands the metaphor, in addition to giving emphasis to the physical basis of Achilles' desire. The metaphor is not employed in Achilles' initial encounter with Polyxena, but later, when he does not go out to fight along with the other Greeks, Albert says it is because he is troubled by a wound of love deep in his chest (*turbatus Achilles / pectoris in camera vulnus amoris habens, Troilus* 3.833–834). Four battles later, the wound is not healed; when Agamemnon begs Achilles to fight, Achilles replies that his incurable wound renders him powerless to do so (*Troilus* 4.237–238, 241):

> I am wounded and carry a hidden weapon in my chest:
> Battle has no place in an injured body.
>
> .   .   .   .
>
> This species of wound is not curable.
>
> Vulneror et clausum porto sub pectore telum,
> Non habet in laeso corpore pugna locum.
>
> .   .   .   .
>
> Vulneris id genus est, quod cum sanabile non sit.

The carnal nature of Achilles' love is underlined by a strong focus on sex in the speech that lures Achilles to the ambush in the temple. Hekabe tempts Achilles with the prospect of deflowering an eager virgin (*Troilus* 4.431–434):

> Our daughter, your darling Polyxena, I say
> loves you as impatiently as you could hope.
> If you are pleased to pluck Love's flowers
> do not delay to enter her embrace, come.
>
> Filia nostra tibi dilecta Polyxena, dico,
> Te, velut optabas, impatienter amat.
> Si te delectat Veneris decerpere flores,
> Eius in amplexu sit mora nulla, veni.

She tells him that Priam will await him in the temple to perform the espousal and adds that "the gorgeous virgin joyfully and gladly awaits your coming with hot desire" (*Nec tepido desiderio pulcherrima virgo / pendet ad adventum laeta libensque tuum,* 4.441–442). When Achilles is in the trap, Albert keeps the link between lust and death well to the fore by drawing a pointed contrast between what Achilles expected to find in the temple and what he actually found (4.483–484): "Instead of a virgin's arms, the man felt fierce war, / instead of a soft bed, hard wounds" (*Vir pro virgineis fera sentit bella lacertis, / Pro molli vero vulnera dura toro*).[111]

In Guido delle Colonne's *Historia* imagery of wounding and sickness pervades the scene in Book Twenty-three in which Achilles falls more deeply in love with Polyxena the longer he keeps his gaze fixed on her. As he first contemplates her beauty, an arrow of desire (*sagitta cupidinis*) suddenly wounds (*vulneravit*) him. He tries to alleviate his desire by gazing on her, but this only enlarges the wound (*maioris scissure vulneris seipsum sibi reddebat actorem*). Since his love for her overwhelms all other concerns, he keeps his sight on her as long as he can; this further enlarges his injuries and deepens the wounds in his heart (*dilatat amplius plagas suas et sui amoris vulnera magis sui cordis attrahit in profundum*). When Polyxena finally leaves, Achilles follows her with the same melting looks (*dulcibus aspectibus*) that were, Guido comments, the first cause of his illness (*causa et principium sui morbi*).[112]

Some words in Achilles' subsequent soliloquy indicate a recognition of illness, but a good Christian reader would find deadly irony rather than a true self-awareness in Achilles' statement that Polyxena is his only possible doctor (*medicus*) and cure (*medela*). The true cure, as the physician Bernardus Gordon tells us (A.D. 1305), would involve a reminder of impending damnation.[113] The cure Achilles has in mind is sexual gratification: he laments that because he has killed her brother he is unlikely to be able to induce Polyxena to budge from her piety (*movere . . . ad lubricum pietatis*) and become pliant (*allicare . . . ad motum flexibilis voluntatis*).[114]

Marriage, it seems, is the only possible means to sexual gratification, and in order to achieve this "cure" Achilles promises to withdraw from and end the war. The second part of the promise, says Guido, is an example of the foolishness all lovers fall into: "It is a fault peculiar to all lovers that, burning with lustful desire, they promise great and impossible things in inconsiderate heat" (*Etenim mos est et proprium vicium omnium amatorum ut, et eorum concupiscencie desiderio estuante, magna sibi et impossibilia inconsulto calore promittant*).[115] The first part, however, is within Achilles' power, and because his lust is so great he keeps his promise for nine months and through seven battles despite the des-

FIGURE 21. Achilles Plays Chess as Greek Embassy Arrives

perate pleas of his friends, one of whom dies in Achilles' own tent while reproaching him for his cruel behavior.[116] In Guido's view, this cruel behavior is generic to lovers, and once again he uses wound imagery to make his point: just as Achilles ignores the Greek need for his prowess, so

> he who is bound in the chains of love lets everything else go. It is customary for all lovers that, cut away from honor by the wounds of love, they flee glory, thinking to displease their mistresses, even if with great ignominy it happens that they hold back from the glory of good works.

> ille qui est amoris vinculis alligatus omnia pretermittit. Est enim mos omnium amatorum ut amoris vulneribus execati honoris laudes effugiant, putantes eorum amatricibus displicere, eciam si cum magna ignominia a bonorum operum laudibus contingeret abstinere.[117]

Guido's "wounds of love" seem more insidious than did Albert's. We can almost visualize *amor* with sword in hand slicing away that part of the lover that was concerned with his own spiritual good and thus dooming him to complete degradation.

Guido in this passage presents a clear opposition between the claims of love and those of the honor and glory that are always associated with

Achilles' name in the Homeric tradition. This opposition is restated in an exchange between Odysseus and Achilles in the subsequent embassy scene. Odysseus urges Achilles not to extinguish his glorious renown (*tante glorie fama*) through his present contrary actions.[118] Achilles rejects Odysseus's plea and chooses a life without danger instead of *fama:*

> Did not most valiant Hektor lose his life pitiably in this war? Thus easily might I also who am not so valiant as he. . . . For I would rather my vigorous reputation be extinguished than my person. Certainly although goodness may be praised, oblivion suddenly overwhelms it.

> Nonne ille fortissimus Hector vitam miserabiliter in hoc bello finivit? Sic de facili possem et ego, qui tante fortitudinis non existo. . . . Nam malo meam strennuitatis famam extingui pocius quam personam. Probitas enim etsi quandoque laudetur, repente oblivio eam submergit.[119]

It is clear that Achilles is choosing physical over metaphysical life. This was not so clear in Guido's source, Benoît's *Roman*. There Achilles had questioned the fact that his *pris* and *los* could be eradicated by his refusal to continue fighting what he now considers a shameful war, and he had said that the praise of men who thought it honorable to die in such

FIGURE 22. Death of Achilles

cause was valueless (19575–19622).[120] Though an earlier indication that Achilles would say or do anything to achieve his desire undermines its effect,[121] the long speech that Benoît gives to Achilles approaches the spirit of Achilles' speech to Odysseus in *Iliad* 9, a speech in which Achilles questioned the very possibility of winning true honor or glory in this corrupt world (*Il.* 9.308–429). Guido's abridgement of Benoît's lengthy speech, while including a condemnation of war as foolish and costly, eliminates Achilles' doubts as to whether one can win honor in such a war or whether present inglorious actions can obliterate earlier glorious ones. Achilles' assumption that both of these questions can be answered in the affirmative is what makes the terms of Guido's choice so clear-cut and the opposition between love and honor so emphatic. Guido's Christian irony is also clear: Achilles' focus on the body will cost him that body along with his honor.

5. LOVE AND WRATH

Throughout the Homeric and non-Homeric traditions alike, what finally returns Achilles to his warrior role is vengeful anger. In the *Iliad* it is anger over Hektor's slaying of Patroklos; in Dares' redactors[122] it is anger over Troilos's victorious slaughter of countless fleeing Greeks. In the *Iliad* a new anger conquers an old anger, but in the alternate tradition anger conquers love. Insofar as anger is the prime emotion of Achilles as warrior, a contest between two opposing emotions inheres in all medieval accounts of Achilles' withdrawal for love of Polyxena. Joseph, for instance, implies such a contest when he says first that the love-struck Achilles "forgets about arms and cares not about battle" (*nec armorum meminit nec prelia curat*, 6.90) and then that the intensity of his renewed onslaught was equivalent to his *ingens ira* (6.304–306).[123] In Albert's account a contest between love and anger is also implied: upon learning of Troilos's carnage Achilles glares savagely (*torve speculatur*, 4.301), and immediately, "just as before the heat of love had overcome his martial spirit, / now love was overcome by the goad of his martial spirit" (*pridem militiam superaverat ardor amoris, / Militiae stimulo nunc superatur amor*, 4.303–304).

Benoît and Guido make this contest between love and vengeful anger explicit. Some 350 lines before Troilos's massacre finally goads Achilles into action, Benoît uses the occasion of one hundred slaughtered Myrmidons to motivate an implicit psychomachia (20702–20812) between Love (*Amors*) and his angry desire for vengeance, here personified as Crime (*Mesfaiz*). Despite Achilles' acknowledgment that "Love does me harm" (20807), *Amors* wins the battle easily and never allows *Mesfaiz* to say a single word. Benoît describes another psychomachia during the next day's battle when the Myrmidons are again being slaughtered. Achilles, enraged,

> many times has it in his heart to
> go out to succor and avenge them.
> But as soon as he decides on this,
> *Amors* prohibits and prevents it:
> Then he suffers mortal pain.
> Whence his valor grows and grows,
> until everything falls into oblivion:
> so furious is he, so very angry,
> that he forgets his love.
> He wishes to go, but immediately
> *Amors* rises so offended
> that he dare not take a step.

> Par maintes feiz a en corage
> D'aler les socorre e vengier,
> Mais ne s'en set vis conseillier,
> Qu'Amors le li defent e viee:
> Por qu'il suefre mortel haschiee.
> E sa proëce le renvie,
> Que tel hore est que toz s'oblie:
> Si est desvez, si est iriez
> Qu'il ne li membre d'amistiez.
> Aler i vueut, mais en poi d'ore
> Li rest Amors si coruz sore
> Qu'il n'i ose le pié porter.
>
> (20842–20853)

Guido, as often, abbreviates and summarizes his predecessor's lengthy dialogue. His Achilles laments over the deaths of his Myrmidons, but his desire to avenge them is restrained by his love for Polyxena:

> But his troublesome love for Polyxena waged fierce resistance, while he pondered that since he loved Polyxena more than himself, a good argument against his desire for revenge was that if he leapt to arms he would

make vain his promise to Polyxena and might be deprived of the joys he hoped for from her.

Sed Polixene amor infestus sibi duro marte resistit, dum cogitat quod, cum Pollixenam diligat plus quam se, contra se est efficax argumentum quod, si forte ad arma prosiliat, Pollixene voto frustrabitur et speratis gaudiis ex ea privari continget.[124]

Achilles' anger at this point is not great enough to overpower his love, but this is only a preliminary skirmish. When Achilles learns of Troilos's bloodbath at the Greek tents, Benoît has him take up arms, "so angry that he remembers neither love nor his beloved" (*Ni le membre, tant a iror, / Adonc d'amie ne d'amor*, 21083–21084). His anger becomes more vivid in Guido's account:

Achilles rises as if raging, his spirit roars, he blazes into anger from his great fury, setting aside his love for Polyxena he seeks arms and puts them on instantly . . . and like a famished wolf upon sheep he throws himself greedily upon the Trojans.

Ad hec igitur Achilles quasi furibundus exurgit, fremit spiritus eius, ex multo furore dum excandescit in iram, amore Polixene postposito arma petit, armatur instanter . . . et velut lupus famelicus inter agnos avidus se ingerit in Troyanos.[125]

As intense anger changes Achilles back into the warrior whose killing of both Hektor and Troilos traditionally ensured the final capture of Troy, love is defeated—not, to be sure, soundly enough to save Achilles' life, but at least for long enough to ensure Greek victory.

We have come a long way from the relatively value-free opposition between lover and warrior found in a classical amatory poet such as Propertius. Love itself, now linked specifically to a body judged anti- thetical to the spirit, has passed through the goatish lust of Quintus's Achilles to emerge as spiritual blindness in the lovesick hero of Guido's stern predecessor, Albert of Stade. Through the Christian efforts of mi- sogynist allegorists such as Fulgentius and Bernardus, Statius's amusing and temporary effeminization of the potential warrior has become in the realized warrior the equivalent of spiritual death and cosmic chaos. Love for an enemy woman, which as originally expressed towards Penthesileia was brief, posthumous, and of little importance in Achilles' sporadic appearances as a classical lover, has become an enduring passion for Priam's daughter and the major element in all late-antique and medieval reincarnations of Dares' doomed lover. Once attention shifted away from Briseis and Deidameia to Polyxena, Achilles' fault could be seen as analogous to that of Samson, who betrayed both his nation and his God when he chose peace with his enemy mistress over war for the Chosen People. Thus it is described first by the courtly Benoît and then by the severe author of the prose *Roman*, who, unlike his predecessor, uses the analogy together with others to Adam and Holofernes explicitly to condemn the fault.

Guido, coming at the end of this developed moralistic tradition, not surprisingly views amorousness as Achilles' principal flaw and largely ignores the towering wrath that for centuries had been depicted as the most serious defect in the hero's character. Dictys, Quintus, and Joseph had broken the original Homeric link between Achilles' wrath and honor, but Guido, in addition to reducing the wrath to a more normal anger, partially realigns it with honor by pitting each against the destructive forces of carnal love. The stage is thus set for the numerous neo-Platonic deployments of irascible and concupiscent passions that occur when Guido's influential redaction of the Troy story comes to compete with a rediscovered *Iliad* for the Achilles of Renaissance poets.

FIGURE 23. Portrait of Achilles

CONCLUSION

We will deny that any of these incidents is told correctly.
(Plato, fourth century B.C.)
Readers may judge to be truer what Dares the Phrygian committed to
memory, he who lived and was a soldier during the time the Greeks
besieged Troy, or they may decide that Homer is to be believed, he who
was born many years after the war was waged.
(Cornelius Nepos, sixth century A.D.)
Listen, wretched Homer, Achilles never . . .
(Guido delle Colonne, thirteenth century A.D.)

These attacks on the *Iliad*'s veracity, recurring roughly three, thirteen,
and twenty centuries after it was composed, attest to the epic's continuing power over the minds and hearts of the communities it had reached
in either its original Greek or its abridged Latin form. This power ensured that as long as war remained a central concern to the societies involved, Achilles, best of Greek warriors, would be a figure to be reck-
oned with, able to be fruitfully manipulated for poetic, political, and
philosophical ends. Changing mores and competing ideologies may
have altered responses to Homer's hero, but they could never consign
him to oblivion.

In the misty origins of Greek heroic tradition, Achilles' superlative
soldiery may have represented the warrior function as described in
Georges Dumézil's tripartite interpretation of Indo-European ideol-
ogy:[1] his clash with Agamemnon may have expressed the disregard or
defiance typically felt by representatives of the second (warrior) function toward those of the first (sacred sovereignty);[2] his extraordinary
wrath may have originated in the combat-induced fury experienced by

the original divine representatives of the warrior function.[3] In other words, the traditional stories of conflict between Achilles and Agamemnon over who is the best of the Achaians[4] possibly arose from a mythic exploration of how a social structure tries to control the forces of coercion that, embodied in autonomous members of the group, are both necessary and dangerous to its well being.

In a realistic epic world that sometimes produces warriors wiser and juster than the king and that often makes the people, whose productivity represents Dumézil's third function, pay with their lives and prosperity for the judgments of leaders they support, the *Iliad* harmonizes all three ideological functions, the three needs that, according to Dumézil, any society must satisfy if it is not to perish.[5] The story of the *Iliad* validates both individual autonomy (Achilles has the power to avenge himself on his society) and the Zeus-given hierarchical social structure (Agamemnon is neither killed by Achilles nor deposed by the group) as well as the welfare of the group (Achilles' power is ultimately turned upon the enemy). Acceptable, therefore, to all classes, it would be especially attractive to the aristocratic warrior class whose "heroic code"— the group's right to apportion honor and wealth according to its estimation of an individual's courage and prowess—has been upheld and ethicized by Achilles' might and whose war tents and feasts, if we may trust Homer's evidence (*Iliad* 9.189; *Odyssey* 1.325–353), furnished the appreciative context for the *Iliad* in its formative years. But although we can thus locate the enduring appeal of the *Iliad*'s plot in the critical problematic of society's relationship to the warrior, this basic problematic does not account for Achilles' tenacious hold on the imaginations of centuries of subsequent poets. For this we must turn to the specific way Homer deploys his society's superlative warrior within the traditional story.

Homer's Achilles, of course, is far from being a simple representative of the warrior function.[6] The *Iliad*'s military hero is used to make a profound statement about the human condition. Because Achilles is not only superlative in prowess and physical beauty but also superlatively complex—possessing the skills of a healer, the uncompromising principles of an idealist, the self-knowledge of a philosopher, the artistry of a poet—readers are emotionally engaged with him as a complete human being. They feel the value of what is at stake when Achilles weighs long life against immortal glory, of what will be the cost when he chooses death for the sake of revenge; they sense the generic implications of the intricate shield he carries on his brutal rampage.

Even when Achilles is at his most inhuman in his rampage, Homer's focus remains the human condition as well as the particular situation, war, in which two societies of humans are operating. The passions that produce the rampage—grief and vengeful anger—are the warrior's normal two-stage response to loss, a response that is highly functional in that it produces vigorous martial activity on the battlefield that is the center of both societies' attention. So it is with Achilles, whose grief and wrath impel him to slaughter masses of the enemy and to ensure Greek victory by killing Hektor—the deed that among the Greeks certifies his claim to be "best of the Achaians." But Homer's vision is somewhat different from that of the bellicose Achaians of tradition.

The poet's vision is different perhaps because he is now composing not for private performance before the aristocratic warrior households that probably formed heroic poetry's first audience but for public performance in the context of the newly emerged *polis*, "city-state." The people of the eighth-century *polis* may have been entranced by stories of their glorious past,[7] but the diversity of the audience and a new spirit of public debate[8] would at least have opened to question the supreme value assigned to aggressive martial excellence by traditional poetry. And the clear and present danger of having one's own city, with its comfortable houses and prosperous families, sacked by invaders[9] would have fostered audience identification and sympathy with the besieged in Troy. Such questioning and such sympathy are, I think, reflected in the way Homer colors Achilles' martial achievement in the *Iliad*.

Continuing to speak in "the antique language of art" that uses stylized animal combats and hunting scenes to depict battlefield death,[10] Homer manipulates the traditional images and similes just enough to intimate that Achilles' deadly wrath, which motivates the merciless slaughter of Hektor and thus in effect wins the war for the Greeks, takes the "best of the Achaians" across the boundaries of the human into the realms of the bestial and the divine. The killing of the enemy champion, therefore, cannot represent highest *human* excellence. With human boundaries again securely established in Book Twenty-Four, Homer suggests what does: communion with the enemy in recognition of common human sorrow. Achilles, best of humans, loses what all humans must: life and happiness, the latter because it is tied to other human beings who are subject to the same inexorable mortality. The epic culminates in a scene that depicts a full comprehension of this sorrowful truth at the same time as it transcends it by something I shall call, for want of a more exact term, greatness of soul.

The charisma of Homer's Achilles, then, emanates from a unique combination of physical and mental qualities. He has continued to live in poets' imaginations because by endowing him with a personality as superior in its complexity as his body is superior in strength and martial technique, Homer made his actions reverberate far beyond the battlefield. It is the force of this archetype that empowers most of the later, more one-sided evocations. Who, for example, would be very much interested in the *Odyssey*'s Achilles if the *Iliad* did not exist? For although in many ways the character is true to the *Iliad*'s—anger, honesty, prowess, glory, concern for honor, all the famous characteristics are there—it lacks depth. The Odyssean Achilles' concern for honor is uncritical, and his glory comes not from granting Hektor's funeral but from the grandeur of his own. In the *Odyssey* the poet's attention is on a more positive aspect of the human condition, and therefore a simplified, one-dimensional Achilles is adequate to supply the desired contrast. A simplified Achilles was adequate to the various political and philosophical purposes of subsequent Greek poets as well, since the veneration accorded the *Iliad* ensured that Achilles would in any case be revered by all. The simplified Achilles seems to have accompanied equally simplified interpretations of the *Iliad* as a whole, interpretations whose supreme valuation of the warrior function was empowered by the charisma of the original hero but reflected little of the complex humanity that created it.

Pindar's evocations of Achilles in fifth-century Greece stressed physical superiority, indicating character only by an unquestioned willingness to fight. They ignored the epic conflict between warrior and sovereign. Using Achilles to bolster his aristocratic system of values, Pindar deployed him as an exemplar of noble genes that reveal themselves on the battlefield by number and greatness of other men killed. Epic Cycle stories of the slayings of the semidivine Kyknos and Memnon were as relevant to this purpose as Homer's description of Hektor's death, for Hektor was but one of three heroes by whose elimination Achilles "cut the sinews of Troy" and earned the hymns of the Muses themselves.

Also relevant was the Epic Cycle account of Achilles' wondrous childhood, which took the hero quite out of the realm of normal humanity. This romantic tradition, in which Achilles represented not the human condition but an elite class whose members are watched over and rewarded by the gods, survives for us outside of Pindar only in vase paintings and in the *Elektra* and *Iphigeneia at Aulis* (where Euripides was concerned to explode the idea that there was anything romantic about war and Achilles' career) until the first century A.D. when Statius's *Achilleid* was produced.

As Pindar focused on only the physical half of the Achilles figure, so in the *Philoktetes* the equally aristocratic, genetically oriented Sophokles focused only on the mental half. Near the end of the fifth century B.C. Sophokles invoked the uncompromising Homeric character as part of what is both a critique and an expression of hope for his contentious city. Self-knowledge is essential to Sophokles' interpretation of this character, but not the kind of self-knowledge Sokrates was then pursuing in his merciless examination of time-honored concepts. Self-knowledge in the *Philoktetes* means only the identification of self with the proper *genos*, "family." Neoptolemos is able to behave correctly—that is, honestly, like his father—only when he learns that "all is disgusting when a person has left his own nature and does things that are not like him."

In the service of dramatizing Neoptolemos's struggle toward this self-knowledge, Sophokles revived the epic conflict between warrior and leader, but the leader in question is portrayed not as a Zeus-sanctioned king but as a demagogue, a man who draws his power from the common people. This conflict is not one between physical might and social status but one perhaps equally traditional in Greek epic, that between might and strategem.[11] Beginning in the early fifth century, this conflict had developed in Athens into a tendency to oppose Achilles to Odysseus as antithetical exemplars of honest deeds and deceitful words, the naturally powerful aristocrat versus the swayer of the masses. In the *Philoktetes* this opposition has the paradoxical effect of separating the warrior class from its function, since, because of the alienation caused by Odysseus to Philoktetes, Neoptolemos's final choice to remain true to his Achillean inheritance means he must abandon the army.[12] It is possible to interpret this separation as the expression of a patriotic aristocrat's fear (or warning) that in order to maintain its integrity his class will be "forced" into noncooperation with the city, which will therefore succumb to the enemy. The play does not, however, end with this despairing vision. Warriors and people are reunited by divine intervention in the form of the deified Herakles, who, as he appears in this play, is a particularly apt expression of Sophokles' hope for Athens. Herakles in myth is the exemplar of physical might, of the aristocratic warrior function;[13] but, as Pierre Vidal-Naquet has pointed out, Herakles' shield and words at the end of the *Philoktetes* identify him as a hoplite,[14] the middle-class citizen warrior of the *polis*. As such he is a vivid symbol of the warrior fully integrated into a purified *polis*. Sophokles' message seems clear: for hoplite power to be strong it needs to be guided by the traditional character of heroes like Achilles.

For Sophokles' play to work most effectively, his audience had to both know and admire Homer's Achilles. Euripides' re-creations of Achilles were predicated on the same two factors but to different ends. The effect of the Achilles ode in the *Elektra*, of his ghost's demand in the *Hekabe*, and of his role in the *Iphigeneia at Aulis* is to force the audience to read Homer more critically, to see martial prowess, the uncompromising temper, and the winning of glory from the victim's point of view. Euripides' motive was antiwar; his main weapons were caricature and parody, and his principal targets were the wrath, the dedication to honor, and the association of glory with deeds of killing.

Why was Euripides Homer's enemy? Citations in the prose writings of the period show that Homeric epic, the *Iliad* in particular, had acquired the quality of myth as defined by Roland Barthes: it was read, that is, as if it gave "an historical situation a natural justification" and as if it were "a system of facts" instead of "a system of values."[15] This reading involved simplification to the point of distortion, a simplification that the *Hekabe* presents both in speeches that recast and reduce the debate of *Iliad* 1 to "sex versus spear" and in Odysseus's manipulations of Achilles' Iliadic terminology. We can summarize the simplified plot of the *Iliad* as follows: "Because a man of war was denied honor he refused to continue to be a man of war, whereupon his side suffered great losses, which showed what a mistake it was to deny honor to the man of war." The concept that is signified by this plot is roughly "In order that men of war will continue to be men of war, nothing whatever should stand in the way of their being given honor commensurate with their deeds; honor commensurate with the deeds of the very greatest warrior is whatever he may demand." This concept, which is empowered by the original *Iliad* that it simplifies and distorts, constitutes a myth that naturalizes and therefore justifies a scale of values that locates the warrior at the very top.

Euripides, who apparently felt that such a scale of values would do little to bring Athens's war with Sparta to a speedy conclusion, unmasks this myth by manipulating it in two ways. First, he contaminates the *Iliad* with the Epic Cycle incident of the sacrifice of Polyxena. Second, he puts the most eloquent expression of Achilles' simplified concepts into the mouth of Odysseus, whom Euripides characterized as a "mob-wooing liar" and who is Achilles' opposite in the tradition. The validity of those concepts is thereby immediately called into question. What Euripides has done is reconstitute the simplified myth so that it must include two inextricable propositions: (1) being a man of war involves trampling on the rights of others, and (2) other things (familial love, Polyxena's "heroism") are of at least equal value to being a man of war. The reconstituted myth restores the sense of contingency that had been eliminated by the original myth: the exaltation of the role of the man of war is a political act, not a natural state.

Although the evidence shows that the Pindaric-Sophoklean evaluation remained strong through the first century B.C., Euripides had at least one spiritual child who assaulted Achilles for the same reasons and in much the same manner. Three centuries later, the Roman Catullus also depicted "heroic" prowess from the victim's point of view, thus continuing Euripides' devaluation of the conqueror's role. In Rome, of course, one did not need to be a pacifist or an anti-imperialist to dislike the conqueror of Troy; nationalist pride made it just as natural for the descendants of the conquered to disparage the killer of Hektor as it had made the Athenians praise him. This chauvinistic ambiguity about Achilles' greatest achievement would make easier Vergil's more complicated pacifist task in the *Aeneid*.

But even in Athens not many years passed before a new assault was begun. The battle against the power of Homer's hero was joined in the fourth century by Plato, who shifted the object of attack from the Athenian war mentality—which does not seem to have concerned him—to the quotidian failure of human beings to control their passions and to their consequent need for role models, which the passionate Homeric portrait most definitely failed to supply. Although Plato used a tripartite schema for his ideal *polis*—philosopher king, guardians, producers—his warrior class was to be quite unlike that of heroic tradition. Achilles' extreme grief, his "insolence" towards Agamemnon, his anger at Apollo, his "greedy" acceptance of ransom for Hektor's body, the attempted mutilation of that body, and the sacrifice of human captives on Patroklos's pyre were not likely to promote the strict obedience and moderation essential to future guardians of his *Polity*. Plato seems to have felt that Achilles' charismatic character was too powerful to be transmuted into either moral lessons or any symbol that would serve his didactic purposes: how else can we account for Achilles' absence from among the Trojan War heroes whom Plato describes choosing new lives in the Myth of Er (*Politeia* 620b–d)? No, Plato would not reincarnate Achilles; rather, he would put an end to the seemingly immortal *kléos* that had kept him alive in Greek hearts. There was room for only one kind of hero in the philosopher's community, one whose passion was directed solely toward the systematic acquisition of wisdom.

Cicero carried the philosophical attack on Achilles' passion into Rome on the heels of Catullus's attack on the warrior role, focusing on the specific passion of anger. Anger, which was apparently the first thing that leapt to mind when people thought of Achilles, was to Cicero closely akin to mental illness; he depicted Achilles, therefore, as a very sick man. A few years later, Vergil, student of philosophy as well as poet, combined the thinking of Plato and Cicero with the sensibilities of Euripides and Catullus to produce a devastating two-pronged attack on Achilles' role and character. The Achilles of his *Aeneid* is the enemy of the Roman state both as the destroyer of ancestral Troy and as the embodiment of that kind of martial heroism whose wellspring is grief and rage. In the skewed version of the *Iliad* presented by the pictures on the temple doors and by the career of Turnus, Achilles becomes a symbol for war itself, for the uncontrolled passion that causes it and for the brutality that is its effect.

Vergil's reading of the *Iliad* may have contributed to his friend Horace's prescription that poets re-creating Achilles should make him "ruthless, angry, violent, and lawless." The dictum certainly received substance from the *Aeneid* and in fact became the norm in literary productions of the Roman empire. The most extreme expression of this brutal portrait was created by a Greek writer of the fourth century A.D., Quintus of Smyrna, whose continuation of the *Iliad*, the *Posthomerica*, merged Achilles with the gigantic god-scorning Kapaneus figure of Aischylos and Statius. An independently achieved but similar creation of a teeth-gnashing, hubristic Achilles by Joseph of Exeter in a twelfth-century Latin version of the Trojan War shows how natural were the affinities between the classical exemplar of martial hubris and an Achilles whose Homeric character had been overwhelmed by wrath and violence.

One counterweight to this wrath and violence was Statius's insistence on linking the characteristic anger to justice in his portrait of the youthful prewar Achilles. Another was a non-Homeric passion that suddenly took on major importance in the first century A.D.: love. Love had played only a minor role in Achilles' literary character up to this point. In the *Iliad* love for Briseis had added depth to Achilles' character but did not motivate any of the action. Outside the *Iliad* there is evidence that Briseis, Deidameia, and Penthesileia, the latter two of whom were characters in Epic Cycle stories, had been continuously viewed as love objects that briefly arrested Achilles' martial activity, but their appearances in the surviving literature are quite subordinate to the more favored motivations of honor, glory, and wrath. Erotic love for Patroklos had been made the basis of Achilles' choice to kill Hektor by aristocratic fifth-century B.C. proponents of homosexuality, but neither this motif nor the homologous one of his desire for Troilos had secured a place in the mainstream tradition by the time of Vergil and Horace.

The apparently increasing importance given to Achilles' love for women in the first century B.C. may be merely due to an accident of survival or it may be due to the choice of more gifted poets, like Propertius and Ovid, to write in the genre of elegiac poetry, whose major concern is amatory behavior. But there is no doubt whatsoever that the first century A.D. marks a sharp change in the status of the amatory motif. This is the century in which Statius produced his gently moralized version of Achilles' youthful affair with Deidameia, depicting him first as effeminized by love and then as returning to a masculine role as warrior. This is also the century that produced the *Ilias Latina*, a Latin abridgement of the *Iliad* that included in its abbreviated embassy scene an Achilles singing to the lyre not to evaluate the heroic code but to soothe the pain of having lost his love, Briseis. These two works, which alone ensured that a positive view of Achilles' prowess and character would survive into the Latin Middle Ages, also ensured that henceforth no part of the tradition would lack the love element.

More influential than these representatives of the romantic and Iliadic traditions, which we have traced from the Epic Cycle and Homer, were two entirely new works created in what I call the rationalistic tradition. The authors who assumed the names of the Trojan priest Dares and the Cretan warrior Dictys utilized a kind of mythologizing different from Euripides', one that was less subtle but, aided by the ever-increasing estrangement between Greece and the Roman empire, in the long run quite effective. Their primary object, which seems to have been *de rigueur* in the first century, was to de-idealize and demystify the Trojan War, and they therefore rid their narrative universe, which they had created by interweaving Homeric, Epic Cycle, and newly invented episodes, of everything extraordinary, everything supernatural.

One result of this rationalization was to deprive Achilles of his goddess parent, of those divine genes which for Pindar automatically made him a superhero. He remained the best Greek warrior, ensuring victory by killing the greatest Trojan champions, but was no longer so superior to his fellows as to avoid being wounded just like them. The monumental wrath of the *Iliad* and its tradition was reduced in Dictys to "a certain thoughtless vehemence and ferocious impatience with customary modes of action." In Dares, who eliminated the temper completely, the Homeric complexity reappeared in the catalogue of portraits as a conglomerate of "mercy," "fierceness in war," and "lovely face" that was totally irrelevant to the plot.

Dares' plot, which in its sixth-century Latin translation became the standard source for Trojan history in the Middle Ages, eliminated the quarrel with Agamemnon and substituted love for Polyxena, Priam's youngest daughter, to motivate Achilles' withdrawal from the fighting. The genesis of this love story out of the sacrifice of a royal virgin on Achilles' tomb, a final act of brutality comparable either to the preliminary brutality of sacrificing Iphigeneia or to Achilles' brutalization of Hektor's corpse, was probably due to two factors: first, the current ascendancy of the amatory theme, and, second, the need to make plausible Achilles' traditional death at the hands of the effeminate Paris within a rationalized universe that now excluded the god who had traditionally guided the arrow. Although the story culminated in a fatal ambush at Apollo's temple, Dares did not present Achilles' love for Polyxena as a flaw in the hero's character but merely as a vulnerability to be taken advantage of by the enemy. As such it was similar to the vulnerable heel that was introduced by Statius into the extant literary tradition a few years later.

Dictys, whose more debased portrayal of the princely actors in the Trojan War did not appeal to the princely audiences of the Middle Ages but whose text nonetheless continued to be consulted in its fourth-century Latin translation for the sake of its postwar narratives, retained the quarrel with Agamemnon over Briseis (now renamed Hippodamia), adding to it an attempted retaliatory ambush on the part of Achilles. He thus transmitted it to Benoît de Sainte-Maure, who, however, would use it only as a flashback in Aias's speech during the judgment of arms. Dictys also made up a story of his own about Achilles' love for Polyxena, and although its details were passed over in favor of Dares' version, his interpretation of Achilles' love as a fatal character weakness was much more appealing to the scholars who later Christianized the tradition than was Dares' theme of simple vulnerability.

In the fifth or sixth century A.D. one such scholar, Fulgentius, merged the vulnerable heel from the romantic tradition with the love story from the rationalistic tradition in an allegory that made them representative of a single Christian weakness: lust. The *Excidium Troiae,* probably composed about this same time, linked the vulnerable heart and heel in a different way, casting Achilles and Polyxena together in the roles of Samson and Delilah and making Paris shoot Achilles in the soles of his exposed feet after Polyxena had discovered his secret and lured him into the temple to pray. This denigration of Polyxena's character bore little literary fruit, but the link between the inner and outer vulnerabilities became a subtradition that later found expression in some fourteenth-century German and English versions of the Troy story.[16] The main tradition, which was formed by redactors of Dares and then of Benoît, eschewed the story of the heel, but the dominant Christian morality of the audience for whom the story was retold ensured that the idea of inner weakness would remain strong.

Benoît de Sainte-Maure's mid-twelfth-century elaboration of Dares' plot marks the next watershed in the tradition. By 1287, the date it was translated by Guido delle Colonne into the Latin version that would henceforth dominate the English and Italian traditions, the *Roman de Troie* had already given rise to a simplified French prose version,[17] had been translated into Spanish[18] and German,[19] and had been used as the source for an Italian version.[20] Before it established this decisive influence on the tradition, Achilles had maintained his superiority to all other warriors, Trojan and Greek, not only in works emanating from the *Ilias Latina* (Odo of Orleans, Godfrey of Rheims, the "Lament for Hektor," Pierre de Saintes, Simon Capra Aurea, and the *Libro de Alexandre*) but also in the major works stemming from Dares (Joseph of Exeter, Albert of Stade). In extant literature composed after 1240 (the date of Albert's *Troilus*), however, Achilles was universally forced to yield the palm of victory to the Trojan champions Hektor, Troilos, and Memnon.

Benoît cast all the warriors at Troy into what the numerous romances of Chretien de Troyes would soon make familiar as the courtly mode of behavior, a mode that was becoming as important for the knightly caste that was just at that moment solidifying itself against the rising bourgeoisie[21] as the heroic code had been for Homer's Greeks. The old Greek distinction between *esthlós*, "noble," and *kakós*, "coward," became a medieval French distinction between courtliness and *villeinie,* behavior suited to the court and tournament versus behavior expected from a rustic laborer. Thus the Hektor of the *Roman en prose* assures Achilles that his offer of an immediate duel is genuine by denying he is making empty threats as a *villeins* would do (thereby cleverly dismissing as spoken *come villeins* Achilles' earlier belligerence, which did not include an immediate call to action) and then sarcastically contrasts the alleged homosexual behavior that the common folk label as *vilanie* with the *courtois* and valiant behavior he expects from Achilles on the battlefield.[22] Acting in a courtly rather than villainous mode, which, it was stressed, was genetically rather than educationally determined, gave knights honor in this world by distinguishing them from the non-knights, and it might, like winning *timē* of old, secure them a favorable place in the medieval equivalent to *kléos,* the elaborate genealogies that were proliferating at the end of the twelfth century.[23] These motives plus the underlying need to close ranks with the ecclesiastical half of the aristocracy provided strong incentive to Benoît's audience to circumscribe the rapacious violence that, as described by eleventh- and twelfth-century ecclesiastics,[24] had made them little different from the brutal, hubristic Achilles of Joseph of Exeter. Benoît made his vernacular version of the Troy story, which was produced for such knights at the court of Henry Plantagenet and Eleanor, relevant to this concern, providing

examples of courtly and villainous behavior for their applause and cat-
calls, and insisting that more important than winning or losing was how
one played the game.

Benoît's Achilles did not play well. Reducing his prowess relative to
Hektor's, Troilos's, and Memnon's had the additional effect of under-
mining his character, making it necessary for his traditional pursuit of
vengeance at any cost to obliterate all sense of honor. His honor is lost
both on the battlefield and in the field of love: anger makes him kill
Hektor by treachery; love for Polyxena makes him abandon the war and
thus earn his friends' opprobrium; anger against Troilos and Memnon
makes him commit a "crime" against his pledge to Polyxena; love for
Polyxena takes away his senses and makes him easy prey to Paris's
vengeance.

Benoît's Achilles cannot play the courtly game well because he is the
plaything of his own twin sexual and aggressive passions. As such he
seems the very incarnation of the medieval conception of aristocratic
"youth" as described by Georges Duby,[25] that passionate, marauding
premarital (though sometimes permanent) stage of life in which, without the control of an established *seigneur* who had added wisdom to his
innate martial ability, the knight would be unable to channel his vigorous energies in productive ways. Hektor, superior prince that he is,
has achieved this wisdom and the courtliness that goes with it; Achilles
neither has it nor will submit to those who do.

Benoît, writing for the court of a prince who was often at odds with
the clergy, produced an essentially secular version of how Achilles became the conqueror of Troy and then died at the hands of Paris. His
translator-adaptor Guido delle Colonne, following in the doctrinal tradition of Fulgentius and Albert of Stade, writing like them in the language of the Church and its literate pupils, and perhaps guided by the
more moralized prose abridgment of the *Roman,* replaced the courtly
condemnation of Achilles' career, especially that part of it pertaining to
his love for Polyxena, with heavy Christian admonishment. The intangible stakes in Guido's "game" were salvation more than status. Achilles,
of course, loses both. His prowess made drastically inferior to Hektor's
in battle, his irrational anger set in contrast to Hektor's philosophical
discourse in the interview scene, his explicit choice in the embassy scene
to forgo honor in order to preserve his physical body (with which he

hoped to enjoy Polyxena), the imagery of disease that pervades the descriptions of his desire for Polyxena—all combine to make Guido's Achilles the very opposite of a perfect Christian knight.

Medieval authors finally succeeded where Euripides, Plato, and Vergil had failed: they deprived Homer's Achilles of his potency as an heroic exemplar. Stripped of his complexity by classical Greek and Roman stereotypes and of his honesty and idealism by the rationalistic authors of late antiquity, Achilles became by the end of the thirteenth century an unprincipled war machine that was turned off and on by crude desires, his major actions depicted as responses to the pain of his body, that is, retaliations for hurts suffered (the killing of Hektor, Troilos, Memnon) or attempts to alleviate sexual frustration (Polyxena). The most positive trait that listeners to the Troy story could note was the excellent condition and appearance of his body. In most countries he would still be accorded the reputation of being a great conqueror, for people were aware that without his having killed Hektor and Troilos Troy could not have been taken. But although the fall of Troy had been ultimately providential in that it made possible the rise of Rome and the Holy Roman Empire (Guido, Book Two, fol. 5v), in the most immediate sense it was a terrible misfortune felt keenly by the descendants of noble Hektor throughout Europe. These descendants in England, Germany, France, and Italy, therefore, listened uncritically to accounts that turned the greatest of the enemy Greeks into a blackguard.

All audiences in Europe were made familiar with the famous prowess, but they were forced either to qualify it with the knowledge of Achilles' magic vulnerability or to judge it as less in comparison with the truly spectacular heroics of Hektor. Even where Achilles could be seen as a true hero, as in the Spanish *Libro de Alexandre,* a severe flaw mars his heroism: Greek *hubris,* Christian pride. This flaw is a mortal one, spiritually as well as physically, and eliminates Achilles as a model for Christian warriors to imitate.

Such an elimination, which seems to be the point of the poem, draws the *Alexandre* into a kind of unity with other medieval versions of Achilles' career, which throughout the thirteenth and fourteenth centuries portrayed Achilles as an example of what not to be. Most auditors of the Troy story in those centuries would no doubt have inferred what the author of the prose *Roman* made explicit—that God himself had brought down the terrible hero specifically to make him a lesson for others:

> The example of Achilles warns us that one should not be ruthless and without mercy in doing as much evil as he can when he is superior. . . . You will see few ruthless and desperate men whose end is not perilous. And this is just, because he who takes pleasure in malice and pursues his sinful desires cannot but harvest the fruit of his deeds. Everything happened because at that time men had very little faith or correct belief. Thus Our Lord showed them many miracles and punished them in this life for their errors, so that their knowledge and their clever reasoning power availed them little. So He acted toward Achilles and toward many others who were knowledgeable and corrupt. For Achilles knew well how he had harmed her who sent for him and that he had broken his promise to her and, this above all, he went off to the meeting on the word of a single servant and without any armor with which he might protect his body among his mortal enemies. This his sin procured. Our Lord was well content that a man as cruel and without pity as he was should be ruthlessly punished and that his pride be debased down to the earth.

> Mult nos defent cist emsample d'Achilles que l'en nie soit trop cruel et sans merci en faire tant de mal come il a de pooir quant il est au dessus. . . . Et mult poi de cruels homes et desesperes verres vos que lor fin ne soit perillouse. Et ce est droit quar qui toute ior se delite en malice et porsut desfreneement ses voluntiers en mal il est impossible chose que le fruit des oeuvres ne le porsivent. Et tout fust il chose que a celui tens les gens n'eussent poi de foi ne de bone creance. Si lor mostroit nostre sires mult de ses miracles et les punissoit temporaument de lor fautes. Si que poi lor valoit lor savoir et lor engignois argumentum. Si come il fist a Achilles et a maint autre qui mult estoient sages et vicious. Quar bien savoit Achille coment il avoit domagie celle qui l'envoia querre et que il l'avoit menti de couvenant et sur tout cen se mist il a aler par parolles d'un seul valet et sans nul garniment dont il peust son cors defendre entre ses mortels henemis. Et ce faisoit son pechie. Et nostre sire soufri bien que si cruel home et sans pitie come il estoit fust cruelment punnis et defacie son orgueil desus la terre.[26]

Not until the Renaissance, when the relearning of the Greek language and the consequent rediscovery of Homer made his classical character as compelling to the poets and audiences of western Europe as it had been to those of Greece and Rome, could Achilles again function as an inspiration for those who would win immortal glory in deadly war. Only then would he cease to be the simple, brutal slayer of heroic ancestors and return to what he was in the classical world: complex, tragic forerunner of contemporary would-be heroes.

The reborn glory of Achilles has maintained its power through our own times, continuing to imbue war death with transcendant value. This power is attested by the continued attacks of antiwar poets, who, just like Euripides, Catullus, and Vergil, are concerned with ranking other, lifegiving values over the ability to kill. The charismatic Iliadic paradigm is again the enemy. A modern East German novelist who seems to question whether the warrior function can continue to hold any place, any rank, in the nuclear age and who has woven her own paradigm of the war hero from the most negative strands of all the various traditions expresses both the goal and its apparent impossibility of fulfillment in the words of her first-person narrator, Kassandra: "If only I could wipe out the name, not merely from my memory, but from the memory of all men living. If I could burn it out of our heads—I would not have lived in vain. Achilles." [27]

NOTES

INTRODUCTION

1. Fascinating delineations of the literary vicissitudes undergone by three popular classical heroes can be found in W. B. Stanford's *The Ulysses Theme* (Oxford, 1963), Raymond Trousson's *Le Thème de Prométhée dans la littérature européenne* (Geneva, 1964), and G. Karl Galinsky's *The Herakles Theme* (Oxford, 1972). Stanford's introductory chapter, "The Adaptability of Mythical Figures," gives an excellent survey of the causes of change in the presentation of archetypal figures.

2. When I use the name "Homer," which is probably a generic name for "poet" (see Gregory Nagy, *The Best of the Achaeans* [Baltimore, 1979] 296–300), I mean the intelligence that created the *Iliad* and the *Odyssey*, the "author" that the literary interpreter who aims at the most probable reading possible must imaginatively reconstruct out of the logic, attitudes, and cultural givens of the "world" of any text, be it anonymous or not. (This is E. D. Hirsch, Jr.'s "speaking subject," "Objective Interpretation" *Publications of the Modern Language Association* 75 [1960] 478). I follow Adam Parry, Cedric Whitman, Michael N. Nagler, and Seth Schein, among others, in believing that the final shaping of the *Iliad* was done by an individual singer of monumental genius with the aid of writing.

3. The earliest and most eloquent proponent of this view is Adam Parry, whose three articles "The Language of Achilles" (*TAPA* 87 [1956] 1–7), "Have We Homer's *Iliad?*" (*Yale Classical Studies* 20 [1966] 177–216), and "Language and Characterization in Homer" (*Harvard Studies in Classical Philology* 76 [1972] 1–22) convincingly challenged the view that the oral-formulaic nature of the epic art-language excluded any individual artistic intent. For a recent and sensitive discussion of the issue, see Seth Schein, *The Mortal Hero* (Berkeley and Los Angeles, 1984) 13–36.

4. The physical prowess that is the source of this power and that makes him "the best of the Achaians" in the tradition that finally produced the *Iliad* is well discussed by Nagy in *The Best of the Achaeans* (26–58, 317–321). Nagy, who

(following Leonard Palmer) derives Achilles' name from *Akhilauos*, meaning "he whose host of fighting men has grief," argues convincingly that the causing of pain both to the Trojans when the hero is at war and to the Achaians when he dies is intrinsic to Achilles' role in myth and epic (69–83). Nagy also discusses Achilles' relationship to cosmic and elemental forces (322–347).

5. Most recently, the Second World War has prompted two feminist meditations on war in which Achilles figures prominently: H. D.'s *Helen in Egypt* (New York, 1961) and Christa Wolf's *Kassandra* (Darmstadt, 1983).

6. For an excellent recent discussion of the theory and practice of literary imitation in the Renaissance, see Thomas M. Greene's *The Light in Troy: Imitation and Discovery in Renaissance Poetry* (New Haven, 1982). Walter Jackson Bate's *The Burden of the Past and the English Poet* (New York, 1973) and Harold Bloom's *The Anxiety of Influence* (New York, 1973) and *A Map of Misreading* (Oxford, 1975) are the most influential studies of the very different relationship between post-Miltonic poets and their predecessors.

CHAPTER ONE
THE ARCHETYPE: HOMER'S ACHILLES

1. Hippolochos said the same thing to his son Glaukos (11.784 = 6.208): αἰὲν ἀριστεύειν καὶ ὑπείροχον ἔμμεναι ἄλλων.

2. For example, at 7.90, 11.506, 15.460. In four places it is defined by the words *máchesthai* or *máchē:* 11.409, 16.292, 16.551, 17.351. Gregory Nagy has well demonstrated that it is an overall Iliadic theme that Achilles is "best of the Achaians" (*Best of the Achaeans* 26–35). Nagy further argues that the *kléos* of Odysseus, who is a contender for the title *áristos Achaiôn* as the actual destroyer of Troy in tradition, is preempted in the *Iliad* by the *kléos* of Achilles. Achilles' superior *bíē* makes him *áristos* in the *Iliad;* Odysseus' superior *mêtis* makes him *áristos* in the *Odyssey* (35–58).

3. Similarly at 1.409–412, when Achilles asks for a Greek defeat so that Agamemnon may know his madness that he did not honor the best of the Achaians; compare 16.269–274.

4. 2.768–770: Achilles is the most powerful, more powerful even than Aias. 4.512–513: Apollo urges the Trojans to fight because Achilles is not fighting against them. 5.788–790: Herê chides the Achaians because when Achilles was fighting the Trojans would never come beyond the Dardanian Gates, so much did they fear his spear. 7.226–228: Aias boasts to Hektor that the Trojan champion will now discover what kind of men are the best of the Danaans "after lionhearted Achilles, breaker of men." 8.224–226 = 11.7–9: Achilles and Aias have positioned ships on either end "trusting in their strength and manhood." 10.105–107: Nestor says that Hektor, who is now giving them so much trouble, will have plenty of troubles of his own if Achilles returns. 13.745–747: Pouly-

damas wants Hektor to regroup forces because he fears reentry of the man who is insatiable of war. 18.257−276: Poulydamas says that he was willing to fight away from the city near the ships while Achilles was angry and the Achaians were easier to fight with, but now that Achilles has returned he judges it best to get back behind the protection of the walls.

5. Milman Parry, *The Making of Homeric Verse* (Oxford, 1971) 92. The other three are *rhēxēnoros* ("man-breaker," three times), *thumoléonta* ("lionhearted"), and *theoîs epieíkel'* ("godlike," six times). For more on Achilles' swiftness and its cosmic affinities, see Nagy, *Best of the Achaeans* 326−328.

6. For example, 17.279 (Aias), 22.370−371 (Hektor).

7. 21.108: οὐκ ὁράᾳς οἷος καὶ ἐγὼ καλός τε μέγας τε.

8. It is used often, however, of parts of the male body, such as skin, eyes, ankles.

9. A millenium later Quintus Smyrnaeus's *Posthomerica*, which ties up all the *Iliad*'s loose ends, describes Nireus's death and comments as follows on his beauty and weakness:

> For the gods do not fulfill all things to mortals
> But from some balance of fate evil is linked to good;
> So to lord Nireus's lovely beauty was added feebleness.
>
> (7.9−12)

10. *Eîdos* without the adjective *kalón* is elsewhere used in reproachful (and unjust) distinctions between admirable appearance and paltry deeds. It is used of the Achaians at 5.787 and 8.228 and of Hektor at 17.142.

11. In Euripides' *Sthenoboia* he kills the woman who traduced him by taking her for a ride on Pegasos and pushing her off. In the *Bellerophontes* he apparently flew to heaven to confront the gods with their injustice because they let him be condemned for the murder of Sthenoboia. The latter seems to be a sympathetic portrayal of a heroic and just man, but we must not forget that he killed a woman by treachery. See Webster, *The Tragedies of Euripides* (London, 1967) 80−84, 109−111.

12. Note that he convenes the one in Book One.

13. Politic but also true to Homeric thought. Compare similar sentiments in Poseidon's remarks to Apollo, 21.440, and Nestor to Agamemnon and Achilles, 1.259.

14. Except for Euchenor, who had the choice either of staying home and dying of a painful sickness or of going to Troy and dying in battle (13.663−670). Somewhat similar is the case of the two sons of Merops. They were told not to go to Troy by their soothsaying father (presumably because they would die there), but they disobeyed him (*oú ti peithésthēn*, 11.328−334) and thus became victims of Diomedes. It is unclear whether they disbelieved their father (this is

one possible translation of *ou peithésthēn*) or made a conscious choice to go and die. But in any case, the element of choice is not stressed. Instead, we are told that their *kêres* of dark death led them (332). Bernard Fenik terms the soothsayer father, who also occurs at 5.148–151, "a ready source of pathetic irony" (*Typical Battle Scenes in the Iliad* [Weisbaden; 1968] no. 24). The difference between all these others and Achilles is clear. Unlike Euchenor, his choice is between life and death; unlike the other soothsayers' sons, he chooses death. Thus irony is absent and the pathos pure.

15. E. T. Owen, *The Story of the Iliad* (Ann Arbor, 1966) 11–12.

16. Schein, "The Death of Simoeisios," *Eranos* 74 (1976) 1, 5.

17. Schein, "Death of Simoeisios," 3.

18. 18.86–90, 19.334–337, 24.540–542. Hektor comes close in his pitying words to Andromache at 6.454–463, but his focus is more the consequences to her of the fall of Troy than his own personal death, and he ends with a fervent wish that he be dead before he hears her crying her loss of freedom (6.464–465).

19. Diomedes and Antilochos have at least equal claims to that distinction; see 14.112, 15.569.

20. So Glaukos, 6.146–149, and Apollo, 21.463–466. Apollo's lofty perspective changes Glaukos's *ándres* to *brotoí deiloí*.

21. The narrative leaves Patroklos sitting beside Eurypylos throughout Books Twelve, Thirteen, Fourteen, and half of Fifteen. "As long as the Trojans were fighting outside the wall, he sat cheering him with words and sprinkling drugs on his grievous wound to allay the pain. But as soon as he perceived that the Trojans had come over the wall," he starts off again for Achilles (15.390–405). See Owen, 118, 141–143.

22. Their primary function, however, is healing. They are never mentioned in the war councils and do not have even brief periods of martial success. Their father is, of course, the mythic founder of the medical art, and in the classical era "sons of Asklepios" is a generic term for physicians.

23. Compare 4.218–219 and 11.830–832.

24. And Apollo: 1.603–604, 24.62–63.

25. That Paris's *kítharis* is not to be distinguished from Achilles' *phórminx* is shown by *Iliad* 18.569–570, where the verb *kitharízō* is used for playing on the *phórminx,* and by *Odyssey* 1.153–155, where the verb *phormízō* is used for playing on the *kítharis.* See Cunliffe, *Lexicon of the Homeric Dialect* (Norman, Okla., 1963), s.v. *kítharis.*

26. For the effect of this conjoining of beauty and blood see Paolo Vivante, *The Homeric Imagination* (Bloomington, Ind., 1970) 158.

27. Nagy, *Comparative Studies in Greek and Indic Meter* (Cambridge, Mass., 1974) 248. On 246–248 he documents the "ubiquitous concatenation [of

kleíō/kléō and *kléomai*] with the notion of 'song,'" and he later argues (254) that the *áphthiton* of *kléos áphthiton* was transferred from the function of the Singer's song—to insure unfailing streams of water, light, etc., from the gods he praised—to the song itself.

28. It is no wonder that when this scene struck the imaginations of later Roman poets, they changed it, providing Achilles with an appreciative audience for his *kléa* (Statius *Achilleid* 1.185—194, has Achilles sing *immania laudum semina* to Cheiron and his mother) or substituting a woman and love as his companion and theme (Ovid *Heroides* 3.113—120; Statius *Achilleid* 1.572—574).

29. Compare Cedric Whitman, *Homer and the Heroic Tradition* (New York, 1965) 193—194; see also 335 n. 36.

30. Whitman, 205. Øivind Andersen ("Some Thoughts on the Shield of Achilles," *Symbolae Osloenses* 51 [1976] 5—18) calls the shield "a kind of mirror for the Iliad" (4), pointing especially to the trial scene (15—18). Leonard Muellner (*The Meaning of Homeric* εὔχομαι [Innsbruck, 1976]), whose thesis is similar to Andersen's, goes so far as to call the man refusing to accept *poinē* in the trial scene an "Achilles-figure." We may also contrast Achilles' shield with the one described in the *Shield of Herakles* 144—317. This shield is also forged by Hephaistos and also attempts universal representation. But its conglomerate of gore, mythology, and occasional social activity lacks the Homeric focus on specifically human activity. For a more lengthy comparison of Herakles' shield with Achilles' see Karl Reinhardt, *Die Ilias und ihr Dichter* (Gottingen, 1961) 408—411.

31. J. T. Sheppard, *The Pattern of the Iliad* (London, 1922) 10; see also 8. Other scholars have described the shield and its significance in a manner similar to Whitman and Sheppard, among them Samuel Bassett, Werner Jaeger, Johannes Kakridis, E. T. Owen, and Wolfgang Schadewaldt. Most recently, Oliver Taplin has written a fine essay, "The Shield of Achilles Within the *Iliad*," (*Greece and Rome* 27 [1980] 1—21), that takes into account the views of all of the above. He focuses on the scenes of peace, which the "two finest things in the *Iliad*—Achilles and Troy—will never again enjoy. . . . The Shield of Achilles brings home the loss, the cost of the events of the *Iliad*" (15).

32. See note 4 above.

33. First, in Book One Agamemnon sends Chryses away against the wishes of the army (22—25); second, in Book Six his cruel call for the destruction without exception of every Trojan male down to babies in the womb (57—60) conquers Menelaos's initial willingness to spare a defeated man; and third, in Book Eleven he slays the pleading sons of Antimachos (131—147).

34. See Charles Segal, *The Theme of the Mutilation of the Corpse in the Iliad* (Leiden, 1971) 17—21.

35. Excellent studies of this technique have been done by James I. Armstrong ("The Arming Motif," *American Journal of Philology* 79 [1958] 337—354), Tilman

Krischer (*Formale Konventionen der homerischen Epik* [Munich, 1971]), Michael N. Nagler (*Spontaneity and Tradition* [Los Angeles, 1979]), and Segal (*Corpse*).

36. The similarity between the two *aristeíai* lies mostly in their heavy concentration of supernatural events. The higher consequence granted to Achilles' actions may most easily be seen in the opening and closing encounters between gods. In Diomedes' case Athene simply persuades her opponent, Ares, to leave the battle and then, at the end, incites and helps Diomedes to wound him. When Achilles takes the field, Athene takes her position one foot on the Achaians' trench, the other one on the seashore (20.49–50); Ares takes his position one foot on the citadel of Troy, the other on the banks of the Simoeis (52–53). The scene is thus invested with the symbolism of earth and water, culture and nature, i.e., the totality of human experience. All the gods are involved, and their initial encounter is marked by Zeus's thundering and Poseidon's shaking the earth so terribly that Hades leaps up and screams in fear that his dark realm will be opened to sight of humans and gods (56–65). The gods withdraw from battle to watch the humans fighting, until Xanthos attacks Achilles, whereupon all reenter the fighting, and, as Whitman says (*Homer* 140), "the whole passage . . . becomes a dumb show of the taking of Troy." One further point: the hostile confrontation between Athene and Ares marks the end of Diomedes' *aristeía;* subsequently the fighting becomes generalized. The *theomachía,* on the other hand, merely ends the first part of Achilles' *aristeía;* the climactic fight is still to come. Whitman (*Homer* 167–168), discusses the contrast between Achilles' and Diomedes' *aristeíai.* See also Owen's discussion of Diomedes' *aristeía* as "background" for Achilles' later behavior (*Story of the Iliad* 47).

37. Fenik, *Battle Scenes* 15. Fenik comments on the list of six slayings near the beginning of Diomedes' *aristeía* in 5.38–83: First, three major Greek heroes (Agamemnon, Idomeneos, Menelaos) execute quick and simple slayings. Then three minor heroes (Meriones, Meges, Eurypylos) perform brutal and grisly slayings.

38. Whitman, 162, and see 157–163 for discussion of Agamemnon's unheroic character. Samuel Bassett ("The Ἁμαρτία of Achilles," *TAPA* 65 [1934] 54–58) offers a similarly unfavorable assessment of Agamemnon's unheroic *aristeía.* For a more balanced view of Agamemnon's strengths and weaknesses see Jasper Griffin's *Homer on Life and Death* (Oxford, 1980) 70–73.

39. Fenik, *Battle Scenes* 15 n. 11.

40. That is, the central section that is relatively free of the supernatural, from after the near fight with Hektor through the flinging of Lykaon's body into the river, 20.381–21.135.

41. Fenik, *Battle Scenes* 85.

42. κλονέω and especially μαιμάω are used predominantly of warriors. See P. Chantraine, *Dictionnaire étymologique* [Paris, 1968] s.vv. κλόνος and μαιμάω.

43. Eleven lines intervene for Agamemnon, ten for Achilles.

44. The earth flows or grows red with blood at several other places: 4.451; 8.65; 10.484; 11.394; 17.360. The identical half-line *rhée d' haímati gaîa mélaina* is found in the battle at the ships, 15.715. The lines about the horses trampling bodies and the chariot being splattered with blood are used earlier to describe Hektor's driving against Aias (20.499–502 = 11.534–537). Their use here provides a good example of how, so often in Homer, "the unique is only a new arrangement of the typical" (Fenik, *Battle Scenes* 58).

45. 11.137, 21.98. All pleas for mercy within the *Iliad* are denied: 6.45–65 (by Menelaos and Agamemnon); 10.454–457 (by Diomedes); 11.128–147 (by Agamemnon); 20.463–472 (by Achilles).

46. Both Sheppard (*Pattern* 190) and J. Griffin (*Homer* 55) find a more positive meaning in Achilles' use of the word *phílos*, viewing it as stemming from, in Griffin's words, "the perspective which puts slayer and slain on a level."

47. Nagler, 147.

48. Compare 11.394–395 (Diomedes); 13.381–382 (Idomeneus); 15.349–351 (Hektor); 17.126–127 (Hektor). Closest in tone is Odysseus's vaunt over Sokos: "Ah, wretch, your father and respected mother will not close the eyes of your corpse, but flesh-eating birds will tear at it, beating close with their wings" (11.452–454).

49. James Redfield, *Nature and Culture in the Iliad* (Chicago, 1975) 200. Jasper Griffin discusses threats to the corpse and compares them to similar Assyrian threats on 44–49 of *Homer on Life and Death*.

50. Whitman, 129. See 128–145 for a thorough discussion of the fire imagery. All of what I will say about fire is either based on or inspired by this discussion.

51. Whitman, 132.

52. Whitman, 138.

53. James I. Armstrong discusses this imagery on 351–352 of "The Arming Motif in the Iliad," his thorough and perceptive comparison of this arming scene with those of Paris, Agamemnon, and Patroklos.

54. So, too, at 18.214, the *sélas* of the divinely-kindled fire reached from Achilles' head to the sky.

55. See Whitman, 132–136.

56. Whitman, 138.

57. See Whitman, 140.

58. Fenik, *Battle Scenes* 24. Emily Vermeule points out that in both art and literature the lion represented "male ambitions to be courageous, dangerous, intelligent and successful" (*Aspects of Death in Early Greek Art and Society* [Berkeley and Los Angeles, 1979] 85–86).

59. Aeneas has a one-line simile at 5.299; Odysseus shares a one-line simile with Diomedes at 10.297.

60. Schadewaldt, *Von Homers Welt und Werk* (Stuttgart, 1959) 147: "ein kraftvoll Wildes, Edles, Mutiges, gefährlich Blutgieriges, Erbarmungsloses."

61. Schadewaldt, 149, and Fränkel, *Die homerischen Gleichnisse* (Gottingen, 1921) 63.

62. Compare Agamemnon's fawn-crunching and gut-gulping lions at 11.113–115, 175–176 (and Whitman's comments, *Homer* 159); Hektor's proud lion whose own courage kills it, 12.41–46 (and E. T. Owen's comments on his "fatal daring," *Story of the Iliad* 120); Menelaos's lion, whose "strong heart freezes" before shouts and spears so that he leaves the sheepfold, 17.109–112; and Aias's enduring lion, who stands up to javelins and fire the whole night before giving way, 11.548–555.

63. Compare Vermeule, *Aspects of Death* 115.

64. Groaning is a common reaction to the death or wounding of a loved one (Priam for Hektor, 24.639; Trojan women and citizens for Hektor, 22.429, 515; 23.1; 24.722, 776; Briseis and others for Patroklos, 19.301, 338; Agamemnon over Menelaos, 4.153) or to being wounded oneself (Teukros, 8.334; Deiphobos, 13.538; Hektor, 14.432; Ares, 21.417). It is also a reaction to mental injury or worry (Achilles, 1.364; Agamemnon, 9.16; 10.16).

65. Fränkel, 93: "nicht nur Trauer, sondern auch wilder Rachedurst zu uns sprechen soll."

66. Erwin Rohde believes that the slaughter of the captives on Patroklos's pyre is a vestige of more primitive times and that Homer without understanding its meaning uses it for his own special purpose to contribute to his depiction of Achilles' superhuman rage and grief (*Psyche,* trans. Hillis [London, 1925] 14–16).

67. Grief (*áchos*) over the death of a comrade in battle often spurs a warrior to increased efforts. An interesting sequence occurs in Book Fourteen (one of the most grisly of the *Iliad*): when Poulydamas kills the Greek Prothoēnor, the Argives feel *áchos* at his boasting (458); in Aias, especially, this stirs up passion (*thumón*, 459). Shortly thereafter, the Trojans feel *áchos* when Aias kills Archilochos and boasts to Poulydamas in return (475). Then it is again the Argives' turn to feel *áchos* after the Trojan Akamas kills Promachos and vaunts (486). And this again rouses passion in a selected Greek (Peneleos), who kills a Trojan and then brutally displays the eyeball stuck on the tip of his spear while he vaunts more nastily than did either Aias or Akamas before him (487–505). In this sequence vengeance-producing *áchos* may be seen as positive insofar as it increases military effort. But insofar as it contributes to a continuous escalation of brutality it may be seen as negative. Such an escalation happens also within the single character of Achilles in Book Eighteen.

68. Krischer also links these three similes as typical of the "moving-out" (*Auszug*) motif that signals the beginning (or a renewed beginning) of an

aristeía (*Formale Konventionen* 40–41). Since this "moving-out" simile is often preceded by a "lustre-of-armor" (*Waffenglanz*) simile (Krischer, 38), and since the simile of the groaning lion (18.318–322), which I have discussed above, is preceded by a "lustre-of-armor" substitute motif (cf. Krischer, 24) at 205–214, we may say that Homer has already created for Achilles in Book Eighteen a submerged "beginning-of-an-*aristeía*." The groaning lion, we may note, is moving out after the man who has taken his cubs. The simile that marks the genesis of Achilles' savage thirst for vengeance thus also signals to the Homeric audience the beginning of its successful accomplishment. For the reader familiar with epic conventions, Achilles is metaphorically already on the battlefield that has come to be his sole object of desire (19.68–70, 146–153, 199–214).

69. The wounding that backfires may possibly look ahead to the death of Pandaros, as Fränkel (63) thought. But the shepherd in the simile escapes death, and it is not even absolutely clear that his sheep are slaughtered, since *kéchuntai* could be translated "huddled together."

70. Compare, for instance, 4.341–344 and 5.535–536.

71. For an excellent discussion of Odysseus's "lucid and melancholy" formulation of the heroic code see Fenik's essay "Stylization and Variety" in *Homer: Tradition and Invention* (Leiden, 1978) 68–90.

72. The difference is that between one typical act of a particular lion and the *customary* behavior of the hero. For a discussion of the atemporal aorist in similes see Chantraine, *Grammaire homerique,* vol. 2 (Paris, 1974) 185–186, no. 274. For *te . . . te* see Chantraine, *Grammaire,* vol. 2, 239–240, no. 352, and J. D. Denniston, *The Greek Particles* (Oxford, 1954) 538, no. 2.

73. A similarly factual either-or occurs in the wounded-leopard simile that images Agenor's tense decision to fight Achilles at 21.573–578. In this case the difference between the animal's spontaneous and the man's intentional action is expressed by grammar rather than vocabulary: the leopard does not give up his fighting strength *prín g' éè xumblémenai éè damênai* (578), "until he comes to blows or is defeated" (*prín* plus the infinitive of temporal relation); Agenor, on the other hand, *ouk éthelen pheúgein, prìn peirésait' Achilêos* (580), "was not willing to flee until he should try Achilles" (*prín* plus the optative of conditional relation).

74. The transition out of the simile leads almost directly into Sarpedon's speech (307–309):

> So at that time his *thumós* incited godlike Sarpedon
> to leap against the wall and break the breastwork.
> And straightway he spoke to Glaukos, son of Hippolochos.

75. Later Attic usage confirms this. Cf. Aischylos *Eumenides* 542; Sophokles *Oedipus at Colonus* 1153; Euripides *Rhesos* 253, 327.

76. See note 64 above.

77. 16.393 (running horses), 489 (bull killed by a lion), 391 (rivers); 2.95, 784 (earth); 23.230 (the sea).

78. In this he is most like Agamemnon at 10.16 and Achilles at 18.33, each of whom *éstene kudálimon kêr.*

79. See 13.767 = 17.117 = 17.683; 16.525.

80. See William Watson Goodwin, *Syntax of the Moods and Tenses of the Greek Verb* (1875; repr. New York, 1965) 180–182, nos. 486, 487; and Chantraine, *Grammaire*, 281–282, nos. 413 and 414.

81. Compare Carroll Moulton, *Similes in the Homeric Poems* [Gottingen, 1977] 112–113.

82. The correspondence of the lion's physical wound and Achilles' emotional one was ignored by the Scholiasts (*pace* Robin R. Schlunk, *The Homeric Scholia and the Aeneid* [Ann Arbor, 1974] 46) but has been noted by K. V. Hartigan, "'He Rose like a Lion,'" *Acta Antiqua* 21 (1973) 227, and Michael Coffey, "The Homeric Simile," *American Journal of Philology* 78 (1957) 117 n. 20. Coffey also notes that the lion's ignoring the attacking townsmen corresponds to Achilles' ignoring the Trojans until Patroklos's death.

83. Hektor's simile at 12.41–48 is the only one besides Sarpedon's that approaches Achilles' in degree of personification. The animal in the simile has a glorious (*kudálimon*) heart (45) and a pride (*agēnoríē*) that doesn't permit retreat (46). But the personifying force of *kudálimon* and *agēnoríē* is weakened by details of the simile. In the first place, the identification between the animal and the hero is necessarily diluted by the fact that here we do not focus on a single animal—Hektor's whirling about is compared to that of a boar *or* a lion. Second, in contrast to Hektor, who is in fact driving the frightened Achaians before him, the boar or lion has been surrounded by men, specifically designated as hunters. Lines 45 and 46 ("and his glorious heart / feels not fear nor flees, but his pride kills him") do indeed make us want to identify this boar or lion with Hektor, of whom Andromache said in Book Six, "Your strength will kill you" (407), and whose city is in fact ringed with enemy "hunters." But this strong connection between the beast and the man is short-lived. The closing of the simile circles back to its beginning as the lion whirls about (*tarphéa te stréphetai*) trying to find a good place to attack the men ranked against him. Hektor is like this beast only in the fact that he whirls (*elísseth'*). Not only is the verb different, he is whirling as he urges on his own men to *attack*. The situations in the simile and the narrative are radically different, and thus the audience is not here encouraged to merge the nature of human hero and beast.

84. Nagy lends support to my interpretation when he says that "the beast's intrinsic behavior is set in the same way as Achilles is driven by his *thūmós*" (*Best*

of the Achaeans 137). Nagy also notes the interesting fact that Achilles and Herakles alone of Homeric heroes are ever called *thumoléōn* (7.228, 5.639) in the *Iliad*. Herakles, even more than Achilles, is marked off from the other heroes by his achievement of superhuman (in the end literally divine) status.

85. Nagler, 147. See also David H. Porter, "Violent Juxtaposition in the Similes of the *Iliad*," *Classical Journal* 68 (1972) 15. William C. Scott (*The Oral Nature of the Homeric Simile* [Leiden, 1974] 119–120) notes that all the similes of peace—20.403 (bull at altar), 20.495 (threshing), 21.257 (man and irrigation ditch), 21.282 (swineherd youth about to be overwhelmed by water), 22.22 (race horse), and 22.26 (evening star)—contrast with "the strange behavior of Achilles," and that this contrast creates a tone opposed to that of "a true heroic *aristeía*."

86. The cultivation and processing of cereals is a mark of human, as opposed to bestial, status. As Jean-Pierre Vernant says, what establishes the difference between animals and beasts is the fact that humans eat cultivated and cooked food whereas beasts eat wild and raw food ("Entre bêtes et dieux," *Mythe et société en Grèce ancienne* [Paris, 1974] 146, 172–173). See also Charles Segal, "The Raw and Cooked in Greek Literature," *Classical Journal* 69 (1974) 291, 299 n. 22, 301. Nagler (147 n. 21) uses this structuralist terminology to state Scott's point (see note 85 above) somewhat differently; he says that "the similes throughout the river fight . . . provide civilized ('cooked') imagery to balance the hero's savage ('raw') behavior."

Only two other similes in the *Iliad* have a similar effect. At 11.67–69 the battle lines of Trojans and Achaians destroying each other are compared to two lines of reapers. In this case the action (*déioun*) is vague enough to save the audience from queasiness. When, however, the men tugging at Patroklos's body are compared to a circle of men stretching an oxhide until the natural moisture goes and the grease sinks in (17.389–393), the audience may feel the same revulsion as here.

87. *Scholia Graeca in Homeri Iliadem*, vol. 5 (Berlin, 1977) 129.

88. But Odysseus, who fights for his life in and against the sea in *Odyssey* 5, is also compared to a sea creature: a tenacious octopus (432–435).

89. In the *Iliad* the cringing Thestor being killed by Patroklos is compared to a fish being hooked by a fisherman (16.406–408), and Euryalos reeling up and backwards from Epeios's victorious fist is compared to a fish leaping out of the water (23.692–693). In the *Odyssey* some of Odysseus's companions are speared like fish by the Laistrygones (10.124), and others later gasp and struggle when hauled onto dry land by a fisherman (12.251–254). The mass of slaughtered suitors is compared to a heap of dead fish on the shore (22.383–388). This last fish simile, which describes the suitors as Odysseus stands and looks at

them, is followed by another simile which describes Odysseus himself as a lion spattered with the blood of an ox (402–405). The heroic nature of Odysseus's action is thus affirmed.

90. Krischer (59–61) places this simile under the rubric of "the victor and his victim" and defines the type as containing a predatory animal (*Raubtier*) and a defenseless (*wehrlos*) victim. One of the situations described by this type of simile is "the bloodbath."

91. I do not accept the view of Walter Leaf (*The Iliad*, vol. 2 [1902; repr. Amsterdam, 1971] 484) and Arthur Adkins (*Merit and Responsibility*, [Oxford, 1960] 31) that *kakós* is never an ethical judgment but refers only to the ill effect of actions on the victim. *Kakà dè phresì mḗdeto érga* (21.19) is the same phrase Homer will use to condemn Achilles' sacrifice of the twelve Trojan youths on Patroklos's pyre (23.176). *Tōn dè stónos ṓrnut' aeikḕs* (21.20) occurs also at 10.482–484, where Diomedes, like a lion *kakà phronéōn* (485–586), slaughters the Thracians. *Aeikḗs* in these cases seems to apply to both the nonheroic mode of slaughter and the mode of dying. When, however, it is used in nearly the identical sentence of the slaughtered suitors in *Odyssey* (22.308–309 = 24.184–185), the shamefulness seems to redound more on the slain than on the slayer. In none of these cases does the idea of human excellence rise to the fore; instead, as the victims die in anonymous heaps, we feel a sense of dehumanization. Segal (*Corpse* 13) supports the view that *kakós* can have an ethical connotation. See A. A. Long, "Morals and Values in Homer," *Journal of Hellenic Studies* 90 (1970) 129–132, for a good analysis of *aeikḗs*.

92. Redfield, *Nature* 201–202, 261 n. 74. At 8.299 *lussētêra* is the epithet of a dog (describing Hektor); Chantraine says (*Dictionnaire*, vol. 3, 651) that though the precise meaning "rabies" ("rage du chien") does not appear until Xenophon, *lússa* does come from the same root as *lúkos* 'wolf,' "rabies (Fr. 'rage') being a disease typical of the wolf." See also Redfield's subchapters "Dogs" and "The Impurity of the Hero," *Nature* 193–204.

93. See Moulton, 113.

94. See Whitman, 156, 340 n. 5.

95. Segal, *Corpse*, 33. Compare Seth Benardete's Trojans, who respond to "civil" *aidṓs*, and his Achaians, who respond to "military" *aidṓs* ("Achilles and the *Iliad*," *Hermes* 91 [1963] 9–11).

96. Achilles as he destroys "civilization" appears to have taken on the nature of Aristotle's fourth-century extrapolitical man who, deprived of or spurning the city that is the proper home of human beings, is "either *thḗrios* or *theós*" (*Politika* 1, 1253a).

97. Compare J. Griffin, *Homer* 138, 177, and W. Marg, "Kampf und Tod in der Ilias," *Die Antike* 18 (1942) 167–179. For an excellent discussion of the *Iliad*

as a critical exploration of the "heroic concept of life" see A. Parry, "Have We Homer's *Iliad?*"

98. See A. Parry's comments on the epithets "king of men" (*ánax andrôn*) and "godlike" (*díos*) in verse 7 (*"*Language and Characterization in Homer" 2–6). See also Adkins, "Values, Goals, and Emotions in the *Iliad,*" *Classical Philology* 77, no. 4 (October 1982) 300.

99. It is stated repeatedly that the "sons of the Achaians" gave the *géra:* 1.162, 276, 368, 392; and see 16.56.

100. See David B. Claus, *"Aidôs* in the Language of Achilles," *Transactions of the American Philological Association* 105 (1975) 23–24.

101. The same sense of betrayal by the group also emerges from Achilles' words at three places in Book Nine. Achilles says that neither Agamemnon nor the other Danaans will persuade him since there was no *cháris* given for endless fighting (315–317). He tells Odysseus to report everything he says clearly so that other Achaians might grow angry if Agamemnon still expects to cheat someone else (369–371). He warns Phoinix not to love those he (Achilles) hates but to care for those who care for him; take half of my *timé,* he says (613–616). See Redfield's comment (*Nature* 103) that Achilles' speech in Book Nine is "the speech of a man who feels himself evicted from his community."

102. See Charles Segal, "Nestor and the Honor of Achilles," *Studi Micenei ed Egeo-Anatolici* 13 (1971) 97–105, and Adkins, "Values, Goals, and Emotions" 311–312. We may perhaps see a veiled reference to Achilles in Nestor's words at 2.344–347: "Do you, Atrides, rule over the Argives as before. But let them perish, those one or two who think apart from the Achaians."

103. This pattern is a major focus of Albert Lord's discussion of the *Iliad* on 186–197 of *The Singer of Tales* (Cambridge, Mass., 1964). Perhaps because his discussion concentrates on universal oral epic patterns (e.g., of bride stealing and rescue; of feuding; of withdrawal, death, and return) rather than on the *Iliad*'s specific critical presentation of the heroic code, his conclusions are rather different from mine: he accuses Achilles of *hubris* in "refusing to accept just return" (189).

104. "These will I give, and with them she whom I took, the girl Briseis" (130–131).

105. Achilles says Agamemnon will not persuade him until he has thoroughly repaid the shame of the insult (386–387), a clearly impossible demand. There are hints, however, that a real apology from Agamemnon could have healed the wound dealt to the code of honor. Whitman (*Homer* 192–193) points out that Achilles seems quite disgusted that Agamemnon did not come in person (372–373) and that in Book Sixteen "he says he would have thrown back the Trojans long ago, 'if Agamemnon would show me a friendly attitude' [721]." See

Whitman (*loc. cit.*) for an eloquent discussion of Achilles' rejection of Agamemnon's bribe.

106. See A. Parry, "Language of Achilles" 1–7. Parry believes (6) that since neither the epic poet "nor the characters he dramatizes can speak any language other than the one which reflects the assumptions of heroic society, . . . Achilles has no language with which to express his disillusionment. Yet he expresses it, and in a remarkable way. He does it by misusing the language he disposes of."

107. See Whitman, 183.

108. See 9.344, 371, 375.

109. For *mênis* as a term signifying specifically *divine* wrath, see P. Considine, "Some Homeric Terms for Anger," *Acta Classica* 9 (1966) 15–25, and Calvert Watkins, "A propos de ΜΗΝΙΣ," *Bulletin de la Societé de linguistique de Paris* 72 (1977) 187–209. Considine concludes (18, 21) that *mênis* is a solemn religious word (21), by which he means that it expresses "the characteristic response of offended deity to human presumption" (18). *Mênis* occurs sixteen times in the *Iliad* and the *Odyssey*. *Iliad:* 1.1, 75; 5.34, 178, 444; 9.517; 13.624; 15.122; 16.711; 19.35, 75; 21.523. *Odyssey:* 3.135; 5.146; 14.283. In the *Iliad* it is used four times of Achilles' anger, three times of Apollo's, three times of Zeus's, and twice of the gods'. In the *Odyssey* it is used twice of Zeus's anger, once of Athene's, and once of the gods'.

110. For an opposing interpretation of Achilles in this scene see Redfield, *Nature* 105. See also Judith A. Rosner, "The Speech of Phoinix: *Iliad* 9, 434–605," *Phoenix* 30 (1976) 314–327, for a discussion of the parallels between Phoinix's whole speech and the life and nature of Achilles.

111. Hektor, it should be noted, does not fight to achieve *timé*. His *kléos* is to be created in another value system, that of *aidôs*, respect for his city's opinions (6.442–443), and also in defense of his family. He says that he has learned to fight always in the foreranks, winning *kléos* for his father and himself (6.444–446), and his primary reason for risking his life is clear: he would rather be dead than see Andromache dragged off a slave (6.464–465). Unlike Achilles (and presumably all the other Achaian leaders except Menelaos), who came to Troy with no personal grievance to settle, Hektor has a personal reason for fighting. Marilyn B. Arthur ("Origins of the Western Attitude Toward Women," *Arethusa* 6 [1973] 11) sees Hektor, like Achilles, as separated from the heroic code and links Hektor's motivation to the new ethics of the *pólis*.

112. Thersites' *dídomen* ("we give") at 2.227–228 supplies evidence that they do participate at least this much.

113. Pindar *I.* 8.22–24 says that Aiakos rendered judgments (*díkai*) even to the gods. Nagy, who quotes this reference, believes that the idea of justice and fair allotments is a "mythological theme that runs through the whole line of Aeacids" (*Best of the Achaeans* 128). In *Iliad* 1 Achilles draws our attention to this

idea by swearing his oath of renunciation upon the royal sceptre, which is, as he says, "carried by the sons of the Achaians when they are busied about justice [*dikaspóloi*], they who guard the ordinances [*thémistas*] from Zeus" (1.237–239).

114. That Homer puts the Trojans in the wrong by having them break the truce in Book Four is irrelevant to what Achilles says in Book Nine. Achilles is not part of the truce-breaking scene, just as Hektor is not part of the scene in which the Trojans decide not to give back Helen (7.345–378). The reader may be aware that the Trojans are morally guilty, but neither Hektor nor Achilles is part of this rightness or wrongness.

115. As Aias's words at 9.636–638 show. Nethercut also notes the radical nature of Achilles' view of Briseis in his discussion of Achilles' journey toward inner value ("The Epic Journey of Achilles," *Ramus* 5 [1976] 2).

116. Vivante, *Homeric Imagination* 55.

117. This is my interpretation of 9.644–648: "Aias, . . . you seemed to speak everything after my own spirit, / but my heart swells in anger whenever I remember / those things, how the son of Atreus degraded me / as if I were a dishonored vagabond."

118. Except when he is mocking Aeneas at 20.178–183: "Do you think Priam will give you a *géras* and *timé* if you kill me? He won't, for he has sons and is of sound mind" (paraphrase). Achilles has learned that it is inherited position, not worth, that wins rewards.

119. This invalidation of categories was foreshadowed in the proem of the *Iliad* (1.1–7). There we are told that a human being's divine wrath (*ménis*) turned other human beings into a banquet for beasts. Redfield ("The Proem of the Iliad," *Classical Philology* 74 [1979] 104), who accepts the stronger reading δαῖτα in line five, comments that it "suggests the deletion of the categorical contrast between men and beasts."

120. *Dionysos Slain,* translated by Mireille Muellner and Leonard Muellner (Baltimore, 1979) 57, and see also the chart included in his "Entre bêtes et dieux," *Nouvelle revue de psychanalyse* 6 (1972) 238.

121. *Contra* Adkins, who staunchly defends his belief that Homer accepts uncritically the traditional valuation of military prowess and concomitant high social position as the highest human value ("Values and Goals" 321–324 and see his earlier *Merit and Responsibility* 31–38). Excellent discussions in Segal, *Corpse* 9–17, and in Long support my contention that the poet may insinuate values somewhat different from the traditional ones of his society.

122. I term the mode of the games comic because every quarrel has a happy ending and because many events, such as Oilean Aias tripping in cow dung, are ludicrous. Their corrective function can be seen in the way Achilles and others stop the disputes from becoming violent:

(1) Achilles settles the angry quarrel (*éris*) between Idomeneus and Oilean Aias over who is going to win the horse race (473–498). Achilles says, "Wait and see the actual result" (495–498).

(2) The greediness of the angry Antilochos makes Achilles smile (555–556).

(3) Antilochos and angry (567, 603) Menelaos patch up their quarrel without fighting, Antilochos confessing his fault (586–595) and Menelaos generously forgiving (596–611).

(4) Nestor is given the respect due him (615–650), and this is put (by Nestor) in the context of honor (*timês*, 649).

(5) "Might" is courteous in the boxing match: Epeios sets upright the dazed Euryalos (694–695).

(6) Achilles stops the wrestling match lest Odysseus or Aias get hurt (735–736).

(7) The sword fight between Aias and Diomedes is stopped lest Aias get hurt (822–823).

123. Owen, 235.

124. See Nagy, *Best of the Achaeans* 218.

125. Athenaeus 12F. Cited by Redfield ("Proem" 96), who argues for retaining *daîta* in 1.5.

126. Redfield, "Proem" 104.

127. Thetis leads the *góos* (18.51), a standard term for the ritual lamentation over a dead person (cf. 24. 723, 747, 761), and when she comes to Achilles she takes his head in her hands (18.71), the standard gesture of the chief female mourner (cf. 24.724). Johannes Kakridis, postulating a lost *Achilleis*, says that Homer has taken "motifs belonging to the dead Achilles and transferred them to the living Achilles" (*Homeric Researches* [Lund, 1949] 72). He presents (69–88) a full discussion of the death and burial of Patroklos in Books Sixteen, Eighteen, and Twenty-Three as based on the death and funeral of Achilles. See also Nagler, 156, and Schein, *Mortal Hero* 129–132.

128. Compare Whitman, 219–220.

129. See Moulton, 101–106.

130. Peleus : Achilles : : Achilles : Patroklos : : Priam:Hektor. Nethercut (14) says that Achilles has a "new sense of what it means to feel like a father." For a discussion of Patroklos not as son but as father figure see Robert Finlay, "Patroklos, Achilleus, and Peleus," *Classical World* 73 (1980) 272–273.

131. Scott, 61. See also Schadewaldt, 348, and Moulton, 114.

132. What I term "society" is expressed in Odysseus's word *stratoû* (14.84).

133. It should be noted that the Hellenistic scholars Aristophanes and Aristarchos rejected 614–617, the lines which describe Niobe weeping eternally even though turned to stone. Kakridis (97) concurs in their judgment because, like the scholiasts (see Hartmut Erbse, *Scholia Graeca in Homeri Iliadem* 5 [Ber-

lin, 1977] 622), he sees an impossible contradiction between Niobe's eating and her petrifaction. This seems silly; it would not contradict logic to envision Niobe being turned to stone *after* she has eaten. But if the lines are indeed an interpolation by someone who wanted to restore the well-known petrifaction, they are, at least, remarkably apt to the poetic situation.

134. Vivante, 20. Or, as Rachel Bespaloff puts it, "The body must take its just revenge on the exhausted soul before the soul can extort new tears from it" (*On the Iliad*, trans. McCarthy [Princeton, 1947], 102).

135. Vivante, 20.

136. Robert Scholes and Robert Kellogg, *The Nature of Narrative* (Oxford, 1966) 210.

137. See Nestor's words at 3.109–113, which list the best of the Greeks who were killed at Troy: Aias, Achilles, Patroklos, and Antilochos. Sophokles will later put these same four names in the mouth of Philoktetes as examples of how only the noblest die in war (*Philoktetes* 331–450).

138. At 9.309–313 he says to Odysseus that he will speak plainly without regard for persons or consequences, for "that man is as hateful to me as the doorway of Hades / he who hides one thing in his heart and says another."

139. This was pointed out to me as a characteristic of Achilles in the *Iliad* by Professor Seth Schein in a private communication.

140. Compare Telemachos's wish that Odysseus had died in Troy so that the Achaians would have heaped up a tomb for him and thus he would have won great *kléos* for himself and his son (1.236–240). Also compare Odysseus's similar wish at 5.308–311.

141. By nonheroic I mean merely nonmartial and not participating in the heroic code of the *Iliad*. Odysseus is fully heroic in his battle against the suitors, but the abilities that got him home and that will get him through the trials still to come are not martial abilities.

CHAPTER TWO

CLASSICAL VISIONS OF THE HOMERIC WARRIOR

1. The summarist's name is Proclus, but scholars are uncertain whether he is a second-century grammarian or the well-known fifth-century Neoplatonist.

2. See Jasper Griffin's thorough comparison of the Epic Cycle to the Homeric poems, "The Epic Cycle and the Uniqueness of Homer," *Journal of Hellenic Studies* 97 (1977) 39–53.

3. Many of the legends no doubt predate Homer; Kakridis, indeed, believes that an already well-known *Aithiopis*, which told of the death of Achilles, is what gives *Iliad* 18 so much of its tragic power (*Homeric Researches* 83–95). But the consensus among scholars is that the rest of the Epic Cycle poems were composed to complement the *Iliad* and the *Odyssey* in the seventh century,

which is when the legends became extremely popular subjects for vase paintings (see K. Friis Johansen, *The Iliad in Early Greek Art* [Copenhagen, 1967] 26–80).

4. For scenes of Achilles' arming in Phthia see K. Friis Johansen, 92–122, and *Lexicon Iconographicum Mythologiae Classicae*, vol. 1 (Zurich, 1981) "Achilleus" nos. 186–203; for Achilles with Cheiron see J. D. Beazley, *The Development of Attic Black-Figure* (Los Angeles, 1951) 10 and *Lexicon Iconographicum* "Achilleus" nos. 19–37.

5. Except where otherwise noted, all references to Proclus's *Chrestomathia* or to Epic Cycle fragments are from Allen's *Homeri Opera*, vol. 5 (Oxford, 1912). A translation of these texts can be found in H. G. Evelyn-White, *Hesiod, The Homeric Hymns and Homerica* (Cambridge, Mass., 1914) 481–533.

6. Hesiod helps us to understand the time scheme. He says that Achilles was a boy being reared by Cheiron when Helen and Menelaos were married (*Suitors of Helen*, frag. 204, *Hesiod: Fragmenta Selecta* edited by R. Merkelbach and M. L. West [Oxford, 1983] 178). We know that ten years elapsed between the elopement and the Achaians' arrival at Troy, since the tenth year of the war is Helen's twentieth year in Troy (*Il.* 24.765–766).

7. This episode, which also includes the magical curing of Telephos, heir of Teuthras, proves especially fruitful in late-antique and medieval versions of the Troy story but was used also by Euripides as the subject of a lost play famous for bringing a king on stage in rags. Jasper Griffin uses this episode of the wound incurable except by the sword that made it as an example of the Epic Cycle's love of the fantastic ("Epic Cycle" 40). Pliny opts for a rational explanation of the magical healing, saying that as a pupil of Cheiron Achilles discovered an herb, henceforth named achilleos after him, with which he cured Telephos's wound. He reports also that others say Achilles was the first to discover that rust is a very useful ingredient in healing plasters and that this is why Achilles is painted scraping it from his spear with his sword onto the wound of Telephos. *Invenisse et Achilles discipulus Chironis qua volneribus mederetur—quae ob id Achilleos vocatur—ac sanasse Telephum dicitur. alii primum aeruginem invenisse utilissimam emplastris—ideoque pingitur ex cuspide decutiens eam gladio in volnus Telephi . . . volunt* [*Nat. Hist.* 25.5.42].

8. καὶ Ἀχιλλεὺς ὕστερον κληθεὶς διαφέρεται πρὸς Ἀγαμέμνονα (*Chrestomathia* 1, p. 104). *Hýsteros kletheis* probably means that Achilles was not invited to participate in some deliberations, perhaps those that decided the fate of Philoktetes after he received his festering wound on Tenedos. For this quarrel, see also *Kypria* frag. 16 (Allen, 123).

9. See later discussion of Euripides' *Hekabe* in this chapter and section on "Polyxena" in Chapter Four for Polyxena's role in the tradition.

10. The lyric poet Stesichoros told a story that included Thetis's giving Achilles the divinely wrought urn she had received from Dionysos in apprecia-

tion for her hospitality (Schol. *Iliad* 23.91). Nagy believes that this urn, which is perhaps the one mentioned in the *Iliad*, is a poetic remnant of Achilles' immortality in hero cult (*Best of the Achaeans* 209).

11. J. Griffin, "Epic Cycle" 43.

12. See Nagy, *Best of the Achaeans*, 174–210. Ibykos and Simonides located his immortal home on the Elysian Plain (Ibyk. frag. 10, *Poetae Melicae Graeci* 151); Pindar placed him on the Island of the Blessed (*O.* 2.79–80), or on a "shining island in the Black Sea" (*N.* 4.49–50).

13. D. L. Page, *Sappho and Alcaeus* (Oxford, 1955) 283.

14. Alk. 42 = Alk. B 10; my translation follows Page's restoration in *Sappho and Alcaeus* 278–279.

15. See frag. B 12, Page, *Sappho and Alcaeus* 281.

16. Page, *Sappho and Alcaeus* 281.

17. See John H. Finley, Jr., *Pindar and Aeschylus* (Cambridge, Mass., 1955) 23–24.

18. See, for example, *N.* 3.40–42.

19. In the *Iliad* Achilles contends only against his fellow men—not deer, as in Pindar, or horses, as here. Homer compares Achilles' running to a prize-winning race horse in full gallop (22.22–23) and thus marks a peak of natural human excellence through evocation of equine excellence. Pindar and Euripides create supernatural excellence by transforming simile into fact.

20. See note 4 this chapter and Chapter Three, note 68.

21. Literally *megalosthenei . . . orphanizoménōi Peleídāi,* "the powerful orphaned son of Peleus." For an account of Achilles' abandonment by his parents, see Chapter Three, note 68.

22. A scholiast opines that *zakátoio* is a pertinent adjective because Achilles' spear was two-pronged and thus inflicted double pain (Scholia to 85, *Scholia Vetera in Pindari Nemea et Isthmia,* edited by E. Abel [Berlin, 1884] 191–193). This is a possible reason for Pindar's choice of the adjective, but, as the scholiast later suggests (*ibid.* 194), the effect is to evoke the famous wrath.

23. Before the fighting with Memnon begins, Proclus says, "Thetis foretold to her son things concerning Memnon" (*Chrestomathia* 2, p. 106). We can perhaps infer from these words that Thetis foretold Achilles' death and thus created a situation similar to that concerning Patroklos in the *Iliad.*

24. See David C. Young, *Three Odes of Pindar* (Leiden, 1968) 32–45.

25. See Mary R. Lefkowitz, *The Victory Ode: An Introduction* (Park Ridge, N.J., 1976) 151–152 for a discussion of how Homer's *kaká* are changed to *pémata* to suit this particular ode's imagery.

26. Lefkowitz (155) has a good discussion of this passage.

27. See Carola Greengard, *The Structure of Pindar's Epinician Odes* (Amsterdam, 1980) 33–34.

28. Greengard, 32.

29. Greengard, 35 n. 27.

30. Bernard M. W. Knox, *The Heroic Temper: Studies in Sophoclean Tragedy* (Berkeley and Los Angeles, 1964) 52.

31. Several plays in which he certainly or possibly appeared are lost: *The Gathering of the Achaians, Aithiopes* or *Memnon, Loves of Achilles, Dolopes, Iphigeneia, Mysians, Shepherds, Dinner Companions, Troilos, Peleus, Priam, Phthian Women, Phrygian Women.* I have used A. C. Pearson's *The Fragments of Sophocles,* 3 vols. (Cambridge, 1917), to make up this list. Volume 1, xvii–xxxi, gives an introductory list; discussions under titles are valuable for determining whether or not Achilles was a character.

32. B. M. W. Knox, *Temper* 124.

33. T. B. L. Webster, *Sophocles: Philoctetes* (Cambridge, 1970) commentary *ad loc.*

34. Compare B. M. W. Knox, *Temper* 125.

35. R. C. Jebb, however, takes *hypourgeîn* as dependent on *deî* in order to smooth over the harsh syntax (*The Philoctetes* [Cambridge, 1890] *ad loc*).

36. Or "in thought" (*gnômēi*) in a moral sense, as Jebb takes it (*loc. cit.*).

37. I should note that Nagy has argued for the existence of an epic tradition, antedating the *Iliad,* in which Achilles and Odysseus contested the title "best of the Achaians" on the basis of superior might versus superior intellect (*Best of the Achaeans* 45–58). If he is correct, then we must view the later poets not as narrowing Homer's vision but as developing an older process of thinking.

38. This fragment was originally attributed to Sophokles' *The Gathering of the Achaians* and as such is discussed by Pearson, *Fragments,* vol. 1, pp. 98–99. For attribution to Euripides, see E. W. Handley and John Rea, "The *Telephus* of Euripides," *Univ. of London Bull. Inst. Classical Studies* Suppl. 5 (1957) 18–39.

39. Quoted from Colin Austin, ed., *Euripidea Nova Fragmenta* (Berlin, 1968) 82. For the context, see E. Handley and J. Rea, "*Telephus* of Euripides" 28–38.

40. We may perhaps cite here as representative of the progressive democrats of this time the opinion with which Thucydides has Diodotos counter Creon's claim that immediate action is the best action. Diodotos says:

> I think there are two things most opposed to soundness of judgment: speed (*táchos*) and anger (*orgē*), of which the former is wont to be found together with lack of understanding (*anoía*), the latter with lack of education (*apaideusía*) and briefest thought (*gnómē*), and whoever maintains that words are not the teachers of deeds is either mindless or disingenuous (*Peloponnesian War* 3.42).

41. For the translation "Right" and "Wrong" see K. J. Dover, *Aristophanes: Clouds* (Oxford, 1970) lviii.

42. The first version of the *Clouds* was produced in 423 B.C., the second in approximately 417. For the dating see Dover, *Aristophanes,* lxxx–lxxxi.

43. My translation is based on an anonymous translation in *Aristophanes: Five Comedies* The Living Library (Cleveland, 1948) 157.

44. Webster, *Philoctetes* 71.

45. See B. M. W. Knox, *Temper* 122–123.

46. Jebb comments (*ad loc.*): "By using oûn, he concedes (at least for argument's sake) what Odysseus has just said. . . . He now demurs to play the part not . . . because it is immoral, but because it is distasteful and difficult."

47. It is used with its most positive connotation in *Il.* 10.225 when Diomedes says that he wants a partner on the night raid because "when two go together one looks ahead to see what is *kérdos.*" Its connotations are least heroic when it is used of Antilochos's "skill" in turning close to the goal-post (*Il.* 23.322, 515).

48. Sophokles stresses Neoptolemos's egocentric dismay here by the emphatic placement of *eîm' egṓ* at the end of 114. Odysseus's reply recognizes and plays to this personal ambition with the framing *sù. . . . soû. Ho pérsōn,* "sacker," is one of the more negative terms in the list of Achillean heroisms Neoptolemos wants to live up to, and it is the one that remains paramount until 1402.

49. B. M. W. Knox, *Temper* 123.

50. Neoptolemos could have said, "I have to fight at Troy to avenge my father" (that is, to kill Paris), but he does not. Since Apollo is mentioned as the sole killer, Neoptolemos has no more reason to fight than had Achilles before Patroklos was killed.

51. As B. M. W. Knox says (*Temper* 123), the lie Neoptolemos tells presents him "as a sort of spurious Achilles; words, mood, and pretended action are all a lying parody of his great-hearted father. Achilles was deprived of his prize by Agamemnon; Neoptolemos claims that the Atreidae denied him his father's armor. Achilles withdrew from the battle and threatened to sail home to Phthia; Neoptolemos claims he has withdrawn from the battle and is sailing home to Scyros (240). And when Philoctetes asks him why he is angry with the Atridae, he speaks with a mock-Achillean fury: 'May I satisfy my anger with this hand, so that Mycenae and Sparta may realize that Scyros too is the mother of warlike men.'"

52. Achilles says very much the same thing, minus the carefully balanced phrases and antitheses, at *Il.* 1.225–244.

53. Achilles says simply: "I do not think Agamemnon or the other Achaians will persuade me" (9.315–316).

54. This fragment was earlier assigned to Aischylos's *Myrmidons* by Vitelli and Norsa, *Papyri Greci e Latini, Publicazioni della Società italiana per la ricerca dei papyri greci e latini in Egitto* II (Florence, 1935) 31211, and D. L. Page, *Greek*

Literary Papyri 1 (Cambridge, 1942) no. 20, p. 136. Cited from H. W. Smyth and Hugh Lloyd-Jones, *Aeschylus* 2 (Cambridge, Mass., 1957) no. 286, pp. 591–592.

55. This Achilles is arrogant in a way that the Homeric Achilles is not. In the *Iliad* Achilles claimed to be the "best of the Achaians"; this Achilles says that he is "everything" (*tà pánta*) to the army (9–11). He also says that there is nothing wrong with his making such a boast since no one of the leaders is of nobler birth (*eugenésteros*) than he (12–14).

56. The translation is Jebb's. See his commentary to 1291.

57. The *Rhesos*, probably written before 440 B.C., i.e., well before the Peloponnesian War, does not show such a totally negative reading. Its plot is similar to that of *Iliad* 10, although as Bernard Fenik points out (*"Iliad X" and "The Rhesus"* [Brussels, 1964] 28), it is built upon non-Iliadic versions. Though the portrait of the Greeks is less favorable than in the *Iliad* (Fenik, *"Iliad X"* 20, 22), neither Hektor nor Achilles is condemned. Achilles, who does not appear in person, is described as *pepúrgōtai* ("massive"), *aíthōn* ("fiery"), and *mēníōn* ("wrathful") at the generals (122, 494–495). For the dating and attribution of the *Rhesos* to Euripides, see G. M. A. Grube, *The Drama of Euripides* (London, 1941) 439–447, and W. Ritchie, *The Authenticity of the Rhesus of Euripides* (Cambridge, 1964). For an overview of Euripides' progressive disenchantment with the Trojan War legends because of an increasing pessimism and antiwar idealism, see Carlo Pacati, "Il significato della guerra troiana nell' opera di Euripide," *Dioniso* 40 (1966) 77–94 and Philip Vellacott, *Ironic Drama: A Study of Euripides' Method and Meaning* (Cambridge, 1975).

58. In *Against Leokrates* 102, Lykourgos says explicitly that Homer's poems were singled out from those of other poets, thus indicating that the *Iliad* and the *Odyssey* were recognized as being by Homer and as superior to the poems of the Epic Cycle.

59. Hesychios, s.v. βραυρωνίοις. Cited by Friis Johansen, 236.

60. The *Iliad* became a popular subject for vase painting starting at the beginning of the sixth century. See K. Friis Johansen, 85–230, and John Boardman, *Athenian Red-Figure Vases* (London, 1975) 230–231.

61. Aischylos turned the *Iliad* into a trilogy (*Myrmidons*, *Nereids*, and *Phrygians* or *Ransom of Hektor*) that dramatized its three major events: the death of Patroklos, the killing of Hektor, and the meeting between Priam and Achilles. See fragments 59–66 and 72–75 in Smyth and Lloyd-Jones, *Aeschylus* 2, and A. Nauck's description of the trilogy under ΜΥΡΜΙΔΟΝΕΣ, *Tragicorum Graecorum Fragmenta* (Leipzig, 1889) 42. Aischylos also wrote a trilogy about Memnon, the middle play of which dealt with the duel between the two goddess-born heroes. See Smyth and Lloyd-Jones, *Aeschylus* 2, p. 421.

62. For a close reading of the ode, a detailed discussion of its implications for the play, and references to other scholarship, see Katherine Callen King, "The Force of Tradition," *TAPA* 110 (1980) 195–212. See also G. B. Walsh, "The First *stasimon* of Euripides' *Electra*," *Yale Classical Studies* 25 (1977) 277–291.

63. See J. D. Denniston's note to verses 443–444 in his edition of *Electra* (Oxford, 1939; reprint 1968) p. 104 for the translation of *móchthous aspistàs . . . teuchéōn*.

64. See Denniston, *Electra* pp. 104–105 for reconstruction of the difficult and partially corrupt verses 445–448.

65. There was apparently an episode in the Epic Cycle that had Thetis bring Achilles immortal arms before he left for Troy. Several vase paintings that illustrate the scene can be found in *Lexicon Iconographicum* "Achilleus" nos. 186–203. In the fourth century B.C. the sculptor Skopas created a statuary group of Poseidon, Thetis, Achilles, and Nereids *supra delphinos et cete aut hippocampos sedentes, item Tritones chorusque Phorci et pistrices ac multa alia marina* (Pliny *Nat. Hist.* 36.5.26); this combination of Nereids on dolphins and dancing sea creatures was probably inspired either by Euripides' ode or by an Epic Cycle incident that had also inspired Euripides.

66. This is the mood that Homer's Agamemnon tries desperately to recall at *Iliad* 8.229–234 and that Thucydides (6.24–25) ascribes to the Athenians at a point not far removed in time from the writing of the *Elektra*.

67. This idea finds expression outside the ode also. Michael J. O'Brien, "Orestes and the Gorgon: Euripides' *Electra*" (*American Journal of Philology* 85 [1964] 23–39), shows convincingly how Orestes becomes a symbol not only of Perseus but also of the Gorgon.

68. When Achilles is at his most inhuman in the *Iliad*, he is still a *natural* force: Homer compares him to fire, a dolphin, a burning city, a star, a sun, a hawk, a hunting dog—all quite ordinary objects.

69. I am indebted for the following remarks to A. C. Pearson's discussion of the issue in his *Fragments of Sophocles*, vol. 2, pp. 161–162. See also Tito Tosi, "Il sacrifizio di Polissena," *Atene e Roma* 17 (1914) 19–38, who considers it absurd to deny a causal link between ghost and sacrifice in the tradition. A more recent summary of the evidence that basically agrees with mine is given by D. J. Conacher in his "Euripides' *Hecuba*," *American Journal of Philology* 82 (1961) 3–5.

70. *Sack of Ilium*: ἔπειτα ἐμπρήσαντες τὴν πόλιν Πολυξένην σφαγιάζουσιν ἐπὶ τὸν τοῦ Ἀχιλλέως τάφον. *Nostoi*: τῶν δὲ περὶ τὸν Ἀγαμέμνονα ἀποπλεόντων Ἀχιλλέως εἴδωλον ἐπιφανὲν πειρᾶται διακωλύειν προλέγον τὰ συμβησόμενα.

71. *Scholia Graeca in Euripidis Tragoedias* vol. 1, ed. William Dindorf (Oxford, 1863) 229–230.

72. *Chrestomathia* 2, p. 107; *Ilias Parva* no. 16, p. 134 (Pausanias 10.27.1); and *Ilias Parva* no. 19, pp. 134–135 (scholiast on Lykophron 1268). Also see Pindar, *Paean* 6.

73. *On the Sublime* 15.7.

74. *Scholia* 220.

75. Frag. 523, Pearson, vol. 2, 164.

76. Henri Weil, in *Sept tragédies d'Euripide* (Paris, 1868) 204, thinks rather that the appearance of the ghost came after the sacrifice at the very end of the play. He conjectures that the ghost in a grand finale warned Agamemnon and the others of the woes awaiting them during the voyage and at home.

77. διασπωμένου αὐτὴν τοῦ Ἀχιλλέως καὶ μελιστὶ ξαίνοντος. Flavius Philostratus, *Heroikos* 56.6–10 (*Flavius Philostratus Heroicus*, edited by L. de Lannoy [Leipzig, 1977] 74–75. Philostratus tells the story in the second or third century A.D. but gives no date for the incident. Arrian has no doubt about the continuing vivacity of Achilles' ghost in the second century A.D. (*Periplous* 23).

78. For summaries of the stories of several other hero-ghosts, both wrathful and beneficent, see Rohde, *Psyche* 132–138. For an account of the hero as a combination of *díkē* ("justice") and *húbris* ("violence") see Nagy, *Best of the Achaeans* 152–156.

79. See Jane Harrison, *Themis* (Cambridge, 1912) 308–316; Rohde, 116–117; A. D. Nock, "The Cult of Heroes," *Harvard Theological Review* 37 (1944) 156–165; D. Gill, "*Trapezomata*," *Harvard Theological Review* 67 (1974) 121–122; Nagy, *Best of the Achaeans* 9, 114, 117; and Herodotos 5.67.5. A possible exception is the ritual human sacrifice that L. R. Farnell says continued to be offered to Diomedes in remote Cyprus through the fourth century B.C. (*Greek Hero Cults* [Oxford, 1921] 290).

80. The ghost of Polydoros offers a good contrast to that of Achilles. Although he has good reason to desire vengeance, his only wish is for burial, and his only emotions are sorrow and pity for his mother. His gentle character is similar to that of Polyxena, whose self-sacrifice will offer another alternative to the "heroism" of Achilles.

81. See Chapter Four for a full discussion of Polyxena's relationship to Achilles.

82. For the meaning of the word *géras*, see Benveniste, 334–339. There is no reason to think that such a term could not be used of the honorific portion reserved for a long-dead king, but I have found no examples (see my article, "The Politics of Imitation," *Arethusa* [1985] n. 24). But although there is not enough evidence to convince me that *géras* was a standard term in hero cult, if it was so used, it would strengthen the effect of the parody in conjoining "civilized" Homer with "primitive" religion.

83. In extant literature, according to H. Liddell, R. Scott, and H. S. Jones (*A Greek-English Lexicon*, 9th ed. [Oxford, 1940] s.v. ἀγέραστος), it occurs only

in Hesiod's *Theogony* 395, Euripides' *Bacchai* 1378, Apollonius's *Argonautika* 3.65, and Lucian's *Tyrannicida* 3. In the first three it is used by gods.

84. Since Agamemnon apparently could have taken ransom as an acceptable substitute for Chryseis with no loss of honor (see *Il.* 1.11–32, 111–115, where Agamemnon's original refusal to return Chryseis is discussed without mention of honor), the honor she confers is obviously interchangeable with the honor wealth confers. Since Agamemnon already has been awarded most of the spoils from previous campaigns (1.162–168) and is certainly the wealthiest of the kings of Troy, it is hard to see how Homer could have meant us to sympathize with Agamemnon's regarding himself as *agérastos*.

85. See *Il.* 6.455–465, 19.290–302; *Od.* 8.523–530.

86. See Chapter One, part two.

87. Compare *Agamemnon* 218 and Sophokles' *Elektra* 573–574.

88. Compare D. J. Conacher ("Euripides' *Hecuba*" 5–6) and James C. Hogan ("Thucydides 3.52–68 and Euripides' *Hecuba*," *Phoenix* 26 [1972] 251), who also stress the political nature of the choice.

89. And compare his statement at 1.113–115 that he prefers Chryseis to Klytaimestra.

90. When Odysseus later contrasts the Trojan "barbarians" with "we Greeks," Euripides' audience, of course, knows who the real barbarians are, for Euripides here makes sure that Athens will be included in that appellation. He deliberately implicates Athens in the barbarity about to be committed by singling out the two sons of her greatest hero to be the only named speakers besides Odysseus to argue for the sacrifice (cf. Gilbert Murray, 87). If we adopt the dating of 424/423 B.C. as roughly accurate for the *Hekabe* (Édouard Delebecque, *Euripide et la guerre du Péloponnèse* [Paris, 1951] 163–164; and Lesky, *History of Greek Literature*, trans. James Willis and Cornelis de Heer [London, 1966] 373), we may speculate that this play is a reaction to the first major atrocities of the Peloponnesian War, those committed in 427 on Mytilene by the Athenians (Thuc. 3.36, 50), on Plataea by the Spartans (Thuc. 3.68), and on Corcyra by democrats (Thuc. 3.81) and oligarchs (3.70) alike.

91. The Greeks clearly accept Nestor's formulation that Agamemnon is automatically *phérteros* (i.e., "more to be respected") because he rules over more people (1.281). See Chapter One, part three.

92. *Acháristoi* also represents the starting point for the *cháris* theme, which Euripides manipulates, in Hogan's words, "to juxtapose a personal view of ethical responsibility and a public view" (254). The first instance of this juxtaposition occurs when Hekabe throws *acháristos* back at Odysseus in line 254, castigating him and all demogogues for ignoring personal debts in favor of winning *timē* and *cháris* from *hoi polloí*.

93. Arthur Adkins ignores this disparity between speaker and speech when

he argues that fifth-century Athenians would have agreed with Odysseus ("Basic Greek Values in Euripides' *Hecuba* and *Hercules Furens*," *Classical Quarterly* 60 [1966] 198). See my discussion in "The Politics of Imitation," n. 38.

94. The consensus among scholars is that Euripides died before completing this play and that his son put on the finishing touches for its posthumous (and victorious) production with the *Bacchai*. There is little consensus, however, on how much of the play is Euripides', how much is his son's, and how much is later interpolation. The ending is clearly spurious (probably Byzantine, says Lesky, *History*, 397) because a fragment of the genuine ending (Aelian *On the Nature of Animals* 7.39) indicates that Artemis appeared at the end to set all to rights. We seem to have two beginnings, one a long, "typical" prologue delivered by Agamemnon, the other a lively exchange between the anxious, self-pitying king and his practical, folk-wise servant. They could both have been created by Euripides (see C. W. Willink, "The Prologue of *Iphigenia at Aulis*," *Classical Quarterly* 65 [1971] 343–364 and Bernard Knox, "Euripides' *Iphigenia in Aulide* 1–163," *Yale Classical Studies* 22 [1972] 239–261) or by someone else (see D. Bain, "The Prologues of Euripides' *Iphigeneia in Aulis*," *Classical Quarterly* 71 [1977] 10–26). Editors generally print them both as genuine parts of the play, sometimes putting the dialogue first (e.g., Paley), sometimes the prologue (e.g., Murray). Other parts of the play are criticized for inexpert metrics, minor inconsistencies, and lack of genius. Since for my purposes what is important is the play that became part of the tradition, I will discuss the play as a unity except for the ending.

95. John Ferguson, "*Iphigeneia at Aulis*," *Transactions of the American Philological Association* 99 (1968) 163.

96. For a more negative view of Agamemnon and Menelaos see H. Siegel, "Self-Delusion and the *Volte-Face* of Iphigeneia in Euripides' *Iphigeneia at Aulis*," *Hermes* 108 (1980) 300–321, and "Agamemnon in Euripides' *Iphigeneia at Aulis*," *Hermes* 109 (1981) 257–265.

97. 124–125:

> καὶ πῶς Ἀχιλεὺς λέκτρων ἀπλακὼν
> οὐ μέγα φυσῶν θυμὸν ἐπαρεῖ
> σοὶ σῇ τ' ἀλόχῳ;

98. Grube, 424.

99. See p. 70 and note 39.

100. Compare *Il.* 16.200–206. Though his men have been muttering, "If you won't let us fight, we might as well go home," there is not a hint that Achilles ever took their views into consideration.

101. 817–818:

δρᾶ γ', εἴ τι δράσεις, ἢ ἄπαγ' οἴκαδε στρατόν,
τὰ τῶν Ἀτρειδῶν μὴ μένων μελλήματα.

102. I omit verses 920–925, a series of reflections on how it is best to react to all things with moderation, as a senseless interpolation. If taken as genuine, they diminish still further the passion of Achilles' anger and increase the contrast with expectation. For a discussion of Achilles' traditional qualities that argues Euripides has improved on the Homeric model see Frederic Will, "Remarks on Counterpoint Characterization in Euripides," *Classical Journal* 55 (1959–60) 341.

103. In taking on his own Myrmidons, he exceeds even the Achilles in the anonymous fragment described in notes 55–56.

104. Compare *Iliad* 1.203, 214; 9.368.

105. Compare *Iliad* 9.646–648; 16.59.

106. 941–943:

ει δι' ἔμ' ὀλεῖται διά τε τοὺς ἐμοὺς γάμους
ἡ δεινὰ τλᾶσα κοὐκ ἀνεκτὰ παρθένος,
θαυμαστὰ δ' ὡς ἀνάξι' ἠτιμασμένη.

107. G. B. Walsh discerns an interesting pattern of role reversal in these sections and in Iphigeneia's later heroism: "As Achilles cannot exercise masculine *aretē* at Aulis, he becomes the representative of the more feminine virtue, *aidōs;* as Iphigenia's feminine *aidōs* does not help her at Aulis, she decides instead to achieve something closer to the masculine *aretē* (*"Iphigenia at Aulis:* Third Stasimon," *Classical Philology* 69 [1974] 246–247).

108. François Jouan, reading his character rather more positively than I do, thinks Achilles is the perfect incarnation of the virtues prized in a young man by the good Athenian society of the day (*Euripide et les légends des chants cypriens* [Paris, 1966] 286–287).

109. Noted by Walsh, who believes that it is part of a major theme of the drama: conflict between public character and "personal desires, strengths, and weaknesses" (*Iphigenia* 245).

110. For an eloquent interpretation of the *Iphigeneia at Aulis* as an antiwar play see George E. Dimock, Jr.'s introduction to his and W. S. Merwin's translation of the tragedy, *Euripides: Iphigeneia at Aulis* (New York, 1978) 3–21.

111. Pindar (*P.* 3.89–92, *N.* 5.34–36, *I.* 6.25, 8.38–40) uses the marriage as an example of how the good are rewarded; Alkaios 42 uses it for contrast with the "marriage" of Helen and Paris, which is "evil" in a way different from Iphigeneia's "marriage" but produces ultimately the same result: the destruction of Troy. See part one of this chapter.

112. Compare Hesiod frag. 1.6–7, Merckelbach and West, 113:

ξυναὶ γὰρ τότε δαῖτες ἔσαν, ξυνοὶ δὲ θόωκοι
ἀθανάτοισι θεοῖσι καταθνητοῖς τ᾽ἀνθρώποις.

113. *Anaklázo* is used of a baying dog by Xenophon (*Kyropaideia* 1.4.15). *Klázo* in fifth-century poets is used of screaming birds, baying dogs, rattling arrows, shrieking seers, and flute music, as well as (less often) of articulate sound such as men singing the paean (*LSJ*, s.v.).

114. No more negative, however, than the stated goal of the enterprise: to destroy Troy utterly. Part of the suitors' oath was *kataskápsein* the city that kept Helen away from her husband (64–65), and Iphigeneia intends her sacrifice to provide *kataskaphaí* for the Phrygians (1379).

115. Euripides describes the Achaians' "lust" for war in nearly the same words as Thucydides uses to describe the mood of the Athenians as they prepared to sail to Sicily. Thucydides writes: *kaì érōs enépese toîs pâsin homoíōs ekpleûsai*, "And a passion for sailing out fell on all alike" (6.24.3). In the *Aulis* Euripides has Achilles say: *hoútō deinòs empéptōk' érōs / têsde strateías Hellád'*, "Such a terrible passion for the expedition has fallen on Hellas" (808–809). Later in the play this passion seems to have escalated: Agamemnon says he cannot control his men because *mémēne d' Aphrodítē tis Hellēnōn stratôi / pleîn hōs táchista barbárōn epì chthóna*, "A violent desire rages in the army to sail instantly against the land of the barbarians" (1264–1265).

116. From a lecture given at the University of North Carolina, February 21, 1974.

117. Siegel argues strongly for interpreting her "decision" as an act of pathetic self-delusion meant only to compensate for a violent death she realizes she cannot in any case avoid ("Self-Delusion," esp. 314–315). Although much of what Siegel says is valid, it is possible to judge some delusions noble, especially when they save the lives of others as Polyxena's saves the lives of Achilles and many Greeks.

118. *Frogs* 1034–1036:

ὁ δὲ θεῖος Ὅμηρος
ἀπὸ τοῦ τιμὴν καὶ κλέος ἔσχεν πλὴν τοῦδ᾽ ὅτι χρήστ᾽ ἐδίδαξεν,
τάξεις, ἀρετάς, ὁπλίσεις ἀνδρῶν;

119. In J. Edmunds *Lyra Graeca* vol. 3 (Cambridge, Mass. 1927) 410–412. Aristotle is hymning his patron Hermias, ruler of Atarneus in Mysia. Hermias's story is told in Lesky, *History* 549.

120. Quoted after the reconstruction of Bruno Snell, who assigns this fragment to Astydamas on the basis of its subject matter and on the other contents of the papyrus on which it was found (*Euripides Alexandros und andere Strassburger Papyri mit Fragmenten griechischer Dichter* [Berlin, 1937] 84–88). Astydamas also wrote a *Hektor,* and it is to this play that Snell assigns it (86).

121. See also *Phaedrus* 248–249, 256a–b.

122. Plato's interpretation of Achilles' cutting off the lock of hair dedicated to Sperchios is also a gross misreading. The hair was dedicated to Peleus to be a thank offering to his native river upon his safe return home. Achilles' giving the lock to Patroklos demonstrates not impious arrogance but a simple awareness that he will never return home to give the lock to Sperchios.

CHAPTER THREE

LOVER OF WAR: CLASSICAL ROME TO MEDIEVAL EUROPE

1. Alexander so revered Homer's hero that he made a special sacrifice at his Trojan tomb on his way to conquer the Persians. It would appear that Alexander saw himself as a second Achilles and only wished he had another Homer to record his glory (Cicero, *Epistolae ad Familiares* 5.12.7, *Pro Archia* 10.24; Plutarch *Alex.* 15.8–9; Arrian *Anabasis* I.12.1–2). Q. Curtius Rufus, a historian of the first century A.D., recounts a gruesome anecdote that, if true, further illustrates Alexander's devotion to Achilles. After Betis was subdued at Gaza, "straps were drawn through his ankles while he was yet alive, and horses dragged him tied to the chariot around the city, while the king gloried that he was imitating Achilles, whose descendant he claimed to be" (*per talos enim spirantis lora traiecta sunt, religatumque ad currum traxere circa urbem, gloriante rege Achillem, a quo genus ipse deducerat, imitatum se esse*) 4.6.29. (Quoted in R. P. Austin, *Aeneidos Liber Secundus* [Oxford, 1966] 130.)

2. There were some exceptions, one of which is Rhianos of Crete (third century B.C.), who wrote at least five epics concerned with heroic themes and apparently modelled the martial prowess of Aristomenes, hero of the *Messeniaka*, on Achilles (see Guiseppe Giangrande, "Das Epyllion Catulls im Lichte der hellenistischen Epik," *L'Antiquité Classique* 41 [1972] 139). Pausanias, who gives us a lengthy summary of the poem, says, "To Rhianos Aristomenes was no less preeminent [*aphanésteros*] than the Iliadic Achilles was to Homer" (Paus. 4.6.3). This is no doubt true, but in spite of the fact that he can slaughter a hundred men in a single battle, Aristomenes, a middle-aged general weighed down with responsibility, who is often wounded and twice captured, is a very different hero from Achilles; as Auguste Couat has indicated, Aristomenes seems a composite of Odysseus, Hektor, and Achilles (*La poésie Alexandrine sous les trois premiers Ptolemeés* [Paris, 1882] 340–342, 352). Achilles did make a few martial appearances in the miniature and composite epic favored by Hellenistic poets, but the extant references, when they are not outright flattery of a patron (see Theokritos 17.55–57), are not so much concerned with militarism as with the importance of poets to great men (Theok. 16.73–75, 22.218–220), seduction (Theok. 29.32–34), and sexual violence: Euphorion's poem on Thrambelos

makes Achilles the unwitting and remorseful instrument of the gods' vengeance on his rapist-murderer cousin (John U. Powell, *Collectanea Alexandrina* [Oxford, 1925] Euphorion frag. 27, p. 35, and Page, *Greek Literary Papyri* 1 [Cambridge, 1942] 494–496), and Apollonios of Rhodes' "Capture of Lesbos" (*Lesbou Ktisis*) makes the lovesick princess of Methumna betray her city to Achilles after extracting his (false) promise to marry her (Powell, Apollonios frag. 12, pp. 7–8). Two poems use him as the slain son of a grieving mother (Kallimachos "To Apollo" 20–21; anon. frag. Cougny *A.P.* iii, 23–24, printed in A. D. Knox, *Choliambic Poets* [Cambridge, Mass., 1946] 281).

3. Rhianos, who was a scholar as well as a poet, published editions of the *Iliad* and the *Odyssey*, and the cumulative efforts of three directors of Alexandria's great library, Zenodotos, Aristophanes, and Aristarchos, produced a standardized text. Aristophanes (257–180 B.C.) also collected and edited Attic tragedy. (For a succinct account of Alexandrian scholarly interests see L. D. Reynolds and N. G. Wilson, *Scribes and Scholars* [Oxford, 1974] 5–15.) The fascination Homer exercised is demonstrated by Sotades' *Iliad*, an unfortunate production in which the epic's dactylic hexameters are rewritten as iambic tetrameters. (The wretched remains can be found in Powell, 239–245.)

4. Achilles' fame actually preceded the Romanizing of his song: Etruscan painting and sculpture reveal a knowledge of the *Iliad* as early as the sixth century B.C., and we are told that in the fifth century B.C. one Lucius Sicinius Dentatus was awarded the name of "Roman Achilles" in tribute to his *ingentem fortitudinem*. (Aulus Gellius II.11.1–2, and see Livy 3.42–43, R. M. Ogilvie, *Commentary on Livy* [Oxford, 1965] 475–476.)

5. *Si malas imitabo, tum tu pretium pro noxa dabis.* Nonius 365.37; Otto Ribbeck, *Tragicorum Romanorum Fragmenta* (Leipzig, 1871) 1.

6. For discussion see J. Vahlen, *Ennianae Poesis Reliquiae* (Leipzig, 1928) cci (the fragments are printed on 118–120); and H. D. Jocelyn, *The Tragedies of Ennius* (Cambridge, 1967) 161–177 (the fragments are printed on 67–70).

7. Vahlen, 120. Jocelyn suggests that this fragment comes from a nondramatic poem rather than a tragedy (*Tragedies of Ennius*, 164).

8. This play covers the events from *Iliad* 12 through 24, from Hektor's *aristeía* to Priam's ransoming his son. It was perhaps a condensation of Aischylos's trilogy, but Ennius may have written it to conform to Homer as Accius did later. For discussion see Vahlen, ccv–ccvii (the fragments are printed on 144–151), and Jocelyn, 290–303 (the fragments are printed on 100–104).

9. Vahlen, p. 150 = Jocelyn, frag. 71, p. 101.

10. For some interesting quotations that couple and contrast *ius* and *virtus*, see Jocelyn, 295.

11. Vahlen, frag. 12, p. 160 = Jocelyn, frag. 95, pp. 107–108. Vahlen (161)

thinks that this passage may have been freely inspired by Euripides' *Iphigeneia* 955–958, in which Achilles reviles Kalchas. Robert A. Brooks, accepting Vahlen's conjecture, argues that the purport of the verses is not so much philosophical as political. He believes that Achilles is referring to *himself* before the feet of Kalchas and that the verses, therefore, reveal Achilles' self-deception in the matter of his and Kalchas's relative power over the army (*Ennius and Roman Tragedy* [Salem, New Hampshire, 1984] 239).

12. *Myr.* 1, Ribbeck, 137. The lines are quoted by Nonius 433.3–8. Vincenzo d'Anto prints, translates, and discusses all the fragments in his recent book *I frammenti delle tragedie* (Lecce, 1980) 65–67, 113–116, 183–191, 509–510, 521–522.

13. *Epinausimache* 7, Ribbeck, p. 177; Nonius 2.24.

14. *Proinde istaec tua aufer terricula atque animum iratum conprime. Telephus* 8, Ribbeck, p. 216; Nonius 227.27.

15. *Ne tum cum fervat pectus iracundiae. Achilles* 2, Ribbeck, p. 136; Nonius 503.36.

16. *Iram infrenes, obstes animis, reprimas confidentiam. Myr.* 5, Ribbeck, p. 138; Nonius 262.16.

17. *Epinausimache* 1, Ribbeck, p. 176; Nonius 233.25. Nonius is proving that *anima* = *iracundia* or *furor* and that *animosi* = *iracundi* (233.19–20), and he also cites Plautus, Cicero, Vergil, and Lucilius.

18. *Ab classe ad urbem tendunt, neque quisquam potest / Fulgentium armum armatus ardorem obtui. Epinausimache* 9, Ribbeck, pp. 177–178; Nonius 495.21–22.

19. Ribbeck, p. 178; Nonius 192.3–4.

20. Also *diotrephés* 'Zeus-nourished' (*Il.* 21.223) and *theós* 'a god' (*Il.* 21.264, 380).

21. Quintilian refers to Achilles' musical accomplishment as validation for contemporary study (*Institutiones Oratoriae* 1.10.30–31), to his shield as a topic for rhetorical exercise (7.2.7), to his beauty as an example of a minor oratorical theme (3.7.11–12); he refers to his size (8.4.24) and battle prowess (7.9.8) in various rhetorical contexts, and he accounts Achilles supreme in war as Homer is supreme in poetry (10.24.65, 12.11.27).

22. The fragments, which come from Books One, Seven, Twelve, Twenty-One, and Twenty-Three, are printed in *Fragmenta Poetarum Latinorum*, ed. W. Morel (Stuttgart, 1927; repr. 1963) 48–49. They are discussed by Ronconi, *Interpreti Latini di Omero* (Turin, 1973) 35–37.

23. The fragments of Ninnius Crassus, one consisting of four words of Patroklos's exhortation to the Myrmidons at 16.270 and the other the sleepy words of Priam at 24.637, are printed in Morel, *Fragmenta* 51.

24. This willingness of Thetis to marry Peleus is, as Fordyce and Curran point out, Catullus's own invention. The *Iliad* tells us she married him *pollà mál'*

ouk ethélousa (18.434). Pindar, in *Nemean* 3.35–36 and 4.62–65, refers to a story that Peleus had to overcome her by wrestling, a story also given in full by Ovid (*Met.* 11.221).

25. Leo C. Curran, "Catullus 64 and the Heroic Age," *Yale Classical Studies* 21 (1969) 191, and see 189 n. 28.

26. *Works and Days* 158–159. M. C. J. Putnam, who sees this poem as a largely autobiographical expression of Catullus's grief over the death of his brother and the infidelity of Lesbia, would disagree. He argues that the Peleus-Thetis relationship represents sexual purity whereas Theseus's behavior represents sexual foulness and that it is only by visualizing the contrast between them "as the tension between the ideal and the real that the full effect of the poem's balance is achieved" ("The Art of Catullus 64," *Harvard Studies in Classical Philology* 65 [1961] 196–198). Friedrich Klingner does not specifically address the undercutting of the Golden Age, but he does note that the intermingling of wedding happiness with bloody death and destruction reveals a refusal to rest content with simplified concepts ("Catullus Peleus-Epos," *Sitzungsberichte der Bayerischen Akademie der Wissenschaften* 6 [1956] 25). Klingner also posits a link with Euripides' earlier (though milder, in his opinion) interjection of the dreadful side of war in the *Iphigeneia*'s Peleus and Thetis ode (*I.A.* 1036–1097). It is, he says, as if Catullus took the concept aroused by γαῖαν ἐκπυρώσων (*I.A.* 1070) and developed it so passionately that indulgence in blood and death becomes the only means by which one can glorify greatest life (24).

27. Kenneth Quinn, *Catullus* (London, 1970) *ad loc.*

28. Theseus is constantly described as *immemor*. See lines 58, 123, 135, 208, 231. Richard Jenkyns (*Three Classical Poets* [London, 1982] 139) is the latest in a series of scholars including Giangrande ("Das Epyllion Catulls" 127) to argue that Catullus is following an obscure version of the myth in which Theseus's forgetfulness was caused by Dionysos and was therefore not his fault.

29. As Curran (181) comments, "It would be difficult to imagine a worse omen for the success of the marriage than the fact that the couch is thus literally shrouded in a covering of such sinister import."

30. *Clarisona . . . voce . . . fuderunt* (320–321). *Clarisona* is a rare word, used outside of this poem only by Cicero for the shrill sound of the North Wind (*Arat.* 280). Earlier in this poem it has been used of Ariadne's shrieks (*clarisonas . . . fudisse . . . voces*, 125). It is roughly analogous to Euripides' jarring *anaklázō* in his own Peleus and Thetis ode (*I.A.* 1062), and its jarring tone here heralds a song whose content is equally jarring in the context of the splendid joy of the wedding feast.

31. Cf. Pindar, *N.* 3.60–61, 51–52.

32. CATULLUS: *cum Phrygii Teucro manabunt sanguine campi*

PINDAR: ὅ καὶ Μύσιον ἀμπελόεν
               αἵμαξε Τηλέφου μέλανι ῥαίνων φόνῳ πεδίον,

Pindar continues: "and made a bridge [*gephúrōse*] to bring the Atreidai home." Catullus continues: *Troiaeque obsidens longinquo moenia bello, / periuri Pelopis vastabit tertius heres.* As Curran points out (187), this last line throws "unfavorable light over the whole Trojan war" and reminds us "that duplicity has been a feature of the Heroic Age" for some time.

33. Curran (188) also finds it significant that "a song celebrating the motherhood of Thetis should dwell upon the disastrous effect her son's birth and life will have upon other mothers and their sons." For an example of Euripides' sudden switching to the point of view of the victim see *Elektra* 464–469 and my discussion in "The Force of Tradition," *TAPA* 110 (1980) 195–212.

34. See *Iliad* 11.67–69, of Trojans and Achaians:

      Οἱ δ᾽, ὥς τ᾽ ἀμητῆρες ἐναντίοι ἀλλήλοισιν
      ὄγμον ἐλαύνωσιν ἀνδρὸς μάκαρος κατ᾽ ἄρουραν
      πυρῶν ἢ κριθῶν· τὰ δὲ δράγματα ταρφέα πίπτει·

Quinn also notes the similarity.

35. Curran, 190.

36. *Iliad* 24.540–542; Pindar, *P.* 3.87–103.

37. The idea of human-divine mingling is also undercut, as Curran notes (185), by the poet's laying "special emphasis on the fact that human and divine guests attend in shifts and do not in fact mingle with each other."

38. Curran (189) would include the third example: he says that the simile that compares Polyxena's death to the death of a sacrificial animal (369–370) casts a shadow on Jupiter's coming in the old days to witness sacrifices of a hundred bulls.

39. Curran, 171.

40. Suetonius tells the story to illustrate Octavian's immoderation in his victory at Perugia (*Divus Augustus* 15), but Appian's account does not mention the sacrifice.

41. Cicero, who supported the assassins of Caesar, for a brief time became an ally of Octavian in order to stop Antony. But when Octavian and Antony joined forces Cicero was doomed. He was proscribed and murdered in December of 43 B.C.

42. They found it useful, according to Cicero, for fighting in battle, for punishing an *improbus cives*, and for forensic oratory (*Tusculan Disputations*, 4.43).

43. Ribbeck prints the fragment as *Ex Incertis Fabulis* no. 13, p. 222.

44. Compare Socrates' attempt to persuade Crito that it will not be him but his body that will remain for disposal after death (*Phaedo* 115c–d).

45. Would that we knew in what work he said this. None of the fragments we have mentions Achilles' anger. Vahlen prints *ira initium insaniae* as *Incerta* no. 18, p. 233.

46. *quid tantum insano iuvat indulgere dolori* ("What help is it to indulge so greatly your insane grief?") 2.776. Indulgence of grief may be said to be the prime mover of the *Iliad*'s action, for Achilles' great wrath was a response to his grief (*áchos*) first at Agamemnon's insult and then at Patroklos's death. Homer, of course, did not call this grief "insane," nor did he ever use a verb such as *indulgere*, which implies a yielding of mastery, to describe Achilles' response. Achilles' passionate behavior was merely an extreme version of the normal and usually productive response of martial heroes to loss and insult. But it has not been productive for Aeneas to indulge his grief in *Aeneid* 2, and it will not be productive ever again. The age in which individual passion was functional is past.

47. *Furor ardentem caedisque insana cupido / egit in adversos* ("Fury and an insane desire for slaughter drew him burning against his enemies") 9.760–761.

48. Brooks Otis, in his superb article "The Originality of the *Aeneid*," describes *Aeneid* 1–6 as "the story of the conversion of a Homeric into a Roman psyche" (*Virgil*, ed. D. R. Dudley [London, 1964] 60).

49. Turnus, alone and unafraid inside the Trojan camp, compares himself to Achilles as he challenges Pandarus (9.741–742): *incipe si qua animo virtus, et consere dextram: / hic etiam inventum Priamo narrabis Achillem* ("Begin, if there is any strength in your spirit, and join battle. You will relate to Priam that here, too, you encountered an Achilles").

50. Turnus vows he will fight Aeneas with courage "even though he surpass great Achilles and wear armor equal to his made by the hands of Vulcan" (*vel magnum praestet Achillem / factaque Volcani manibus paria induat arma / ille licet*) 11.438–440.

51. At the banquet in Carthage, Dido keeps pressing Aeneas to tell her the story of what happened at Troy; she asks about the Trojans Priam, Hektor, and Memnon, and she asks about Greeks (1.752): *nunc quales Diomedes equi, nunc quantus Achilles* ("What were Diomedes' horses like? How big was Achilles?"). Aeneas describes how the Trojans were taken in by Sinon (2.196–198):

> credita res, captique dolis lacrimisque coactis
> quos neque Tydides nec Larisaeus Achilles,
> non anni domuere decem, non mille carinae.

The matter was believed and we were captured by guile and forced tears, we whom neither Diomedes nor Larissaean Achilles, neither ten years, nor a thousand ships had conquered.

Turnus, using sarcasm to convict Drances of hyperbole in extolling the power of Aeneas and his men, says (11.403–404): *nunc et Myrmidonum proceres Phrygia arma tremescunt, / nunc et Tydides et Larisaeus Achilles* ("And indeed now the leaders of the Myrmidons tremble at Phrygian arms, now indeed both Diomedes and Larissaean Achilles"). A fourth reference, in which a Latin warrior taunts Aeneas (10.581–583), helps explain the prominence of Diomedes:

> non Diomedis equos nec currum cernis Achilli,
> aut Phrygiae campos; nunc belli finis et aevi
> his dabitur terris.

Not here do you see Diomedes' horses or the chariot of Achilles or Phrygian fields. Now an end to your war and your life will be given in this land.

Liger seems to mean that he will conquer Aeneas as Diomedes did (*Iliad* 5.302–317) and as Achilles was about to (*Iliad* 20.158–339) and that this time there will be no gods to rescue him. Diomedes shares with Achilles the honor of having defeated Vergil's hero.

52. When Vergil describes the Trojan exploration of the deserted Greek camp, he mentions first the place where the Dolopians and ferocious Achilles pitched their tents (*hic Dolopum manus, hic saevus tendebat Achilles*, 29). These are the only names mentioned. From this particular, Vergil moves, contrary to his usual practice, to the general location of ships and battle (see Austin, *Liber Secundus, ad* 30: *classibus*).

53.   cum Troia Achilles
> exanimata sequens impingeret agmina muris,
> milia multa daret leto, gemerentque repleti
> amnes nec reperire viam atque evolvere posset
> in mare se Xanthus.

Lines 804–806 sum up the action of *Iliad* 21.526–611, especially 527–528 and 540–543, in which the Trojans fled in panic to and into the walls with Achilles chasing them, the *lussa* upon him. Lines 806–808 recall Skamander's complaint to Achilles that he could not roll (*prochéein*) his stream forward to the sea because his waters were full and choked with corpses (*Iliad* 21.218–220). Thus, even though no emotive epithets are used, Neptune's words bring forward the full terror of Achilles' awesome sweep through the Trojan ranks in the *Iliad*.

54. Oddly enough, this episode, which was extremely popular with vase painters from the seventh century on, does not survive in literary expression anywhere but here and in some abstruse verses of the Hellenistic Lykophron (see below Chapter Four, note 5), though the indefatigable Sophokles apparently wrote a tragedy on the subject (for the fragments see Pearson, vol. 2,

p. 255–262). The story, which was told in the *Kypria* (Allen, 105), was probably as follows: Troy was fated not to fall if Troilos could attain the age of twenty, so Achilles ambushed him at night while he was exercising his horses (or, alternatively, accompanying his sister Polyxena to fetch water). Achilles speared the youth; his horses bolted and dragged him. Troilos is mentioned only once in the *Iliad*, as one of the noble sons Priam complains Achilles has killed (*Il.* 24.257). For an excellent discussion of conflicting variants and the scanty evidence, see Pearson, vol. 2, pp. 253–255).

55. Lykophron uses this version (*Alex.* 269–270). According to a scholiast on *Iliad* 22.470–473, Aischylos's *Ransom of Hektor* included a scene in which gold was weighed out on stage. See Augustin Cartault, *L'Art de Virgile* (Paris, 1926) 165–166, 121 n. 4, for a list of monuments that illustrate such a scene.

56. Bernard M. W. Knox, "The Serpent and the Flame," *Vergil: A Collection of Critical Essays* (Englewood Cliffs, N.J., 1966) 137 (also *AJP* 71 [1950] 395).

57. Aeneas repeats this phrase at 3.87.

58. Jupiter is predicting the final defeat of the Achaian Confederacy in 146 B.C., but although Argos and Mycenae are used as terms for Greece in general, Phthia has a more specific meaning. In Book Six, Anchises refers to a future Roman general's victory over *Argos Agamemnoniasque Mycenas / ipsumque Aeaciden, genus armipotentis Achilli* ("Argos and Agamemnonian Mycenae, and the scion of Aiakos himself, offspring of Achilles strong in battle") 6.838–839. Vergil here devotes a whole line to the descendant of Achilles, thereby emphasizing Achilles' preeminent role in Troy's defeat. Aemilius Paullus, to whose victory over Perseus at Pydna in 168 B.C. these lines refer, conquered only the descendant of Achilles, but Vergil elaborates this into a victory over all the Greek enemy who warred on Troy.

59. Noted by Cartault, 122. See also W. R. Nethercut, "The Imagery of the *Aeneid*," *Classical Journal* 67 (1971–72) 142.

60. 1.4, 1.11, and 12.830–831, as well as her actions in general, invite us to do so.

61. Compare W. R. Johnson, *Darkness Visible* (Berkeley and Los Angeles, 1976) 133. For more on the complexities of the *Aeneid*'s intertextual relationship with the *Iliad*, see my article "Foil and Fusion: Homer's Achilles in Vergil's *Aeneid*," *Materiali e discussioni per l'analisi dei testi classici* 7 (1983) 31–57 and the bibliography therein.

62. This epistle, also known as the *Ars Poetica*, was probably composed between 19 and 15 B.C.

63.   sed noctem sermone trahunt, virtusque loquendi
         materia est: pugnas referunt hostisque suasque,

· · · · · · · · · · · · · · ·
                        quid enim loqueretur Achilles,
         aut quid apud magnum potius loquerentur Achillem?

64. It is, however, implicit in Achilles' reaction to the bloody war shield Odysseus puts out to trick him into betraying himself (1.852–863).

65. See Chapter One, part three.

66. See, for example, θρασύφρων (1.4), ὄβριμος (2.499), ποδάρκης (1.130) δῖος (2.404).

67. See Chapter Two, part one. This fabulous boyhood soon became a popular topic. Philostratus Lemnius (born c. 191), for example, in his *Eikones* (2.2) describes a fictional series of paintings illustrating the subject (*Philostrati Maioris Imagines*, ed. Benndorf and Schenkel [Leipzig, 1893] 63–66).

68. Pindar does not tell the story of why Achilles was abandoned by his parents but says only that Achilles was "orphaned" (ὀρφανιζόμενος, P. 6.22). The most complete version occurs in the *Argonautika* of Apollonios of Rhodes (third century B.C.): "For she used to burn away his mortal flesh in the fire's flame during the night; in the day she would anoint his soft body with ambrosia so that he might become immortal and avoid the wrinkles of old age. But Peleus, leaping out of bed, saw his dear son gasping through the flames, and he screamed in horror when he saw her, the big fool. When she heard him she took and hurled Achilles shrieking to the ground and, like a breeze or a dream, she was gone swiftly from the house and rushed angrily into the sea. And she never came back again" (4.869–879). Apollodoros's briefer account (first or second century A.D.) is similar and adds that Peleus then gave the baby to Cheiron, who fed him on lion guts and bear marrow (*Bibliotheca* 3.13.6). Lykophron's abstruse *Alexandra* (third century B.C.) followed a variant which told of six earlier sons who had died in similar fires while Thetis was testing their immortality (177–179). (For further details and references see J. G. Frazer, *Apollodorus* [Cambridge, Mass., 1921], vol. 2 no. 4, and Pearson, vol. 1, p. 106–107, note to fragment 151. For a possible seventh-century illustration of Achilles' baby food see J. D. Beazley, *The Development of Attic Black-Figure* (Los Angeles and Berkeley, 1964) 10–11 and pl. 4. Statius does not mention this story since he uses yet another variant on Thetis's attempts to make her son immortal: at 1.134 and 480–481 he refers to her dipping Achilles in the Styx to make his body invulnerable. This version is the one that seems to have produced the ankle or heel as Achilles' one vulnerable spot, a story clearly followed by Hyginus, who probably lived in the second century A.D. (H. J. Rose, *Hygeni Fabulae* [Leiden, 1934] vii–viii), and elucidated in the fourth century A.D. by Servius, who says that Achilles' "whole body was invulnerable except for that part by which he was held" (*toto corpore invulnerabilis fuit, excepta parte qua tenutus est*), commentary to *Aeneid* 6.57. A sixth-century Chalcidean vase that depicts Achilles prostrate on a battlefield with an arrow in his heel (*Lexicon Iconographicum* no. 850) may be evidence of an early origin for this story (see figure 7).

69. Lines 2.163–165:

> edocuit monitusque sacrae sub pectore fixit
> iustitiae, qua Peliacis dare iura verenda
> gentibus atque suos solitus pacare biformes.

70. See Chapter Four for further discussion of the theme of love versus war.

71. See Chapter Two.

72. The god-defier Oilean Aias, however, is twice compared to Titans while he is in the sea undergoing Athene's punishment for violating the sanctity of her altar (14.550, 582–585).

73. The references in Vergil's works are *Eclogues* 4.36; *Georgics* 3.91; *Aeneid* 11.438; in Ovid's works, *Meta.* 8.309; 12.163, 615; 13.30, 133, 134; *Ars Amatoria* 2.711; *Tristia* 1.9.29.

74. The works of both Apollodoros and Hyginus are to be dated to the first or second century A.D. On the grounds of style and language, H. J. Rose puts Hyginus in the second century during the age of the Antonines, A.D. 138–192 (Prolegomena, *Hygini Fabulae* vii–viii), a date which would place him well after Statius (A.D. 48–96). C. Robert locates Apollodoros in the early part of the second century (*De Apollodori Bibliotheca* [Berlin, 1873] 40–44).

75. O. A. W. Dilke, "'Magnus Achilles' and Statian Baroque," *Latomus* 22 (1963), 503, and see especially 500–502 for a discussion of the aspect of size.

76. *Od.* 11.311–316. Homer tells us in this passage that they were at least twelve feet wide and fifty-four feet tall at that age.

77. See Chapter Four, note 70.

78. A version similar to this seems to have become part of the tradition by the time of Horace, who in *Ode* 4.6.1–12 links Achilles with two other hubristic victims of Apollo, Niobe and Tityos. Hyginus seems to allude to this version when he says that Apollo killed Achilles in anger over his boasting that he would conquer Troy single-handedly (*Fab.* 107). Achilles always yields to the gods in the *Iliad*, but his angry retort to Apollo that he would take vengeance for being tricked if he had the power (*Il.* 22.19–20) was interpreted by Plato, for one, as arrogance (*hyperēphanía*, 891c) and may have formed the basis of a story that he was killed for *hubris*. Francis Vian discusses the traditional variants of Achilles' death in *Recherches sur les Posthomerica de Quintus de Smyrne* (Paris, 1959) 33–35.

79. ὁ κόμπος δ᾽ οὐ κατ᾽ ἄνθρωπον φρονεῖ (425).

80. The combination of gentleness with strength is reminiscent of Zeus's description at *Il.* 17.204, and the idea of being nice to everyone recalls Menelaos's description at *Il.* 17.670–671.

81. Various other characters in the *Posthomerica* are also given to outbursts of stoic moralizing, e.g., the narrator about Nestor (3.7–9), Kalliope (3.642–643),

Odysseus (5.595–597). The combination of such moralizing with frequent scenes of violence is reminiscent of the Silver Latin rhetoric of Seneca and Lucan.

82. For more on Polyxena see Chapter Four.

83. To Lollius Maximus. Edward Morris dates it between 24 and 20 B.C. (Horace, *Satires and Epistles,* 28–29).

84. Troiani belli scriptorem, Maxime Lolli
dum tu declamas Romae, Praeneste relegi,
qui quid sit pulchrum, quid turpe, quid utile, quid non,
planius ac melius Chrysippo et Crantore dicit.

85. The practice of creating or alluding to works "written" by participants in the Trojan War in order to contradict Homer seems to have become fashionable by the second century A.D. For examples see Nathaniel Griffin, *Dares and Dictys* (Baltimore, 1907) 14–15 n. 4, 80–81 n. 2, and Otmar Schissel von Fleschenberg, *Dares-Studien* (Halle an-der-Salle, 1908) 87.

86. Ut legentes cognoscere possent, quomodo res gestae essent: utrum verum magis esse existiment, quod Dares Phrygius memoriae commendavit, qui per id ipsum tempus vixit et militavit, cum Graeci Troianos obpugnarent, anne Homero credendum, qui post multos annos natus est, quam bellum hoc gestum est. (Prologue to *Daretis Phrygii De Excidio Troiae Historia,* ed. Ferdinand Meister [Leipzig, 1873] I.9–14.)

A statement very similar to this occurs ten centuries later in the preface to a French translation of Dares published in 1592: "Après avoir cognu Dàres Phrigius avoir plus succinctement et véritablement escript de toute la querelle entre les Grecs et les Troyens que nul autre, j'ay bien voulu le traduire en nostre langue, et communiquer à ung chascun. . . ." ("After having seen that Dares the Phrygian had written more succinctly and truly about the whole quarrel between the Greeks and the Trojans than had any other, I very much wanted to translate it into our language and to communicate it to everyone"). The French is quoted by Nathaniel Griffin, *Dares and Dictys* 7 n. 1, in a note that also contains an interesting quotation from Joseph of Exeter (c. A.D. 1187) attesting to Dares' eyewitness veracity. A similar sentiment is expressed by Benoît de Sainte-Maure (c. A.D. 1160), in the Prologue to *Le Roman de Troie,* vv. 45–94 (ed. Leopold Constans [Paris, 1904–1912] vol. 1 pp. 3–6).

87. The translator identifies himself as Lucius Septimius. Nathaniel Griffin dates the translation to the fourth century because of the style and moral sentiment and in particular because of frequent allusions to Sallust, Vergil, and Hellenistic authors, which betoken "a period prior to the disruptions of relations with the literary past" (*Dares* 3 n. 2). There is also the use of the word *consularis* instead of *proconsul* to mean "governor of a province," a meaning it did

not acquire until Constantine (A.D. 323–337) (*Dares* 3–4 n. 2). As for the date of the Greek composition, it can be narrowed down to between A.D. 66, when the author of the preface says it was discovered, and A.D. 205, the date of the papyrus on which a fragment survives (R. M. Frazer, Jr., *The Trojan War* [Bloomington, Ind., 1966] 10–11). Nathaniel Griffin argues that it was composed soon after the reign of Nero because the occasional variations between what he thinks must have been the original Dictys and what is in the fragment of A.D. 205 can be accounted for only by a long interval of time ("The Greek Dictys," *American Journal of Philology* 29 [1908] 335).

88. The translator claims to be one Cornelius Nepos, who happened upon the Greek manuscript while studying in Athens. Nathaniel Griffin dates the extant text of Dares to the sixth century by (1) the barbarousness of the Latin; (2) occasional references to the First Vatican Mythographer (who wrote of the destruction of Troy by Herakles); (3) a reference to Dares by Isidore of Seville *Origines* 1.41 (*Dares* 5–6 n. 4). R. M. Frazer, Jr., following Schissel von Fleschenberg, arrives at the sixth-century date on the basis of the expanded portions of the text: sections 5–10 are clearly based on Dracontius's late-fifth-century *Romulea*, and sections 1–3 form the basis for a Latin work composed about fifty years after Dracontius (*The Trojan War* 12–13). The date for the Greek composition is set in the first century A.D. because there was a reference to Dares in Ptolemaios Chennos's *Kainè Historía*, written around the turn of the century (N. Griffin, *Dares* 81 n. 2 [cont.]).

Evidence for the existence of a Greek original exists, first, in the fact that the catalogue description of the heroes and heroines has the same source as does the description in the work of the late-sixth-century Byzantine Malalos, who seems to have known no Latin (see N. Griffin, *Dares* 52–53, 105–108 and Schissel von Fleschenberg 84), and, second, in the fact that the wording seems influenced by Greek (Schissel von Fleschenberg 85–86).

89. See Nathaniel Griffin, *Dares* 15 n. 2, and J. R. Berrigan, "The Trojan War in the *Chronicon* of Benzo d'Alessandria," *Classical Journal* 61 (1966) 220. As for the quality of Dares' *History*, it is perhaps best summed up in Griffin's opinion that it "consists of an ill-sorted aggregation of meagre details, written in forty-four short chapters of barbarous Latin" (*Dares* 4).

90. Agamemnon for the most part comes off better than he does in Homer's verse or in Euripides'. He is willing to give up command rather than sacrifice Iphigeneia (1.19), and he apologizes heartily for his rash and stupid behavior to Achilles over the women (2.48–49). However, he does participate in the treachery at the end and helps cheat Aias out of the Palladium as a favor to Odysseus for persuading the army not to kill Helen as Aias had suggested (5.14). He also is possibly implicated in the subsequent murder of the angry Aias.

91. I cannot accept the view of Nathaniel Griffin (*Dares* 10 n. 1 and 15 n. 2)

and R. M. Frazer that the reason for the greater popularity of Dares was that "the Latin speaking West had inherited a pro-Trojan bias from the Romans, who claimed descent from the Trojans" (Frazer, 3). Dictys is not anti-Trojan, he is anti-everybody—Trojan royal family, Greek princes, the mass of Greek soldiers—with the significant exception of the Trojan commoners (see esp. 1.8). E. Collilieux, on the other hand, argues that Dares himself is anti-Trojan (*Étude sur Dictys et Dares* [Grenoble, 1886] 88–90).

92. With the help of Antenor and Aeneas, the Greeks negotiate with the Trojan Council a false peace treaty complete with a trick oath-taking ceremony. They accept a huge tribute from the Trojans before they sail away only to return at night to slaughter and burn everyone and everything in sight (4.22–5.13).

93. The complete description is as follows: *hic in primis adulescentiae annis, procerus, decora facie, studio rerum bellicarum omnes iam tum virtute atque gloria superabat, neque tamen aberat ab eo vis quaedam inconsulta et effera morum impatientia.*

94. This version of Hektor's death is so unheroic that Benzo d'Alessandria, a fourteenth-century historian who took Dictys as his main source for the events of the Trojan War, thinks that Dictys must here have gotten his information from unreliable sources and that Dares gives the truer account: *tum quia verisimilius videri debet tam insignem virum, Achillem videlicet, nequaquam ad tam probrosum actum deduci potuisse ut insidiis interimeret Hectorem* ("first because it must seem closer to the truth that such an illustrious man, namely Achilles, could never be brought to do such a shameful thing as to kill Hektor by sneak attack") (Benzo's *Chronicon* fol. 245r, as quoted by Berrigan, "The Trojan War" 221).

95. His plot is foiled by Odysseus.

96. Enraged at her having dared to transgress the bounds of her sex, Diomedes prevails upon the Greeks not to let Penthesileia die naturally from her wounds but instead to throw her into the river while she is still alive enough to have feeling (4.3). Achilles is against torturing the Amazon and in general is nice to women (see 2.19, 3.27).

97. These are the same Trojans who, in Dictys' account, abetted the Greek treachery *in spite of* Priam's yielding.

98. For more on Polyxena see Chapter Four.

99. ἔπειτα ἀναχθέντες Τευθρανίᾳ προσίσχουσι καὶ ταύτην ὡς Ἴλιον ἐπόρθουν. Τήλεφος δὲ ἐκβοηθήσας, Θέρσανδρόν τε τὸν Πολυνείκους κτείνει καὶ αὐτὸς ὑπὸ Ἀχιλλέως τιτρώσκεται. ἀποπλέουσι δὲ αὐτοῖς ἐκ τῆς Μυσίας χειμὼν ἐπιπίπτει καὶ διασκεδάννυνται. Ἀχιλλεὺς δὲ Σκύρῳ προσσχὼν γαμεῖ τὴν Λυκομήδους θυγατέρα Δηιδάμειαν. ἔπειτα Τήλεφον κατὰ μαντείαν παραγενόμενον εἰς Ἄργος ἰᾶται Ἀχιλλεὺς ὡς ἡγεμόνα γενησόμενον τοῦ ἐπ' Ἴλιον πλοῦ.

Then having put to sea they landed at Teuthras's city and sacked it thinking it was Troy. Telephos came to help, killed Thersander Polyneikes' son,
and was himself wounded by Achilles. As they sailed away from Mysia, a
storm fell upon them and scattered them. Achilles put to land at Skyros
and married Deidameia, daughter of Lykomedes. Then when an oracle
had brought Telephos to Argos, Achilles healed him so that he would
guide their voyage to Troy. (*Kypria,* Proclus *Chrestomathia* 2, p. 104)

100. *Aeneid* 1.475.

101. The older tradition is present only in the fact that Troilos is thrown
from his horse, thus making it easier for Achilles to kill him. For an account of
the older tradition, see n. 54 above.

102. See Chapter Four.

103. Dares' complete description is as follows: *Achillem pectorosum ore venusto
membris valentibus et magnis iubatum bene crispatum clementem in armis acerrimum vultu hilari largum dapsilem capillo myrteo* (Meister, 16). ("Achilles had a
large chest, a beautiful face, large strong limbs, very curly hair; he was gentle,
very fierce in battle, very generous, with a cheerful look and dark brown hair.")

104. Dictys's rationalistic account follows in the tradition of Euhemeros (fl.
311–298 B.C.), whose imaginary travelogue *Hierà Anagraphḗ* ("Holy Inscription") presented "evidence" that the gods of the Greek pantheon were originally magnificent but quite human kings. Herakleidos's *Allegory of Homer,* which
turns the angry Apollo of *Iliad* 1 into the hot summer sun and makes Achilles
end the plague through his healing skills, was written in the same tradition, perhaps in the same period as Dares and Dictys. See also Dio Chrysostomos's Eleventh Oration and my discussion in Chapter Four.

105. Dares 19, 32–33. In Dictys he must share this honor with Aias (2.3, 9, 12,
16–19, 42–43; 4.13).

106. See B. Bischoff, "The Study of Foreign Languages in the Middle Ages,"
Mittelalterliche Studien 2 (1967) 231–232, 234–235; L. D. Reynolds and N. G.
Wilson, *Scribes and Scholars* (Oxford, 1974) 105–107, 240; and R. R. Bolgar, *The
Classical Heritage and its Beneficiaries* (Cambridge, 1954; repr. 1977) 122–123.

107. Medieval scholars entitled it *Homerus Latinus* and considered it to be
the work of one Theban Pindar. On the basis of acrostics in the first and last
eight lines it is now attributed to an unknown Italicus, sometimes alleged to be
the orator and poet Silius Italicus, who died in A.D. 101. For a good discussion
of dating and authorship see F. Plessis' introduction to his edition of the *Ilias
Latina* (Paris, 1885) i–ii, vii–xvii.

108. The epithet is used four times (60, 71, 860, 995), twice as often as
any other.

109. The poem is printed by A. Boutemy in "Trois oeuvres inédites de
Godefroid de Reims," *Revue du Moyen Age Latin* 3 (1947) 335–364. For a discus-

sion of the whole verse epistle, see Boutemy, "Autour de Godefroid de Reims," *Latomus* 6 (1947) 231–255; the section called "Hector and Achilles" is described on 251.

110. See E. P. M. Dronke, "Functions of Classical Borrowing in Medieval Latin Verse," *Classical Influences on European Culture, A.D. 500–1500,* ed. R. R. Bolgar (Cambridge, 1971) 163. Dronke, who first brought my attention to this poem, will discuss it in a forthcoming work as an example of cross-fertilization between classical *planctus* and popular ballad. The poem has been most recently edited by M. de Marco, *Aevum* 29 (1955) 119–23.

111. Boutemy, "Autour" 251.

112. See Boutemy, "Autour" 251.

113. *I.L.* 933. The poet's giving the plea to Andromache instead of to Priam may reflect influence from Dares' *Historia,* chapter 24. Andromache's passionate plea to Hektor in Book Six of the *Iliad* is not mentioned in the *Ilias Latina* (see 564–574).

114. He is also credited with "fighting and killing Lapiths" (*Lapithes ferit pugnando,* 19), a detail from an entirely different cycle of myth, that which centers on Theseus. The source of this intermingling of disparate legends is most likely Book Twelve of Ovid's *Metamorphoses,* in which Nestor tells the story of the Lapiths and Centaurs to relaxing warriors around a Greek campfire at Troy.

115. For the identification especially in the last battle, see Nethercut, "Imagery" 137. For the identification in Book Ten and for further bibliography see my article "Foil and Fusion: Homer's Achilles in Vergil's *Aeneid.*

116. It exists in a verse epistle written by Godfrey of Rheims c. 1065. The text is printed in A. Boutemy, "Trois Oeuvres de Godefroid de Reims" 350–351. For the dating and a brief discussion of the poem see Boutemy's "La poème '*Pergama flere volo . . .*' et ses imitateurs du XII⁰ siècle," *Latomus* 5 (1946) 233–234.

117.   Quantus pro Danais ferus exsurrexit Achilles
         Pro Teucris quantus martius Hector erat.
                        Godefroid de Reims 2.257–258.

118. The poem's 124 lines are printed in *Poésies populaires latines antérieures au douzième siècle,* ed. du Méril (Paris, 1843) 400–405. They begin with Paris's rape of Helen and end with the founding of Rome by Aeneas.

119. Pierre declares (83–84): "I will be another Homer, or greater than Homer himself, / when I am able to describe so many misfortunes" (*Alter Homerus ero vel eodem major Homero, / tot clades numero scribere si potero*) (du Méril, 404).

120. Praesidium fidum stetit urbis in Hectore, qui, dum
      stabat, Dardanidum robor erat validum.
      Cuspide Pelidae simul idem defuit Idae,
      studebant trepide praelia Dardanidae.

                              (du Méril, p. 403)

      A faithful prop for the city was Hektor; while
      he stood, Dardanian strength was firm.
      As soon as Achilles' spear took Hektor from Ida,
      Dardanian battle zeal turned to alarm.

Other heroes are mentioned—Agamemnon, Aias, Diomedes, Neoptolemos—
but only later, in the fighting that ensues after the wooden horse is in the city.

    121. I adopt du Méril's conjectural reading of *exitio* for the ms. *exilio* in 42
(403).

    122. Two other very brief poetic summaries of the Trojan War written in the
Iliadic tradition in the twelfth century—"Pergama flere volo" and "Fervet
amore Paris," both anonymous—fail to mention Achilles, and the only reason
to place them in the Iliadic rather than the Dares tradition is that in addition to
mentioning the Trojan horse in couplets 9–10, "Pergama flere volo" was apparently the inspiration for Pierre de Saintes (see Boutemy, "Pergama" 240) as well
as for "Fervet amore Paris." The poems are printed in *Carmina Burana*, vol. 1,
pt 1, ed. Alfons Hilka and Otto Schumann (Heidelberg, 1941), nos. 101 and 102,
pp. 139–165. Three other well-known poems that fail to mention Achilles in
their accounts of the Trojan War can be placed in neither tradition: "*Quis partus
Trojae*" and "*Bella minans Asiae*" (both printed in E. Faral's "Le manuscrit 511 du
'Hunterian Museum,'" nos. 6 and 21, *Studi Medievali* 9 (1936) 21–22, 33–34) are
concerned with the events that lead to the war rather than with the fighting;
Hugo Primat's "*Urbs erat illustris*" is concerned with the dismal aftermath and
mentions only Hekabe, Ganymede, Paris, Helen, and Diomedes, though v. 52
seems to refer to Neoptolemos's sacrilege during the sack of the city (printed by
William Meyer in "Die Oxforder Gedichte des Primas [des Magisters Hugo von
Orleans]" *Nachrichten von der Königlichen Gesellschaft der Wissenschaften zu Göttingen* [Berlin, 1907] 136–137).

    123. During his many years as poet at the court of Henry, Count of Cham-
pagne, Simon published three versions of the Troy story. The first contained the
adventures of Paris and the siege of Troy. The second version appended to the
first a summary of the *Aeneid*. The third version greatly amplified both parts of
the second version (increasing its three hundred verses to nearly a thousand) by
adding details and fleshing out the episodes previously only sketched in. The
portion covering the Trojan War closely follows the *Ilias Latina*, with the significant addition of Achilles' love for Polyxena, included in the final version (see
Chapter Four). The first version is printed following Albert of Stade's *Troilus*,

ed. T. Merzdorf (Leipzig, 1875) pp. 199–203, vv.i–152 and *Patrologia Latina* vol. 171, cols. 1447–1451. The third version is printed in Boutemy, "La version Parisienne du Poème de Simon Chèvre d'Or sur la guerre de Troie," *Scriptorium* 1 (1946–1947) 269–286. A convenient summary of Simon's work may be found in F. J. E. Raby, *A History of Secular Latin Poetry in the Middle Ages* vol. 2 (Oxford, 1957) 70–71.

124. *PL* 171, col. 1450; Merzdorf, 202 (137–140).

125. 219–220:

> Quod punire parat tanto discrimine crimen
> Rex reus Atrides non iterare timet.
> (Boutemy, "La version" 273.)

126. 324: *Hii Danaum virtus, Dardanidumque tremor* (Boutemy, "La version" 274). In this final version Simon also inserts between the couplets forty-four lines of invective against Odysseus (279–322).

127. See Chapter Two, part two.

128. See 275–276 (Boutemy, "La version," 273): *At ferus Eacydes ut venit et Hectora vicit, / Vergit ad Eneam spes viduata Frigum* ("But when fierce Achilles came and conquered Hektor, the Phrygians' widowed hope turned to Aeneas").

129. 207–208:

> Si cor si vires, si bella requires Achillis,
> Ut doceam paucis, Hectore maior erat.
> (Boutemy, "La version" 272).

Compare Merzdorf, p. 202, vv. 135–136.

130. There is a general consensus that the poem, whose main source is the Latin *Alexandreis* (1180), was written in the first decade of the thirteenth century (see Jesús Cañas Murillo, "Introducción," *Libro de Alexandre* [Madrid, 1978] 19–25), although R. S. Willis, in his review of Ian Michael's work, seems to suggest a date after 1248 ("The Artistry and Enigmas of the *Libro de Alexandre*," *Hispanic Review* 42 [1974] 35–36).

131. See note 1 above. The Poet's decision to use this tradition was no doubt suggested by the mention of Homer in the Latin *Alexandreis* (1.479), as R. S. Willis points out (*The Relationship of the Spanish "Libro de Alexandre" to the "Alexandreis" of Gautier de Chatillon* [Princeton, 1934] 58–59).

132. Ian Michael, *The Treatment of Classical Material in the Libro de Alexandre* (Manchester, 1970) 261.

133. So M. R. Lida de Malkiel argues in *La idea de fama en la edad media castellana* (Mexico and Buenos Aires, 1952) 172–187.

134. *Classical Material* 19, 28–87.

135. *Ibid.* 279–284.

136. The poet says so explicitly at the end of the poem, stt. 2670–2671. For a good discussion of the Christianization of the poem's classical base see Michael's article "The Description of Hell" in *Medieval Miscellany Presented to Eugene Vinaver* (Manchester, 1965) 220–229 and his *Classical Material* 88–142.

137. The text cited and quoted is that of Cañas Murillo.

138. E. Bagby Atwood has shown that the provenance of this scene is the *Excidium Troiae* (for which see Chapter Four, note 84) rather than Statius, because a prophecy of Achilles' necessity replaces rumors of his might ("The Story of Achilles" *Studies in Philology* 39 [1942] 492–493). The prophecy appears also in other later vernacular works: Alfonso el Sabio's *General estoria*, ed. Solalinde, Kasten, and Oelschlager (Madrid, 1961), vol. 2, pt. 2, chap. 543, p. 125; Konrad von Würzburg's *Der Trojanische Krieg*, ed. A. von Keller (Stuttgart, 1858) vv. 27108–27115; the *Göttweiger Tojanerkrieg*, ed. A. Koppitz (Berlin, 1926) vv. 14976–14980; the *Seege or Batayle of Troy* ed. Mary E. Barnicle (London, 1927) 1192–1199; and Leomarte's *Sumas de historia Troyana*, ed. A. Rey (Madrid, 1932) chap. 91, p. 179.

139. In the *Ilias Latina* Nestor welcomes them back and Agamemnon praises them (737–740).

140. The *Alexandre* poet adds this simile, just as he subtracts all the actions— like tearing his clothes and flinging himself on the corpse (*I.L.* 846–848)—that indicated the extremity of Achilles' grief in the *Ilias*. Michael, who gives a good description of the changes (though he neglects to mention the simile), thinks they were made in order to render the scene acceptable to a thirteenth-century audience (*Classical Material* 185–186). Whatever the reason, the effect is once again to eliminate the erotic element from Achilles' story and leave the reader free to focus on the sin of pride.

141. *Ibid.*, 200.

142. See, for example, Otto of Freising, *Two Cities* (New York, 1928) 1.4; Hugo of St. Victor, "Sermon 38," in *Patrologia Cursus Completus* (Paris, 1844– 1864) vol. 77, cols. 994–999.

143. As Michael points out (*Classical Material* 121), there is no God mentioned in the source for the soliloquy of stt. 677–678 (*I.L.* 932–934) and stt. 685–688 are based on a rhetorical question about what help Hektor can find now (*I.L.* 970–971).

144. Achilles' nostrils flare in anger (st. 696c); after a failed attack he is *fieramente irado* (st. 699b); he balances his spear *con ira* (st. 701a); and when the battle is over *por vengarse de ira olvidó piedad*, "to avenge his anger he forgets mercy" (st. 713b) and drags Hektor around the city three times.

145. Michael, *Classical Material* 268.

146. E. Bagby Atwood and Virgil K. Whitaker believe that the provenance

of this story in medieval redactions is the *Excidium Troiae* (*Excidium Troiae*, Cambridge, Mass., 1944, xlv–xlvii), but the poet could as well have gotten the story directly from Hyginus or Servius (see note 68 above).

147. Ovid does something similar with Cygnus's armor (*Meta.* 12.88–90), but such consistency is not practiced by all authors who use the story. Konrad von Würzburg, for instance, emphasizes Achilles' invulnerability to the point of having it twice save him when Hektor beats his armor off him (31168–31181, 31200–31203, 36400–36427), but he has Achilles so gravely wounded when he fights Hektor in their third battle that he would have died had he been wounded any more (39626–39629). The *General estoria* includes the story of Thetis making Achilles invulnerable (chap. 546, p. 127) but never mentions it thereafter. Leomarte uses the episode at the beginning of his narrative and then forgets it in order to follow Benoît and Guido; at the end he returns to it briefly by mentioning an "alternative" version of Achilles' death, one that has him killed via his feet (chap. 148, p. 247).

148. Michael, *Classical Material* 155–156.

149. The poet says that Paris had heard the story many times but had forgotten it in his sadness.

150. The most common title for Joseph's three-thousand-line work is *Frigii Daretis Iliados libri sex.* It is also referred to as *Frigii Daretis Historia belli Troiani, Liber Daretis,* and the *De bello Troiano.* The manuscript seems not to have borne Joseph's name until the fourteenth and fifteenth centuries, and it was generally thought to be the original translation of Cornelius Nepos (see note 88 above). The first printed texts (Basle 1541, 1558, 1583) all attribute the work to Cornelius. (See L. Gompf, *Joseph Iscanus* [Leiden, 1970] 10–15; G. Roberts, *The Iliad of Dares Phrygius* [Capetown, 1970] xi–xii; and R. K. Root, "Chaucer's Dares," *Modern Philology* 15 [1917] 3–5.) Citations are to Gompf's 1970 edition.

151. For the dating c. A.D. 1185 see Roberts, x, and Gompf, 19–22. It should be noted that despite the difference in their primary sources (Dares versus "Homer"), the poets are similar in that they use the same supplementary sources: Vergil, Ovid, and Statius.

152. 5.485–488:

> Excitat ergo
> Eaciden; non ille quidem certamina tanto
> Temptasset conferre viro, sed Iuno negantem
> Sollicitat, stimulat Pallas.

(She urged on Achilles; he himself would not have tried to fight with such a man, but as he refused, Juno provoked and Pallas goaded him.)

153. Joseph's *Audax, munificus, hilaris, pius* (4.108) seems pretty much equivalent to Dares' *clementem in armis acerrimum vultu hilari largum dapsilem* (13, Meister, p. 16).

154. W. B. Sedgwick has demonstrated that Statius's Silver Latin is in fact a major model for Joseph's Latin and that his *Thebaid* appears to be Joseph's model for how to write a proper epic ("The *Bellum Troianum* of Joseph of Exeter," *Speculum* 5 [1930] 49–69). As Sedgwick says, Joseph's "meter, grammar, and vocabulary are essentially Classical; he does but carry further the process of elaboration which marks the whole succession of Latin poetry" (66).

155. 4.353–355:

> Interea Eaciden stimulantibus excitat ausis
> Impaciens languere animus, furor intima pulsat
> Martius et residem mens arguit effera dextram.

Meanwhile, Achilles' spirit impatient of doing nothing prodded him with the thought of doing deeds, the war god's *furor* pounded within, and his savage mind censured his idle hand.

In Dares 16 (Meister, 20) Achilles and Telephos are sent (*mittuntur*) to plunder Mysia; the expedition is not their own idea.

156.
> Missilis innocui mixta pudor asperat ira
> Eaciden, frendit atque ignescentia torquens
> Lumina.
>
> (4.396–398)

These lines appear to be a conglomerate of *Aeneid* 12.666–668, 101–102 (Turnus, insane with grief, rage, and shame) and Ovid, *Meta.* 8.437: *tumida frendens Mavortius ira* (Meleager, about to kill his uncles). Lines 397–398 re-create, most remarkably, Achilles' behavior in Homer's *Iliad* as he armed to take vengeance for Patroklos: "He was grinding his teeth and his two eyes shone like the glare of fire" (19.364–367; see Chapter One, part two). The parallel with the *Iliad* is intriguing since there is no evidence that Joseph had access to Homer, but there is no grinding of teeth in the *Ilias Latina* or in either of Statius's epics. Joseph has Achilles grind his teeth in battle rage twice elsewhere (5.206, 6.304).

157. Translated by Gildas Roberts, *The Iliad of Dares Phrygius* (Cape Town, 1970) 49.

158. Resemblance to Quintus, like that to Homer, is probably fortuitous, since there is no evidence that Joseph read Greek.

159. 6.344–348:

> servior instat
> Mirmidonum princeps, sic mens acceptaque suadent
> Vulnera. Iam trepidos longum quesisse tirannos,

> In vulgi iugulum nolens furit, impetus iram
> Mutat et ultricem cogit plebescere dextram.

The prince of the Myrmidons pressed on more savagely, goaded by his spirit and the wounds he had received. It now took too long to seek out the trembling princes, and reluctantly he turned his fury on the throats of the plebs; his passion deflected his rage and compelled his avenging right hand to go slumming. (Roberts translation, 72)

We should compare this with 6.270–280, in which Troilos's mounting passion makes him scorn the easy slaughter of plebeians in favor of battling bejewelled kings and leaders, even though the crowd of common soldiers makes it difficult to reach the leaders.

160. Gaudet . . .

> Nupturam pepulisse Thetin; pallore minori
> Flegreos montes Flegreaque tela timeret.
>
> (Roberts translation, 72.)

161. Joseph declares that the sky-scaling citadel of Priam's rebuilt Troy deserved Jove's retaliation as much as did the tower of Babel and the giants of Phlegra (1.488–502).

162. *Ipsa virum strages numerat natoque superbit / Inmemor, heu, fati mater— sic gloria vincit.*

163. The *Troilus* contains well over five thousand lines, divided, like Joseph's poem, into six books. Albert himself gives us the date in Book Six, lines 671–672. I have used Merzdorf's 1875 edition. Albert's models for his treatment of Achilles are Dares, Joseph, and the *Ilias Latina*.

164. The episode of Teuthras's death is brief: Achilles gives Teuthras *vulnera dira* (2.322), and when he is about to finish him off, Telephos interposes his shield (2.323). Achilles asks why (325–326), Telephos explains about the claims of past hospitality (327–334), and that is the end of the matter. Hektor's fighting is equal to Achilles' except in their final battle.

165. Dares 24, 33; Joseph 5.490–505, 6.304–322, 330–343; Albert 3.481–544, 4.323–340, 344–356.

166. L. Constans discusses the dating in vol. 6, pp. 182–191, of his edition of Benoît, placing the publication of the *Roman* between 1155 and 1160 (190). Citations are to this edition.

167. Guido gives the date at the conclusion of his work. N. E. Griffin, the editor of the only modern edition of Guido's *Historia*, gives his surname as "de Columnis" (de Columpnis). M. E. Meek gives a useful discussion of the work and its context in the introduction to her translation. All citations will be to Griffin's edition, *Historia Destructionis Troiae* (Cambridge, Mass., 1936).

168. Nearly all of the increasingly nationalistic European countries claimed

to have been settled by Trojan refugees: Italians knew on the authority of Vergil that Rome had been founded by Aeneas; Germans believed that they were descended from a nephew of Priam; the French derived their name from Hektor's son Francus, the British theirs from Brutus, the grandson of Aeneas (see Frank Borchardt, *German antiquity in renaissance myth* [Baltimore, 1971] 85, 196–199; and Egidio Gorra, *Testi inediti di storia trojana preceduti da uno studio sulla leggenda Trojana in Italia* [Turin, 1887] 68.) In addition, many noble families traced their individual lineages back to specific companions of the great Trojan founders (see Gorra, 91–100).

169. Benoît 10684–10724, 11270–11294, 11541–11556, 12507–12550, 12789–12796, 14148–14203, 14491–14504, 16180–16199. Compare Guido Book 16, fol. 77 (N. E. Griffin, *Historia* 149–150); Guido 17 fol. 78 (Griffin, 152), fol. 79 (Griffin, 154); Guido 18, fol. 81 (Griffin, 159); Guido 20, fol. 86 (Griffin, 168), fols. 86–87 (Griffin, 170), Guido 21, fol. 88 (Griffin, 174–175).

170. Benoît makes Achilles visit Hektor in Troy (13121–13185); Guido makes Hektor visit the Greek camp and stop to chat at Achilles' invitation (Guido 19, fols. 82–83, N. E. Griffin, *Historia* 161–162).

171. As I have indicated in my discussion of the "Lament for Hektor," the end of the *Aeneid* is not, of course, as simplistic as my words here suggest. In addition to the references I cited there, see W. R. Johnson, *Darkness Visible,* and M. C. J. Putnam, *The Poetry of the Aeneid* (Cambridge, Mass., 1965).

172. C. P. Bock, "Lettres à M. L. Bethman sur un manuscrit de la bibliothèque de Bourgogne, intitulé *Liber Guidonis*," *Annuaire de la bibliothèque royale de Belgique* 12 (1851) 97–98 n. 1. Bock, who believes that the song may have had a long oral tradition before Guido of Pisa wrote it down in 1119 (*loc. cit.*), terms it a "romance populaire" on 60.

173. The text I print here is based on Bock's (61) as emended by E. P. M. Dronke, who brought the poem to my attention, in a private communication. My one deviation from Dronke's punctuation occurs in verse 5 as noted.

174. Dronke reads: *Achilles "propera!"* while I have punctuated to read *turba* as the subject of *clamat*. It would also be possible to take Hektor as the subject, coupling the resulting sarcasm with that of the succeeding couplet.

175. Bock prints: *At Hector fugat et sauciat.*

176. Bock: *At* (both here and in verse 7).

177. This work has been published as the *Anonymi Historia Troyana Daretis Frigii* by Jürgen Stohlmann (Dusseldorf, 1968). The text, which is printed on 266–327, is preceded by a thorough discussion and followed by notes and glossary.

178. *considerabat enim Achilles nisi Hectorem occideret plures de Graecorum numero eius dextera perituros* (24, Meister, p. 30).

179. *fit pugna maior, clamor ab oppido et a toto exercitu surgit. Hector Achillis femur sauciavit. Achilles dolore accepto magis eum persequi coepit nec destitit, nisi eum occiderit* (24, Meister, p. 30). Both Joseph and Albert interpret *dolore accepto* as "because of his pain" (Joseph, 5.502–504; Albert 3.515–518).

180. Benoît, as Stohlmann has convincingly argued (166–172), knew the abridgement.

181. There are some differences in detail: Achilles decides to attack Hektor not for the immediate salvation of perishing Greeks but to make possible ultimate victory; the actual attack is spurred specifically by a desire to take vengeance for Policenes (Polypoetes); Achilles is wounded in the groin (*inguine*) instead of the thigh (Guido 21, fol. 88, N. E. Griffin, *Historia* 174–175).

182. Guido 21, fol. 88, N. E. Griffin, *Historia* 175.

183. Guido 17, fol. 78, Griffin, *Historia* 151.

184. Albert, who may not have been familiar with Benoît (M. A. Joly, at least, sees no direct connection, *Benoît de Sainte More et le Roman de Troie* [Paris, 1870] 865), interprets this incident in similarly sinister fashion: Agamemnon lists the men Hektor has killed and concludes, "'Let all Greek fighters conspire to kill hot Hektor'. What he said was pleasing" (*Hectoris in jugulum ferventis tota juventus / Dorica conspiret. Dixerat, idque placet*, 2.773–774). Joseph, on the other hand, transfers the decision to gang up on Hektor from the deliberative quiet of a council to the heat of the battlefield; the attack is a spontaneous reaction to the deaths in quick succession of three important leaders, and since it merely makes Hektor laugh, one assumes that Achilles, Aias, and Diomedes are not meant to be among the attackers (5.306–315).

185. Troilos: Benoît 21411–21443, Guido 26, fol. 99 (N. E. Griffin, *Historia* 203–204); Memnon: Benoît 21559–21589, Guido 26, fol. 100 (Griffin, 205–206).

186. Achilles can be seen as actually more heroic than Aeneas, who deliberately brings Mezentius's horse down. Achilles aims for Troilos himself, but the horse rears and takes the blow intended for its master (6.313–318).

187. Compare *Troilus* 4.325 and 331–332 with *Aeneid* 10.722 and 707–708.

188. Guido 26, fol. 99, N. E. Griffin, *Historia* 203–204. The episode of Achilles' dragging the corpse is taken from Benoît (21447–21450), who also has Troilos surrounded by Myrmidons but who makes Achilles kill his enemy when he falls with his slain horse and loses his helmet (21426–21443).

189. Guido 26, fols. 99–100, N. E. Griffin, *Historia* 204–205.

190. *Attende, miser Homere, quod numquam Achilles virum strenuum nisi proditorie interfecit* (Guido, 26, fol. 100, N. E. Griffin, *Historia* 206).

191. Dares 13: *ore venusto* (Meister, 16); Benoît 5157: *Achillès fu de grant beauté;* Guido 8, fol. 45: *mira pulchritudine fuit decorus* (N. E. Griffin, *Historia* 83); see also Joseph "*Ilias*" 4.108–109; *Troilus* 2.71, 4.505. For Achilles as most beautiful of the Greeks in Homer, see Chapter One, part one.

192. Guido 8, fol. 45: *Nullus Grecorum tunc fortior ipso fuit* (N. E. Griffin, *Historia* 83).

193. See *Ilias Latina* 931–932, "*Viribus arte minis*" 43–44, Simon Capra Aurea 273–274, Benoît 16580–16594, Joseph 5.525, Guido 22, fol. 89 (N. E. Griffin, *Historia* 178–179).

CHAPTER FOUR

SOLDIER OF LOVE: ARCHAIC GREECE TO MEDIEVAL EUROPE

1. Notable exceptions are Jasper Griffin, who uses Achilles' Epic Cycle *affaires* to illustrate the "over-heated" and "perverse" quality of those epics ("The Epic Cycle and the Uniqueness of Homer," *Journal of Hellenic Studies* 97 [1977] 43–45), and C. Fontinoy, who surveys Achilles' posthumous marriages to support his theory that the conception of Polyxena as "bride" derived from an archaic funerary ritual that gave a dead unmarried hero the bride that was necessary to his happiness in the underworld ("Le sacrifice nuptial de Polyxene," *L'Antiquité Classique* 19 [1950] 389–390).

2. Aischylos' *Myrmidons* contained the following lines in Achilles' lament over the dead Patroklos (frag. 135):

You had no reverence for the holy majesty of your thighs,
O most ungrateful for my frequent kisses.

σέβας δὲ μηρῶν ἁγνὸν οὐκ ἐπῃδέσω,
ὦ δυσχάριστε τῶν πυκνῶν φιλημάτων

Quoted from *Tragicorum Graecorum Fragmenta*, ed. A. Nauck, 44. I think it quite possible that this play is one Ovid had in mind when, complaining that other authors could write about sex without being banished, he wrote that a tragic poet who had created a "love-soft Achilles" had not been harmed by having "weakened strong deeds through his verse" (*nec nocet auctori, mollem qui fecit Achillem, / infregisse suis fortia facta modis, Tristia* 2.409–412).

3. In the *Symposium* Phaidros tells us that Aischylos portrayed Achilles as Patroklos's lover, and he himself declares that Patroklos was Achilles' lover (179e–180a). Diotima, who later refers to Achilles' sacrificing his life for Patroklos, does not term their relationship either erotic or nonerotic.

4. Aischines in the oration *Against Timarchos* (345 B.C.) attempts to demonstrate with the examples of Achilles and Patroklos that homosexual love is practiced by *hoi sōphrones,* "men of sound mind," while heterosexual love is practiced by *hoi hubristai,* "licentious men" (141–150).

5. The lines, no more enigmatic than most of Lykophron's, are as follows:

ὦ σκύμνε, τερπνὸν ἀγκάλισμα συγγόνων
ὅς τ' ἄγριον δράκοντα πυρφόρῳ βαλὼν
ἴυγγι τόξων, τὸν τυπέντα δ' ἐν βρόχοις

μάρψας ἀφύκτοις βαιὸν ἀστεργῆ χρόνον,
πρὸς τοῦ δαμέντος αὐτὸς οὐ τετρωμένος,
καρατομηθεὶς τύμβον αἱμάξεις πατρός.

Oh cub, delightful darling of your siblings,
who, casting at the wild dragon with the flame-bearing
charm of arrows and for a short time having
caught in an inseparable snare the implacable one now stricken,
yourself not wounded by the one you conquered,
you will have your throat cut and bloody the tomb of your father.

Tzetzes confirms that these verses do indeed refer to Troilos, who, Tzetzes says, fled from Achilles to the altar of Apollo (his real father), where he was killed. Tzetzes is cited from *Lycophronis Chalcidensis Alexandra, obscurum poema. Cum Graeco Isaaci, seu Joannis, Tzetzae commentario* (Oxford, 1702) 39–40.

6. Servius *ad Aeneid* 1.474: *veritas quidem hoc habet: Troili amore Achillem ductum palumbes ei quibus ille delectabatur obiecisse, quas cum vellet tenere, captus ab Achille in eius amplexibus periit. sed hoc quasi indignum heroo carmine mutavit poeta* ("The true story is this: Achilles, who fell in love with Troilos, brought down the dove in which be delighted, but when he tried to hold him, his captive died in his loving embrace. But the poet changed the story as unworthy of epic") *Servianorum in Vergilii carmina commentariorum volumen 2* (Lancaster, 1946) 219–220.

7. Bion (Poem 12) classes Achilles and Patroklos in the ranks of true friends along with such other famous pairs as Theseus and Pirithoos and Orestes and Pylades (Gow 163). Theokritos (*Idyll.* 29.33–34) is ambiguous as to whether friendship or erotic love is indicated by the reference to "Achillean friends." Sporadic references to the homosexual relationship continue to occur in Latin poetry, e.g., Ovid *A.A.* 1. 743, and in the twelfth century A.D. Benoît de Sainte-Maure resurrects it in the form of an insult delivered to Achilles by Hektor (*Roman de Troie* 13183–13184).

8. The tone of Bacchylides' poem is quite serious: the Iliadic episode, in which Hektor brings fire to the ships, is used to illustrate the greatness of Achilles by depicting what he had prevented before as well as the greatness of Aias by depicting his valiant efforts in the absence of his cousin.

9. This play, transmitted in the manuscripts of Seneca, could certainly not have been published until after Nero's death in A.D. 68, and, since it correctly prophesies Nero's death (619–631), it was probably not written until then either. It is therefore not by Seneca, who died in A.D. 65, but by a contemporary poet who managed to survive Nero's reign. See Lucile Y. Whitman's discussion in her introduction to *The Octavia* (Bern and Stuttgart, 1978) 5–12.

10.

> Fecit et in capta Lyrneside magnus Achilles,
>   cum premeret mollem lassus ab hoste torum.

Illis te manibus tangi, Brisei, sinebas,
   imbutae Phrygia quae nece semper erant.
An fuit hoc ipsum quod te, lasciva, iuvaret,
   ad tua victrices membra venire manus?

Achilles [used his free hand well] with his captive Lyrnessan
   when he pressed the soft bed tired from the enemy.
You, Briseis, allowed yourself to be touched by those hands
   which were often dripping with Phrygian blood.
And was it because this made you happy, wanton one,
   that his victorious hands came to your limbs?

Quoted from *P. Ovidi Nasonis, Amores, Medicamina Faciei Femineae, Ars Amatoria, Remedia Amoris,* ed. E. J. Kenney (Oxford, 1973).

11. Tzetzes's commentary (*Lykophronos* 23) assures us that Lykophron's verses refer to Achilles, and Pausanias (second century A.D.) confirms the union between Achilles and Helen in *Lakonia* 19.13. This marriage makes Achilles an otherworldly bigamist since Lykophron elsewhere makes Medea Achilles' wife (174, 798), as does Apollodoros (*Epit.* 5.5). The location of Achilles' posthumous marriages is always the White Island.

12. This is a variant of the story of how and why Achilles killed Tenes. The version in Apollodoros (*Epit.* 3.23–26) relates that Tenes tried to stop the Greeks from landing at Tenedos by throwing stones at them, and then Achilles stabbed him in the chest. In both versions (neither of which appears in extant fragments of the Epic Cycle) the killing of Tenes has dire consequences for Achilles: death at the hands of Apollo. Thetis had apparently forewarned Achilles of this fated consequence, but in the heat of passion he forgot.

13. Although starting around 700 B.C. Attic vase painting offers numerous illustrations of Achilles fighting with or killing Penthesileia, there are no clear indications of a love story until some early-fourth-century south Italian painters begin to include Aphrodite in their representations of the episode (see *Lexicon Iconographicum* "Achilleus" no. 740). Six early-fifth-century Attic vases probably show Achilles delivering the death blow while Penthesileia pleads for mercy (*Lexicon Iconographicum* "Achilleus" nos. 729, 731–736); since in one of these cases her helmet is definitely off (no. 733), it is possible to assume that Propertius's version (see below) is not yet current. On the other hand, one late-sixth-century vase shows Achilles carrying Penthesileia's body in a manner similar to the familiar one of Aias carrying the body of his beloved cousin (*Lexicon Iconographicum* "Achilleus" no. 725). This kindly treatment of his enemy's body may reflect some of the genuine warmth of feeling expressed in an Epic Cycle story that did not become popular until much later. See also Kossatz-Diesmann's discussion of "Achilleus" no. 716 (*Lexicon Iconographicum* vol. 1, pt. 2, p. 162), which assumes that the love story was being illustrated in the early seventh century.

14. At least for the moment: after Achilles kills Thersites, Penthesileia is never mentioned again.

15. See note 94.

16. So A. C. Pearson believes (*Fragments,* vol. 2, p. 193). Deidameia is not mentioned by Homer, and in the *Iliad* Achilles is clearly unmarried; their son Neoptolemos, however, is very much Achilles' concern—second only to Peleus—when he foresees the effect of his death in the *Iliad* (19.326–327) and questions Odysseus in the *Odyssey's* Hades (11.492–493, 506–540).

17. χειμὼν ἐπιπίπτει καὶ διασκεδάννυνται. Ἀχιλλεὺς δὲ Σκύρῳ προσσχὼν γαμεῖ τὴν Λυκομήδους θυγατέρα Δηιδάμειαν.

A storm fell upon them and scattered them. Achilles, when he landed at Skyros, married Deidameia, the daughter of Lykomedes (Allen, 104).

The *Little Iliad* apparently also dealt with this episode; see fragment 4 (Allen, 130). There exists probably one illustration of part of this story: a red-figured vase from 450 B.C. pictures Achilles, helmet in hand, saying farewell to Deidameia, who holds a libation basin, while Lykomedes and four other young women, no doubt Deidameia's sisters, look on (see figure 17). The characters are not named, but the interpretation is strengthened by the named picture on the other side of the vase: Neoptolemos leaving Skyros for Troy (see Kossatz-Deismann's discussion, *Lexicon Iconographicum* "Achilleus" no. 176). It is interesting that it is just about this same time, i.e., the mid-fifth century, that illustrations of Thetis bringing Achilles armor in Phthia (see *Lexicon Iconographicum* "Achilleus" nos. 186–205) disappear. The lack of illustrations of arming in Phthia after 440 B.C. perhaps reflects the growing popularity of the newer story about Achilles' being hidden in Skyros and leaving for Troy from there; however, the Skyros episode also lacks other illustrations until after Statius made the story extremely popular in Roman times.

18. Pearson cites Euripides fragment 682 as decisive for this plot. He also discusses the possibility that Sophokles' *Skurioi* was on this same subject but decides instead that it was about the extraction of Neoptolemos (191–193).

19. Quoted with minor modification from *Bucolici Graeci,* edited by A. S. F. Gow (Oxford, 1952) 157–158.

20. For more on Ovid's depiction of rape in the *Ars Amatoria* see Julie Hemker, "Rape and the Founding of Rome," *Helios* 12 (1985) 41–47.

21. See *Heroides* 9. In Greek legend, Herakles was forced to be the slave of Queen Omphale for a certain period of time as punishment for killing his friend Iphitos, whereupon Omphale set him to do many labors, including some humiliating feminine tasks. Love, therefore, had nothing to do with his temporary effeminization. The first hint of an erotic relationship occurs in Propertius 3.11, where Herakles and Omphale are included in a list of role-reversed couples, the

rest of whom were definitely lovers. Ovid made the hint blatant and thus changed the tradition forever. According to Ovid's jealous Deianira, Omphale was mistress of Herakles' heart as well as of his body, and this was why he was willing to spin wool and to amuse her with stories of his past greatness while she preened in his lion skin (*Her.* 9.73–118). The story next surfaces in chap. 21 of Boccaccio's *Legend of Famous Women,* but Iole, whom Herakles wanted so much that he killed her father and sacked her whole city to get her (Soph. *Trachiniai*), is here substituted for Omphale. It is thus, with Iole in the role of domineering mistress and Herakles in that of effeminized lover, that the story is immortalized by Tasso and Spenser (*Gerusalemme liberata* 16.3, *Faerie Queene* 5.5.24).

22. The reverse may also be true: Deidameia wants to go to war with Achilles (1.949–950).

23. *Scholia Graeca in Euripides Tragoedias I,* vol. 1, 229–230:

ὁ δὲ τὰ Κυπριακὰ ποιήσας φησὶν ὑπο. ᾽Οδυσσέως καὶ Διομήδους ἐν τῇ τῆς πόλεως ἁλώσει τραυματισθεῖσαν ἀπολέσθαι, ταφῆναι δὲ ὑπὸ Νεοπτολέμου, ὡς Ὑλαῦκος γράφει.

This evidence is actually thirdhand since it reports what Glaukos of Rhegium (c. 400 B.C.) said that the *Kypria* said.

24. Richard Förster, "Zu Achilleus und Polyxena," *Hermes* 18 (1883) 477: "Dass aber Polyxena von Neoptolemos einen τάφος erhält, kann doch nur als Act der Pietät des Sohnes gegen den Vater gefasst werden. Mithin muss schon in den Kyprien Achill die Polyxena begehrt haben."

25. E.g., A. Rzach, s.v. "*kyklos,*" *Real-Encyclopaedie der Klassischen Altertumswissenschaft* (Stuttgart, 1922) 2394; vol. 2, Wilhelm Kroll, *C. Valerius Catullus* (Leipzig, 1923; repr. Stuttgart, 1968) 190; Curran, "Catullus 64" 189–190; and, possibly, L. Meridier, *Euripide,* vol. 2 (Paris, 1956) 166.

26. Nearly two hundred illustrations of this scene beginning in the late seventh century are reproduced and/or discussed in *Lexicon Iconographicum* "Achilleus" nos. 206–388.

27. See Förster, "Achilleus und Polyxena. Zwei unedirte Deklamationen des Choricius," *Hermes* 17 (1882) 193, esp. n. 3; also "Zu Achilleus" 476.

28. Förster believes that the story of her being sacrificed by Neoptolemos developed later in the lyric poets out of the love story indicated by the vase paintings and the burial recorded by the scholiast ("Zu Achilleus" 477).

29. E.g., F. Welcker, *Die griechischen Tragödien,* vol. 1 (Bonn, 1839) 183–184 n. 6; Weil, *Sept tragédies d'Euripide* 204–205; E. Ciaceri, *La Alessandra di Licofrone* (Catania, 1901) 177, commentary to 323; C. Robert, *Die griechische Heldensage,* vol. 3 (Berlin, 1923) 1189–1190; Fontinoy, 389–90, and Elaine Fantham, *Seneca's Troades* (Princeton, 1982) 238 commentary to 195.

30. For extensive references see Margaret Alexiou and Peter Dronke, "The Lament of Jephtha's Daughter," *Studi Medievali* 3d ser., 12, no. 2 (1971) 819–841; and Richmond Lattimore, *Themes in Greek and Latin Epitaphs* (Urbana, 1962) 192–197. I owe much to both works for their citations of literary references and funerary epigrams.

31. Σῆμα Φρασικλείας· κούρη κεκλή[σο]μαι αἰεί
ἀντὶ γάμου παρὰ Θεῶν τοῦτο λαχοῦσ᾽ ὄνομα.

The tomb of Phrasikleia: I shall be called a maiden always, having received from the gods this name instead of marriage. (*Epigrammata Graeca*, ed. G. Kaibel [Berlin, 1878] no. 6, p. 4)

Also quoted in Lattimore, *Themes* 192.

32. ἀκμὴν δ᾽ οὐ γενετῆρες ἐμήν, οὐκ ἐσθλὸς ὅμαιμος,
οὐ πόσις, ἀλλ᾽ ᾿Αίδης λυγρὸς ἐκαρπίσατο.

There plucked the fruit of my youth not my parents or my noble brother or a husband, but baneful Hades. (Kaibel, no. 157–158, p. 52)

Also quoted in Lattimore, *Themes* 193. Compare Kaibel no. 325.11–15, pp. 125–126; no. 381, p. 151.

33. νυμφοκόμοις στολίδεσσι σύνοικος [ἔ]ο[ν] γὰρ ἄωρος ("Untimely come, I dwell here in bridal robes"). *Sammelbuch Griechischer Urkunden aus Aegypten*, ed. F. Preisigke and F. Bilabel (Strassburg, 1915) 6178.3 Quoted by Lattimore, *Themes* 185.

34. Sarah B. Pomeroy, *Goddesses, Whores, Wives, and Slaves* (New York, 1975) 62.

35. As this passage indicates, wedding imagery was used in laments for young men as well as women, but not nearly as often. See Lattimore, *Themes* 193–194. Compare Kaibel, no. 236, p. 88.

36. Alexiou and Dronke, 838.

37. Alexiou and Dronke, 839. For a useful summary of the correspondences between wedding ritual and funerary ritual see J. Redfield, "Notes on the Greek Wedding," *Arethusa* 15 (1982) 188–190.

38. For the accentuation of pathos in such a case see Lattimore, *Themes* 192.

39. The above passages are cited also by Lattimore, *Themes* 192, and Alexiou and Dronke, 825–826.

40. Alexiou and Dronke cite this passage in a very interesting note that discusses possible allusions to the motif in Aischylos, 829 n. 7.

41. Alexiou and Dronke cite this passage, 827.

42. ἦλθε δ᾽ ὁ δυσ[πε]νθὴς ῾Αίδης καὶ ἀπήγαγε [σ᾽] ὠκύ,
καλλ[ο]σύνην τὴν σὴν ἰσιδὼν [καὶ] [ἦ]θος ἄμεμπτον.

Lamentable Hades came and swiftly snatched you when he saw your beauty and blameless character.

Inscriptiones Creticae, ed. M. Guarducci (Rome, 1935) 1, 5, 41, 3–4. Quoted in Lattimore, *Themes* 194.

43. Werner Peek, *Griechische Vers-Inschriften* vol. 1 (Berlin, 1955) no. 1989, p. 626. Theiophila complains that she had many suitors, but Hades seized her first "because he fell in love with me, seeing a Persephone better than Persephone" (ἔφθασε δ᾽ἁρπάξας ᾽Αΐδης, ἠράσσατο γὰρ μευ, Φερσεφόνας ἐσιδὼν κρέσσονα Φερσεφόναν, 3–4). Later on, the maiden laments that she shares Persephone's husband (Κόρης σύλλεκτρος) rather than the man picked out for her (9–11). H. J. Rose connects the idea of Hades as bridegroom with his role as "giver of the good gifts of the earth" whose fertility would be increased by the unused fertility of the dead virgin, and he surmises that Persephone is in fact a projection of all the maidens carried off by Hades ("The Bride of Hades," *Classical Philology* 20 [1925] 242).

44. In the *Trojan Women* Kassandra has not been raped so she is also a virgin (see line 453), but she is reserved for Agamemnon, who as usual exerts his prerogatives as king.

45. See my article "The Politics of Imitation: Euripides' *Hekabe*," *Arethusa* 18 (1985) 47–66.

46. I.e., Neoptolemos, who, according to Lykophron, is the son of Iphigeneia (*Alex.* 183–185).

47. Some take the next three lines also as referring to Polyxena, but since the grammar and sense more logically point to Iphigeneia, in this particular case I would rather follow Tzetzes and understand *Kandion* in 328 as Ares rather than Hephaistos and the wolves in 329 as the Greeks at Aulis rather than at Troy (commentary to 323, pp. 40–41).

48. See note 11.

49. The phrase is Alexiou and Dronke's, 824.

50. M. C. J. Putnam, "The Art of Catullus 64," *HSCP* 65 (1961) 193.

51. Putnam, 194. Putnam also notes the correspondence of *acervis* and *coacervatum*. Putnam's words are worth quoting further: "The image is so skillfully wrought by the poet that the reader's eye climbs the tomb—which instead of being polished or round becomes a heap of blood-red carnage—only to find the white-limbed virgin on top, sacrificed to the ideal of heroism which lives in spirit though dead in the flesh" (194).

52. Curran does think that the sacrifice of Polyxena is an allusion to a wedding and that her mock wedding associates her with Ariadne as an ironic counterpart to the wedding of Peleus and Thetis (Curran, "Catullus 64" 189–190). His arguments are interesting but are unfortunately based on the supposition that the wedding was a firm part of the tradition. Curran refers to Wilhelm Kroll's commentary to line 362, which states that already in the Epic Cycle

Achilles demanded Polyxena be sacrificed as his bride so that he could be her husband in the afterworld (*C. Valerius Catullus* [Stuttgart, 1959] 190).

53. Euripides may have inspired this passage, as Otto Korn has pointed out (*Ovid: Metamorphosen,* vol. 2 [Zurich and Dublin, 1966] commentary *ad loc.*). Euripides' Polyxena says that she wants not to be constrained by the soldiers as she dies, for she who is a princess would be ashamed to be called a slave among the dead (Hek. 548–550).

54. *cinis ipse sepulti / in genus hoc saevit; tumulo quoque sensimus hostem* ("Entombed, his ashes themselves rage against this family; we feel his enmity even from the grave").

55. This mediocre poet produced his work between 70 B.C., when Meleager's *Garland* was published, and A.D. 40, when Philip of Thessalonica published a new *Garland* comprising epigrams subsequent to those included in the earlier anthology. (See Pierre Waltz, *Anthologie Grecque,* pt. 1, vol. 1 [Paris, 1960] xii–xviii for a discussion of the two anthologies.) Gow and Page do not believe that Flaccus was in fact a contributor to Philip's *Garland,* but their only suggested date (the first decade of the first century A.D.) does not affect my chronology (A. S. F. Gow and D. Page, *The Greek Anthology: The Garland of Philip and Some Contemporary Epigrams,* vol. 1 [Cambridge, 1968] 451).

56. πένθιμον ἡνίκα πατρὶ Πολυξείνης ὑμέναιον / ἤνυσεν ὀγκωτοῦ Πύρρος ὕπερθε τάφου ("Above the heaped-up grave Pyrrhus accomplished a mournful wedding of Polyxena with his father"). Verses 3–4 describe Hekabe and 5–8 give her a lament very similar to her lament in Ovid (*Met.* 13.503–504).

57. Gow and Page, 454, commentary to VI.1.

58. ταύτης ὑμεν[αῖος ὅδ'] ἐστιν. *Monumenta Asiae Minoris Antiqua,* vol. 3 (London, 1928–) 793.3. The fragment, which is of uncertain date, is quoted by Alexiou and Dronke, 834, who also point out that ὑμεναῖος is used similarly in Achilles Tatius's prose romance "The Story of Leukippe and Kleitophon" (second century A.D.). As part of their discussion of expressions that have become formulaic Alexiou and Dronke (839) quote the following sentence from a lament in Achilles Tatius 1.13: γάμος δὲ ὁ θάνατος. θρῆνος δὲ ὁ ὑμέναιος. ὁ δὲ κωκυτὸς οὗτος τῶν γάμων ᾠδαί ("Your wedding is death, a dirge your wedding song. This wailing is your wedding hymn").

59. Similar "Iliadic" sentiments of wrath and honor are revived in the fourth and fifth centuries A.D. by two Greek authors who may well be consciously attempting a return to early Greek sources (see W. F. J. Knight, "Iliupersides," *Classical Quarterly* 26 [1932] 178–189) and who ignore Seneca's subsequent wedding imagery and the love story in Dares and Dictys. Tryphiodoros in his *Taking of Troy* concludes his description of the atrocities committed by the Greeks with their "pouring Polyxena's blood on the tomb, to appease the wrath

[*mênin*] of the dead Achilles" (οἱ δὲ Πολυξείνης ἐπιτύμβιον αἷμα χέαντες / μῆνιν ἱλασσάμενοι τεθνειότος Αἰακίδαο, 686–687). Quintus makes Achilles demand Polyxena as his share of the spoils (14.213–214), and Neoptolemos, when he reports his father's ghostly visitation, terms her a *géras* (14.240). Koechly believes that *géras* also appeared in Achilles' speech in the one-line lacuna between lines 214 and 215 (580, commentary to 14.215).

60. Seneca's *Agamemnon* 641, which describes Polyxena as *Haemonio desponsa rogo*, "betrothed to the Haemonian grave," suggests that *cineribus* is the indirect object of *desponsa*, not of *mactetur*, and therefore that *desponsa* must not be translated absolutely as, for example, "my fiancée."

61. Funeral torches that ought to have been wedding torches constitute another recurrent theme in the epigrams and inscriptions, e.g., Meleager *Palatine Anthology* 7.182.7–8; Peek (note 3 this chapter) 1989.7–8, translation in Alexiou and Dronke, 837; *Carmina Latina Epigraphia*, ed. F. Buecheler (Leipzig, 1895–1897) 383.1–4, quoted in Lattimore, *Themes* 194; and *Corpus Inscriptionum Latinarum* (Berlin, 1862) 6315, cited by L. B. Lawler, "Some Lesser Lights," *Classical Journal* 30 (1934) 72.

62. Elaine Fantham (382, commentary to 1157) compares Polyxena's hostile fall to a Roman curse that was used to invert the standard blessing *sit tibi terra levis* ("may the earth rest light upon you"). She suggests that Ausonius (fourth century A.D.) was inspired by Seneca's description when he wrote the following literary epitaph (*Epitaphia Heroum* 26):

> Troas Achilleo coniuncta Polyxena busto
> malueram nullo caespite functa tegi.
> non bene discordes tumulos miscetis, Achivi:
> hoc violare magis, quam sepelire fuit.

> I, Trojan Polyxena, joined in Achilles' tomb,
> would have preferred to be covered with no earth when dead.
> You do not well, Achaeans, to mingle discordant graves:
> this was violation, not burial.

The epitaph is printed in *Decimi Magni Ausonii Burdigalensis Opuscula*, edited by Sextus Prete (Leipzig, 1978) 64.

63. Lattimore, Themes 193.

64. *Iliad* 22.359–360; *Aithiopis*, Allen, 106; *Aeneid* 6.56–58; Ovid *Met.* 12.600–606; Apollodoros *Epit.* 5.3. For Apollo alone as killer see Aischylos frag. 350 (Plato *Republic* 383b, Nauck 105), Soph. *Philoktetes* 334–336; Horace *Odes* 4.6.1–12; Hyginus *Fab.* 107; Quintus of Smyrna *Posthomerica* 3.37–92.

65. This appears to be the interpretation put on Achilles' demand by at least one version extant in the fourth century A.D. The Vergilian commentary of Servius contains a summary (*ad Aen.* 3.322):

Cum Graeci victores in patriam vellent reverti, e tumulo Achillis vox dicitur audita querentis quod sibi soli de praeda nihil impertivissent. De qua re consultus Calchas cecinit, Polyxenam Priami filiam, quam vivus Achilles dilexerat, eius debere manibus immolari; quae cum admota tumulo Achillis occidenda esset, manu Pyrrhi aequanimiter mortem dicitur suscepisse. Inventur enim apud quosdam, quod etiam ipsa Achillem amaverit, et ea nesciente Achilles fraude et insidiis sit peremptus.

The story goes that when the victorious Greeks were about to return home, Achilles' voice was heard from the tomb complaining that to him alone they had given no share of booty. When they consulted Kalchas about this, he interpreted it to mean that Polyxena, daughter of Priam, whom Achilles had loved when he was alive, must be sacrificed as an offering to his ghost. It is said that when Polyxena was brought to Achilles' tomb to be killed she accepted death at the hand of Pyrrhus calmly. Indeed, some authors relate that she herself returned Achilles' love and it was without her knowledge that Achilles was killed by deceit or treachery.

(*Servianorum in Vergilii carmina commentariorum volumen 3* [Oxford, 1965] 127)

Tzetzes' twelfth-century commentary on Lykophron also makes love the motive, relating that Achilles appeared in a dream to the Greek leaders and asked for Polyxena "because he still loved her even after death" (ὡς καὶ μετὰ θάνατον ἐρῶν αὐτῆς), p. 41 comm. to 323.

66. The last sentence of the Servian commentary quoted above (note 65) indicates that some other authors did implicate Polyxena in the plot, and this involvement would certainly have provided a motive for hate. Servius's earlier commentary to the same passage in the *Aeneid* implies such a motive:

Quam cum Troiani fraude promisissent, Paris post Tymbraei Apollonis simulacrum latuit et venientem Achillem ad foedus missa vulneravit sagitta. Tum Achilles moriens petiit, ut, devicta Troia, ad eius sepulchrum Polyxena immolaretur.

After the Trojans had deceitfully promised her, Paris hid behind the statue of Thymbrian Apollo and, when Achilles came with regard to the contract, shot and wounded him with an arrow. Then Achilles asked as he died that once Troy were overthrown Polyxena be sacrificed on his grave.

(Servius, vol. 3, p. 126) In Dictys' *Journal* no motive is suggested: though the love story is fully developed, the sacrifice is told in one sentence of a long account of who got whom in the divisions of the spoils (5.13). Dares' *History* makes Neoptolemos sacrifice her as the cause of Achilles' death (*cuius causa pater eius perierat*, 43), thus suggesting a motive of revenge for her involvement even though that involvement seems to have been innocent (see Dares 34).

67. Seneca fails also to have Agamemnon bring forward a version that has Achilles killed while on a love mission, a version that would have fit in nicely with his disparagement of Neoptolemos as "conceived from the secret defilement of a woman" (342).

68. See 68–69 for a good summary of the argument based on plausibility. Cited from *Dionis Chrysostomi Orationes*, ed. G. de Bude (Leipzig, 1916) 168–169.

69. Dio does mention the sacrifice in his Sixth Oration, however, as part of a point Diogenes supposedly made about the benefits of onanism. The Greeks so overvalued sexual intercourse with women, said Diogenes, that they not only sacked cities for them but even considered it necessary to give Achilles a woman after he was dead (6.18; de Bude, 110): τοὺς δὲ Ἀχαιοὺς οὕτως εἶναι ἄφρονας ὥστε καὶ τοὺς νεκροὺς νομίζειν προσδεῖσθαι γυναικῶν καὶ τὴν Πολυξένην σφάττειν ἐπὶ τῷ τάφῳ τοῦ Ἀχιλλέως ("The Achaians were so senseless that they thought even dead men needed women, and they sacrificed Polyxena on Achilles' grave").

70. The earliest clear version of this variant occurs in Horace *Odes* 4.6.1–12, where Achilles is linked with Niobe and Tityos, other hubristic victims of Apollo. Hyginus (*Fab.* 107) makes Apollo, disguised as Paris, kill Achilles in anger for his bragging that he will conquer the city all by himself. Quintus of Smyrna follows Hyginus. The motive for this version is expressed perfectly by C. A. Sainte-Beuve in a laudatory comment on Quintus: "C'est une manière ingénieuse de louer Achille, même dans sa mort, et de faire entendre qu'un tel homme ne pouvait être atteint par la main et l'arme d'un mortel" (*Etude sur Virgile, suivie d'une étude sur Quintus de Smyrne* [Paris, 1891] 417).

71. See Chapter Three part two.

72. The story of Achilles and Polyxena occurs in those chapters (11–43) which Otmar Schissel von Fleschenberg's analysis has established to be from the original Greek Dares (*Dares Studien* [Halle-an-der-Salle, 1908] 84–157).

73. Later on, Hektor's mutilation of Patroklos's body provides a second and still more potent motive for his anger and eventual revenge (3.10–11).

74. Compare *Aeneid* 4.1, 68, 531; 7.462–465; 12.5.

75. Compare *Iliad* 24.515–524, 552–571 with Dictys 24. In the *Iliad* the topic of conversation is generic human woe (*Il.* 24.525–542, 599–620); in Dictys' *Journal* it is the causes of the war, or, rather, how Priam could have been so foolish as to let the war start and then continue.

76. In later Byzantine tradition, the suspicions of the Greek soldiers would seem to be well-founded. In the sixth century A.D. a rhetorician named Choricius wrote a pair of set speeches whose hypothesis was that "after Hektor's death Achilles, having fallen in love with Polyxena, sent an embassy to the Trojans offering an alliance [*summachian*] as the price for marriage" (μετὰ τὴν Ἕκτορος τελευτὴν ἐρασθεὶς Ἀχιλλεὺς τῆς Πολυξένης πρεσβεύεται πρὸς τοὺς

Τρῶας μισθὸν ἐπαγγελλόμενος τοῦ γάμου τὴν συμμαχίαν). The speeches are printed in Förster *Hermes* 17 (1882) 208–238; the passage quoted from the hypothesis appears on 208. In the speeches which praise and oppose the proposal (delivered by Poulydamas and Priam, respectively) it seems that Achilles actually means to fight on the side of the Trojans.

77. The organs veinally connected to the heel are the kidneys or loins (*renes*), the thighs, and the *membrum virile*. Quoted from *Fabii Planciadis Fulgentii V. C. Opera*, ed. R. Helms (Leipzig, 1898) 70–72.

78. Achilles, of course, is not quite "Everyman." He is more strongly fortified than most and as such exemplifies the fact that even the most excellent of human beings should not be complacent in the face of the powerful enemy within. For another example of lust as the fatal flaw in an otherwise excellent human being, see Joseph of Exeter's comments on Helen's excellence being reduced to naught because of an overactive liver (= seat of passions) whose tickling she could not resist (4.193–205). This one part not only overwhelmed her but also goaded the whole world into war (4.206–207). For the liver as seat of passions see, for example, Lactantius *De Opificio Dei* chap. 14.

79. In this he is following St. Augustine, who believed that every act of sin was the exact equivalent of Adam's yielding to Eve in the primal Fall (*De Trinitate* 12). Similarly, Gregory the Great, sixth-century theologian and pope, viewed Job as typifying Christ and his despairing wife as typifying the temptations of the flesh (*Moralia in Job;* cited in Rand, *Founders of the Middle Ages* [New York, 1957] 31).

80. *The Commentary on the First Six Books of the Aeneid of Vergil Commonly Attributed to Bernardus Silvestris: A New Critical Edition*, ed. J. Jones and E. Jones (Lincoln, Nebraska, 1977) 12.

81. It should, of course, be noted that Propertius's poem itself shifts from amused disapproval to stern condemnation as he develops a diatribe against the promiscuous eastern queen who nearly parlayed her conquests of Caesar, Pompey, and Antony into a conquest of Rome.

82. In the eleventh-century "Letter from Deidameia to Achilles" (*"Deidamia Achilli,"* printed by J. Stohlmann, "Eine Ovid-Imitation aus dem 11.Jahrundert," in *Litteratur und Sprache im Europäischen Mittelalter*, Darmstadt: 1973, 224–231), Deidameia couches her repeated complaints that Achilles has succumbed to Briseis's charms in the language of this topos: *Victus ab ancilla diceris esse tua* ("You are said to be conquered by your serving girl," 68); *Victorem Frigum vincit amica virum* ("A girlfriend has conquered the conqueror of Phrygian men," 70); *Tu nunc captiva frueris plus captus amica* ("Now more as a captive you enjoy your captured girlfriend," 81). Simon Capra Aurea in his late-twelfth-century poem "Divitiis, regno, specie" says of Achilles' withdrawal on account of Briseis that soft love had pierced the breast impenetrable by steel (*et*

quem nemo potest vincere vincit amor. / *Pectus Pelyde nullo penetrabile ferro,* / *Mollis amor penetrat,* 228–230). And later, when Polyxena enters the story, Simon remarks on the fact that the conqueror who set Troy aflame was himself set on fire by a beautiful virgin who conquered him (*Pulchra soror Paridis Pelide pectus adurit,* / *Hic Troye flammas, suscitat illa duci.* / *De victore Frigum Polissena virgo triumphat,* 329–331, Boutemy, "La Version" 273, 274). Albert of Stade in the mid-thirteenth century similarly evokes the irony of a hero like Achilles, a man who laid low so many, being himself trampled by the tender feet of a single girl (*Qui totiens socios, totiens perterruit hostes,* / *Iactat sub teneros unica virgo pedes,* *Troilus* 3.719–720). In the late thirteenth century Guido delle Colonne's Achilles self-pityingly laments that he who is so strong not even Hektor could conquer him is conquered by the sight of a weak girl: *Ve michi, quia me, quem viri fortissimi et robusti vincere minime potuerunt, quem nec etiam ille fortissimus Hector, qui fortissimos omnes excessit, unius fragilis puelle devicit et prostravit intuitus* (Guido 23, fol. 92, p. 185).

83. *Le Roman de Troie en prose,* chap. 198, ed. L. Constans and E. Faral (Paris, 1933) 161–162. For the dating in the mid-thirteenth century see Constans's edition of Benoît, vol. 6, pp. 313–314.

84. A. E. Atwood and V. K. Whitaker, editors of the *Excidium Troiae* (Cambridge, Mass., 1944), believe that the original composition of this work is to be dated to late-antiquity (fourth to sixth centuries), but our earliest manuscript belongs to the ninth century and the language is vulgar Latin of the medieval period (xi–xv). This clumsy chronicle of the Trojan War and the founding of Rome is based on a wide variety of Greek and Latin sources and gives Dares and Dictys no particular preference.

85. Achilles sees and falls in love with her as she bends over the city wall to throw her jewelry into the scale of gold that is being measured against the weight of Hektor's body (*Excidium Troiae* 11.25–12.10). This part of the story is also found in Vatican Mythographer 2, p. 205 (*Scriptores Rerum Mythicarum Latini Tres Romae nuper reperti,* ed. G. H. Bode [Darmstadt, 1834; repr. Hildesheim, 1968] 143).

86. *Excidium Troiae* 12.12–25.

87. *Excidium Troiae* 12.25–13.5. Polyxena later comes to a horrible end: to punish her betrayal Neoptolemos imprisons her alive in Achilles' coffin (20.1–5).

88. I have come across only one other expression of this story, an Italian sonnet, one of seven that introduce a fourteenth-century copy of Petrarch's *Triumph of Love,* in the Codex Laurentiano Strozziano 174. The first half of this sonnet, which begins *Io sono l'oltramirabile d'Achille,* is devoted to Achilles' military prowess; the second is devoted to Polyxena:

> E questa è Pulisena [mia] sposa,
> la quale i' miro con tanto dilecto;
> per certo ch' i' l'amay sopr' ogni cosa.

Finite fu le noçça del mio lecto;
et fu palese a questa frescha cosa
ancor di mi persona ogni difecto;
bench' a suo dì mori nel mio conspecto.

The sonnet is quoted by E. Gorra, *Testi inediti di storia Trojana* (Turin, 1887) 61–62 note 4.

89. Benoît, *Le Roman de Troie* 26466–26470, Albert of Stade 6.665–6.666, and Guido delle Colonne Book 30, fol. 113, p. 236, all assert her innocence. Joseph of Exeter does not do this explicitly, but he does label her being turned over to Pyrrhus a *scelus ingens* (6.878) and calls her *infelix preda* (6.879); Benoît (21227–21233) and Guido (Book 26, fol. 99, p. 203) say that she is unhappy at the news of Achilles' re-entering battle because she wants him as a husband. Benoît reports her sadness at Achilles' death (26467) and has her revile her mother for having caused it (22449–22460); in addition, a mourning image of her is set up on Achilles' tomb (22435–22444). The earliest account of reciprocal love occurs in Flavius Philostratus's *Heroikos* (c. A.D. 200). According to Philostratus, Achilles and Polyxena fall in love when Priam brings her with him to negotiate for Hektor's body (50). The story then proceeds as in Dictys until after Achilles is killed. At this point Philostratus' narrative has Polyxena flee from the deserted temple to the Greek camp, where she lives for three days under the protection of Agamemnon. Then "she ran to his grave at night and fell on a sword, greatly lamenting in the manner of a wife and asking Achilles to remain her lover and to be true to their marriage" (δραμεῖν ἐπὶ τὸ σῆμα ἐν νυκτί, ξίφει τε αὐτὴν ἐπικλῖναι πολλὰ εἰποῦσαν ἐλεεινὰ καὶ γαμικά, ὅτε δὴ καὶ δεῖσθαι τοῦ Ἀχιλλέως ἐραστήν τε μεῖναι καὶ ἀγαγέσθαι αὐτὴν μὴ ψευσάμενον τὸν γάμον) *Her.* 51b (Lannoy 65).

90. Book 31, fol. 112, p. 236.

91. It is interesting that Dares feels compelled to give Achilles a double motive: love for Polyxena and anger at the army over Palamedes' being chosen over him to replace Agamemnon as commander (27). No subsequent author uses the double motive. Guido restores the anger but makes it a result of the love: when the army rejects Achilles' advice to end the war, Achilles is *iracundia multa motus* and orders his Myrmidons to stay out of the fighting. Guido 24, fol. 93, p. 189.

92. See Chapter Three, note 103, for Dares' complete description. This portrait remains basically constant throughout the redactors, the only real change occurring in the addition of eyes (see below) and in the color of his hair: dark brown in Dares, Joseph (4.111), and Albert (2.73), auburn in Benoît (5161), blond in Guido (Book 8, fol. 45, p. 83).

93. Guido 8, fol. 45, p. 83: *oculis glaucis et grossis sed amorosi aspectus*. This replaces Benoît's *Les ieuz . . . hardiz e fiers* (5160). As W. B. Wiggington comments, thus "Albert and Guido make clear that the eventual downfall of Achilles . . . may be traced to a weakness in his character—his amorousness" (*The Nature and Sig-*

nificance of the Late Medieval Troy Story: A Study of Guido delle Colonne's Historia Destructionis Troiae, Ph.D. dissertation, Rutgers, 1964, p. 136).

94. *Primum autem in hoc peccato est aspectus oculorum quo mulier pulchra aspicitur* (*Job* 31 Lectio 1, cited by Wiggington in connection with Paris's falling in love with Helen, p. 104.) Compare St. Ambrose *Explanation of Psalm 118* 5.29. Secular statements about the ocular origins of love abound. Andreas Capellanus goes so far as to assert that blind persons cannot fall in love (*De Amore* 1, 5). Guillaume de Lorris's *Amors* shoots his arrow through the poet's eyes to lodge its barb of *Biauté* permanently in his heart (*Roman de la Rose*, 1689–1720; ed. Félix Lecoy [Paris, 1968] vol. 1, p. 52). This conception of the visual source of love was not merely a theological and literary one. Scientists, too, like Bernardus Gordonius (fl. A.D. 1285) and the Arab physician al-Damiris (fl. A.D. 1400) subscribed to it and included it in their medical treatises when discussing the mental illness or *mania* of love (see the quotations in J. L. Lowes, "The Loveres Maladye of Heroes," *Modern Philology* 11 [1913–1914] 491–546, esp. 499 and 516).

95. See D. L. Robertson, *Preface to Chaucer* (Princeton, 1962) 191. St. Ambrose inveighs as follows against the disturbing and fallacious information transmitted by the eyes (*De bono mortis* 9.40):

> Vidisti meretricem, captus es vultus eius, et forma decoram putasti: erraverunt oculi tui, perversa viderunt, alia nuntiaverunt. Nam si vere vidissent, vidissent deformem meretricis affectum, inhorentem procaciam, indecentem impudicitiam, marcentes libidines, tetram colluvionem, animae vulnera, conscientiae cicatrices. . . . [qui adulterium requisivit] videre enim quaesivit ut concupisceret, non ut verum cognosceret. Errat igitur oculus, ubi errat affectus. Affectus ergo deceptio est, deceptio visus.

> You see a whore and you are captivated by her face, and you think her body is beautiful: your eyes err, they see perversely, they report other things. For if they had seen truly, they would have seen the ugly passion of a whore, bristly impudence, indecent shamelessness, indolent pleasures, loathsome swill, wounds of the soul, scars of the conscience. . . . [He who searches for adultery,] seeks to see in order to desire, not in order to know the truth. The eye accordingly errs, where passion errs. An act of passion therefore is an act of deception, an act of deception is an act of seeing.

The Latin is quoted from J.-P. Migne, vol. 14 (1982) col. 586.

96. A scholium to 718 indicates that *tempora tria* refers to the past present and future and explains: *praeteritum oblivioni tradidit, praesens non curavit, futurum non prospexit* ("He forgot the past, cared not for the present, and did not look to the future"), *Troilus, ad loc.*

97. Isaiah 42.7, 43.8, 59.9–10; Mark 6.52, 8.17–18.

98. For blindness of heart see Mark 3.5, 6.52, 8.17; for synonymity of *cor* and *mens* see Hebrews 10.16. In Ephesians 1.18 Paul prays that God may give the Ephesians *illuminatos oculos cordis vestri*.

99. tenebris obscurantum habentes intellectum, alienati a vita Dei per ignorantiam, que est in illis, propter caecitatem cordis ipsorum, qui desperantes, semetipsos tradiderunt impudicitiae, in operationem immunditiae omnis in avaritiam.

100. *The Revised Medieval Latin Word List* (London, 1965), the sole Medieval Latin lexicon to contain the verb, defines *tiresio* as "to change sex" and dates it to 1200, which is roughly Albert's time. Unfortunately, this lexicon gives no citations.

101. "Divitiis" 92–93, Boutemy "La version" 271.

102. In fairness it must be noted that Alfred Adler, who discusses the various love stories (Helen and Paris, Troilos, Briseida and Diomedes, and Achilles and Polyxena) in terms of how *Amor* and *Militia* feed on each other and yet destroy each other, apparently sees no Christian message at all in Benoît's account of Achilles' passion for Polyxena. Instead, he sees Achilles' love for Polyxena as the triumph of real (i.e., courtly) love over Achilles' homosexual love for Patroklos and Antilochos ("*Militia et Amor* in the *Roman de Troie*," *Romanische Forschungen* 72 [1960] 23). Adler accepts as a precept for Benoît's world Andreas Capellanus's later (c. 1200) formulation that without courtly love *nihil boni operatur in orbe*, and he sees Achilles' yielding to love as entirely proper (21), as, indeed, is Briseida's yielding to Diomedes (19).

103. *Le Roman de Troie en prose* ed. L. Constans and E. Faral (Paris, 1922) 161.

104. For the bizarre medieval story of Vergil's embarrassing escapade with the Emperor's daughter, see Domenico Comparetti, *Vergil in the Middle Ages*, trans. E. F. M. Benecke (London, 1875; repr. New York 1929) 326–335.

105. *diabolum vero amoris et luxuriae auctorem esse, Scripture referente cognovimus* (*De Amore* 3, ed. S. Bataglia [Rome, 1947] 380). St. Jerome, the great fourth-century expositor and translator of Scripture, gives a lengthy explication of the Devil's intimate connection with the sexual organs (*Epistle* 22 ["To Eustochium"] 11).

106. This evil is mentioned also by Albert, *Troilus* 4.448.

107. *cunctis amor in vita poenam intolerabilis praestat hominibus et maiores in immensum poenas post mortem facit subire defunctos* ("*Amor* imposes unbearable punishment on all men in this life and makes dead men undergo immensely greater punishment after they die") *De Amore* 3, p. 372).

108. The most striking and ethically significant example of the Classical Latin *topos* is Vergil's application of the image to the doomed Dido and Turnus (*Aeneid* 4.1–2, 12.4–5, 45–46). The metaphor is frequent in Ovid's amatory poetry.

109. A sermon written by St. Bonaventure, a respected thirteenth-century theologian, bestows the sanction of the Church on the metaphor: if you go to public celebrations to gaze at women, warns the cardinal, "you must get a deadly wound in your heart" (*toties letale vulnus in corde tuo habuisti*). The statement, from the Sermon *De Sancto Nicolai*, is quoted by Wiggington, 139, n. 15.

110. *Roman de la Rose,* 4567–4569, Lecoy vol. 1, p. 141.

111. Lest we think that submission to marriage eliminates the fault that medieval readers would have seen in Achilles' lustful desire, we should remember that even in marriage carnal delight could scarcely be treated as a *culpa* without *crimen.* So says Andreas *De Amore* 3, p. 378, and he is backed up by the stern pronouncements of Jerome *Ep.* 22.21–22.

112. Guido 23, fols. 91–92, pp. 184–185.

113. *verecundetur cum verbis et amonitionibus ostendendo pericula seculi: diem iudicii: et gaudia paradisi* (*Lilium medicinae* chap. 20; Lowes, 501).

114. Guido 23, fol. 92, p. 185. Sexual gratification is the cure recommended by the Muslim physician Razi (fl. 900), whose works were widely read and cited after being translated into Latin in the thirteenth century (see Lowes, 506–507).

115. Guido 23, fol. 93, pp. 187–188. Achilles makes no such foolish promises in Dares' account but merely hopes that if he refuses to fight the rest of the Greeks will give up and go home (*History* 27). The promise is taken from Dictys' *Journal* 3.3, where Achilles promises Hektor to end the war. Dictys' Achilles does not attempt to carry out his promises, because Hektor immediately escalates his demand to include assassination and betrayal. Guido again links foolishness with *inconsultus calor* in Book Twenty-Seven when he comments that Achilles in accepting Hekabe's summons to the ambush was deceived by *amoris inconsulto calore,* "the inconsiderate heat of love," which deprives the wise of their senses (fol. 101, p. 207).

116. Guido 25, fols. 94–95, pp. 192–193.

117. Guido 25, fol. 95, p. 193.

118. Guido 25, fol. 95, p. 195.

119. Guido 25, fol. 96, p. 195.

120. The bare bones of the embassy scene are found in Dares' *History* 30, and Achilles' sentiments about the stupidity of the war are found in chapter 27. No mention of honor or glory is made in either place.

121. At 18062–18064 Achilles declares that to accomplish his *grant desirier* there is nothing under the sun that he won't do (*soz ciel n'a rien que jo n'en face*), and he does not care if people hate him for it afterwards.

122. Dares himself implies that the motive is simply rescue and does not mention anger (*Historia* 33).

123.   Frendit atrox, quantumque ingens dabat ira, lacertum
         Erigit Eacides ac toto robore nisus
         Iam responsuros parat ictus.

He grinds his teeth savagely, raises his arm to the height of his huge anger, and leaning with all his strength prepares to deliver answering blows.

124. Guido 26, fol. 98, p. 200.

125. Guido 26, fol. 99, p. 202.

CONCLUSION

1. As expounded in *Mythe et épopée. L'idéologie des trois fonctions dans les épopées des peuples indo-européens*, 3 vols. (Paris, 1968, 1971, 1973). See especially vol. 3, p. 203.

2. Georges Dumézil, *Heur et malheur du guerrier* (Paris, 1969) 46. "Disregard" and "defiance" are Alf Hiltebeitel's translations of *méconnaissance* and *mépris* in the English edition of this work: *The Destiny of the Warrior* (Chicago and London, 1970) 43. Subsequent citations will be to the English edition.

3. Dumézil, *The Destiny of the Warrior* 22.

4. See Nagy, *Best of the Achaeans* 26–48.

5. Dumézil *Mythe et épopée* vol. 1, p. 632.

6. Dumézil himself has pointed this out in *Mythe et épopée* vol. 3, p. 633.

7. A. M. Snodgrass, *The Dark Age of Greece* (Edinburgh, 1971) 431–434.

8. See J.-P. Vernant, *The Origins of Greek Thought* (Ithaca, N.Y., 1982) 51. This work was originally published as *Les origines de la pensée grecque* (Paris, 1962).

9. Snodgrass, *Dark Age* 435.

10. Emily Vermeule, *Aspects of Death* 84–93. Vermeule illustrates this "language" with an eighth-century vase painting that depicts two lions devouring a warrior on a battlefield (p. 86, fig. 5).

11. See Nagy, *Best of the Achaeans* 48.

12. Pierre Vidal-Naquet interprets the conflict as one between the values of the city as opposed to those of the family, and he gives Neoptolemos's choosing to desert the army and take Philoktetes home the same political import that Antigone's choosing to bury her brother had in Sophokles' earlier play. "Sophocles' *Philoctetes* and the Ephebeia," *Tragedy and Myth in Ancient Greece*, translated by Janet Lloyd (Sussex and New Jersey, 1981) 185.

13. Dumézil, *The Stakes of the Warrior*, trans. David Weeks (Berkeley and Los Angeles, 1983) 123–133.

14. Vidal-Naquet, *op. cit.* 186–187.

15. Roland Barthes, *Mythologies*, trans. A. Lavers (New York, 1972) 142, 131. For how one unmasks such a myth, see 135.

16. Atwood and Whitaker, xlvi and notes.

17. The prose *Roman*, composed about 1250, was widely copied and was substituted for the original translation of Dares in the *Histoire ancienne jusqu'à Cesar*, a work that remained popular through the fifteenth century (see Paul Meyer, "Les Premières compilations françaises d'Histoire ancienne," *Romania* 14 [1885] 1–81).

18. The *Historia troyana en prosa y verso* was composed in 1270 (published by R. Menéndez Pidal, Madrid, 1934). In addition, the historians commissioned by Alfonso the Wise (ruler of Leon and Castille from 1252 to 1284) to write the

vernacular *General estoria* (published by Solalinde, Kasten, and Oelschläger, Madrid, 1961) used Benoît as their source for the Trojan events.

19. The *Leit von Troye* by Herbort of Fritslar was composed between 1210 and 1217 (published by G. Fromman, Leipzig, 1837), and the *Trojanische Krieg* by Konrad of Würzburg was left uncompleted in 1287 (its 40,000 verses have been published by A. von Keller, Stuttgart, 1858).

20. The *Intellegenzia,* composed probably in the late thirteenth century in Florence, contains 423 verses devoted to the Trojan War that used Benoît as source. The verses are printed in *Documents inédits pour servir à l'histoire littéraire de l'Italie depuis le VIIIe siècle jusqu'au XIIIe,* ed. A. F. Ozanam (Paris, 1850), pp. 391–401.

21. Georges Duby, *The Three Orders: Feudal Society Imagined,* trans. A. Gold-hammer (Chicago, 1980), pp. 298–299.

22. Chap. 136; *Roman de Troie en prose* 108.

23. Georges Duby, *Le chevalier, la femme et le prêtre* (Paris, 1981), pp. 242–244.

24. Duby, *The Chivalrous Society,* trans. C. Postan (Los Angeles, 1980), pp. 47–49.

25. Duby, *The Three Orders* 45–47, 302–303.

26. This passage occurs in the second half of the *Roman de Troie en prose* that Constans and Faral failed to publish. The text I print here is based on my own reading of Paris Bibliothèque Nationale French Mss. 1612 (fols. 98v–99r) and 1627 (61v), both transcribed in the late thirteenth century. My translation was aided by an Italian translation in a manuscript (Paris Bibliothèque Nationale Italian Ms. 120, fols. 83v–84r) transcribed in the fifteenth century. The passage is interjected by Benoît's abridger before Achilles' death, just after he has accepted Hekabe's proposal. The sentiment receives further explicit expression in fifteenth-century England by John Lydgate (*Troy Book* 3213–3222), who also co-opts God as Paris' partner in killing Achilles.

27. Christa Wolf, *Cassandra,* trans. Jan van Heurck (New York, 1984) 9.

BIBLIOGRAPHY

Adkins, Arthur. *Merit and Responsibility: A Study in Greek Values.* Oxford, 1960.

———. "Basic Greek Values in Euripides' *Hecuba* and *Hercules Furens.*" *Classical Quarterly,* 60 (1966) 193–219.

———. "Values, Goals, and Emotions in the *Iliad.*"*Classical Philology* 77 (1982) 292–325.

Adler, Alfred. "*Militia et Amor* in the *Roman de Troie.*" *Romanische Forschungen* 72 (1960) 14–29.

Aischylos. *Aeschylus.* Edited and translated by H. W. Smythe and H. Lloyd-Jones. Vol. 2. Cambridge, Mass., 1957.

———. *Myrmidons, Nereides, Phrygians:* Fragments. In *Tragicorum Graecorum Fragmenta* (see Nauck) 42–47, 49–50, 84–87.

Alarcos Llorach, E. *Investigaciones sobre el Libro de Alexandre.* Madrid, 1948.

Albert of Stade. *Troilus.* Edited by T. Merzdorf. Leipzig, 1875.

Alexiou, Margaret, and Peter Dronke. "The Lament of Jephtha's Daughter: Themes, Tradition, Originality." *Studi Medievali,* 3d ser., 12, no. 2 (1971) 819–863.

Alfonso el Sabio. *General estoria.* Edited by A. G. Solalinde, L. A. Kasten, and V. R. Oelschläger. Vol. 2, pt. 2. Madrid, 1961.

Andersen, Øivind. "Some Thoughts on the Shield of Achilles." *Symbolae Osloenses* 51 (1976) 5–18.

Andreas, Capellanus. *De Amore.* Edited by Salvatore Bataglia. Rome, 1947.

———. *The Art of Courtly Love.* Translated by John J. Parry. New York, 1941.

d'Anto, Vicenzo. *L. Accio. I frammenti delle tragedie.* Leece, 1980.

Apollonios of Rhodes. *Argonautica.* Edited by Robert C. Seaton. Oxford, 1929.

Aristophanes. *Clouds.* Edited by K. J. Dover. Oxford, 1970.

———. *Aristophanes: Five Comedies.* The Living Library. Cleveland, 1948.

Armstrong, James I. "The Arming Motif in the Iliad." *American Journal of Philology* 79 (1958) 337–354.

Arthur, Marilyn B. "Origins of the Western Attitude toward Women." *Arethusa* 6 (1973) 7–58.

Atwood, E. Bagby. "The Story of Achilles in the *Seege of Troye*." *Studies in Philology* 39 (1942) 489–501.

Atwood, E. Bagby, and Virgil K. Whitaker, eds. *Excidium Troiae*. Cambridge, Mass., 1944.

Austin, Colin. *Euripidea nova fragmenta in papyris reperta*. Berlin, 1968.

Austin, R. G. *P. Vergili Maronis Aeneidos Liber Secundus*. Oxford, 1966.

――――. *P. Vergili Maronis Aeneidos Liber Sextus*. Oxford, 1977.

Bain, D. "The Prologues of Euripides' *Iphigeneia in Aulis*." *Classical Quarterly* 71 (1977) 10–26.

Barlow, Shirley A. *The Imagery of Euripides: A Study in the Dramatic Use of Pictorial Language*. London, 1971.

Barnicle, Mary E. Introduction and Appendix B. *The Seege or Batayle of Troye*. London, 1927.

Barthes, Roland. *Mythologies*. Translated by A. Lavers. New York, 1972.

Bassett, Samuel E. "Achilles' Treatment of Hector's Body." *Transactions of the American Philological Association* 64 (1933) 41–65.

――――. "The Ἁμαρτία of Achilles." *Transactions of the American Philological Association* 65 (1934) 48–69.

Beazley, J. D. *The Development of Attic Black-Figure*. Berkeley and Los Angeles, 1951.

――――. *Attic Red-Figure Vase-Painters*. 2d ed. Oxford, 1963.

Benardete, Seth. "Achilles and the *Iliad*." *Hermes* 91 (1963) 1–16.

Benoît de Sainte-Maure. *Le Roman de Troie*. 6 vols. Edited by Leopold Constans. Paris, 1904–1912.

Benveniste, Emile. *Indo-European Language and Society*. Translated by Elizabeth Palmer. London and Coral Gables, Florida, 1973.

Bernardus. *The Commentary on the First Six Books of the Aeneid of Vergil Commonly Attributed to Bernardus Silvestris: A New Critical Edition*. Edited by J. W. Jones and E. F. Jones. Lincoln, Nebraska, 1977.

Berrigan, J. R. "The Trojan War in the *Chronicon* of Benzo d'Alessandria." *Classical Journal* 61 (1966) 219–221.

Berschin, Walter. *Griechisch-Lateinisches Mittelalter von Hieronymus zu Nikolaus von Kues*. Bern and Munich, 1980.

Bespaloff, Rachel. *On the Iliad*. Translated by Mary McCarthy. Washington, D.C., 1947.

Bion. *Bucolici Graeci*. Edited by A. S. F. Gow. Pp. 153–165. Oxford, 1952.

Bischoff, B. "The Study of Foreign Languages in the Middle Ages." *Mittelalterliche Studien* 2 (1967) 227–245.

Bly, P. A., and A. D. Deyermond. "The Use of *figura* in the *Libro de Alexandre*." *Journal of Medieval and Renaissance Studies* 2 (1972) 151–181.

Bock, C. P. "Lettres à M. L. Bethman sur un manuscrit de bibliothèque de

Bourgogne, intitulé *Liber Guidonis.*" *Annuaire de la bibliothèque royale de Belgique* 12 (1851) 43–204.

Bolgar, R. R. *Classical Influences on European Culture, A.D. 500–1500.* Cambridge, 1971.

————. *The Classical Heritage and Its Beneficiaries.* Cambridge, 1954; repr. 1977.

Borchardt, Frank L. *German Antiquity in Renaissance Myth.* Baltimore, 1971.

Boutemy, André. "Autour de Godefroid de Reims." *Latomus* 6 (1947) 231–255.

————. "Le poème 'Pergama flere volo' et ses imitateurs du XIIeme siècle." *Latomus* 5 (1946) 233–244.

————, ed. "Trois oeuvres inédites de Godefroid de Reims." *Revue du Moyen Age Latin* 3 (1947) 335–366.

————. "La version parisienne du poème de Simon Chèvre d'Or sur la guerre de Troie (Ms. Lat. 8430)." *Scriptorium* 1 (1946–1947) 267–288.

Brand, Charles Peter. *Torquato Tasso: A Study of the Poet and of His Contributions to English Literature.* Cambridge, 1965.

Brooks, Robert A. *Ennius and Roman Tragedy.* Salem, New Hampshire, 1984.

Brown, Peter. *The Cult of the Saints: Its Rise and Function in Latin Christianity.* Chicago, 1981.

Buchthal, Hugo. *Historia Troiana: Studies in the History of Medieval Secular Illustration.* London, 1971.

Buffière, Félix. *Les Mythes d'Homère et la pensée grecque.* Paris, 1956.

Bury, J. B. *The Nemean Odes of Pindar.* London, 1890.

Camps, W. A. *An Introduction to Virgil's Aeneid.* Oxford, 1969.

Cañas Murillo, J. Introduction and notes to *Libro de Alexandre.* Madrid, 1978.

Carlesso, Giuliana. "La versione Sud del 'Roman de Troie en prose' e il volgarizzamento di Binduccion dello Scelto." In *Atti dell'Istituto veneto di Scienze Lettere ed Arti.* Vol. 124 (1965–1966) 519–560.

Carmina Latina Epigraphia. Vols. 1 and 2. Edited by Franz Buecheler. Leipzig, 1895–1897.

Cartault, Augustin. *L'Art de Virgile dans l'Énéide.* Paris, 1926.

Caxton, William. *The Recuyell of the Historyes of Troye.* Vol. 2. Edited by H. Oskar Sommer. London, 1894.

Chantraine, P. *Dictionnaire étymologique de la langue grecque.* 4 vols. Paris, 1968–1980.

————. *Grammaire homérique.* Vol. 2. Paris, 1963.

Ciaceri, E. *La Alessandra di Licofrone: testo, traauzione, e commento.* Catania, 1901.

Cicero. *M. Tulli Ciceronis Tusculanae Disputationes.* Edited by Michelangelo Giusta. Turin, 1984.

Clarke, Howard. *Homer's Readers: A Historical Introduction to the Iliad and the Odyssey.* Brunswick, N.J., 1981.

Claus, David B. "*Aidōs* in the Language of Achilles." *Transactions of the American Philological Association* 105 (1975) 13–28.

Clogan, Paul M. *The Medieval Achilleid of Statius, edited with introduction, variant readings, and glosses.* Leiden, 1968.

Coffey, Michael. "The Function of the Homeric Simile." *American Journal of Philology* 78 (1957) 113–132.

Collilieux, E. *Étude sur Dictys de Crête et Darès de Phrygie.* Grenoble, 1886.

Comparetti, Dominico. *Virgil in the Middle Ages.* Translated by E. F. M. Benecke. London, 1875; repr. New York, 1929.

Conacher, D. J. "Euripides' *Hecuba*." *American Journal of Philology* 82 (1961) 1–26.

Considine, P. "Some Homeric Terms for Anger." *Acta Classica* 9 (1966) 15–25.

Constans, L. See Benoît de Sainte-Maure.

Constans, L., and E. Faral. See *Roman de Troie en prose.*

Couat, Auguste. *La Poésie Alexandrine sous les trois premiers Ptolemées, 324–322 av. J.-C.* Paris, 1882; repr. Brussels, 1968.

Crotty, Kevin. *Song and Action: The Victory Odes of Pindar.* Baltimore, 1982.

Cunliffe, R. J. *A Lexicon of the Homeric Dialect.* London, 1924; repr. Norman, Okla., 1963.

Curran, Leo C. "Catullus 64 and the Heroic Age." *Yale Classical Studies* 21 (1969) 171–192.

Curtius, Ernst R. *European Literature and the Latin Middle Ages.* New York, 1953.

Daretis Phrygii De Excidio Troiae Historia. Edited by Ferdinand Meister. Leipzig, 1873.

Davison, J. A. "Peisistratos and Homer." *Transactions of the American Philological Association* 86 (1955) 1–21.

de Blasi, Nicola. "Il rifacimento napoletano trecentesco dell'Historia Destructionis Troiae." *Medioeva Romanzo* 6 (1979) 98–134.

Delebecque, Édouard. *Euripide et la guerre du Péloponnèse.* Paris, 1951.

de Lorris, Guillaume and Jean de Meun. *Le Roman de la rose.* 2 vols. Edited by Félix Lecoy. Paris, 1968.

de Marco, Maria. "Un 'Planctus' sulla morte di Ettore." *Aevum* 29 (1955) 119–123.

Denniston, J. D. *Electra.* Oxford, 1939; repr. 1968.

———. *The Greek Particles.* 2d. ed. Oxford, 1954; repr. 1966.

Detienne, Marcel. *Dionysos Slain.* Translated by Mireille Muellner and Leonard Muellner. Baltimore, 1979.

———. "Entre bêtes et dieux." *Nouvelle revue de psychanalyse* 6 (1972) 231–246. Reprinted and translated as chapter 3 of *Dionysos Slain.*

Dictys Cretensis Ephemeridos Belli Troiani Libri a Lucio Septimo ex Graeco in Latinum Sermonem Translati. Edited by Werner Eisenhut. Leipzig, 1958.

Dictys Cretensis Ephemeridos Belli Troiani Libri Sex. Edited by Ferdinand Meister. Leipzig, 1872.

BIBLIOGRAPHY

Diehl, Ernst. *Anthologia Lyrica Graeca.* 3d ed. Leipzig, 1954–1955.

Dilke, O. A. W. "'Magnus Achilles' and Statian Baroque." *Latomus* 22 (1963) 498–503.

Dimock, G. E., Jr. Introduction to *Euripides: Iphigeneia at Aulis.* New York, 1978. 3–21.

Dio Chrysostomos. *Dionis Chrysostomi Orationes.* Edited by G. de Bude. Leipzig, 1916.

Dolce, Lodovico. *L'Achille et l'Enea.* Vinegia, 1572.

Dover, K. J. Introduction and commentary. *Aristophanes: Clouds.* Oxford, 1970.

Dronke, E. P. M. *Poetic Individuality in the Middle Ages: New Departures in Poetry, 1000–1150.* Oxford, 1970.

———. "Functions of Classical Borrowing in Medieval Latin Verse." In R. R. Bolgar, ed., *Classical Influences on European Culture.* Cambridge, 1971. 159–164.

Duby, Georges. *Le chevalier, la femme et le prêtre.* Paris, 1981.

———. *The Chivalrous Society.* Translated by Cynthia Postan. Berkeley and Los Angeles, 1980.

———. *The Three Orders. Feudal Society Imagined.* Translated by Arthur Goldhammer. Chicago: 1980.

Dumézil, Georges. *Heur et malheur du guerrier.* Paris, 1969. (Translated by Alf Hiltebeitel as *The Destiny of the Warrior.* Chicago, 1970.)

———. *Mythe et épopée. L'idéologie des trois fonctions dans les épopées des peuples indo-européens.* 3 vols. Paris, 1968–1973.

———. *The Stakes of the Warrior.* Translated by David Weeks. Berkeley and Los Angeles, 1983.

Durling, Robert M. "The Epic Ideal." In *The Old World: Discovery and Rebirth.* Edited by D. Daiches and A. Thorlby. London, 1974.

Ennius, Quintus. *Ennianae Poesis Reliquiae.* Edited by Ioannes Vahlen. Leipzig, 1928.

Epicorum Graecorum Fragmenta. Edited by Godfrey Kinkel. Leipzig, 1877.

Epigrammata Graeca. Edited by G. Kaibel. Berlin, 1878.

Erbse, Hartmut, ed. *Scholia Graeca in Homeri Iliadem.* Vol. 5. Berlin, 1977.

Escher-Burkli, J. "Achilleus." In Pauly, Wissowa, Kroll (see below), vol. 1.1 (1890) cols. 221–245.

Euripidea nova fragmenta. See Austin, Colin.

Excidium Troiae. Edited by E. Bagby Atwood and V. K. Whitaker. Cambridge, Mass., 1944.

Fantham, Elaine. *Seneca's Troades: A Literary Introduction with Text, Translation, and Commentary.* Princeton, 1982.

———. "Statius' Achilles and His Trojan Model." *Classical Quarterly* 73 (1974) 457–462.

Faral, E. "Le manuscrit 511 du 'Hunterian Museum' de Glasgow." *Studi Medievali* n.s. 9 (1936) 18–121.

Farnell, Lewis R. *Greek Hero Cults and Ideas of Immortality.* Oxford, 1921.

———. *The Works of Pindar.* 3 vols. London, 1930–1932.

Fenik, Bernard. *"Iliad X" and "The Rhesus," The Myth.* Brussels, 1964.

———. "Stylization and Variety: Four Monologues in the Iliad." In *Homer: Tradition and Invention,* edited by Bernard Fenik, 68–90. Leiden, 1978.

———. *Typical Battle Scenes in the Iliad: Studies in the Narrative Techniques of Homeric Battle Descriptions.* Wiesbaden, 1968. (= *Hermes Einzelschriften* 21.)

Ferguson, John. "*Iphigeneia at Aulis.*" *Transactions of the American Philological Association* 99 (1968) 157–163.

Finlay, Robert. "Patroklos, Achilleus, and Peleus: Fathers and Sons in the *Iliad.*" *Classical World* 73 (1980) 267–273.

Finley, John H., Jr. *Pindar and Aeschylus.* Cambridge, Mass., 1955.

Fleischer, C. "Achilleus." In Roscher, *Ausfürliches Lexicon,* vol. 1.1. (1884–1886) cols. 11–66.

Fontinoy, C. "Le sacrifice nuptial de Polyxène." *L'Antiquité Classique* 19 (1950) 383–396.

Fordyce, Christian J. *Catullus.* Oxford, 1961.

Förster, Richard. "Achilleus und Polyxena. Zwei unedirte Deklamationen des Choricius." *Hermes* 17 (1882) 193–238.

———. "Zu Achilleus und Polyxena." *Hermes* 18 (1883) 475–478.

Fraccaroli, Giuseppe. *Le Odi di Pindaro.* Verona, 1894.

Fragmenta Poetarum Latinorum Epicorum et Lyricorum Praeter Ennium et Lucilium. Edited by W. Morel. Stuttgart, 1927; repr. Leipzig, 1982.

Fränkel, Hermann. *Die homerischen Gleichnisse.* Göttingen, 1921.

Frazer, J. G. Translation and commentary to *Apollodorus. The Library.* 2 vols. Cambridge, Mass., 1921.

Frazer, R. M., Jr. *The Trojan War: The Chronicles of Dictys of Crete and Dares the Phrygian.* Bloomington, Ind., 1966.

Friedman, Lionel. "Gradus Amoris." *Romance Philology* 19 (1965) 167–177.

Friis Johansen, K. *The Iliad in Early Greek Art.* Copenhagen, 1967.

Fulgentius, Fabius Planciades. *Expositio Vergilianae Continentiae.* Translated and with introduction by Lynn C. Stokes. *Classical Folia* 26 (1972) 28–63.

———. *Fabii Planciadis Fulgentii V.C. Opera.* Edited by Rudolf W. O. Helm. Leipzig, 1898.

Giangrande, Giuseppe. "Das Epyllion Catulls im Lichte der hellenistischen Epik." *L'Antiquité Classique* 41 (1972) 123–147.

Gill, D. "*Trapezomata:* A Neglected Aspect of Greek Sacrifice." *Harvard Theological Review* 67 (1974) 117–137.

Gompf, Ludwig. See Joseph of Exeter.

Goodwin, William Watson. *Syntax of the Moods and Tenses of the Greek Verb*. 1875; repr. New York, 1965.

Gorra, Egidio. *Testi inediti di storia trojana preceduti da uno studio sulla leggenda trojana in Italia*. Turin, 1887.

Der Göttweiger Trojanerkrieg. Edited by Alfred Koppitz. Berlin, 1926. (= *Deutsche Texte des Mittelalters* 29.)

Gow, A. S. F., and D. Page. *The Greek Anthology: The Garland of Philip and Some Contemporary Epigrams*. Vol. 1. London, 1968.

Greek Literary Papyri. Vol. 1. Edited and translated by D. L. Page. Cambridge, 1942.

Greene, Thomas. *The Descent from Heaven: A Study in Epic Continuity*. New Haven, 1963.

Greengard, Carola. *The Structure of Pindar's Epinician Odes*. Amsterdam, 1980.

Griffin, Jasper. "The Epic Cycle and the Uniqueness of Homer." *Journal of Hellenic Studies* 97 (1977) 39–53.

———. *Homer on Life and Death*. Oxford, 1980.

Griffin, Nathaniel E. *Dares and Dictys: An Introduction to the Study of Medieval Versions of the Story of Troy*. Baltimore, 1907.

———. "The Greek Dictys." *American Journal of Philology* 29 (1908) 329–335.

Grube, G. M. A. *The Drama of Euripides*. London, 1941.

Guido de Columnis (Guido delle Colonne). *Historia Destructionis Troiae*. Edited by N. E. Griffin. Cambridge, Mass., 1936. (= Medieval Academy of America Publications, no. 26.)

———. *Historia Destructionis Troiae*. Translated and edited by Elizabeth Meek. Bloomington, 1974.

Handley, E. W., and John Rea. "The *Telephus* of Euripides." *University of London Bulletin of the Institute of Classical Studies*. Suppl. 5 (1957).

Harrison, Jane E. *Themis: A Study of the Social Origins of Greek Religion*. Cambridge, 1912.

Hartigan, K. V. "'He Rose like a Lion': Animal Similes in Homer and Vergil." *Acta Antiqua* 21 (1973) 223–244.

Hartung, A. E., ed. *A Manual of the Writings in Middle English, 1050–1500*. Vol. 6. Hamden, 1980.

Hemker, Julie. "Rape and the Founding of Rome." *Helios* 12 (1985) 41–47.

Herbort von Fritslar. *Herbort's von Fritslâr Liet von Troye*. Edited by Georg K. Fromman. Quedlinburg and Leipzig, 1837.

Hesiod. *Hesiodi Theogonia Opera et Dies Scutum*. Edited by F. Solmsen. *Fragmenta Selecta*. Edited by R. Merkelbach and M. L. West. 2d ed. Oxford, 1983.

Hirsch, E. D., Jr. "Objective Interpretation." *Publications of the Modern Language Association* 75 (1960) 463–479.

Histoire de la destruction de Troie. Geneva, 1481. British Library, Department of Printed Books, press mark IB.38427.

Histoire de la guerre de Troye (= *Le Roman de Troie en prose*). Paris, Bibliothèque Nationale, French Manuscripts 1612 and 1627.

Historia troyana. Edited by Kelvin M. Parker. Santiago de Compostela, 1975.

Historia troyana en prosa y verso texto de hacia 1270. Edited by R. Menendez Pidal. Madrid, 1934.

Hogan, James C. "Thucydides 3.52–68 and Euripides' *Hecuba.*" *Phoenix* 26 (1972) 241–257.

Homer. *Iliad.* In *Homeri Opera,* 3d ed., vols. 1–2, edited by D. B. Monro and T. W. Allen. Oxford, 1920.

———. *Odyssey.* In *Homeri Opera,* 2d ed, vols. 3–4, edited by T. W. Allen. Oxford, 1917, 1919.

Homeric Hymns. In *Homeri Opera,* vol. 5, edited by T. W. Allen, 1–92. Oxford, 1912.

Horace (Quintus Horatius Flaccus). *Satires and Epistles.* Edited by Edward P. Morris. 1939; repr. Okla., 1967.

Hugo of St. Victor. "Sermon 38." In *Patrologia Cursus Completus: Series Completa.* Vol. 77, cols. 994–999. Edited by J.-P. Migne. 221 vols. Paris, 1841–1902.

Hyginus. *Hygini Fabulae.* Edited by H. J. Rose. Leiden, 1934.

Ilias Latina. Italici Ilias Latina. Edited by Frederic Plessis. Paris, 1885.

Inscriptiones Creticae. Edited by Margherita Guarducci. Rome, 1935–.

"La 'Istorietta Troiana'." Edited by Mario Marti and Cesare Segre. In *La Prosa del Duecento.* Milan, 1959.

Jaeger, Werner. *Paedeia: The Ideals of Greek Culture.* Vol. 1. Translated by Gilbert Highet. New York, 1965.

Jauss, Hans Robert. *Aesthetic Experience and Literary Hermeneutics.* Translated by Michael Shaw. Minneapolis, 1982.

Jebb, R. C. *The Philoctetes.* Part 4 of *Sophocles: The Plays and Fragments.* Cambridge, 1890.

Jenkyns, Richard. *Three Classical Poets: Sappho, Catullus and Juvenal.* London, 1982.

Jocelyn, H. D. *The Tragedies of Ennius. The fragments edited with an introduction and commentary.* Cambridge, 1967.

Johnson, W. R. *Darkness Visible: A Study of Vergil's Aeneid.* Berkeley and Los Angeles, 1976.

Joly, M. A. *Benoît de Sainte More et le Roman de Troie.* Paris, 1870.

Joseph of Exeter. *The Iliad of Dares Phrygius.* Translated by Gildas Roberts. Cape Town, 1970.

———. *Joseph Iscanus: Werke und Briefe.* Edited by Ludwig Gompf. Leiden, 1970.

Jouan, François. *Euripide et les légends des chants cypriens. Des origines de la guerre de Troie à l'Iliade*. Paris, 1966.

Kaibel, Georg. *Epigrammata Graeca ex lapidus conlecta*. Berlin, 1878.

Kakridis, Johannes. *Homeric Researches*. Lund, 1949.

Kates, Judith A. "The Revaluation of the Classical Heroic in Tasso and in Milton." *Comparative Literature* 26 (1974) 299–317.

Kemp-Lindemann, Dagmar. *Darstellungen des Achilleus in griechischer und römischer Kunst*. Bern and Frankfurt, 1975.

King, Katherine Callen. "Foil and Fusion: Homer's Achilles in Vergil's *Aeneid*." *Materiali et discussioni per l'analisi dei testi classici* 7 (1983) 31–57.

———. "The Force of Tradition: The Achilles Ode in Euripides' *Electra*." *Transactions of the American Philological Association* 110 (1980) 195–212.

———. "The Politics of Imitation: Euripides' *Hekabe* and the Homeric Achilles." *Arethusa* 18 (1985) 47–66.

Kirk, Geoffrey S. *The Songs of Homer*. Cambridge, 1962.

Kitto, H. D. F. *Greek Tragedy: A Literary Study*. New York, 1950.

Klingner, Friedrich. "Catulls Peleus-Epos." *Sitzungsberichte der Bayerischen Akademie der Wissenschaften* 6 (1956) 1–92.

Knapp, Gerhard P. *Hector und Achills; Die Rezeption des Trojastoffes im deutschen Mittelalter*. Bern, 1974.

Knight, W. F. J. "Iliupersides." *Classical Quarterly* 26 (1932) 178–189.

Knox, Alfred D. *Herodes, Cercidas and the Greek Choliambic Poets (Except Callimachus and Babrius)*. Cambridge, Mass., 1946.

Knox, Bernard M. W. "Euripides' *Iphigenia in Aulide* 1–163 (in that order)." *Yale Classical Studies* 22 (1972) 239–261.

———. *The Heroic Temper: Studies in Sophoclean Tragedy*. Berkeley and Los Angeles, 1964.

———. "The Serpent and the Flame." In *Virgil: A Collection of Critical Essays*. Edited by Steele Commager. Englewood Cliffs, N.J., 1966. Originally printed in *American Journal of Philology* 71 (1950) 374–400.

Konrad von Würzburg. *Der Trojanische Krieg*. Edited by A. von Keller. Stuttgart, 1858. (= *Bibliothek des Litterarischen Vereins in Stuttgart* 44.)

Korn, Otto, and Michael von Albrecht. *Ovid: Metamorphosen*. Vol. 2. Edited and with commentary by Otto Korn. Zurich and Dublin, 1966.

Krischer, Tilman. *Formale Konventionen der homerischen Epik*. Munich, 1971. (= *Zetemata* 56.)

Kroll, Wilhelm. *C. Valerius Catullus*. Leipzig, 1923; repr. Stuttgart, 1959.

Latham, R. E., ed. *Revised Medieval Latin Word List from British and Irish Sources*. London, 1965.

Lattimore, Richmond. *The Iliad of Homer*. Chicago, 1951; repr. 1970.

———. *Themes in Greek and Latin Epitaphs*. Urbana, 1962.

The Laud Troy Book: A Romance of About 1400 A.D. Edited by J. E. Wulfing. London, 1902.

Lawler, Lillian B. "Some Lesser Lights." *Classical Journal* 30 (1934) 62–77.

Leaf, Walter, ed. *The Iliad.* 2d ed. 2 vols. 1900, 1902; repr. Amsterdam, 1971.

Lefkowitz, Mary R. *The Victory Ode: An Introduction.* Park Ridge, N.J., 1976.

"Leomarte." *Sumas de historia troyana.* Edited by A. Rey. Madrid, 1932.

Lesky, Albin. *Greek Tragedy.* Translated by H. A. Frankfort. London and New York, 1975.

———. *A History of Greek Literature.* Translated by James Willis and Cornelis de Heer. London, 1966.

Levenson, J. T. "The narrative format of Benoît's *Roman de Troie.*" *Romania* (1979) 54–70.

Lexicon Iconographicum Mythologiae Classicae. Vol. 1, pts. 1 and 2. Zurich, 1981.

Libro de Alexandre. Edited by J. Cañas Murillo. Madrid, 1978.

Lida de Malkiel, M. R. *La idea de fama en la edad media castellana.* Mexico and Buenos Aires, 1952.

Lloyd-Jones, H. *The Justice of Zeus.* Berkeley and Los Angeles, 1971.

Long, A. A. "Morals and Values in Homer." *Journal of Hellenic Studies* 90 (1970) 121–139.

Lord, Albert B. *The Singer of Tales.* Cambridge, Mass., 1960.

Lowes, John Livingston. "The Loveres Maladye of Hereos." *Modern Philology* 11 (1913–1914) 491–546.

Luschnig, C. A. E. "Euripides' *Hecabe:* The Time is Out of Joint." *Classical Journal* 71 (1975–1976) 227–234.

Lydgate, John. *Lydgate's Troy Book, A.D. 1412–20.* Edited by H. Bergen. *Early English Text Society* Extra Series vols. 97 (1906), 103 (1908), and 106 (1910).

Lykophron. *Alexandra.* Edited by L. Mascialino. Leipzig, 1964.

———. *The Alexandra of Lycophron.* Edited and translated by George W. Mooney. London, 1921; repr. New York, 1979.

MacCary, W. T. *Childlike Achilles: Ontogeny and Philogeny in the Iliad.* New York, 1982.

Marg, W. "Kampf und Tod in der Ilias." *Die Antike* 18 (1942) 167–179. (Revised and expanded in *Würzburger Jahrbücher für die Altertumswissenschaft,* n.s. 2 [1976] 7–19.)

Mazzatini, G. "La *Fiorita* di Armannino Giudice." *Giornale di Filologia Romanza* 3 (1880) 1–55.

Méridier, Louis. *Euripide.* Vol. 2. Paris, 1956.

Meyer, Paul. "Les premières compilations françaises d'Histoire ancienne." *Romania* 14 (1885) 1–81.

Meyer, William. "Die Oxforder Gedichte des Primas (des Magisters Hugo von Orleans). II: no. 1–15 und no. 23." In *Nachrichten von der Königlichen Gesell-*

schaft der Wissenschaften zu Göttingen. Philologisch-historische Klasse aus dem Jahre 1907, 113–230. Berlin, 1907.

Michael, Ian. "The Description of Hell in the Spanish *Libro de Alexandre.*" In *Medieval Miscellany Presented to Eugene Vinaver,* edited by F. Whitehead, A. H. Diverres, and F. E. Sutcliffe, 220–229. Manchester, 1965.

———. *The Treatment of Classical Material in the Libro de Alexandre.* Manchester, 1970.

Monumenta Asiae Minoris Antiqua. Vol. 2. London, 1928–.

Moore, John C. *Love in Twelfth-Century France.* Philadelphia, 1972.

Morel, Willy. See *Fragmenta Poetarum Latinorum.*

Morel-Fatio, A. "Recherches sur le texte et les sources du *Libro de Alexandre.*" *Romania* 4 (1875) 7–90.

Moulton, Carroll. *Similes in the Homeric Poems.* Gottingen, 1977. (= *Hypomnemata* 49.)

Muellner, Leonard. *The Meaning of Homeric* ΈΥΧΟΜΑΙ *Through Its Formulas.* Innsbruck, 1976.

Murray, Gilbert. *Euripides and His Age.* New York, 1913.

Nagler, Michael N. *Spontaneity and Tradition: A Study in the Oral Art of Homer.* Berkeley and Los Angeles, 1979.

Nagy, Gregory. *The Best of the Achaeans: Concepts of The Hero in Archaic Greek Poetry.* Baltimore, 1979.

———. *Comparative Studies in Greek and Indic Meter.* Cambridge, Mass., 1974.

Nauck, A. *Tragicorum Graecorum Fragmenta.* Leipzig, 1889.

Nethercut, William R. "The Epic Journey of Achilles." *Ramus* 5 (1976) 1–17.

———. "The Imagery of the *Aeneid.*" *Classical Journal* 67 (1971–1972) 123–143.

Nock, A. D. "The Cult of Heroes." *Harvard Theological Review* 37 (1944) 141–173.

Nonius. *Nonii Marcelli Peripatetici Tubursicensis De Compendiosa Doctrina* Edited by Louis Quicherat. Paris, 1872.

Notopoulos, James A. "Homeric Similes in the Light of Oral Poetry." *Classical Journal* 52 (1957) 323–328.

O'Brien, Michael J. "Orestes and the Gorgon: Euripides' *Electra.*" *American Journal of Philology* 85 (1964) 13–39.

Ogilvie, Robert M. *A Commentary on Livy: Books 1–5.* Oxford, 1965.

Origen. *Contre Celse.* Vol. 2. Edited by Marcel Borret. Paris, 1968.

Otis, Brooks. "The Originality of the Aeneid." In *Virgil,* edited by Donald R. Dudley, 27–66. London, 1964.

Otto of Freising. *Chronica Sive Historia de Duabis Civitatibus.* Edited by Adolfus Hofmeister. Hanover, 1912.

———. *The Two Cities: A Chronicle of Universal History to the Year 1146 A.D.* Translated by C. C. Mierow. New York, 1928.

Ovidius Naso, Publius. *Metamorphoses.* Edited by Rudolfus Ehwald. Leipzig, 1916.

————. *P. Ovidi Nasonis Amores, Medicamina Facei Femineae, Ars Amatoria, Remedia Amoris.* Edited by E. J. Kenney. Oxford, 1973.

Owen, E. T. *The Story of the Iliad.* 1946; repr. Ann Arbor, 1966.

Ozanam, Antoine F. *Documents inédits pour servir a l'histoire littéraire de l'Italie depuis le VIIIᵉ siècle jusqu'au XIIIᵉ.* Paris, 1850.

Pacati, Carlo. "Il significato della guerra troiana nell'opera di Euripide." *Dioniso* 40 (1966) 77–94.

Page, D. L. *Sappho and Alcaeus: An Introduction to the Study of Ancient Lesbian Poetry.* Oxford, 1955; repr. 1965.

Painter, Sidney. *French Chivalry: Chivalric Ideas and Practices in Medieval France.* Baltimore and Ithaca, 1964.

Panofsky, Erwin. *Studies in Iconology: Humanistic Themes in the Art of the Renaissance.* 1939; repr. New York, 1969.

Parry, Adam. "Have We Homer's *Iliad?*" *Yale Classical Studies* 20 (1966) 177–216.

————. "Language and Characterization in Homer." *Harvard Studies in Classical Philology* 76 (1972) 1–22.

————. "The Language of Achilles." *Transactions of the American Philological Association* 87 (1956) 1–7.

Parry, Milman. *The Making of Homeric Verse: The Collected Papers of Milman Parry.* Edited and with introduction by Adam Parry. Oxford, 1971.

Patrologia Latina. Patrologiae Cursus Completus: Series Latina. Vol. 171. Edited by J.-P. Migne. Paris, 1893.

Pauly, A., G. Wissowa, and W. Kroll. *Real-Encyclopädie der klassischen Altertumswissenschaft.* Stuttgart, 1890–.

Pearson, A. C. *The Fragments of Sophocles.* 3 vols. Cambridge, 1917.

Peek, Werner. *Griechische Vers-Inschiften.* Vol. 1. Berlin, 1955.

"Pergama flare volo." In *Carmina Burana,* edited by Alfons Hilka and Otto Schumann, vol. 1, pt. 2, no. 101, pp. 139–141. Heidelberg, 1941.

Philostratus, Flavius. *Flavius Philostratus Heroicus.* Edited by L. de Lannoy. Leipzig, 1977.

Philostratus, Lemnius. *Philostrati Maioris Imagines.* Edited by Otto Benndorf and Carl Schenkel. Leipzig, 1893.

Pierre de Saintes. "Viribus arte minis." In *Poésies populaires latines antérieures au douzième siècle,* edited by M. E. du Méril, 400–405. Paris, 1843.

Pindar. *Pindari Carmina cum fragmentis.* 2d ed. Edited by C. M. Bowra. Oxford, 1947.

Pliny. *C. Pliny Secundi Naturalis Historiae.* 5 vols. Edited by Karl Mayhoff and Ludwig von Ian. Stuttgart, 1897–1933; repr. 1967–1970.

Poésies populaires latines antérieures au douzième siècle. Edited by M. E. du Méril. Paris, 1843.

Poetae Melici Graeci. Edited by D. L. Page. Oxford, 1962.

Pomeroy, Sarah B. *Goddesses, Whores, Wives, and Slaves.* New York, 1975.

Porter, David H. "Violent Juxtaposition in the Similes of the *Iliad*." *Classical Journal* 68 (1972) 11–21.

Porter, H. N. Introduction to *The Odyssey*. Bantam edition, 1–20. New York, 1962.

Powell, John U. *Collectanea Alexandrina*. Oxford, 1925; repr. 1970.

Proclus. *Chrestomathia*. In *Homeri Opera*, vol. 5, edited by T. W. Allen, 93–109. Oxford, 1912.

Propertius. *Sexti Properti Carmina*. 2d. ed. Edited by E. A. Barber. Oxford, 1960.

Putnam, M. C. J. "The Art of Catullus 64." *Harvard Studies in Classical Philology* 65 (1961) 165–205.

———. *The Poetry of the Aeneid*. Cambridge, Mass., 1965.

Quinn, Kenneth. *Catullus: The Poems*. London, 1970.

Quintus Smyrnaeus. *Quinti Smyrnaei Posthomericorum Libri XIV*. Edited by Arminius Koechly. 1850; repr. Amsterdam, 1968.

Raby, F. J. E. *A History of Secular Latin Poetry in the Middle Ages*. 2 vols. Oxford, 1957.

Rand, Edward K. *Founders of the Middle Ages*. New York, 1957.

Redfield, J. *Nature and Culture in the Iliad: The Tragedy of Hector*. Chicago, 1975.

———. "Notes on the Greek Wedding." *Arethusa* 15 (1982) 181–201.

———. "The Proem of the *Iliad*: Homer's Art." *Classical Philology* 74 (1979) 95–110.

Reinhart, Karl. *Die Ilias und ihr Dichter*. Gottingen, 1961.

Reinhold, Meyer. "The Unhero Aeneas." *Classica et Medievalia* 27 (1966) 195–207.

Rey, Agapito. Introduction. *Sumas de historia troyana*, by "Leomarte." Madrid, 1932.

Reynolds, L. D., and N. G. Wilson. *Scribes and Scholars: A Guide to the Transmission of Greek and Latin Literature*. 2d. ed. Oxford, 1974.

Ribbeck, Otto. *Tragicorum Romanorum Fragmenta*. Leipzig, 1871.

Ritchie, William. *The Authenticity of the Rhesus of Euripides*. Cambridge, 1964.

Rivier, Annie. *La vie d'Achille illustrée par les vases grecs*. Lausanne, 1936.

Robert, Carl. *De Apollodori Bibliotheca*. Berlin, 1873.

———. *Die griechische Heldensage*. Vol. 3. Berlin, 1923.

Roberts, Gildas. See Joseph of Exeter.

Robertson, Durant W., Jr. *A Preface to Chaucer: Studies in Medieval Perspective*. Princeton, 1962.

Rohde, Erwin. *Psyche: The Cult of Souls and the Belief in Immortality Among the Greeks*. Translated by W. B. Hillis. London, 1925; repr. New York, 1966.

Le Roman de Troie en prose. Edited by L. Constans and E. Faral. Paris, 1922.

Ronconi, Alessandro. *Interpreti Latini di Omero*. Turin, 1973.

Root, Robert Kilburn. "Chaucer's Dares." *Modern Philology* 15 (1917) 1–22.

Roscher, Wilhelm H. *Ausführliches Lexicon der griechischen und römischen Mythologie*. Leipzig, 1884–1937; repr. Hildesheim, 1965.

Rose, H. J. "The Bride of Hades." *Classical Philology* 20 (1925) 238–242.

———. Prolegomena, commentary, and appendices to *Hygini Fabulae recensuit, prolegomenis commentario appendice instruxit.* Leiden, 1934.

Rosner, Judith A. "The Speech of Phoenix: *Iliad* 9, 435–605." *Phoenix* 30 (1976) 314–327.

Roussel, P. "Le rôle d'Achille dans l'*Iphigénie à Aulis.*" *Revue des Études Grecs* 28 (1915) 234–250.

Rzach, A. "*kyklos.*" In Pauly, Wissowa, Kroll, *Real-Encyclopädie*, vol. 11 (1922) cols. 2347–2435.

———. *Hesiodi Carmina.* Leipzig, 1902.

Sabbadini, Romigio. *Storia e critica di testi latini.* 1914; repr. Padua, 1971.

Sainte-Beuve, Charles A. *Étude sur Virgile, suivie d'une étude sur Quintus de Smyrne.* Paris, 1891.

Sale, W. "Achilles and Heroic Values." *Arion* 2 (1963) 86–100.

Sammelbuch Griechischer Urkunden aus Aegypten. Herausgegeben in Auftrage der Wissenschaftlichen Gesellschaft in Strassburg. Edited by F. Preisigke and F. Bilabel. Strassburg, 1915.

Schadewaldt, Wolfgang. *Van Homers Welt und Werk.* 3d ed. Stuttgart, 1959.

Schein, Seth. "The Death of Simoeisios." *Eranos* 74 (1976) 1–5.

———. *The Mortal Hero.* Berkeley and Los Angeles, 1984.

Scherer, Margaret R. *The Legends of Troy in Art and Literature.* New York, 1963.

Schissel von Fleschenberg, Otmar. *Dares Studien.* Halle-an-der-Salle, 1908.

Schlunk, Robin R. *The Homeric Scholia and the Aeneid: A Study of the Influence of Ancient Homeric Literary Criticism on Vergil.* Ann Arbor, 1974.

Scholes, Robert, and Robert Kellogg. *The Nature of Narrative.* New York, 1966.

Scholia Graeca in Euripidis Tragoedias. Vol. 1. Edited by William Dindorf. Oxford, 1863.

Scott, William C. *The Oral Nature of the Homeric Simile.* Leiden, 1974.

Sedgwick, Walter B. "The *Bellum Troianum* of Joseph of Exeter." *Speculum* 5 (1930) 49–76.

The Seege or Batayle of Troye. Edited by Mary E. Barnicle. *Early English Text Society* 172. London, 1927.

Segal, Charles. "*Kleos* and Its Ironies in the *Odyssey.*" *L'Antiquité Classique* 52 (1983) 22–47.

———. "Nestor and the Honor of Achilles." *Studi Micenei ed Egeo-Anatolici* 13 (1971) 90–105.

———. "The Phaeacians and the Symbolism of Odysseus' Return." *Arion* 1 (1962) 17–64.

———. "The Raw and Cooked in Greek Literature: Structure, Values, Metaphor." *Classical Journal* 69 (1974) 289–308.

BIBLIOGRAPHY

————. *The Theme of the Mutilation of the Corpse in the Iliad.* Leiden, 1971. (Cited in notes as *Corpse*)

Segre, Cesare, and Mario Marti, eds. *La Prosa del Duecento.* Milan, 1959.

Seneca, Lucius Annaeus. *L. Annaei Senecae Tragoediae.* Edited by R. Peiper and G. Richter. Leipzig, 1902.

————. *The Octavia: Introduction, Text, and Commentary,* by Lucile Y. Whitman. Bern and Stuttgart, 1978. (= *Noctes Romanae* 16.)

Servius. *Servianorum in Vergilii carmina commentariorum volumen 2.* Editionis Harvardianae. Lancaster, 1946. *volumen 3.* Oxford, 1965.

Severyns, Albert. *Sur de début des chants cypriens.* Amsterdam, 1965.

Sheppard, J. T. "The *Electra* of Euripides." *Classical Review* 32 (1918) 137–141.

————. *The Pattern of the Iliad.* 1922; repr. London and New York, 1969.

Siegel, H. "Agamemnon in Euripides' *Iphigeneia at Aulis.*" *Hermes* 109 (1981) 257–265.

————. "Self-delusion and the *Volte-Face* of Iphigeneia in Euripides' *Iphigeneia at Aulis.*" *Hermes* 108 (1980) 300–321.

Silvestris, Bernardus. *See* Bernardus.

Simon Capra Aurea. "*Divitiis, regno, specie.*" In "La Version Parisienne du poème de Simon Chèvre D'Or sur la guerre de Troie," by André Boutemy. *Scriptorium* 1 (1946–1947) 267–288.

Sinos, Dale. "The Entry of Achilles into Greek Poetry." Ph.D. dissertation, Johns Hopkins, 1975.

Smyth, H. W., and Hugh Lloyd-Jones, eds. and trans. *Aeschylus.* Vol. 2. Cambridge, Mass., 1963.

Snell, Bruno. *Euripides Alexandros und andere Strassburger Papyri mit Fragmenten griechischer Dichter.* Berlin, 1937.

Snodgrass, A. M. *The Dark Age of Greece: An Archaeological Survey of the Eleventh to the Eighth Centuries.* Edinburgh, 1971.

Solmsen, Friedrich. "The 'Gift' of Speech in Homer and Hesiod." *Transactions of the American Philological Association* 85 (1954) 1–15.

Statius. *P. Papini Stati Thebais et Achilleis.* Edited by Heathcote W. Garrod. Oxford, 1906.

Steadman, John. "The Arming of an Archetype: Heroic Virtue and the Conventions of Literary Epic." In *Concepts of the Hero in the Middle Ages and the Renaissance,* edited by Norman T. Burns and Christopher J. Regan. Papers of the 4th and 5th Annual Conferences of the Center for Medieval and Early Renaissance Studies, State University of New York at Binghamton, 2–3 May 1970; 1–2 May 1971. Albany, 1975.

Stohlmann, Jürgen. *Anonymi Historia Troyana Daretis Frigii.* Ratingen, Dusseldorf, 1968.

————. "*Deidamia Achilli:* Eine Ovid-Imitation aus dem 11. Jahrhundert." In

Litteratur und Sprache im Europäischen Mittelalter. Festschrift für Karl Langosch zum 70. Geburtstag, 224–231. Darmstadt, 1973.

Stokes, L. C. Introduction to "*Expositio Vergilianae Continentiae.*" *Classical Folia* 26 (1972) 28–29.

Storie de Troia e de Roma. Edited by Mario Marti and Cesare Segre. In *Prosa del Duecento.* Milan, 1959.

———. Edited by Ernesto Monaci. In *Miscellanea della Società Romana di storia patria.* Rome, 1920.

Taplin, Oliver. "The Shield of Achilles Within the *Iliad.*" *Greece and Rome* 27 (1980) 1–21.

Thomson, George. *Studies in Ancient Greek Society: The Prehistoric Aegean.* New York, 1965.

Tosi, Tito. "Il sacrifizio di Polissena." *Atene e Roma* 17 (1914) 19–38.

Tragicorum Graecorum Fragmenta. See Nauck.

Tryphiodorus. *The Taking of Ilium.* In *Oppian, Colluthus Tryphiodorus,* edited by A. W. Mair. London and New York, 1928.

Türk. "Polyxena." In Roscher, *Ausfürliches Lexicon,* vol. 3, no. 2 (1902–1909) 2718–2742.

Tzetzes, Johannes. Commentary. *Lycophronis Chalcidensis Alexandra, obscurum poema. Cum Graeco Isaacii, seu Joannis, Tzetzae commentario.* Oxford, 1702.

Vahlen, J. *Ennianae Poesis Reliquiae.* 3d ed. Leipzig, 1928.

Van der Valk, M. *Researches on the Text and Scholia of the Iliad.* 2 vols. Leiden, 1963–1964.

Vatican Mythographers. *Scriptores Rerum Mythicarum Latini Tres Romae nuper reperti.* Edited by G. H. Bode. Darmstadt, 1834; repr. Hildesheim, 1968.

Vellacott, Philip. *Ironic Drama: A Study of Euripides' Method and Meaning.* Cambridge, 1975.

Vergil. *The Aeneid of Virgil.* Edited by R. D. Williams. London, 1973.

Vermeule, Emily Townsend. *Aspects of Death in Early Greek Art and Poetry.* Berkeley and Los Angeles, 1979.

———. Introduction to *Electra.* In *Euripides,* III, edited by R. Lattimore and D. Grene, 3, pp. 204–208. New York, 1963 (reprint of 1959 edition).

Vernant, Jean-Pierre. *Mythe et Société en grèce ancienne.* Paris, 1972. Translated by Janet Lloyd as *Myth and Society in Ancient Greece.* Sussex and New Jersey, 1980.

———. *Les Origines de la pensée grecque.* Paris, 1962. Translated by Janet Lloyd as *The Origins of Greek Thought.* Ithaca, N.Y., 1982.

Vian, Francis. *Recherches sur les Posthomerica de Quintus de Smyrne.* Paris: 1959.

Vidal-Naquet, Pierre. "Bêtes, hommes et dieux chez les Grecs." In *Hommes et Bêtes: Entretiens sur le racism,* ed. Leon Poliakou, 129–142. Paris, 1975.

BIBLIOGRAPHY

————. "Sophocles' *Philoctetes* and the Ephebeia." In *Tragedy and Myth in Ancient Greece*, edited by J.-P. Vernant and Pierre Vidal-Naquet and translated by Janet Lloyd. Sussex and New Jersey, 1981.

Vitelli, G., and M. Norsa. *Papyri Greci e Latini. Publicazioni della Società italiana per la ricerca dei papyri greci e latini in Egitto* 11. Florence, 1935.

Vivante, Paolo. *The Homeric Imagination: A Study of Homer's Poetic Perception of Reality.* Bloomington, Ind., 1970.

Walsh, G. B. "The First Stasimon of Euripides' *Electra.*" *Yale Classical Studies* 25 (1977) 277–291.

————. "*Iphigenia in Aulis:* Third Stasimon." *Classical Philology* 69 (1974) 241–248.

Waltz, Pierre. *Anthologie Grecque.* Pt. I, vol. 1, 2d. ed. Paris, 1960.

Watkins, Calvert. "A propos de ΜΗΝΙΣ." *Bulletin de la Societé de linguistique de Paris* 72 (1977) 187–209.

Webster, T. B. L. *Sophocles: Philoctetes.* Cambridge, 1970.

————. *The Tragedies of Euripides.* London, 1967.

Weil, Henri. *Sept tragédies d'Euripide.* Paris, 1868.

Welcker, Friedrich G. *Die griechischen Tragödien.* Vol. 1. Bonn, 1839.

Whitman, Cedric. *Homer and the Heroic Tradition.* 1958; repr. New York, 1965.

Wiggington, W. B. *The Nature and Significance of the Late Medieval Troy Story: A Study of Guido delle Colonne's Historia Destructionis Troiae.* Ph.D. dissertation, Rutgers, 1964.

Will, Frederic. "Remarks on Counterpoint Characterization in Euripides." *Classical Journal* 55 (1959–1960) 338–344.

Willink, C. W. "The Prologue of *Iphigenia at Aulis.*" *Classical Quarterly* 65 (1971) 343–364.

Willis, R. S. "The Artistry and Enigmas of the *Libro de Alexandre:* A Review Article." *Hispanic Review* 42 (1974) 33–42.

————. *The Relationship of the Spanish "Libro de Alexandre" to the "Alexandreis" of Gautier de Châtillon.* Princeton, 1934.

Wolf, Christa. *Cassandra: A Novel and Four Essays.* Translated by Jan van Heurck. New York, 1984.

Young, Arthur M. *Troy and Her Legend.* Pittsburgh, 1948.

Young, David C. *Three Odes of Pindar: A Literary Study of Pythian 11, Pythian 3 and Olympian 7. Mnemosyne Suppl.* 9. Leiden, 1968.

Zambrini, Francesco. *Le opere volgari a stampa dei secoli XIII e XIV.* Bologna, 1866.

Zarker, J. W. "King Eetion and Thebe as Symbols in the *Iliad.*" *Classical Journal* 61 (1965) 110–114.

Zumthor, Paul. *Histoire littéraire de la France medievale.* 1954; repr. Geneva, 1981.

CHARACTER AND PLACE NAME INDEX

Achilles: arms of, 18, 52, 61, 82–83, 133, 157 (*see also* Achilles, shield of); arrogance of, 89–90, 109, 113–114, 160, 232, 272n78; beauty of, 3–4, 169, 220, 265n21, 285n191; as best of the Greeks, 1, 2–13, 133, 149, 150–153, 170, 221, 256n55; and Biblical figures, 206; birth of, 51; bloody hands of (*see* Blood); childhood of, 56–58, 69, 129, 131, 223, 271; as city sacker, 4, 52, 141; compassion of, 2, 142; conception of, 115; confronting army, 76–77; deceitfulness of, 140–141, 166–167, 169; description of, 275n93, 276n103, 282n153, 299n92; as divine, 39, 221; as Dog Star, xix, 18; as dolphin, 24–25; duel with Hektor, 25–28, 156; embassy to, 143, 197, 210, 213; as *eugenés* ("noble"), 75; and fatherhood, 42; feminization of, 180–183, 201–202, 206; and fire, 15, 17–18, 19, 20, 24; foreknowledge of, 5, 6, 33, 46; funeral of, 47, 130, 222; funeral games for, 52; and generic human activity, 41; ghost of, 46–47, 86–88, 138, 258n76, 258n80; greed of, 109; grief of, 113, 221, 226, 268n46 (*see also* Achilles, laments); grief of, as humanizing, 42, 55–56; groans of, 19–20; in Hades, 45–48; as healer, 7–10, 70, 141, 220, 252n7; heel of, 201–202, 203–204, 228–229, 271n68; heritage of, 56–59, 95–96; and heroic song, 10–11, 132–133, 181, 238n25, 238–239n27 (*see also* Achilles, and lyre); as homosexual, 162–163, 171–172, 301n102; *hubris* of (*see* Achilles, arrogance of); immortality of, 53–54, 59–60, 157–158, 281n147 (*see also*

Achilles, as superhuman); inferiority of, 166–170; and Juno, as linked with, 126; and justice, 34; and Kapaneus, merged with, xviii, 136–137, 160, 227; lamenting criticized, 109; laments Myrmidons, 215–216; laments Patroklos (*see* Achilles, grief of; Patroklos, Achilles mourns); laments Peleus, 6; and lyre, 10, 58 (*see also* Achilles, and heroic song); as mad dog, 25; and *mênis* (see *mênis*); moral superiority of, 223; as mortal, 98; musical accomplishment of, 265n21; name of, 135–136n4; and obedience in *Philoktetes*, 71–72; promises of, 302n115; rampage of, 1, 13–28, 122, 160, 199, 221; and reconciliation with Priam, 2, 37–45, 143, 199–200; and sex, 44; shield of, 11–13, 82–83, 156, 221, 239nn30, 31, 265n21; shield of, and fire, 18; shield of, lions of, 13, 83; shield of, and Tower of Babel, 156; as short-lived, 5, 7, 36, 66, 220–221, 237–238n14; as short-lived, in *Iphigeneia at Aulis*, 99–100; short-lived, in *Apology*, 105–106 (*see also Character Index* Thetis, foreknowledge of; Thetis, laments Achilles); size of, 134–137, 160, 265n21; and sleep, 44; and social convention, 98; as subhuman, 19, 24, 26, 37 (*see also* Lion similes); as superhuman, 19, 24, 26, 37, 134, 223; and suppliant, 13, 16 (*see also* Suppliant); swiftness of, 3, 4, 57, 134, 253n19; swiftness of, in *Elektra*, 83–84; swiftness of, in Epic Cycle, 51; swiftness of, in Dares, 141; swiftness of, in *Iphigeneia in Aulis*, 95; on temple doors,

GENERAL INDEX

Academics, 119, 121
Accius, 113, 119–120, 133; *Achilles* of, 113; *Battle of the Ships* of, 113, 121; *Myrmidons* of, 112–113, 121; *Telephus* of, 113
Achilleid. See Statius: *Achilleid*
Achilles (character). *See Character Index*
Achilles, of Astydamas, 104–105
Achilles, of Livius, 111
Achilles Aristarchi, 111
Adkins, Arthur, 246n91, 249n121, 259–260n93
Adler, Alfred, 301n102
Aeneid, xix–xx, 121–128, 146–147, 225, 226, 278n123, 282n156, 294n64, 296n74, 301n108; Achilles in, 268–269n51, 269n52; temple doors in, 122–124, 126, 127. *See also* Vergil; *Character Index under* Aeneas
Agamemnon, 90
Agricultural scenes, 13, 117, 189
Aischines, 78, 171
Aischylos, 104, 136, 171, 264n8, 270n55, 294n64; *Agamemnon* of, 90; *Myrmidons* of, 286n2
Aithiopis, 52, 61–62, 174–175, 294n64
Ajax, 77–78
Albert of Stade, xix, 208, 299n89. See also *Ilias Latina; Troilus*
Alexander the Great, 110, 150–152, 158, 263n1; and Achilles, 150, 151–158; death of, 157; *Libro de Alexandre,* xviii, 149–158, 232; as warrior, 150, 154
Alexandra, 134, 171, 174–176, 188, 271n68, 288n11
Alexiou, Margaret, 186
Alfonso el Sabio: *General estoria,* 280n138, 304n18
Alkaios, 50, 53–56, 62–63, 261n111
Andersen, Øivind, 239n30
Andreas Capellanus, 208, 300n94, 301n102, 302n111

Andronicus, Livius, 110–111
Anger, sin of, 158
Animal similes, 189, 245n88, 245–246n89. *See also* Dog Star; Dolphin; Fish similes; Lion similes
Anonymi Historia Troyana, 165–166
Antigone, 186
Antipater, 150
Apollodoros, 271n68, 272n74, 288n11, 294n64
Apollonios of Rhodes, 264n2, 271n68
Apology, 105–106, 107
Appian, 118, 267n40
Aquinas, Thomas, 205
Aristarchos, 111
aristeia ("period of preeminence in battle"), 14–15, 20, 24–25, 32, 37, 123, 240n36, 243n68, 245n85, 264n8
aristeúein. See *áristos*
Aristophanes, 71, 78, 104
áristos ("best"), 2–4, 21, 37, 45, 133, 196, 236n2
Aristotle, 104, 150
arma ("arms," "battle"), 124, 127, 128, 142, 145, 165, 265n18, 268n50, 268–269n51, 270n58, 282n153; versus love, 172, 181, 214, 216
Armstrong, James I., 241n53
Arrian, 258n77
Ars Amatoria, 173, 180–184, 272n73, 287n7
Arthur, Marilyn B., 248n111
Astydamas, *Achilles* of, 104–105
Athenian democracy, 70–71
Atwood, E. Bagby, 280n138
Aulus Gellius, 264n4
Ausonius, 294n62
Austin, R. G. P., 125

Bacchylides, 172, 178, 287n8
Barthes, Roland, 224
Bassett, Samuel, 240n38

Designer: Mark Ong
Compositor: G & S Typesetters, Inc.
Text: Linotron 202 Galliard
Display: Forum
Printer: Maple-Vail Book Mfg. Group
Binder: Maple-Vail Book Mfg. Group